THE DEMOCRATIC ASPECTS OF TRADE UNION RECOGNITION

The long ascendancy of pluralism and 'collective laissez-faire' as a guiding ideology of British labour law was emphatically shattered by the New Right ideology of Thatcher and Major. When New Labour was finally returned to power in 1997, it did not, however, attempt to resurrect the pre-Thatcher preference for pluralist non-intervention in collective industrial relations. Instead, it purported to follow a 'Third Way'. A centrepiece of this new approach was the statutory recognition provision, introduced in Schedule A1 Trade Union and Labour Relations (Consolidation) Act 1992. By breaking with the tradition of voluntarism in respect of recognition of trade unions, New Labour sought to provide a model of collective labour law which combined legal support with control through juridification. A closer study of both the history of approaches to recognition and the current provisions opens up fundamental questions as to the nature of this new model and the ones it aimed to replace.

This book uses political philosophy to elucidate the character of those historical approaches and the nature of the 'Third Way' itself in relation to statutory union recognition. In particular, it traces the progressive eclipse of civic republican values in labour law, in preference for a liberal political philosophy. The book articulates and defends a civic republican philosophy in terms of freedom as non-domination, the intrinsic value of democratic participation through deliberative democracy, and community. This can be contrasted with the rights-based individualism and State neutrality characteristic of the liberal approach. Despite the promise of civic community in the 'Third Way' rhetoric, this book demonstrates that the reality of New Labour's experiment in union recognition was an emphatic reassertion of liberalism in the sphere of workers' collective rights. This is the first monograph to offer a sustained critical analysis of legal approaches to trade union recognition. It will be of particular interest to labour lawyers, but also a wider audience of scholars in political philosophy and industrial relations.

The Democratic Aspects of Trade Union Recognition

Alan Bogg

·HART·
PUBLISHING
OXFORD AND PORTLAND, OREGON
2009

Published in North America (US and Canada) by
Hart Publishing
c/o International Specialized Book Services
920 NE 58th Avenue, Suite 300
Portland, OR 97213–3786
USA
Tel: +1 503 287 3093 or toll-free: (1) 800 944 6190
Fax: +1 503 280 8832
E-mail: orders@isbs.com
Website: http://www.isbs.com

Hart Publishing Ltd, 16C Worcester Place, Oxford, OX1 2JW
Telephone: +44 (0)1865 517530 Fax: +44 (0)1865 510710
E-mail: mail@hartpub.co.uk
Website: http://www.hartpub.co.uk

British Library Cataloguing in Publication Data
Data Available

ISBN: 978-1-84113-790-2

Typeset by Columns Design Ltd, Reading
Printed and bound in Great Britain by
TJ International Ltd, Padstow, Cornwall

This book is dedicated to my wife, Sarah,
and my mum, Jean, with love.

Acknowledgments

I have incurred many debts along the way in the lengthy gestation period of this book, and it is a great pleasure to record them. Many of the ideas in this book emerged in an embryonic form in the preparation of a DPhil thesis at the University of Oxford. I am particularly grateful to the Arts and Humanities Research Council for an award that permitted me to undertake graduate research study. Without those first steps, this journey could never have been undertaken. My largest intellectual debt is to Sandy Fredman. Many years ago she was kind enough to take a chance on offering a place to read law to an unpolished teenager from East Lancashire at Exeter College, Oxford. She has variously performed the roles of college tutor, BCL tutor, DPhil supervisor, referee, Faculty mentor, and now a senior colleague in the Oxford Law Faculty. She has performed all of those roles with unstinting kindness and uncompromising intellectual rigour. It has been my tremendous good fortune to have Sandy as a mentor and a friend.

Other lawyers have been exceedingly generous in their intellectual support. In Oxford, my Faculty colleagues have been especially supportive. It is a pleasure to thank Nick Barber, Cathryn Costello, Paul Craig, Anne Davies, Mark Freedland, Wanjiru Njoya and Alison Young. They have all been on hand to discuss ideas and/or comment on drafts of my work, and their support has been invaluable. Alistair Fletcher, a Hertford labour lawyer of growing eminence, has provided fantastic research assistance. Beyond Oxford, I am particularly grateful to Rob Cryer, Paul Davies, Ruth Dukes, Keith Ewing, Martin George, Colin Manchester, Tonia Novitz, Jake Rowbottom, Bob Simpson and John Stanton-Ife. In different ways they have each been a source of intellectual inspiration and support. Beyond these shores, Matt Finkin, Bill Gould and Tom Kohler have been unfailingly patient in illuminating the arcane intricacies of US labour law. In institutional terms, Hertford College (its fellows and students) has provided a stimulating, collegial and good humoured environment for my work. It also provided a term of sabbatical leave that enabled this book to be completed. I am lucky to have had Alison Young as my law colleague and friend. She exemplifies all of the republican virtues of good citizenship that I defend in this book. The Oxford Law Faculty has also been a perfect intellectual home for me, as an undergraduate, then a graduate, now a lecturer.

Hart Publishing has been a joy to work with. In particular, Richard Hart and Rachel Turner have combined consummate professionalism with an unstuffy and helpful demeanour at every twist and turn of the project.

My personal debts are undoubtedly the greatest of all. I would like to thank my mum, Jean, for her support over many years. The subject-matter of this book owes much to her. For most of her life, she combined backbreaking and underpaid work with being a single mum and a long-standing NUPE member and activist. For her, as for countless others, the working class struggle was a way of life rather than a fancy set of theoretical propositions to be dissected in the academy. I should certainly record my gratitude to the staff and players of Blackpool Football Club. The last two years have seen Championship football at Bloomfield Road for the first time in nearly 30 years. My fortnightly trips to the Fylde Coast, with my fellow lawyer and tangerine Franklin Meisel, have been a welcome escape from the pressures of the book. By the time this book is on the shelves, tangerines everywhere will know the Championship fate of our beloved club. Finally, and most of all, I would like to thank my wonderful wife, Sarah Green. She has tolerated regular absences, both work and football related, with patience and good humour. As a legal critic, best friend and wife, she is second to none.

Contents

Table of Abbreviations

ACAS	Advisory, Conciliation and Arbitration Service
AFL	American Federation of Labor
APEX	Association of Professional, Executive, Clerical and Computer Staffs
ASTMS	Association of Scientific, Technical and Managerial Staffs
BAJ	British Association of Journalists
CAC	Central Arbitration Committee
CIR	Commission on Industrial Relations
CLF	collective laissez-faire
CO	Certification Officer
CSEU	Confederation of Shipbuilding and Engineering Unions
DPA	default procedure agreement
DTI	Department of Trade and Industry
ECtHR	European Court of Human Rights
EEF	Engineering Employers Federation
EPA	Employment Protection Act
ICER	Information and Consultation of Employees Regulations
ILO	International Labour Organisation
IRA	Industrial Relations Act
IRC	Industrial Relations Commission
NALGO	National Association of Local Government Officers
NAT	National Arbitration Tribunal
NIRC	National Industrial Relations Court
NLRA	National Labor Relations Act
NLRB	National Labor Relations Board
NUGMW	National Union of General and Municipal Workers (Wales)
QIP	Qualified Independent Person
TASS	Technical, Administrative and Supervisory Section
TGWU	Transport and General Workers' Union
TUC	Trades Union Congress
TULRA	Trade Unions and Labour Relations Act
TULRCA	Trade Union and Labour Relations (Consolidation) Act
UKAPE	United Kingdom Association of Professional Engineers
USDAW	Union of Shops Distributive and Allied Workers

Table of Cases

LITIGATION

European Convention on Human Rights

European Union

United States of America

CENTRAL ARBITRATION COMMITTEE

Table of Legislation

International

United States of America

CODES OF PRACTICE

Introduction

The long ascendancy of pluralism and 'collective laissez-faire' as a guiding ideology of British labour law was emphatically shattered by the New Right ideology of Thatcher and Major. When New Labour was finally returned to power in 1997, it did not, however, attempt to resurrect the pre-Thatcher preference for pluralist non-intervention in collective industrial relations. Instead, it purported to follow a 'Third Way'. A centrepiece of this new approach was the statutory recognition provision, introduced in Schedule A1 Trade Union and Labour Relations (Consolidation) Act 1992. By breaking with the tradition of voluntarism in respect of recognition of trade unions, New Labour sought to provide a model of collective labour law which combined legal support with control through juridification. A closer study of both the history of approaches to recognition and the current provisions opens up fundamental questions as to the nature of this new model and the ones it aimed to replace. This book uses political philosophy to elucidate the character of those historical approaches and the nature of the 'Third Way' itself in relation to statutory union recognition. In particular, it traces the progressive eclipse of civic republican values in labour law, in preference to a liberal political philosophy. The book articulates and defends a civic republican philosophy in terms of freedom as non-domination, the intrinsic value of democratic participation through deliberative democracy, and community. This can be contrasted with the rights-based individualism and State neutrality characteristic of the liberal approach. Despite the promise of civic community in the 'Third Way' rhetoric, this book demonstrates that the reality of New Labour's experiment in union recognition was an emphatic reassertion of liberalism in the sphere of workers' collective rights.

This is a book in three parts. Part one begins with a historical perspective on the relation between union recognition and legal regulation. Chapter one begins, as any treatment of union recognition must, with the framework of collective laissez-faire as articulated and defended by Otto Kahn-Freund. For Kahn-Freund, what was distinctive about British labour law's relationship with union recognition was the *form* of State support for collective bargaining. In particular, there was a marked preference for indirect over direct methods of auxiliary support (such as a directly enforced legal duty to bargain, US-style). Collective laissez-faire, and its corresponding theory of indirect auxiliary support, has been subjected to a range of powerful theoretical critiques in recent years. Chapter one argues that once the underlying pluralist political theory of collective laissez-faire is brought into view, these critiques are ultimately unsuccessful. As an interpretive account of British labour law's preference for indirect auxiliary support, collective laissez-faire continues to provide the most coherent theoretical elucidation of that tendency. Fundamentally, the political virtue of the indirect method was its respect for the pluralist principle of group autonomy. This was a principle of political freedom, holding that the social groups in civil society should be free to determine their own bargaining constituencies and to formulate their own norms, free from State interference and control. By contrast, direct forms of auxiliary support imperilled group autonomy by giving the State a more pronounced role in the specification of bargaining units and bargaining agents, and the enforcement of good faith standards in the collective bargaining process itself.

If chapter one is testament to the *coherence* of collective laissez-faire, chapter two is testament to its *resilience*. One of the major themes in British industrial relations in the post-war period was an increasingly urgent questioning of the value of group autonomy as a political ideal. In particular, the freedom of the bargaining parties to set their own priorities regardless of the public interest came under increasing scrutiny in public discourse. Allan Flanders' *civic* theorisation of collective bargaining was an exemplar of this tendency. This alternative political discourse, emphasising the civic responsibility of trade unions and employers to be attentive to the common good in their bargaining activities rather than their absolute freedom to pursue their own self-interest, countenanced a much more pronounced role for the State in the previously sacrosanct sphere of free collective bargaining. At the theoretical level, this shift had profound implications for the choice between direct and indirect modes of auxiliary support. Once the State's role in vindicating the common good acquired growing legitimacy in political terms, then so would direct modes of auxiliary support that necessitated more intensive State engagement with the collective bargaining process. At a superficial level, that is indeed what occurred from the Donovan Commission onwards until 1979. British labour law experimented with a series of direct modes of auxiliary support for collective bargaining. And at a superficial level, it is tempting to present this as a simple linear progression away from the principle of group autonomy. Nevertheless, collective laissez-faire continued to exert a deep and profound gravitational pull on the design and implementation of directly enforced legal duties to bargain. This was manifested particularly in the failure of legal standards of good faith to take root in the British system of bargaining regulation. This was testament to the resilience of group autonomy, and thus of collective laissez-faire, in the British industrial relations imagination. In the context of State auxiliary intervention, at least, collective laissez-faire was alive and well in British industrial relations.

Part two of the book distinguishes between two alternative political models for framing collective labour law issues in the post-1997 'New Labour' era. These two models began to emerge as tentative political alternatives to the dominant political pluralist paradigm in British industrial relations during the 1960s and 1970s, but they were certainly more clearly formed in third way rhetoric in the lead up to New Labour's election victory. On the one hand, there was a liberal paradigm that emphasised State neutrality and respect for individual autonomy and freedom of choice. On the other hand, there was a civic paradigm that emphasised civic virtues and responsibilities and the need for citizens to honour the common good through participation in self-government. These two political models provided alternative possible trajectories for the 'third way' experiment in collective labour law. Following Stuart White, the assumption of this book is that, in political terms at least, there was not one third way but there were in fact many. According to Stuart White, 'the nature of the third way remains fundamentally vague and elusive. It is not really a concept or an ideology, but, to use Steven Lukes' phrase, a *rhetorically defined space*'.[1] This 'rhetorically defined space' contained intimations of both understandings of politics within it.

Chapter three focuses on the liberal paradigm in industrial relations. Its first task is to address the possibility that New Labour's project is *neo-liberal* in inspiration. Various influential critiques have pointed to the legislative continuities between the previous Conservative Government's legislative programme and New Labour's legislative programme. From this, they conclude that New Labour shares a common ideological underpinning that is best characterised as neo-liberal. Chapter three casts doubt on this argument, pointing to the pervasive presence of incompletely theorised agreements in labour law. Instead, I argue that a 'State neutrality' model of liberalism offers the best interpretive characterisation of New Labour's regulatory approach in the trade union context. While this 'State neutrality' model is descriptively powerful as a way of making sense of New Labour's particular liberal trajectory, it is vulnerable to many of the civic and communitarian critiques that have been levelled at the liberal viewpoint in recent years. The chapter then explores various liberal alternatives to this unrefined 'State neutrality' model that are less vulnerable to the civic charge that liberalism is based upon an unattractive foundation of asocial individualism. Drawing upon the work of contemporary liberals such as Kymlicka, White and Raz, I argue that there is fertile scope for imaginative law reform that is simultaneously faithful to liberal values while also offering a framework of regulation that is more supportive of collective goods such as trade unionism and collective bargaining.

In chapter four, I set out the civic republican alternative in labour law in terms of three overarching values: community, collective self-rule and freedom as non-domination. Despite the recurrent appeals to civic republican rhetoric in third way thinking, this conception of politics has singularly failed to influence any of New Labour's major reform initiatives in the trade union context. In relation to the value of community, New Labour's legislative reforms have continued to endorse a view of trade unions as associations based merely on the voluntary consent of their members. This has eclipsed the civic understanding of trade unions as thickly constituted communities bound together by obligations of solidarity that inculcate important civic virtues amongst their members. This has generated an impoverished set of legal concepts for regulating matters as diverse as the closed shop, the treatment of dissentient union members, secondary industrial action and the protection of workers from anti-union discrimination.

[1] S White, 'The Ambiguities of the Third Way' in S White (ed), *New Labour: The Progressive Future?* (Basingstoke, Palgrave, 2001) 3 (emphasis added).

In relation to the civic value of collective self-rule, civic republicanism defends the position that civic participation in deliberative democracy is a public good of great intrinsic significance. In the industrial sphere, this is allied with a legal agenda that promotes the radical democratisation of the industrial sphere. Once again, however, the values and assumptions that have structured New Labour's legal reforms have led to a public conception of collective bargaining that is democratically impoverished and ill-suited to enabling workers to regain democratic control over their working lives. Finally, the republican good of non-domination, so prominent in contemporary accounts of republican theory, has failed to exert any practical influence over New Labour's reform agenda in labour law. Subordination in working life has been pushed from the core to the penumbra of the labour law agenda, and it appears only very peripherally on New Labour's industrial relations radar. This has led to the legitimisation of a diverse range of voice mechanisms tainted by employer domination or control. Chapter four traces the yawning gaps between the civic rhetoric and the liberal reality of New Labour's reform agenda in collective labour law, and over the course of the chapter it offers a practical manifesto for realising a civic conception of collective labour law at the level of practical legal reforms.

Part three uses the political framework outlined in Part two to engage in a systematic analysis and critique of the Schedule A1 recognition procedure. Chapter five focuses on legal regulation of the ballot process. It identifies the underlying normative model of the recognition ballot as based upon a liberal conception of the 'cultural marketplace'. The success of the trade union depends on its ability to attract sufficient support amongst workers in the bargaining unit to reach the majority support thresholds, and the State's role is confined to ensuring that the cultural marketplace created by the Schedule A1 recognition procedure establishes a level playing field for unions and employers. Drawing upon US and Canadian comparisons, chapter five identifies various ways in which the cultural marketplace in Schedule A1 falls short of the liberal ideal of a level playing field in respect of employer unfair practices and union access during the ballot procedure. The conclusion points the way to a civic realignment of the underlying political basis of the ballot procedure as a powerful alternative to the liberal 'cultural marketplace' model.

Chapter six then challenges the normative premise underlying the Anglo-American model of statutory recognition, that workers' preferences should be sovereign in the allocation of bargaining rights, and that the State should remain neutral in simply aggregating those preferences. The civic conception of politics rejects this faith in the benign effects of pluralist democracy. Certain preferences seem distorted by adaptation to what is possible. If my preferences are causally driven by perceptions of which options are realistically available to me, and those background restrictions on options are unjust, those preferences seem to lack autonomy. The absence of desire for unavailable options may be more to do with the reduction of cognitive dissonance associated with frustrated aspirations than anything else. Should the law defer to such preferences? There would seem to be no welfare loss in respecting the preference since the citizen gets what she wants. But matters are less straightforward where collectively binding decisions are concerned. Citizens can legitimately expect to be bound by collective decisions that are not the product of preferences distorted by unjust background constraints. Chapter six argues that there is such an 'adaptive preference' problem in the context of the collective decision whether or not to unionise. As such, it explores five strategies for countering such adaptive preference effects in a legal recognition procedure. While Schedule A1 has elements of these civic strategies in its regulatory armoury, more work needs to be done in formulating a comprehensive regulatory response to the civic problem of preference distortion in the context of union recognition.

Finally, chapter seven looks at the tension between pluralist and deliberative democracy in conceptualising State regulation of the collective bargaining process itself. On the pluralist view, the parties should be free to pursue their own self-interest through interest-group bargaining. The republican perspective rejects this understanding of industrial politics. On this alternative deliberative view, the parties should engage in shared deliberation with a sense of civic responsibility to promote the common good. The first part of chapter seven offers a normative defence of deliberative democracy in the industrial sphere. Criticism of the deliberative conception rests on a faulty understanding of deliberative democracy and its regulatory implications in collective bargaining law. Then, the legal concept of good faith bargaining in North America is subjected to a searching critique. Despite appearances, the deliberative potential of the good faith duty has been undermined by deeply rooted pluralist democratic assumptions that shape public regulation of the collective bargaining process. This is manifest in the legal definition of 'good faith' bargaining, the narrow scope of bargaining duties and the precariousness of the right to strike. Finally, the bargaining duty in Schedule A1 is analysed. Despite New Labour's concept of 'social partnership' paying some lip service to the deliberative model of democracy in its broad rhetoric, the British legal framework is similarly infused with pluralist values and assumptions. Consequently, the realisation of 'social partnership' based on deliberative democratic principles seems likely to remain unfulfilled without systematic legal reform. The chapter concludes by setting out a series of specific legal reforms that would be well-suited to promoting deliberative engagement in the industrial sphere.

Part 1:

Historical Perspectives on Union Recognition and the Law

1

Reappraising Kahn-Freund: The Coherence of Collective Laissez-Faire

I INTRODUCTION

IT IS GENERALLY accepted that British labour law had an exceptional relationship with the social structures and practices of collective bargaining in the post-war period. In particular, there was no directly enforceable legal duty to bargain as existed in other countries such as the US and Canada. Instead, there was a range of 'indirect' auxiliary props to the social system of collective bargaining, and this 'indirect' method of intervention marked a distinctive British preference. The ruling theory of British labour law was articulated by Otto Kahn-Freund and became known as 'collective laissez-faire' (CLF). It offered a rationalisation of this 'indirect' pattern of auxiliary support for union recognition that has, in recent years, been subject to three distinctive critiques. So impressive have been the challenges, and so eminent the challengers, one might be forgiven for concluding that CLF has had its day as an interpretive account of British labour law. The purpose of this chapter is to reappraise CLF by elucidating its underlying political philosophy. Once elucidated, it can be seen that CLF still offers the most compelling theoretical rationalisation of the pattern of auxiliary intervention in the post-war period. The three critiques, while containing many interesting insights, leave the inner core of the theory intact.

II CLF AND ITS CRITICS

> British collective labour law is in one respect unique among the legal systems of the larger industrial countries. Trade union 'recognition' was achieved in this country by purely industrial as distinct from political and legislative action. No Wagner Act, no Weimar Constitution, no Front Populaire legislation has imposed upon British employers the duty to enter into negotiation with trade union representatives. The proud edifice of collective labour regulation was built up without the assistance of the 'law'.[1]

[1] O Kahn-Freund, 'Collective Agreements under Wartime Legislation' (1943) 6 *Modern Law Review* 112, 143 (Kahn-Freund, 'Wartime Legislation').

So ended one of Otto Kahn-Freund's earliest essays on the nature of British labour law. Decades later, Kahn-Freund reiterated this view: 'The absence of direct sanctions, then, is characteristic of British labour law, and it is perhaps not inapposite here to emphasize what an extraordinary phenomenon this is in our contemporary world.'[2]

The historical absence of a legal duty to bargain, so singular in comparative terms, was reflective of Britain's particular social heritage. The British working class achieved industrial enfranchisement through voluntary action long before it secured political enfranchisement. This shaped the distinctively 'non-interventionist' character of British labour law. At certain points, Kahn-Freund came perilously close to a teleological view of British labour history. In his teleological moments, recognition of trade unions by employers seems to emerge naturally through the invisible hand of spontaneous social forces, under the watchful gaze of a neutral and indifferent State. Labour relations had evolved organically from 'primitive' to 'mature' patterns of interaction,[3] with union recognition shifting from the 'contested' to the 'accepted' sphere in civil society as the British system reached its *telos* of 'maturity' in the post-war period. Once this evolution had occurred, once intergroup relations had 'developed into a higher community',[4] legal norms were of peripheral significance in the shaping of intergroup relations. Thus, 'the recognition of the trade unions, then, which is the linchpin of industrial relations today, does not rest on a "legal" foundation.'[5] Or again, 'In Britain trade-union recognition was achieved almost entirely by "industrial" action … Elsewhere … the partly "political" origin of union recognition has left its permanent mark on the pattern of intergroup conflicts and their settlement: the role of the law in these matters has remained very much more conspicuous than it is in Britain.'[6] This 'social' character of union recognition, so prominent in Kahn-Freund's mature analytical work, was integral to the genetic code of CLF.

Elsewhere, Kahn-Freund drew back from this teleological view to emphasise the distinctive *form* of British auxiliary support for union recognition. Kahn-Freund's schema acquired its definitive shape in a spectacular troika of work published in the 1950s. In 'Legal Framework', he offered a panoramic view of British labour law's main structural features; in 'Intergroup Conflicts' and 'Labour Law'[7] he proffered a theoretical rationalisation of that pattern. The

[2] O Kahn-Freund, 'Industrial Relations and the Law: Retrospect and Prospect' (1969) 7 *British Journal of Industrial Relations* 301, 306 (Kahn-Freund, 'Retrospect').

[3] O Kahn-Freund, 'Intergroup Conflicts and their Settlement', in O Kahn-Freund, *Selected Writings* (London, Stevens & Sons, 1978) 41 (Kahn-Freund, 'Intergroup Conflicts').

[4] Kahn-Freund, 'Intergroup Conflicts' 54.

[5] O Kahn-Freund, 'Legal Framework', in A Flanders and HA Clegg (eds), *The System of Industrial Relations in Great Britain* (Oxford, Blackwell, 1954) 42, 53 (Kahn-Freund, 'Legal Framework').

[6] Kahn-Freund, 'Intergroup Conflicts' 44.

[7] O Kahn-Freund, 'Labour Law', in O Kahn-Freund, *Selected Writings* (London, Stevens & Sons, 1978) 1 (Kahn-Freund, 'Labour').

outstanding characteristic of that structure identified in 'Legal Framework' was the relative insignificance of direct legal intervention in shaping collective labour relations. The real puzzle for Kahn-Freund was not that there was no auxiliary support for collective bargaining, but *why* auxiliary State support for collective bargaining had emerged in a distinctively British form.

The crux of the matter rested upon Kahn-Freund's famous analytic distinction between direct and indirect forms of legal intervention:

> [T]here is a difference between saying to the employers: 'You act unlawfully if you refuse to recognize unions and to bargain with them in good faith' (the American attitude) and saying to them 'It is for you to decide whether or not you wish to bargain collectively, but if you do not we may impose upon you terms and conditions of employment which you must observe' (the British attitude).[8]

The 'American attitude' consisted of a statutory duty to bargain in good faith, defined and enforced by an administrative agency, and backed ultimately by coercive judicial remedies. The 'British attitude', by contrast, consisted in the use of 'indirect inducements' that often involved the imposition of substitute terms and conditions of employment on recalcitrant employers.[9] The remainder of 'Legal Framework' offered a microscopic analysis of the particular species of legal technique that fell within the British genus of 'indirect inducement': machinery for ensuring the compulsory normative effect of qualifying collective agreements, wages councils, fair wages clauses, extension of collective agreements and compulsory arbitration, and State provision of dispute resolution machinery.

For Kahn-Freund, this attitudinal difference was neither inconsequential nor arbitrary; it touched upon something fundamental, a 'point of principle'.[10] This was the principle of 'industrial autonomy'.[11] Now that 'Legal Framework' had mapped the legal topography, it was left to 'Intergroup Conflicts' and 'Labour Law' to render the map coherent by refracting that pattern through this core principle. In part, the principle of industrial autonomy embodied a universal axiom of labour market regulation in developed legal systems: that non-State law created by autonomous organisations in civil society was at least as important as State law in regulating the economic sphere (in Ehrlich's evocative phrase, the 'living law'),[12] and that States should accordingly augment the normative capacities of such organisations. Yet it also embodied a more particularistic sense, particularistic because it spoke to the distinctness of 'industrial autonomy'

[8] Kahn-Freund, 'Legal Framework' 55.
[9] *Ibid,* 62.
[10] *Ibid,* 55.
[11] *Ibid,* 44.
[12] E Ehrlich, *Fundamental Principles of the Sociology of Law* (New Brunswick and London, Transaction, 1999).

in the British legal and political system.[13] Specifically, it highlighted the *especially wide latitude* given by the British State to the 'free play of collective forces of society' in comparative terms.[14] The 'British attitude' of 'indirect' auxiliary support was more solicitous of that latitude than other, more direct techniques of supportive State intervention.

This, in essence, is the rationalisation offered by Kahn-Freund. For decades, the acuity of CLF's historical analysis seemed unassailable. More recently, however, Kahn-Freund's theorisation of CLF has stimulated a lively critical debate. It has been subjected to three kinds of critique: we might term these the abstentionist critique, the neutrality critique, and the coherence critique. First, the abstentionist critique has alleged that CLF rested upon a faulty materialist understanding of the relation between social power and legal norms, that is that social power exists independently of legal norms. Hugh Collins has been most prominent in pushing this line.[15] Secondly, the neutrality critique alleges that CLF has vastly underestimated the significance of the British State's role in promoting union organisation and collective bargaining. CLF postulated State neutrality towards the social practice of collective bargaining. In reality, however, the State's presence in collective labour relations has been systematic, enduring, and crucial to the stability of collective bargaining. Ewing[16] and Howell[17] have adopted variants of this broad critique. Finally, the coherence critique questions the analytical utility of the direct/indirect distinction as a way of making sense of the British State's distinctive relationship with collective bargaining. Most notably, Davies and Freedland seem sceptical of its analytical coherence.[18] Each of these critiques asserts, in different ways, the visibility of the State in British industrial relations, in contradistinction to the thesis of State invisibility allegedly at the heart of CLF. A closer examination of CLF's intellectual heritage suggests, however, that these criticisms are misplaced.

The next step in the argument is to explore the political basis of CLF. Kahn-Freund's rationalisation of the British attitude, reflected in the primacy of 'indirect' methods of auxiliary support, was rooted in his account of Britain's 'pluralistic constitution'. The main elements of his interpretation of this constitutional pluralism are set out. Then, its connections to theories of political pluralism are explained and defended. Once these political connections are

[13] See R Dukes, 'Constitutionalizing Employment Relations: Sinzheimer, Kahn-Freund, and the Role of Labour Law' 35 (2008) *Journal of Law and Society* 341, 352–5 on the methodological distinction between universal and particularistic propositions in labour law.

[14] Kahn-Freund, 'Labour Law' 8.

[15] H Collins, 'Against Abstentionism in Labour Law', in J Eekelaar and J Bell (eds), *Oxford Essays in Jurisprudence* (Oxford, Oxford University Press third series, 1987) 79.

[16] KD Ewing, 'The State and Industrial Relations: "Collective laissez-faire" Revisited' (1998) 5 *Historical Studies in Industrial Relations* 1.

[17] C Howell, *Trade Unions and the State: The Construction of Industrial Relations Institutions in Britain, 1890–2000* (Princeton, Princeton University Press, 2005).

[18] P Davies and M Freedland, *Labour Legislation and Public Policy* (Oxford, Oxford University Press, 1993) ch 1.

understood, the chapter uses its underlying political theory to defend CLF against each of the critiques. Of course, it is important to remember that Kahn-Freund's theorisation of CLF was dynamic rather than static. Kahn-Freund was not afraid to change his mind if a change of facts required it. Consequently, the primary focus will be on the framework articulated by Kahn-Freund in the 1950s, although his earlier and later work will be considered where relevant.

III CLF AND THE 'PLURALISTIC CONSTITUTION'

A Introduction

For Kahn-Freund, the constitutional basis of CLF could be traced to 'the rapidly developing pluralistic character of the British Constitution'.[19] It was this crucial constitutional element that Dicey had missed when he predicted that State intervention in the economic sphere would increase in tandem with the growing power of the labour movement and the widening franchise. As Kahn-Freund observed, the reverse was true, such that 'the spectacular rise of the trade unions since the First World War ensured in many areas the defeat of the principle of State intervention.'[20] The institutional manifestation of this pluralistic approach was that 'the line between "State" and "society" has been blurred very deliberately, or to put it differently, the "pressure" of the pressure groups has been so organised as to work inside the legislative, administrative, judicial and policy making processes'.[21] This pluralism was reflected in, amongst other things, the inclusion of 'representative organisations' in the machinery of investigation,[22] adjudication,[23] and regulatory processes leading to the creation of binding normative standards enforceable by legal sanction;[24] above all, the settled practice of State agencies eliciting the active consent of 'representative organisations' in the governance of the labour market.[25]

In effect, then, the pluralistic constitution envisaged the devolution of regulatory tasks to autonomous groups in civil society, such as trade unions. Did this deliberate 'blurring' of State and society imply the integration of British trade unions into the apparatus of the State? After all, this pluralism seemed to envisage the incorporation of trade unions into the public structures of governance, whereas CLF would seem more naturally aligned with a strict delineation

[19] Kahn-Freund, 'Labour Law' 8.

[20] *Ibid.*

[21] *Ibid*, 10.

[22] See, eg, the procedures for triggering the operation of the Cotton Manufacturing Industry (Temporary Provisions) Act 1934. For an excellent discussion, see D Brodie, *A History of British Labour Law 1867–1945* (Oxford, Hart Publishing, 2003) 200–201.

[23] See, eg, Industrial Court Act 1919 s 1.

[24] See, eg, the approach to minimum wage fixing machinery in the Wages Councils Act 1945.

[25] Kahn-Freund, 'Labour Law' 20.

of 'State' from 'society'. Such an integrationist interpretation of pluralism would, of course, have been entirely unthinkable to Kahn-Freund.[26] It was also inconsistent with his observation that the British trade unions' aversion to direct legal support gave them 'a position of strength in the British Constitution which is hardly paralleled elsewhere'.[27] The key to elucidating the nature of the British 'pluralistic constitution' lay in its deeper connections to theories of political pluralism that were prevalent at that time, particularly given that CLF 'was located in the established mainstream of liberal political thought in the Britain of the 1950s'.[28]

B Collective Bargaining as Industrial Democracy: The Influence of American Political Pluralism

The inter-connectedness of political pluralism and industrial relations pluralism has been explored by Hyman[29] and, more recently, Ackers.[30] Elements of American political pluralist thought were particularly influential in Clegg's and Kahn-Freund's conceptualisation of the collective bargaining process. American political pluralism 'came to assign key significance to intermediate groups between the state and the individual: a protection against the social atomism of the "mass society" in which citizens were susceptible to totalitarian manipulation'.[31] Democratic theorists such as Schumpeter and Dahl affirmed the democratic virtue of free political competition. For Schumpeter, the essence of the democratic method lay in periodic elections between competing political parties.[32] Democratic competition was the principal bulwark against totalitarianism, and the operation of the democratic marketplace ensured that governments remained responsive to citizens' aggregated preferences. Dahl's theory complemented this focus on elites by exploring the role of groups in the democratic process.[33] The competitive clash between fixed interests in bargaining between pressure groups and the State ensured that a wide range of individuals could exercise some influence over public decision-making. The self-interest of citizens,

[26] It would, of course, have been unthinkable in the light of Kahn-Freund's Weimar experiences, and the catastrophic political consequences of the integration of German trade unions into the coercive apparatus of the State. For further discussion, see R Dukes, 'Otto Kahn-Freund and Collective Laissez-Faire: An Edifice without a Keystone?' (2009) 2 *Modern Law Review*, 220–46.

[27] Kahn-Freund, 'Labour Law' 24.

[28] R Lewis, 'Kahn-Freund and Labour Law: An Outline Critique' (1979) 8 *Industrial Law Journal* 202, 217.

[29] See the seminal R Hyman, 'Pluralism, Procedural Consensus, and Collective Bargaining' (1978) 16 *British Journal of Industrial Relations* 16.

[30] P Ackers, 'Collective Bargaining as Industrial Democracy: The Political Foundations of British Industrial Relations Pluralism' (2007) 45 *British Journal of Industrial Relations* 77.

[31] Hyman, above n 29, 19.

[32] JA Schumpeter, *Capitalism, Socialism and Democracy*, 2nd edn (London, George, Allen and Unwin, 1947).

[33] RA Dahl, *A Preface to Democratic Theory* (Chicago, University of Chicago Press, 1956).

pressure groups, and their ruling elites was thus revealed as the motor-force of politics, the basis of political equilibrium, and the guarantor of democratic values.

These political alignments helped to shape the motifs of CLF: the democratic need for trade unions to perform an oppositional role in industry; the protective function of collective bargaining as a process for vindicating workers' rights and interests; the centrality of collective bargaining as a form of interest group bargaining between trade unions and management; the risks inherent in participative schemes of worker involvement in diluting unions' independence from management; the inherent democratic inferiority of consultation; and the institutionalisation of conflicts of interest through collective bargaining and its potential for securing equilibrium and consensus.[34]

As an account of the 'pluralistic constitution', this interface between American political pluralism and CLF explains much of significance. Nevertheless it was incomplete in important ways. In particular, British trade unions operated primarily as *industrial* rather than *political* pressure groups despite having sufficient leverage to do the latter. One of the major themes of American political pluralism was its conception of legitimate group activity in politics. As Hirst argues, these theories postulated as an ideal-type of the democratic process, 'a process of political competition [which] tends to treat the state and government as intermediary networks through which competing interests strive to influence policy and through which the objectives of the dominant organized interests on any particular issue are carried out'.[35] Such a view of industrial politics was utterly alien to the envisaged relation between trade unions and the State in CLF. In fact, whilst American political pluralism elucidated the role of trade unions *within* the British system of industrial relations, it was unable to explain the nature of the State's relationship to the autonomous actors operating within that system. That crucial relationship is elucidated through understanding CLF's less conspicuous, but no less important, connections to English political pluralism.

C The State and Collective Bargaining: The Influence of English Political Pluralism

As Roy Lewis has argued, CLF also signified 'a limitation on the sovereignty of the state, and specifically that "groups" in society (such as religious organizations and trade unions) should be independent from the State. The existence of the independent or autonomous groups disperses power and so, it is argued,

[34] The classic treatment along these lines is HA Clegg, *A New Approach to Industrial Democracy* (Oxford, Blackwell, 1960).

[35] PQ Hirst, 'Introduction', in PQ Hirst (ed), *The Pluralist Theory of the State: Selected Writings of GDH Cole, JN Figgis, and HJ Laski* (London, Routledge, 1993) 3. See also D Nicholls, *The Pluralist State: The Political Ideas of JN Figgis and his Contemporaries*, 2nd edn (London, Macmillan, 1994) 134.

safeguards freedoms against an all-powerful state'.[36] This offered an account of State and civil society that was rooted in the anti-statist philosophy of the English political pluralists. It was a natural political alignment for one such as Kahn-Freund who had witnessed at first hand the catastrophic consequences of an overweening State in the Weimar years.[37]

English political pluralism was an eclectic movement that was inspired by a distrust of State power.[38] It spanned a diverse set of political thinkers, including the theologian JN Figgis, and (in their early work, at least) the political philosophers GDH Cole and Harold Laski. In turn, the English movement had derived intellectual support from Otto von Gierke's legal historical analysis of the position of groups and corporations in German law.[39] Gierke had attacked the idea, which he ascribed to the influence of Roman law concepts in the German juristic tradition, that associations derived their fictitious existence solely through the conferral of legal personality by a legal act of the State.[40] Rather, and contrary to this 'concessionist' view of corporate personality, these associations were real entities that enjoyed inherent rights and privileges against the State. The conferral of legal personality through State recognition was simply a means of rendering the legal position of groups concordant with their social reality. English political pluralism thus set its face against, on the one hand, the atomising tendencies of liberal individualism, and on the other hand, the excessive collectivist reliance on State regulation. It was therefore opposed in equal measure to classical liberals such as Dicey, and technocratic Fabians such as the Webbs.[41]

The English political pluralists were fundamentally committed to the value of autonomous group life in civil society. The various groups and associations of civil society provided a forum where citizens could express and realise their inherent social natures while pursuing their own conceptions of the good with like-minded others. More importantly, this web of autonomous associations provided an effective bulwark against State encroachment on individual liberty, and provided an institutional safeguard against totalitarianism. The various tasks of social life were, as far as possible, to be executed by cooperative group action in civil society, rather than by State regulation and legal enactment:

[36] Lewis, above n 28, 114.

[37] Dukes, above n 26.

[38] D Nicholls, *Three Varieties of Pluralism* (London, Macmillan, 1974) 6.

[39] For an account of Gierke's influence see PP Craig, *Public Law and Democracy in the United Kingdom and the United States of America* (Oxford, Oxford University Press, 1990) 141. See also Hirst, above n 35, 17.

[40] See O Von Gierke, *Political Theories of the Middle Age* (Cambridge, Cambridge University Press, 1900), translated and with an introduction by FW Maitland.

[41] Its resonance with collective laissez-faire should thus be immediately apparent, as a careful reading of 'Labour Law' makes clear.

> Central to pluralism were the belief in the vitality and the legitimacy of self-governing associations as means of organizing social life and the belief that political representation must respect the principle of function, recognizing associations like trade unions, churches and voluntary bodies. In the pluralist scheme it is such associations that perform the basic tasks of social life. Pluralism is strongly anti-statist in its basic principles.[42]

These basic anti-statist principles consisted of two more specific themes: first, a critique and rejection of monistic concepts of State sovereignty; secondly, a defence of the view that associations were 'real' *sui generis* entities, not reducible to the actions of individual members, and reflected in a 'realist' view of corporate personality. Given the importance of English political pluralism as a normative backdrop to Kahn-Freund's pluralistic constitution, a closer examination of each of these elements is warranted.

(i) Sovereignty and Pluralism

First, let us take the pluralist critique of sovereignty. English political pluralism arose, at least in part, in opposition to the ruling theory of politics and constitutional law in nineteenth century England: the doctrine of sovereignty. Sovereignty implies 'that some agency enjoys of right a plenitude of power, that it may make any rule or policy within a given territory and put it into effect'.[43] This doctrine facilitated, both ethically and legally, the assertion of supremacist claims by the State. The English political pluralists challenged both kinds of supremacist claim.

It was Laski who attacked the ethical theory of sovereignty most forcefully.[44] He had a clear perception of the devastating threat ethical sovereignty posed to autonomous group life in the polity. If the State was to achieve ethical primacy in the lives of its citizens, then the very existence of more particularistic attachments and solidarities arising in the multiplicity of social unions in civil society raised a significant challenge to the State's totalising project. For Laski, it was both futile and unconscionable for States to ignore the plurality of legitimate ethical loyalties that encumbered the lives of conscientious citizens. These social attachments, such as membership of trade unions or churches, penetrated the very identities of those who participated in these various social unions.[45] The

[42] Hirst, above n 35, 2.

[43] *Ibid*, 23.

[44] See Lord Wedderburn, 'Laski's Law behind the Law: 1906 to European Labour Law', in R Rawlings (ed) *Law, Society and Economy* (Oxford, Oxford University Press 1997) 25, at 39, where Wedderburn notes the close personal contact between Laski and Kahn-Freund towards the end of World War II. See also R Lewis, 'Collective Agreements: the Kahn-Freund Legacy' (1979) 42 *Modern Law Review* 613, 618.

[45] Figgis also defended such a view. See JN Figgis, 'The Great Leviathan', in PQ Hirst (ed), *The Pluralist Theory of the State: Selected Writings of GDH Cole, JN Figgis, and HJ Laski* (London, Routledge, 1993) 125.

continuous potential for conflicting allegiances, which presented citizens with genuine ethical dilemmas, was perfectly natural; and such conflicts could not be eradicated by assuming a priori that legal obligations ethically trumped all other particularistic attachments. Thus, Laski argued that 'every community has groups of citizens to whom certain things are fundamental. They will fight for the preservation of those things ... There are English men (*sic*), I think, who would resist an attempt to abolish the enfranchisement of the working class, or the right to industrial combination, or the re-establishment of limitations upon freedom of religious belief.'[46] Given the ethical legitimacy of conscientious disobedience in the pluralist theory, this erected a presumptive cautionary norm for public decision-makers: that wherever the State legislated *against* the group's particular will and conscience, this intervention was likely to be ineffective in shaping human conduct. Worse still, the potential social backlash against such intervention and the resulting civil disorder could undermine the very authority of the State. As Figgis put it in an ecclesiastical context, 'the Roman government did not destroy the living unity of the church by denying its claim to exist; but it nearly destroyed itself in the attempt'.[47]

The pluralists' rejection of ethical sovereignty also underpinned their rejection of legal sovereignty. At first glance, the incompatibility of legal sovereignty and English political pluralism is not obvious. For example, neither Figgis nor Laski denied the formal subordination of common law to legislation as a source of law.[48] Moreover, it is important not to confuse the anti-*statist* impulse of political pluralism with the anti-*legal* position associated with certain strands of Marxist theory.[49] Political pluralists such as Figgis defended the need for public coordination of the various self-governing associations in civil society, and they also accepted that the principal technique for securing social coordination was through the exercise of legal authority. What the pluralists argued for, however, were entrenched constitutional limits on the State's legislative and administrative capacities. Without entrenched limits, the possibility always remained that the State could 'deny the plural interests and wills of a complex society ... and use bureaucracy to carry out comprehensive programmes of reconstruction of the "private" sphere, secure in the state's right to legislate over every circumstance'.[50] Thus, the English political pluralists rejected the logic of legal illimitability that was central to the concept of legal sovereignty. Instead, they endorsed the crafting of constitutional limits on State action to ensure that the self-governing activities of associations were protected.

[46] HJ Laski, 'Law and the State', in PQ Hirst (ed), *The Pluralist Theory of the State: Selected Writings of GDH Cole, JN Figgis, and HJ Laski* (London, Routledge, 1993) 206.

[47] Figgis, above n 45, 126.

[48] Nicholls, above n 35, 50.

[49] Hirst, above n 35, 29.

[50] PQ Hirst, *Associative Democracy: New Forms of Economic and Social Governance* (Cambridge, Polity, 1994) 28.

(ii) The Real Personality of Groups and Pluralism

This critique of sovereignty was complemented by the pluralists' adoption of a 'realist' interpretation of corporate personality. This 'realist' theory emerged as a counterpoint to 'fiction' theories of corporate personality. On the one hand, 'fiction' theories argued that while groups could sometimes acquire legal personality (for example, through the legal act of incorporation) so that they could be the independent bearers of legal rights and duties, this extension of juristic capacity was predicated on a fiction. This legal 'person' did not correspond to anything real that existed in the world. Rather, the State simply extended juristic capacity beyond the central case of natural persons in certain circumstances where the State deemed it expedient to do so. This involved treating corporate bodies as if they really existed, but only for specific juristic purposes as a concession by the State. On the other hand, 'realist' theories argued that the conferral of legal personality on groups simply brought the law into alignment with social reality. For Laski, this concessionist view that groups were brought into existence and could be extinguished solely by a legal act of recognition by the State was a distortion: 'to your ordinary man it is a strange notion that a Roman Church, a Society of Jesus, a Standard Oil Trust—the most fundamentally unified persons, so he would say, in existence—should be thus devoid of group will because, forsooth, certain mystic words have not been pronounced over them by the state'.[51] Groups were organic *sui generis* entities that enjoyed a unitary life beyond the several lives of their individual constituents. Legal personality was ancillary to this social truth, and it needed to be developed by the lawyers so as to reflect it.

Understood as a metaphysical claim, the 'realist' theory now seems rather quaint.[52] However, as HLA Hart acknowledged, the debates about corporate personality were often not 'the battle-cries of analytical jurists. They were ways of asserting or denying the claims of organized groups to recognition by the State'.[53] In other words, the realist theory was political as well as metaphysical in nature. The political form of the realist theory involved the moral advocacy of free group life vis-à-vis the claims of the State. This moral advocacy embraced two distinct elements. First, it offered a variant of the futility objection raised by the political pluralists in their critique of ethical sovereignty. Just as coercive intervention would seldom be effective in bending the group's will to the State's

[51] HJ Laski, 'The Personality of Associations', in PQ Hirst (ed), *The Pluralist Theory of the State: Selected Writings of GDH Cole, JN Figgis, and H J Laski* (London, Routledge, 1993) 174.

[52] See M Cohen, 'Communal ghosts and other perils in social philosophy' (1919) 16 *The Journal of Philosophy* 673, for a convincing demolition of realism as a metaphysical claim concerning groups. Other proponents of CLF have rejected the realist position as a matter of metaphysics: see KW Wedderburn, 'Corporate Personality and Social Policy: the Problem of the Quasi-Corporation' (1965) 28 *Modern Law Review* 62, 70–71.

[53] HLA Hart, *Essays in Jurisprudence and Philosophy* (Oxford, Oxford University Press 1983) 25.

own purposes, so indeed would a denial of the group's very existence in law. At best, this interference and suppression would be ineffectual in shaping human conduct and would necessitate oppressive State tactics to achieve its goals; at worst, it would undermine respect for the law if dissentient citizens resisted such interference with public acts of disobedience. This was recognised by the legal historian Maitland, who observed that 'group personality is no purely legal phenomenon. The law-giver may say that it does not exist, where, as a matter of moral sentiment, it does exist. When that happens, he incurs the penalty ordained for those who ignorantly or wilfully say the thing that is not.'[54] Laski also defended this presumptive cautionary norm against State interference.[55]

The second element was a vigorous normative defence of the group's democratic right to be autonomous and self-determining. As Laski perceived, beyond the clutter of metaphysical distractions, the denial of the group's democratic right was an interpretative tendency that flowed ineluctably from the fiction theory of corporate personality: 'The corporation is given personality for certain purposes to be found in its history, in its charter, its constituting act, its articles of association … The corporation is a creature of the state. Its will is a delegated will; its purpose exists only because it has secured recognition.'[56] Thus, the realist theory derived its salience as a political defence of the group's liberty to define its own purposes and internal mode of existence, free from State control. If the group's organic growth was stultified, the free development of the individual personality was stultified also. As such, the disagreement between realists and concessionists was of great practical significance. Both realism and concessionism were 'active doctrines of legal interpretation'.[57] But whereas the concessionists advocated strict fidelity by the group to its narrowly defined purposes policed through the judicial technique of ultra vires, the realists defended the democratic value of group self-determination and its free organic growth. Thus the realist notion of groups as living persons was, in the final analysis, a metaphor in service of concrete political ends.

At the intersection of the political pluralist theories of sovereignty and group personality was its overriding political value: the maximisation of liberty through the liberal principle of respect for group autonomy.[58] This was to be achieved through the pluralistic constitution giving maximum latitude to the self-governing activities of voluntary groups in civil society. It is here that the overlap of English political pluralism and CLF is most striking. For example, Kahn-Freund's famous insight in 'Labour Law' that the British labour movement had been the heir to a liberal as much as a socialist political tradition is acutely

[54] FW Maitland, 'Moral Personality and Legal Personality', reprinted as an appendix in D Nicholls, *The Pluralist State: The Political Ideas of JN Figgis and his Contemporaries*, 2nd edn (London, Macmillan, 1994) 177.

[55] Laski, above n 51, 179–80.

[56] *Ibid*, 165.

[57] Hirst, above n 35, 18.

[58] Nicholls, above n 38, 5.

perceptive of this overlap.[59] It is also reflected in Flanders' authoritative interpretation of CLF

> the values of voluntarism bring us back to the theme of democracy—as trade unions interpret it. They want to order their own affairs according to their own preferences with as little outside interference as possible ... The extent to which external aid, including legislation, is sought depends on the need for it, and trade unions try to assess how much they will be losing or gaining control over what they take to be their own affairs.[60]

IV CLF DEFENDED: THREE CRITIQUES OF CLF

Articulating the political theory of CLF provides the key to grasping its coherence as an interpretive account of the historical structure of British collective labour law. Now that this political theory has been elucidated, we can evaluate the abstentionist, neutrality, and coherence critiques of CLF. In different ways, each of these critiques miscarries. Properly understood, and contrary to its critics, CLF continues to provide the most coherent explanatory account of the State's historical role in British industrial relations.

A The Abstentionist Critique

In his less guarded moments, Kahn-Freund certainly emphasised the law's abstemiousness in British industrial relations. Hugh Collins' 'abstentionist' critique purports to identify Kahn-Freund's rationalisation of this tendency, and then offers a critique of that rationalisation.[61] Collins' argument proceeds in the following way. In labour law systems historically based on industrial pluralism, of which Britain was the paradigm case, there was a wise aversion to the use of law to promote union recognition and collective bargaining. In Britain, where that aversion was at its most extreme, organised labour abjured direct legal support in the form of a statutory duty to bargain. Instead, the law abstained from interfering with the spontaneous social forces of inexorable union growth. This fostered the prized vigour of the British system of collective bargaining, which operated (largely) independently of positive legal supports. Even in industrial pluralist systems such as the US where there was a longstanding statutory duty to bargain, the efficacy of this legal intervention was questionable. For industrial pluralists, this elaborate statutory structure served 'as much to frustrate the aspirations of the employees as to impose the pluralist model on the enterprise'.[62]

[59] Kahn-Freund, 'Labour Law' 8.
[60] A Flanders, 'The Tradition of Voluntarism' (1974) 12 *British Journal of Industrial Relations* 352, 362–3.
[61] Collins, above n 15.
[62] *Ibid*, 83.

Thus, the industrial pluralists were forced to conclude that collective bargaining prospered best where the law had least to do with it. CLF represented the apex of this wise anti-legal pragmatism.

What was the basis of this sceptical attitude towards the use of law as an instrument for effectuating social change? For Collins, it was based in a faulty materialist understanding of the relation between legal norms and social practices that had its roots in Marxist social theory. Crudely, this position was based on a view that legal norms were impotent in steering economic and social relations. This was predicated on a perception of the law, on the one hand, and society and the economy, on the other hand, as entities that were hermetically separate from each other. For Collins, 'these theories of the relation between law and society infuse and guide the abstentionist labour law tradition, so much so that they are treated as rudimentary truisms, beyond the reach of criticism'.[63]

Collins' challenge to this abstentionist thesis was simple and powerful. When we talk of the social power of capital and organised labour, this takes place against the backdrop of a legal baseline that allocates proprietary and contractual entitlements. The social power of capital derives from its ownership of the means of production; and this ownership, in turn, is defined by the legal incidents of a system of private property. Similarly, the social power of organised labour is dependent on the legal rules regulating workers' combination and collective action. Sometimes this legal baseline is so taken for granted it seems invisible. But Collins joins forces with a diverse band of legal realists,[64] critical labour lawyers,[65] and republican legal theorists,[66] in arguing that this invisibility is an illusion: 'Since it is impossible to distinguish the economic relations of production from their legal definition, it makes little sense to speak of the law regulating social power or being separate from capital and labour, for the law determines in the first instance who should hold power, the strength of that power, and to what ends it may be used.'[67] With this materialist spell broken, all sorts of possibilities in the positive use of labour law to bring about desirable patterns of social change are opened up.

Collins' 'abstentionist' critique, while profoundly influential, has attracted vehement counterattacks from defenders of CLF.[68] While these challenges create significant problems for the 'abstentionist' critique, I propose to adopt a different tack. Hugh Collins' view that legal norms perform a constitutive role in establishing the social power of actors in the labour market provided an

[63] *Ibid*, 86.

[64] MR Cohen, 'Property and Sovereignty' (1927) 13 *Cornell Law Quarterly* 8.

[65] K Klare, 'Workplace Democracy and Market Reconstruction: An Agenda for Legal Reform' (1988) 38 *Catholic University Law Review* 1.

[66] C Sunstein, *The Partial Constitution* (Cambridge Massachusetts, Harvard University Press, 1993).

[67] Collins, above n 15, 87.

[68] See, eg, Lord Wedderburn, 'Collective Bargaining or Legal Enactment? The 1999 Act and Union Recognition' (2000) 29 *Industrial Law Journal* 1, 8–12.

important and powerful insight into the potential utility of law as an instrument of social justice.[69] In this respect, Collins' analysis unequivocally validated labour law as a worthwhile practical regulatory activity, and the importance of Collins' essay in the development of labour law theory should not be under-estimated. However, this 'constitutive' view of legal norms was entirely consistent with, and indeed implicit in, Kahn-Freund's theorisation of CLF. While Kahn-Freund certainly counselled caution in the use of law as an instrument of social change in certain clearly defined contexts, this did not amount to a general scepticism about the law's utility as a regulatory tool.

In fact, a careful reading of Kahn-Freund's work discloses a richly differentiated account of the law's regulatory capacities. For Kahn-Freund, the potential efficacy of legal norms was evident in three ways. First, when Kahn-Freund emphasised the relative insignificance of legal sanctions in the sphere of collective labour relations, he was speaking as a comparatist. Thus, and by way of contrast to the British experience, in the US the law had left an unmistakeable imprint on the industrial relations system. Bargaining units were defined through administrative procedures; bargaining agents were selected through a State administered ballot procedure; and those legally sanctioned bargaining agents were subject to a legal duty of fair representation to give equal protection to the interests of all their worker constituents.[70] Moreover, US unions had enjoyed favourable experience of legal support in the early years of the Wagner Act, and this generated a more positive attitude by those unions towards the use of law to promote recognition.[71] This British exceptionalism was reinforced through an appreciation of the law's more pronounced role in jurisdictions as diverse as Australia, France, Germany and Sweden. Time and again, Kahn-Freund emphasised he was explicating 'a characteristic peculiar to the British industrial scene'.[72] This touches a point of fundamental methodological significance missed by the 'abstentionist' critique: 'needless to say the question what contribution the law can make to the ordering of industrial relations *cannot be asked in the abstract, but only with reference to a particular society and a particular system of industrial relations*'.[73] This is irreconcilable with Collins' view that CLF (as a species of 'industrial pluralism') was based on a universal axiom postulating a generic truth about labour law in general—namely the materialist separability of legal norms from social and economic forces in society. This would be to confuse Kahn-Freund the comparatist with Kahn-Freund the social theorist.

[69] The question arises whether this constitutive view of legal norms is inconsistent with the materialist analysis. For a compelling view that there is no such inconsistency, see GA Cohen, 'Base and Superstructure: A Reply to Hugh Collins' (1989) 9 *Oxford Journal of Legal Studies* 95.

[70] Kahn-Freund, 'Intergroup Conflicts' 48–9; Kahn-Freund, 'Legal Framework' 53 and 55.

[71] Flanders, above n 60, 369.

[72] Kahn-Freund, 'Legal Framework' 45.

[73] Kahn-Freund, 'Retrospect' 301 (emphasis added).

Secondly, Kahn-Freund's work demonstrates a sensitive assessment of the pros and cons of legal regulation in particular substantive domains: dogmatic presumptions for or against legal regulation in general were rejected. This was reflected in Kahn-Freund's observation that 'all legal development must be along a diagonal in a parallelogram of forces, one of the sides of which is a formulated policy directed towards a defined aim, the other of which is traced by what is practicable in a society in the light of traditions, habits, and available means'.[74] Thus, within the domain of regulating internal trade union affairs, he concluded that it was proper to enact legal rights for union members not to be arbitrarily excluded or expelled from union membership.[75] By contrast, the specific difficulties with imposing a prescriptive legal template for the election of union leaders were significant. Models of political democracy did not translate well into the context of internal union affairs. Kahn-Freund was forced to conclude that 'this must surely be a matter which the law should severely leave alone'.[76]

And again, the Donovan Commission (wisely, in his view) did not recommend compelling the legal enforceability of the contractual aspect of collective agreements, or the enactment of a legal duty to bargain in good faith (this was the Royal Commission on Trade Unions and Employers Associations, popularly known as the Donovan Commission on account of it being chaired by Lord Donovan). For various context-specific reasons, Kahn-Freund's parallelogram of forces pointed towards a less direct route to desired social change. By contrast, after a balanced appraisal of the virtues and vices of British collective agreements, Kahn-Freund argued strenuously for a comprehensive legislative code of regulatory norms governing the legal incidents of the contract of employment.[77] The direct legislative route was both possible and desirable. All of this denotes an altogether more multifaceted attitude in Kahn-Freund's work towards social change through legal enactment.

Thirdly, Kahn-Freund was scrupulously attentive to the *form* of legal intervention and, in particular, the interplay between legal form and the efficacy of law as an instrument of social change. This is particularly important in his discussion of the characteristic British preference for 'indirect' modes of auxiliary support for collective bargaining, and its correlative aversion to the use of civil or criminal sanctions to directly compel the recognition of unions.[78] These indirect modes variously consisted in the use of fair wages clauses, institution building either through wages councils or administrative intervention by the Ministry of Labour, or extending the normative scope of collective agreements. For Kahn-Freund, the unifying theme of the indirect mode was its basis in 'organized persuasion'.[79]

74 *Ibid*, 308.
75 O Kahn-Freund, 'Trade Unions, the Law and Society' (1970) 33 *Modern Law Review* 241.
76 *Ibid*, 264.
77 Kahn-Freund, 'Retrospect' 311–13.
78 *Ibid*, 303–8.
79 *Ibid*, 304.

Moreover, this preference for indirect intervention had proven to be a smart regulatory choice in Britain: 'the law has been conspicuously unsuccessful where it sought to promote bargaining and peace through direct compulsion', whereas indirect strategies had been 'astonishingly successful'.[80] Once again, Kahn-Freund's highly positive evaluation of the social effects of 'indirect' legal intervention belies the 'abstentionist' characterisation of CLF. Legal abstentionism would be equally sceptical of the social efficacy of legal intervention in either its direct or indirect forms.

If the law *could* be successful as a regulatory tool in various contexts, which social and economic elements impeded its efficacy? It is here that the political theory of CLF provides an answer. In one of Kahn-Freund's mature contributions to the debate concerning the law's role in industrial relations, he observed:

> Certain aspects of labour relations *cannot be controlled by the law*. The law is likely to be a failure whenever it seeks to counteract habits of action or of inaction adopted by large numbers of men and women in pursuance of established social custom, norms of conduct or ethical or religious convictions ... Legal norms have their social effect through legal sanctions, and sanctions cannot be applied to counteract the spontaneous conduct of amorphous masses.[81] (emphasis added)

In essence, this mirrors the English political pluralists' thesis concerning the possibilities (and limits) of State regulation of groups in civil society. To recap, the English political pluralist critique of ethical sovereignty and its defence of the real personality of groups converged on a vitally significant cautionary norm for public decision-makers: that whenever the State legislated contrary to individual conscience or the group's will, or whenever the State withheld legal recognition from a social group that pressed for it, such acts were likely to be oppressive, futile, and counterproductive. If resistant groups met such measures with civil disobedience, the very existence of the State might be threatened. The pluralist State therefore needed to proceed carefully where group regulation was concerned. That was a pragmatic reason in favour of the primacy accorded by pluralists to the group's right of self-determination.

This provides a more lucid rationalisation of Kahn-Freund's attitude towards law as a regulatory tool than the materialist characterisation of the 'abstentionist' critique. In particular, it explains Kahn-Freund's generally cautious attitude towards the use of law in the sphere of collective labour relations, particularly where group autonomy was concerned; and, by contrast, his generally more sanguine attitude towards its use where individual employment rights were

[80] *Ibid*, 305. Kahn-Freund is more circumspect about the efficacy of wages councils. However, this is not driven by latent law-aversion or blind ideological closure. It is based in a concrete assessment of their particular regulatory effects. In 'Retrospect', Kahn-Freund is more positive about the social effects of fair wages clauses, by contrast.

[81] Kahn-Freund, above n 75, 241.

concerned.[82] It also illuminates his attitude to one of the great regulatory controversies of the post-war period: the use of direct legal sanctions against striking workers to enforce industrial peace. The evidence presented to the Donovan Commission by Sir Harold Emmerson, concerning mass resort to penal sanctions against striking miners at Betteshanger Colliery under Order 1305, was a vivid empirical demonstration of the English political pluralist thesis.[83] When the criminal law collided with the conscientious actions of 'amorphous masses', it did so unsuccessfully. In the end, Kahn-Freund's caution and Emmerson's note persuaded Lord Donovan in rejecting reliance on legal sanctions in this context.

In fairness to the 'abstentionist' critique, many of Kahn-Freund's observations taken singly are consistent with the thrust of its materialist characterisation of CLF. Thus, we find in *Labour and the Law* the famous statement that 'the law has important functions in labour relations but they are secondary if compared with the impact of the labour market (supply and demand) and, which is relevant here, with the spontaneous creation of a social power on the workers' side'.[84] Or again, 'everywhere the effectiveness of the law depends on the unions far more than the unions depend on the effectiveness of the law'.[85] Nevertheless, the broad canvass of Kahn-Freund's work is inconsistent with the 'abstentionist' critique's characterisation. It seems to me that in Kahn-Freund's seeming materialist moments in *Labour and the Law*, he was simply emphasising the impact of non-legal labour market factors such as the level of unemployment on patterns of union membership growth and decline. That there is such an impact, and that legal norms have little direct influence over it, is undeniable. It is quite mistaken to equate this sensible insight with a generalised scepticism about law's regulatory efficacy in collective labour relations. In retrospect, Collins' positive thesis that legal norms can be effective in mitigating bureaucratic subordination in employing organisations remains compelling. However, this thesis involved no inconsistency with the political elements of CLF.

B The Neutrality Critique

Keith Ewing[86] and, more recently, Chris Howell[87] have urged an alternative line of attack on CLF. The main thrust of this critique is that CLF has systematically

[82] Compare A Wilson, 'Contract and Prerogative: A Reconsideration of the Legal Enforcement of Collective Agreements' (1984) 13 *Industrial Law Journal* 1, who mistakenly assumes that CLF was based upon an undifferentiated hostility to all forms of State intervention in the sphere of labour law.

[83] Royal Commission on Trade Unions and Employers' Associations 1965–1968 Report (Cmnd 3623, 1968) 340–41.

[84] PL Davies and MR Freedland (eds), *Kahn-Freund's Labour and the Law*, 3rd edn (London, Stevens & Sons, 1983) 19.

[85] *Ibid*, 21.

[86] Ewing, above n 16.

[87] Howell, above n 17.

underestimated the role of the State in British industrial relations. In particular, it has failed to identify the State's positive role in constructing and supporting bargaining institutions. The most damaging legacy of this is that it has led unions to devalue the importance of securing positive State support for effective bargaining activities. Yet both Ewing and Howell argue that bargaining structures in Britain have rarely thrived in the absence of strong State support, but have instead tended to wax and wane in tandem with State intervention and withdrawal. If the State's active support was so integral to the maturity of British collective bargaining in the mid-twentieth century, how did a theorist of Kahn-Freund's eminence manage to miss this giant elephant standing in the middle of the British industrial relations room? The analysis offered by the 'neutrality' critique is elegant.

As an exemplar of this critique, let us evaluate Keith Ewing's argument. Ewing draws a distinction between two alternate models of political theory that might underpin a system of worker-protective labour law. On the one hand, 'social liberalism' envisaged ameliorative intervention by the State to mitigate the worst excesses of unequal bargaining power between individual workers and employers. As a liberal political theory, it was aligned with a defence of State neutrality; as a worker-protective theory, it likewise acknowledged that genuine neutrality could only be achieved by legislative exclusion of the common law impediments to collective action. But beyond these 'negative' statutory exclusions, the 'social-liberal' State should defer as far as possible to the collective forces in industrial civil society. For Ewing, 'a strong echo of this is to be found in the theory and practice of "collective laissez-faire", which is based on the premise of a largely but not wholly passive state'.[88] Moreover, the essence of the State's role in CLF 'is by definition one of political indifference, in the sense that while the state may remove the impediments which prevent trade unions from operating, it is largely indifferent to the success or failure of trade-union organization'.[89]

On the other hand, 'social-interventionism' rejected the strictures of State neutrality espoused by social liberals. Instead, the State's role was unashamedly positive, with social interventionists advocating the use of public power to promote the social and economic welfare of citizens. This corresponded to a distinctive legal structure. 'Negative' statutory exclusions of common law doctrines were insufficient. Active State support was needed 'to ensure that the institutional structures are in place to facilitate trade-union involvement in the decision-making process, using the law or other forms of state apparatus in a positive sense where necessary'.[90] This countenanced statutory intervention as an auxiliary prop to collective bargaining, but it was equally comfortable with other forms of 'administrative' intervention by the State where these were likely to prove effective.

[88] Ewing, above n 16, 4.
[89] *Ibid*, 5.
[90] *Ibid*, 6–7.

According to Ewing, CLF went wrong in mistaking the normative character of the British State. CLF erroneously adopted the 'social-liberal' characterisation because it was seduced by the historical absence of a legal duty to bargain. It was perhaps a natural error to equate this absence with State neutrality, for the pre-eminent modus operandi of the State is legislative enactment. In its failure to legislate, the British State was behaving as a social-liberal state might behave. Nevertheless, according to Ewing, CLF went wrong in failing to appreciate that *the legal duty to bargain might have functional equivalents in other forms of non-statutory State intervention.*

Once these functionally equivalent modes of State intervention were brought into view, the full extent of the State's critical role in the industrial relations system was exposed. In particular, Ewing focuses on the administrative activities of the Ministry of Labour in the inter-war period. The Whitley Committee unequivocally identified collective bargaining as a normatively attractive basis for British industrial relations. The State, through the medium of the Ministry of Labour, was to take responsibility for encouraging the voluntary formation of Joint Industrial Councils by unions and employers' associations or, where union organisation was weak, through the formation of Trade Boards under the Trade Boards Act 1918. This technique of public dialogue and persuasion, conducted in the shadow of legal compulsion provided by the system of trade boards, proved remarkably successful. Ewing is surely correct when he claims that the spectacular coverage of collective wage-setting mechanisms in the immediate aftermath of World War II (in excess of 85 per cent) 'seems impossible to achieve without a strong steer from the state'.[91] Contrary to the social liberal postulate of State neutrality, the British State's enduring role in supporting and extending the system of collective bargaining could only be accounted for by the social-interventionist theory of the State. Its primary mode of intervention was through the administrative activity of *institution-building*, in dialogue with other industrial relations actors in civil society. Refracting this sphere of social life through the narrow lens of legal enactment, represented by a statutory duty to bargain, ultimately distorted the State's pivotal historical role in British industrial relations.[92]

The richness of the historical evidence upon which the 'neutrality critique' is based is difficult to dispute. If CLF was predicated on the notion of State neutrality towards collective bargaining, then Ewing's critique of CLF as a descriptive-explanatory theory of British labour law is compelling. The countervailing evidence is too strong to sustain the 'social liberal' characterisation of the State's role. On closer examination of Kahn-Freund's framework, however, one may begin to question the identification of CLF with a social-liberal political theory. In fact, Kahn-Freund was acutely aware of the British State's distinctive

[91] *Ibid*, 31.
[92] *Ibid*, 7.

mode of positive intervention. It was rooted in his perceptive elucidation of the concept of 'organized persuasion':

> The collective bargaining process itself and the observance of concluded agreements are supported by a series of legislative measures, of institutions, and of administrative practices. The gist of these is that they provide a statutory framework for organized persuasion ... Persuasion and indirect sanction, that is promise of benefits and threat of disadvantages, are the ways by which in this country the law traditionally exercises its function as an auxiliary to collective bargaining.[93]

As Kahn-Freund himself acknowledged, the persuasive efforts of the Ministry of Labour in this regard were 'a conspicuous success'.[94]

Confusingly, Kahn-Freund was equally forthright in his characterisation of the law's aspiration to neutrality in collective labour relations. In particular, it was in the context of the regulation of trade disputes that the policy of legal neutrality between the warring parties was most prominent.[95] What are we to make of this apparent inconsistency in CLF's schema? Is it possible for the law simultaneously to reject and endorse a policy of neutrality in collective labour relations, or does this simply betray theoretical incoherence? One way of teasing out this distinctive political orientation is to consider the controversial position of compulsory arbitration in the theory and practice of CLF. As Wedderburn has reminded us, it is an 'undervalued' fact that Britain has had some four decades' experience of compulsory arbitration in the war and the post-war period.[96] For Kahn-Freund, compulsory arbitration occupied an ambiguous and problematical place in the free institutions of liberal democracies, whichever precise form it took. The theoretical statement of this position can be found in 'Intergroup Conflicts': 'of the various methods of legal intervention ... the only one intrinsically antithetic to the principle of group autonomy is that known as compulsory arbitration ... It cannot be justified from the point of view of the principle of intergroup autonomy.'[97] Elsewhere in his early work, Kahn-Freund was equally uncompromising in his rejection of compulsory arbitration as 'incompatible with voluntary trade unionism' and his view that 'it has a close affinity to Fascist legal institutions'.[98] Consequently, it was Kahn-Freund's fervent hope that compulsory arbitration would be discontinued at the end of the war—it was irredeemably 'an undesirable institution'.[99]

[93] Kahn-Freund, 'Retrospect' 304.
[94] *Ibid.*
[95] Kahn-Freund, 'Labour Law' 23; see also, Kahn-Freund, 'Legal Framework' 44.
[96] Lord Wedderburn, *Labour Law and Freedom* (London, Lawrence & Wishart, 1995) 11.
[97] Kahn-Freund, 'Intergroup Conflicts' 73.
[98] Kahn-Freund, 'Wartime Legislation' 121 n 30.
[99] *Ibid*, 120. On this issue in particular, Kahn-Freund's views were not static. In his later work, Kahn-Freund was more open-minded to the possibility that compulsory arbitration might have useful functions that did not entail unacceptable risks to political freedom. This was clear in the final edition of *Labour and the Law* (above n 84), where he pointed to the vigorous independence of Australian trade unions under a general system of compulsory arbitration (at 147–53). The social effects of legislation

What was the basis of this early hostility, and what does it tell us about the politics of CLF? If we examine Kahn-Freund's analysis of Order 1305,[100] there is an illuminating contrast in his attitude towards two different legal aspects of that provision. First, there were the provisions dealing with the compulsory settlement of trade disputes to ensure unimpeded production in the circumstances of wartime. Article 4 deemed all strikes and lockouts a criminal offence except where 21 days had elapsed and the Minister had not referred the dispute for settlement in that time. Once the trade dispute had been referred for settlement, and any voluntary methods of settlement had been exhausted, the Order provided for binding arbitration administered by the National Arbitration Tribunal (NAT). It was this legal aspect of Order 1305—the compulsory settlement of trade disputes—which Kahn-Freund found repugnant. It was repugnant because it entailed the transformation of social organisations pursuing private purposes through free bargaining, into subordinated instruments of State-led social and economic policy. Its social effect was the destructive integration of free organisations into the apparatus of the State.

This was why the status of the arbitrating body was so important in Kahn-Freund's attitude towards different schemes of compulsory arbitration. Where the arbitrator was formally insulated from governmental directives specifying desirable social and economic public policies, as under the tripartite constitution of the NAT, the risks to union autonomy and self-government were reduced. Where ministerial directives bound the arbitrator, as under the Weimar system of compulsory arbitration, the risks to union autonomy and industrial self-government could be catastrophic. It seems to me that when Kahn-Freund was defending State neutrality he was simply emphasising the virtues of private ordering through free collective bargaining. This enabled unions (and employers) to pursue their own conceptions of the good through an unimpeded regulatory process, and it minimised the threats to liberty posed by a State that pursued perfectionist ideals in disregard of citizens' (and, more importantly, their groups') preferences. Liberal neutrality, and the corresponding respect for the freedom of bargainers to formulate their own norms guided by their own lights, was the surest safeguard against totalitarianism.

The contrast with Kahn-Freund's attitude towards the parallel provisions dealing with 'recognised terms and conditions' in Article 5 is striking. Article 5 stipulated the norm that employers were required to observe the recognised terms and conditions or such terms and conditions as were not less favourable. Recognised terms and conditions were those set down in collective agreements by organisations 'representative respectively of substantial proportions of the employers and workers' in the relevant trade or industry and district. Furthermore, Article 5(2) provided a technical definition of 'not less favourable' that was

could only be measured by a total view of its social and political context. I am grateful to Ruth Dukes for pressing me on this point.

[100] The Conditions of Employment and National Arbitration Order (SR & O 1940/1305).

tied to alternative sources of applicable collectively agreed terms and conditions that the employer could choose to observe instead.

For Kahn-Freund, the political difference between legal enforcement of the normative effect of collective agreements and compulsory arbitration of trade disputes was of the first magnitude. The former involved the State deferring to the regulatory capacities of industrial actors in civil society and underwriting autonomously created norms in collective agreements; the latter involved the State overriding those regulatory capacities in pursuit of publicly determined objectives. Indeed, and in contrast to other scholars,[101] Kahn-Freund refused to apply the term 'compulsory arbitration' to the legal enforcement of recognised terms.[102] This refusal was less to do with definitional exactitude, and much more to do with the need to preserve the term's distinctive moral opprobrium for any legal measure that imperilled the autonomy of unions from the State. Legal enforcement of recognised terms respected CLF's political neutrality because the State declined to interfere with the parties' own determination of the good, as reflected in the parameters of their collective agreement. The State's role was confined to the legal enforcement of the norms legislated for by the parties, rather than attempting to modify those norms to suit publicly defined goals. As a mode of intervention, then, it was 'merely a reflection in the law of a change in bargaining habits which has occurred in society, but it is not an attempt to transform those habits or their effect'.[103] And note that this understanding of neutrality has little in common with the conception of neutrality deployed in Ewing's critique. For Kahn-Freund, *it was an important point in Article 5's favour that it promoted collective bargaining*[104] And it would have been odd for it to be otherwise given Kahn-Freund's view of collective bargaining as an industrial relations good.

The sense of neutrality deployed in CLF did not preclude positive State measures to promote collective bargaining. What it set itself against were measures that threatened the parties' freedom of collective contract, and their ability to determine and pursue their own purposes free from State scrutiny or interference. Once we examine English political pluralism, we see precisely this distinction at work. English political pluralists advocated a limited role for the State. The guiding principle of the political pluralists was the liberal principle of respect for the organisational autonomy of associations in civil society. The pluralist State was to abstain from any articulation of a common good, for this courted tyranny.[105] The State's vocation was procedural rather than substantive

[101] See, eg, Wedderburn above n 96.

[102] O Kahn-Freund, *Selected Writings* (London, Stevens & Sons, 1978) 126–7.

[103] Kahn-Freund, 'Intergroup Conflicts' 73.

[104] Kahn-Freund, 'Wartime Legislation' 142.

[105] As Nicholls has pointed out, liberty was the overriding end of pluralist governance. The articulation of a common good by the State was thought to imperil liberty. As such, 'The British pluralist writers believed that individual freedom is most likely to be preserved when a large number of associations coexist in the state, and when the state does not itself pursue some national policy

in nature. Its task was to create a procedural framework within which individuals could form associations for the pursuit of shared ends. As far as possible, the State was to respect the autonomy of these self-governing associations, and to delegate the execution of social tasks to the associations of civil society. The pluralist State was thus a neutral State. It was permitted a role in encouraging and supporting the growth of associational life and buttressing weak associations.[106] But beyond this, civil society rather than the State was the proper sphere for the articulation and pursuit of goods. The contours of the pluralist State can be encapsulated in the following terms

> a state which is both a public power, able to ensure public peace, and a legal order, which sustains that peace through the rule of law ... The pluralist State will be a minimal state but one whose primary task is to create the conditions for associations, and through them individual citizens, to be free to pursue their purposes. A pluralist legal order, in defining the rights of associations, would pay due regard to their autonomy and their right to develop as determined by their own internal decision procedures.[107]

Properly understood, CLF complements the arguments offered by Ewing and Howell. Ewing and Howell are surely correct in identifying 'institution-building' as the paradigmatic mode of intervention by the British State. But CLF offered a compelling rationalisation of *why* that mode was so appropriate. 'Institution-building' enabled the State to support the growth of self-governing associations in civil society while at the same time respecting the freedom of those groups to be self-determining entities in the collective bargaining process. It enabled the State, that is, to promote collective bargaining while remaining scrupulously neutral towards the parties' self-determined conceptions of the good. In fact, Kahn-Freund would have agreed wholeheartedly with the 'neutrality' critique's central conclusion, that what was interesting and distinctive about the British State's historical role was the *form* of its auxiliary intervention.

C The Coherence Critique

In fact, Kahn-Freund famously argued that what was distinctive about British labour law was its preference for indirect auxiliary modes. This direct/indirect distinction was most famously presented in 'Legal Framework',[108] but it was also reiterated much later in Kahn-Freund's career.[109] It was thus a settled part of

which purports to realise a common good ... Pluralist writers disliked coercive authority, believing that people should be encouraged to form self-governing associations to pursue the ends which they think valuable, rather than waiting for governments to act. They agreed with Proudhon that government is at best a necessary evil.' Nicholls, above n 35, 15.

[106] *Ibid*, xix.

[107] Hirst, above n 35, 29.

[108] Kahn-Freund, 'Legal Framework' 55, 62.

[109] Kahn-Freund, 'Retrospect' 303–7.

CLF's canon. For Davies and Freedland, the line between direct compulsion and indirect inducement was an elusive one, and Kahn-Freund offered no precise formula for drawing that line.[110] Davies and Freedland are right to place the direct/indirect distinction under theoretical scrutiny and pressure. Indeed, they suggest that the existence of auxiliary support for collective bargaining 'posed a major theoretical problem for the abstentionist analysis of labour law'.[111] However, I want to argue that the 'direct-indirect' distinction is a coherent one in the light of CLF's political theory. Let us begin by considering Kahn-Freund's rationalisation of the historical absence of a legal duty to bargain in British labour law. For Kahn-Freund, there were two distinct arguments that explained the British preference; one was pragmatic and the other political.

(i) The Legal Duty to Bargain I: The Pragmatic Objection to Direct Auxiliary Support

The argument from pragmatism can be found in a neglected piece of analysis written by Kahn-Freund for an American legal audience on minimum wage-fixing machinery.[112] Here Kahn-Freund distinguished between two distinct kinds of regulatory problem in countries with developed systems of collective bargaining.[113] First, there was a basic failure of collective bargaining at its inception. This might have various causes, such as unwillingness to bargain by hostile individual employers or the absence of cohesive bargaining organisations on either side of the bargaining table—let us call this a type (a) recognition problem. Secondly, there was a failure of normative effect of intergroup collective agreements. This would generally occur where bargaining organisations were too weak to use social sanctions either to prevent defection internally (by federated entities) or externally (by non-federated entities)—let us call this a type (b) recognition problem.

In the US the recognition problem emerged in a particular way and assumed a particular form so as to necessitate a particular kind of regulatory solution. It was, in essence, a type (a) recognition problem, with a specific cause: 'a refusal of individual employers to negotiate with a strong and representative union'.[114] This corresponded with the main elements of the legal technique in the National Labor Relations Act (NLRA): a statutory criterion of union representativity based upon a majoritarian concept of democracy; a publicly administered procedure for determining the bargaining unit; and an 'unfair labor practice' jurisdiction outlawing various practices which were antithetical to employees' freedom to choose collective bargaining. Type (b) recognition problems did not

110 Davies and Freedland, above n 18, 27–8.

111 *Ibid*, 11.

112 O Kahn-Freund, 'Minimum Wage Legislation in Great Britain' (1949) 97 *University of Pennsylvania Law Review* 778.

113 *Ibid*, 780.

114 *Ibid*.

often arise because the standard bargaining pattern was not predicated on *intergroup* relations. The US collective agreement was usually concluded between a single employer and a trade union and confined to a single plant.

Kahn-Freund argued, in unusually categorical terms, that it was '*impossible*' for the British legislator to adopt the American regulatory technique of a legal duty to bargain.[115] The nature of what constituted a recognition problem in a given country, and hence an appropriate regulatory response, was shaped by the complex history of its bargaining organisations. In Britain recognition problems displayed two distinctive features that rendered the American regulatory response inapposite. First, type (a) recognition problems generally arose out of institutional failures on the workers' side: there was no stable workers' organisation for the employers' association to bargain *with*; hence the legal duty to bargain would have been superfluous. Thus, type (a) problems had a different cause than in the American context. Furthermore, the intergroup nature of British industrial relations entailed that type (b) recognition problems were equally important. Defection by individual employers from the normative effect of the collective agreement undermined the regulatory authority of the bargaining organisations. Where those organisations were strong, social sanctions against defectors would usually suffice. Where those organisations were weak, particularly in circumstances of economic depression, legal support for the normative effect of collective agreements might be necessary. Without legal underpinning, the erosion of institutional authority would lead to the collapse of collective bargaining structures and thus a failure of recognition. As Howell has convincingly argued, in Britain union recognition was transmitted indirectly through the medium of employers' associations, and this was facilitated by legal support for intergroup collective agreements.[116]

The practical unsuitability of the US regulatory technique in the British context was matched by the emergence of functionally equivalent modes of intervention that were particularly responsive to the British version of the recognition problem. Type (a) recognition problems were addressed by the 'institution-building' measures analysed by Ewing, namely the system of wages councils and discretionary intervention of the Ministry of Labour. If the main cause of type (a) failure in Britain was the inability of bargaining organisations on the workers' side to take root, then 'institution-building' techniques were the smart regulatory response. Type (b) recognition problems were addressed through the various initiatives to ensure the compulsory normative effect of intergroup collective agreements: the Cotton Manufacturing Industry (Temporary Provisions) Act 1934; the relevant legal mechanisms in Orders 1305 and 1376; section 8 of Terms and Conditions of Employment Act 1958; and the Fair Wages Resolution 1946. Once again, if the main cause of type (b) failure in

115 *Ibid.*
116 Howell, above n 17, 97.

Britain was the inability of social sanctions to prevent the defection of individual employers from the intergroup collective agreement, then the provision of substitute legal sanctions in certain circumstances was the smart regulatory response.

This argument from pragmatism, while powerful, was never conclusive. For example, multi-employer bargaining units have always been 'a common if not dominant bargaining pattern' in the United States, in certain industries such as clothing, newspaper printing, and longshore and maritime industries.[117] While the US statutory procedure does not specifically authorise multi-employer units, the National Labor Relations Board has always in practice certified such units and this has been sanctioned by the Supreme Court. Thus, there is no inherent incompatibility between a statutory duty to bargain and multi-employer bargaining structures. Moreover, once it became clear that industry-wide bargaining was a façade and that plant-level bargaining was of greater significance in Britain, the argument from pragmatism diminished in significance. However, in an article written after his realisation of the great structural changes afoot in British collective bargaining, Kahn-Freund mounted a separate *political* argument against the adoption of a US-style legal duty to bargain and in defence of the British preference for 'indirect' methods of support.

(ii) The Legal Duty to Bargain II: The Normative Argument against Direct Auxiliary Support

It is worth setting this argument out in full:

> The American experience … shows that it is impossible to give the courts the power of deciding in what cases an employer or union should bargain without including the power of saying with what union, at what level, and about what subjects the employer, and also of saying about what subjects a union has to bargain. This amounts in fact to the conferment upon the courts of a regulatory power, a power of determining the substance of the bargaining process and its form, and to some extent even the structure of the unions—a power for the exercise of which the courts are not equipped.[118]

Superficially, at least, this is simply a restatement of CLF's distrust of the ordinary courts' involvement in collective bargaining, and this certainly weighed heavily in Kahn-Freund's objection to a US-style good faith bargaining duty. However, I would suggest that this institutional caveat did not exhaust Kahn-Freund's concerns. Another critical issue for Kahn-Freund was the negative impact of juridification on group autonomy entailed by a legal bargaining duty. In the light of Kahn-Freund's political pluralism, juridification through a good faith bargaining duty posed unacceptable risks to political freedom.

[117] RA Gorman and MW Finkin, *Labor Law: Unionization and Collective Bargaining*, 2nd edn (St Paul Minnesota, Thomson West, 2004) 105.
[118] Kahn-Freund, 'Retrospect' 307.

If we take first the question of determining the scope of the bargaining unit and the identity of the bargaining representative, the British system embodied a particularly strong attachment to group autonomy in that 'the scope of application of collective intergroup standards is … determined by the autonomous decision of the groups themselves'.[119] In the US, by contrast, the scope of the bargaining unit and the identity of the bargaining representative were determined through public administrative procedures culminating in a ballot of the workers in the bargaining unit.[120] It is difficult to overestimate the tectonic shift involved in the transition to this juridified scheme for designating legitimate bargaining representatives in the US. In Tomlins' masterly history of the juridification of US labour relations, he traces the fate of two conceptions of collective bargaining in the years before and after the implementation of the legal duty to bargain under the NLRA.

On the one hand, the American Federation of Labor (AFL) conceived of collective bargaining as a fundamentally private activity. From this perspective, unions themselves were real entities, principals with their own jurisdictional 'property' rights rooted in established bargaining structures. Tomlins has termed this 'a *gesellschaft* model of society and politics'.[121] A corollary of this *gesellschaft* model was the AFL's claim to an exclusive right to determine its members' jurisdiction scope based on 'tradition, custom, "property rights" accumulated by a particular organization in the course of its development as an organic representation of a particular craft'.[122] On the other hand, this *gesellschaft* model was progressively eclipsed as an alternative legal discourse took hold in the early years of the NLRA scheme. This discourse conceived of collective bargaining as a matter of public rather than private right.[123] That public right, conferred by and defined in accordance with the statute, was based upon the worker's individual civil right to choose to authorise an exclusive bargaining agent. Since unions were not considered to be real entities with their own institutional interests and proprietary prerogatives, the 'union's claim to legitimacy could not reside in any organic relationship which it might argue existed between itself and its constituency'.[124] Instead, unions were treated as agents rather than principals, acquiring their representational legitimacy through the principle of majority rule as determined in a government-supervised ballot of the bargaining unit members.

[119] Kahn-Freund, 'Intergroup Conflicts' 48.

[120] *Ibid*, 49.

[121] CL Tomlins, *The State and the Unions: Labor Relations, Law, and the Organized Labor Movement in America, 1880–1960* (New York, Cambridge University Press, 1985) 77.

[122] *Ibid*, 118.

[123] On the public right doctrine in the context of US labour relations law, see K Klare, 'Judicial Deradicalization of the Wagner Act and the Origins of Modern Legal Consciousness' (1978) 62 *Minnesota Law Review* 265, 310–18.

[124] Tomlins, above n 121, 116.

With the history of the US legal duty to bargain presented in this way, it is perhaps easier to comprehend Kahn-Freund's sceptical attitude in the British context. The *gesellschaft* conception of the bargaining unit that pre-dated the NLRA framework was highly solicitous of group autonomy, and in this respect it reflected similar values and concerns to the English political pluralists. Significantly, this *gesellschaft* model was aligned with a 'realist' view of corporate personality and it set itself against the 'concessionist' view. If unions were real entities with their own institutional interests and jurisdictional 'property' rights, as was envisaged by the *gesellschaft* model, then it followed that patterns of legal regulation should be deferent to those existing social structures and practices. Once collective bargaining was conceptualised as a matter of public right originating in the statute itself, however, the 'concessionist' view gained much greater currency. If the parameters of collective bargaining were *created and defined* by legislation as a matter of public right, in the manner of a concession by the State, then it followed that those parameters could be *redefined* by legislative enactment in the public interest. As Tomlins has argued, the NLRA framework eventually 'made collective bargaining a matter of public concern, conducted by institutions with statutorily defined rights and responsibilities within a framework shaped by state agencies. While this represented a major encouragement to collective bargaining, it also represented what was potentially a severe encroachment upon union autonomy.'[125]

Even once bargaining rights had been allocated through the government-supervised ballot, further encroachment on union autonomy was an inevitable effect of the State's enforcement of good faith bargaining duties. First, the interest-group bargaining paradigm used by CLF as a model for the collective bargaining process was deeply anti-paternalistic. It envisaged that groups 'come to the political process with preselected interests that they seek to promote through political conflict and compromise … Moreover, efforts to alter or shape preferences … assume the status of tyranny.'[126] This partly explains the elusiveness of publicly enforced good faith standards to regulate the bargaining process. It was for the groups themselves to determine what was in their respective interests, and to promote those interests vigorously through bargaining. This interest group theory of politics furnished no objective yardstick by which the State could distinguish hard bargaining from bad faith bargaining.

Secondly, English political pluralism converged on this scepticism about public values and good faith bargaining in the following way. The formulation of good faith standards in the bargaining process depended upon a much richer normative role for the State than would have been legitimate in the English political pluralist tradition. It would have required the State to make controversial judgements about which bargaining positions and strategies were objectively

125 *Ibid*, 101.
126 C Sunstein, 'Interest Groups in American Public Law' (1985) 38 *Stanford Law Review* 29, 32.

reasonable, in the light of the State's own vision of desirable social and economic goals. This would have inevitably violated the pluralist State's commitment to liberal neutrality in its dealings with groups in civil society. Ultimately, then, and contrary to his earlier tentative view in 'Intergroup Conflicts', the enforcement of good faith bargaining shared more in common with the 'fascistic' institutions of compulsory arbitration than more innocent 'institution building' measures that were characteristic of the British preference for 'indirect' methods.

Understanding CLF's normative rejection of the 'direct' method points us towards an explanation of the distinctness and political appeal of the 'indirect' method. *This lay in its adoption of the* gesellschaft *model that had been eclipsed by juridification in the United States.* A paradigm of the 'indirect' method of auxiliary support can be found in Article 1 (a) of the Fair Wages Resolution of 1946:

> The contractor shall pay rates of wages and observe hours and conditions of labour not less favourable than those established for the trade or industry in the district where the work is carried out by machinery of negotiation or arbitration to which the parties are organizations of employers and trade unions representative respectively of substantial proportions of the employers and workers engaged in the trade or industry in the district.

This measure was designed to mirror and reinforce the *gesellschaft* bargaining structures administered by 'representative' bargaining organisations. From the perspective of CLF it had two important advantages. First, it respected the autonomy of the 'representative' bargaining organisations to determine the regulatory scope of the bargaining unit. It was thus aligned with a view of bargaining organisations as real entities with their own institutional interests. Secondly, it ensured that the State did not trespass on the bargaining process itself. The content of the obligation was shaped entirely by the relevant collective agreement. In turn, this had been shaped by the free play of social forces in the autonomous processes of negotiation. It thus enabled the State to remain neutral towards the substantive outcomes embodied in the collective agreement. This avoided the difficulties inherent in the enforcement of good faith bargaining duties.

The nature of clause 4 of the Fair Wages Resolution 1946 reinforces this view. This clause protected 'the freedom of his workpeople to be members of trade unions'. Interestingly, the Industrial Court maintained that clause 4 protected union membership per se; it did not extend to a refusal by the employer to recognise the union. For this reason, Bercusson was forced to conclude that 'in terms of the protection of trade union rights, clause 4 has been useless.'[127] Why this strict adherence to a static conception of union membership in an ostensibly collectivist measure? After all, if union recognition had been included within the scope of clause 4 and its protective remit, the sanction for non-compliance was quintessentially indirect in Kahn-Freund's taxonomy.

[127] B Bercusson, *Fair Wages Resolutions* (London, Mansell, 1978) 345.

The reason, I would suggest, is the same reason that underlay Kahn-Freund's early aversion to compulsory arbitration and his persistent and settled aversion to a legal duty to bargain. The enforcement of recognition would have necessitated public scrutiny of the parties' bargaining interaction. This was inconsistent with CLF because it required the State to eschew neutrality and exercise a moral judgement when scrutinising the parties' bargaining interaction. This would have transformed the Fair Wages Resolution 1946 into a 'direct' form of auxiliary intervention quite apart from its reliance on 'indirect' sanctions.

The other kind of indirect technique—'institution-building' through, for example, wages councils, was faithful to this political pluralist *gesellschaft* model in three ways.[128] First, the statutory process of wage fixing replicated the autonomous process of joint regulation through collective bargaining. While a Ministerial order was needed to give compulsory normative effect to wages councils' determinations, the State's role was subordinate to the democratic will of the parties. The Minister could not modify the parties' substantive proposals. Secondly, in some wages council industries the pluralist preference for supporting established bargaining organisations was feasible, since one trigger condition for the establishment of a wages council was an *anticipated* failure of current bargaining structures. In the baking industry, for example, voluntary organisation was relatively strong but it had proved difficult for the bargainers to exercise control over night work practices in the industry.[129] Finally, what of wages councils industries where there were no bargaining structures in place? According to Bayliss, three unions in particular were heavily involved in the operation of wages councils in industries where they had few members: the TGWU, the NUGMW and the USDAW.[130] These examples vividly demonstrate a *gesellschaft* model of representational legitimacy. Once the right to collective bargaining was conceptualised as the worker's individual civil right to choose a bargaining representative, the close connection between majority rule and representational legitimacy was natural. Only if unions were treated as real entities with their own organic legitimacy was it defensible to disconnect the conferral of regulatory powers on trade unions from individual worker consent, as had happened under the wages council framework.

V CONCLUSION

We began with Kahn-Freund's often quoted statement from 'Collective Agreements under Wartime Legislation' emphasising the exceptional absence of a legal duty to bargain in British labour law. By reappraising Kahn-Freund's legacy, it has been argued that CLF still offers a compelling theorisation of the State's role

128 See, generally, FJ Bayliss, *British Wages Councils* (Oxford, Blackwell, 1962).
129 HA Clegg, *The System of Industrial Relations in Great Britain* (Oxford, Blackwell, 1978) 357–8.
130 Bayliss, above n 128, 106.

in British industrial relations. Consequently, contemporary critiques have failed to undermine CLF's credentials as a *descriptive-explanatory theory* of British labour law's historical development. Of course, CLF as a *normative theory* did face serious challenges in the post-war period. No scholar was more keenly aware of this than Kahn-Freund himself. In this respect, it is worth revisiting his conclusion in 'Collective Agreements under Wartime Legislation' and quoting its rarely cited and often-forgotten final words: 'The proud edifice of collective labour regulation was built up without the assistance of the "law". *After the war the relationship between collective bargaining and the law may have to be redefined.*'[131]

This redefinition was precipitated by the increasingly fraught relationship between State economic planning and free collective bargaining. By the time of 'Intergroup Conflicts', it remained an open question for Kahn-Freund whether reconciliation might be achieved between these aims within the political framework of CLF. The spectre of fascism had given Kahn-Freund an almost unshakeable love of political freedom through free collective bargaining; and an instinctive distrust of State encroachment on free collective bargaining. The challenge of 'redefinition' was one that various governments would approach in radically different ways. This was reflected not only in the rise of incomes policies and coordinated wage restraint, but also in the emergence of legal bargaining duties in the 1970s. It was also reflected in the deregulatory agenda pursued by the New Right Conservative Government from 1979 onwards. Whatever the eventual fate of CLF as a normative theory, this contested process of 'redefinition' in the post-war period inevitably took place against the political benchmark that CLF had set.

[131] Kahn-Freund, 'Wartime Legislation' 143 (emphasis added).

2

The Rise of the Legal Duty to Bargain: The Resilience of Collective Laissez-Faire

I INTRODUCTION

THE DISTINCTIVE MARK of collective laissez-faire (CLF) was its preference for indirect over direct methods of auxiliary State support for collective bargaining. The preference for indirect methods reflected the underlying political values of CLF, for the indirect approach respected the fundamental principle of *group autonomy*. This principle demanded that the scope of the bargaining unit and the identity of the bargaining agent should be a matter for the autonomous decision of the groups themselves. It also demanded a commitment to free collective bargaining such that the State did not interfere with the autonomous social processes of norm creation. Where collective agreements had been shaped by the free play of social forces in the autonomous processes of negotiation, this enabled the State to remain neutral towards the substantive outcomes embodied in the collective agreement. To adopt Tomlins' terminology from chapter one, the British indirect method represented a *gesellschaft* model of the relation between State and industrial civil society, which was the surest guarantee of political freedom in the liberal polity.

We ended the previous chapter by identifying a tension that would prove to be epochal for CLF in the post-war period: how to reconcile the principle of group autonomy with State-led social and economic planning. As Davies and Freedland's authoritative history of that period emphasises, the voluntary heritage of CLF was increasingly subject to a variety of political pressures. These pressures 'posed a powerful set of problems for traditional collective *laissez-faire*; cumulatively, they destroyed it'.[1] These pressures necessitated a more prominent role for the State in industrial civil society, in order to promote social and economic objectives which collective bargaining was either impeding or failing to deliver: non-inflationary pay settlements, sustainable economic growth based on rising productivity, gender equity in the labour market. The rise of incomes policies was perhaps the clearest manifestation of this challenge to group autonomy, and the implications of incomes policies for CLF have been the subject of scholarly

[1] P Davies and M Freedland, *Labour Legislation and Public Policy* (Oxford, Oxford University Press, 1993) 59.

attention elsewhere.[2] Given the challenge to group autonomy, these political forces also placed intense pressures on the British preference for indirect auxiliary support. For example, if chaotic bargaining structures or selfishly acquisitive bargaining behaviour undermined desirable social and economic objectives pursued by the State, the principle of group autonomy no longer presented an irresistible argument against State intervention. This was because the freedom of groups in industrial civil society to pursue their own purposes was no longer the overriding political value. Once this foundational political principle began to be eroded, the way was opened up for the enactment of *direct* methods of auxiliary support that were less solicitous of group autonomy.

It was Allan Flanders who articulated what we might term the *juridification dilemma* posed by direct methods of auxiliary support most pithily: 'collective bargaining has been made the subject of little legal regulation, but it has also been afforded little legal support. And, by and large, the second condition has been readily accepted in order not to prejudice the first. It has been realised that greater legal support would most certainly bring greater legal regulation in its train.'[3] Once the normative way was clear for more intensive legal regulation of the collective bargaining process as competing public interests acquired greater legitimacy, it followed that direct methods of auxiliary legal support also simultaneously acquired greater legitimacy too. Of course, what were considered acceptable trade-offs between direct legal support and the corresponding loss of group autonomy were likely to be very different for the State, trade unions, and employers. Nevertheless, one of the outstanding characteristics of the historical period from the beginnings of the Donovan Commission in 1965 through to the election of a Conservative Government in 1979 was the increasing prominence of the legal duty to bargain as a direct technique of auxiliary support.

Superficially at least, the rise of direct methods alongside the more traditional indirect pattern of auxiliary support, and the corresponding challenge to group autonomy, appears to lend further support to Davies and Freedland's thesis of CLF's cumulative destruction in the post-war period. That is not, however, the argument of this chapter. Once we examine the shifts and permutations in patterns of auxiliary support during this period, what we find is an altogether more complex and contradictory set of tendencies at work. This is certainly true if we make comparisons *between* distinct phases within the period under review (for example, the Conservative Government's Industrial Relations Act 1971 (IRA) recognition procedure compared with the Labour Government's Employment Protection Act 1975 (EPA) section 11 recognition procedure). More interestingly, perhaps, it also true that *within* particular historical phases different State institutions—the government, the judiciary, third party industrial relations

[2] See, in particular, the editors' introduction, in PL Davies and MR Freedland (eds), *Kahn-Freund's Labour and the Law*, 3rd edn (London, Stevens & Sons, 1983).

[3] A Flanders, *Management and Unions: The Theory and Reform of Industrial Relations* (London, Faber and Faber, 1970) 95.

agencies—often pursued distinct and sometimes discordant political agendas within the same regulatory context.

As a framework for this chapter, we can distinguish two different facets of group autonomy that might be undermined by direct methods of auxiliary intervention. The first facet looks to the designation of the bargaining unit and the identity of the bargaining agent; the second facet looks to the regulation of the collective bargaining process itself. In relation to this first facet, the general tendency from 1965 onwards was decisively against group autonomy. Increasingly, bargaining units and bargaining agents were determined in accordance with publicly decided criteria of legitimacy, formulated and enforced by third party industrial relations agencies and with an increasingly heavy accent upon ensuring order and rationality in the public designation of units and agents. These criteria were often intensely contested, particularly in relation to bargaining agents. Nevertheless, the *gesellschaft* model that envisaged the groups themselves having exclusive authority to determine the structure of bargaining units and the identity of bargaining agents was in retreat.

Given the eclipse of this *gesellschaft* model, two alternative approaches competed for ascendancy as a public basis for allocating bargaining rights through direct methods of auxiliary support. On the one hand, the *liberal* approach would only countenance the allocation of bargaining rights to a bargaining agent where it had demonstrable majority support amongst workers within the bargaining unit. This was particularly characteristic of the IRA recognition procedure, and it also struck a chord with the judiciary in judicial review proceedings under the EPA. On the other hand, the *civic* approach pointed to the social malleability of citizens' preferences.[4] Where workers' preferences had adapted to a non-union status quo and where it was anticipated that their preferences might adapt accordingly if they were exposed to the experience of collective bargaining and unionisation, it might be appropriate to allocate bargaining rights where there was less than arithmetical majority support in the bargaining unit. This was characteristic of the approach of the various third party industrial relations agencies during the period under review. Between 1965 and 1979, there was an almost incessant seesaw between these two approaches under various pieces of recognition machinery. Nevertheless, the general point remained: bargaining units and agents were no longer private matters beyond the legitimate reach of public regulation.

By contrast, in relation to the second facet of group autonomy—the freedom of the bargaining parties to formulate their own norms guided by their own lights—this continued to exert a powerful influence on the parameters of institutional design and implementation. This was reflected most strongly in the

[4] I term this a civic approach because Cass Sunstein has identified the adaptive preference model, and the corresponding need to ameliorate adaptive preference effects, as characteristic of civic republican conceptions of politics: see C Sunstein, 'Beyond the Republican Revival' (1988) 97 *Yale Law Journal* 1539, 1548–9.

failure of legal good faith bargaining duties to take root in the British system. It was also reflected in the State's reticence in pursuing other, less direct modes of steering bargaining conduct: state registration of trade unions and employers' associations to promote alignment between private and public purposes, civic education of bargaining parties to promote responsiveness to public interests in bargaining activity, and regulation and restriction of economic weaponry. It is important not to impose procrustean uniformity on the entire period. There were important and salient differences in the regulatory choices made by different governments during distinct historical phases, and these will be highlighted where appropriate. Nevertheless, the dominant tendency of regulatory initiatives post-Donovan was to defer to the parties' bargaining freedom despite recurrent lip service being paid by governments to the importance of 'responsible' bargaining in the public interest. In this respect, reports of the death of CLF were, by the time we reach 1979 at least, greatly exaggerated in the particular domain of direct auxiliary intervention. Hence, as far as the autonomy of the collective bargaining process itself was concerned, CLF proved to be a resilient living ideology in the face of competing political pressures.

It is tempting to present these political pressures on group autonomy as barbarians at the gate of CLF. However, this would do a disservice to the depth and richness of the pluralist tradition in British labour law and industrial relations. As Hyman's seminal work has made clear, there was no single concept of pluralism in British industrial relations.[5] Rather, it spanned a diverse cluster of loosely connected methods, ideas and values that defied reduction into a simple unifying definition. As a prelude to considering the rise of direct auxiliary methods during the 1960s and 1970s and their analytical significance, it is worth revisiting the complex theoretical cross-currents internal to the industrial pluralist tradition. In particular, the contrasting visions of Hugh Clegg and Allan Flanders provided a microcosmic representation of the more general political force field operating on CLF during this period. This provided the normative context to the Donovan Commission's Report, which was to mark a watershed in respect of the emergence of direct methods of auxiliary intervention. It is to that theoretical microcosm that we now turn.

[5] R Hyman, 'Pluralism, Procedural Consensus, and Collective Bargaining' (1978) 16 *British Journal of Industrial Relations* 16.

II TWO CONCEPTIONS OF INDUSTRIAL RELATIONS PLURALISM: PLURALIST AND CIVIC VOLUNTARISM, AND THE DONOVAN COMMISSION REPORT

A Flanders, Clegg and the 'Oxford School' of Industrial Relations

Along with Alan Fox, Hugh Armstrong Clegg and Allan Flanders constituted the intellectual backbone of the so-called 'Oxford School' of industrial relations. Nevertheless, their contrasting visions of pluralist industrial relations were very different. The differences reflected distinct political philosophies. In each case, the political philosophy structured a distinctive view of the State's role in industrial relations, and the underlying justification and procedural character of collective bargaining in industrial civil society. On the one hand, Hugh Clegg defended what might be termed a *pluralist* voluntarist paradigm.[6] In common with Kahn-Freund, Clegg's theory of industrial democracy was formulated with an acute sensitivity to the dangers of the totalitarian State.[7] Rooted in a traditional liberal 'distrust of power', it emphasised the oppositional role of trade unions as self-interested pressure groups in civil society operating under the free institutions of liberal democracy. Clegg's theory also evinced a sceptical attitude towards the notion of an overarching public interest defended by the State against sectional democratic pressures.[8] Clegg's theorisation of collective bargaining therefore corresponded to maximal latitude for collective freedom of contract.

On the other hand, Allan Flanders defended what might be termed a *civic* voluntarist paradigm. In intellectual terms, Flanders espoused a faith in rational deliberation and reason as the basis of a just social order. As such, Flanders' conception of collective bargaining emphasised its integrative potential through the practice of reasoned dialogue. Further, Flanders envisaged a far richer notion of the common good than would have been possible within Clegg's cautious and sceptical liberalism. It therefore extended beyond a narrowly circumscribed concern to promote industrial peace or stability, as was characteristic of the pluralist voluntarists, to encapsulate a public concern for the entire social, economic, and civic well-being of citizens.[9] In Kelly's words, 'he had adopted the

[6] Two of Clegg's contributions are of particular theoretical significance: HA Clegg, *A New Approach to Industrial Democracy* (Oxford, Blackwell, 1960) (Clegg, *Democracy*); HA Clegg, 'Pluralism in Industrial Relations' (1975) 13 *British Journal of Industrial Relations* 309.

[7] Clegg, *Democracy* 19–21.

[8] See P Ackers, 'Collective Bargaining as Industrial Democracy: The Political Foundations of British Industrial Relations Pluralism' (2007) 45 *British Journal of Industrial Relations* 77, where Ackers draws attention to Clegg's annotation in Clegg's copy of Sidney and Beatrice Webb, *Industrial Democracy*. Adjacent to the paragraph outlining the Webbs' assertion of an overarching national interest in the sphere of collective bargaining, Clegg has inscribed 'nonsense' in the margin (80).

[9] For a mature and systematic elaboration of this civic conception, see A Flanders, 'Collective Bargaining: Prescription for Change', in A Flanders, *Management and Unions: The Theory and Reform of Industrial Relations* (London, Faber and Faber, 1970) 155–211.

supra-class category of the "public interest" as a third party with a legitimate interest in the outcomes of wage bargaining'.[10] This corresponded to a less stringent regard for free collective bargaining where vital elements of the common good were at stake; and the State was the appropriate agency to vindicate the common good. Given this emphasis on deliberation and the common good, Flanders' theory was closely aligned with a civic conception of politics.

These abstract political ideologies had concrete institutional and regulatory implications. This is especially important given the pivotal role of the 'Oxford School' in the formulation of public policy in the post-war period. Thus, while the pluralist voluntarists Clegg and Kahn-Freund sat on the Donovan Commission and were instrumental in crafting its main proposals, the civic voluntarist Flanders' written evidence to the Commission was pivotal in the Commission's thinking. In this way, pluralist and civic voluntarism marked out the ideological terrain upon which the reform of collective bargaining law was to unfold. Flanders' work in particular demands close attention, for it embodied a radical civic challenge to the entrenched liberal institutions of British industrial relations, as defended by Clegg and Kahn-Freund.

The watershed between pluralist and civic voluntarism rested above all on their competing philosophies of collective bargaining. For pluralist voluntarists such as Clegg, the democratic virtue of collective bargaining was rooted in its oppositional character. In this way, workers' divergent interests would be vindicated through a contractual process of bargaining. As Clegg perceived, this protective rationale 'tends to emphasize disagreement … The emphasis of differences may appear to be stupid and obstructive. Its justification lies in the basic assumption of democracy: that even the most enlightened authorities tend to ignore the interests of others.'[11] This protective theory of democracy also tended to legitimise sectional democratic behaviour. As Gutmann and Thompson have put it, 'on a bargaining conception citizens do not have any reason directly to promote the well-being of other citizens. This conception authorizes citizens to try to maximize their own or their group's advantage even at the expense of the well-being of other citizens.'[12] The trade union's overriding moral purpose was to maximise its members' self-interest through bargaining, even where this blinkered pursuit might have wider anti-social consequences. For civic voluntarists such as Flanders, by contrast, the virtue of collective bargaining lay in its *deliberative* potential. In contrast to the bargaining conception of democracy, deliberative democracy might be defined as 'public deliberation focused on the

[10] J Kelly, 'Social Democracy and Anti-Communism: Allan Flanders and British industrial relations in the early post-war period', in A Campbell, N Fishman, and J Mcilroy (eds), *British Trade Unions and Industrial Politics: The Post-War Compromise, 1945–64* (Aldershot, Ashgate, 1999) 192, 205.

[11] Clegg, *Democracy* 109.

[12] A Gutmann and D Thompson, *Democracy and Disagreement* (Cambridge, Harvard University Press, 1996) 58.

common good'.[13] Public deliberation is predicated upon the exchange of reasons, rather than the exercise of pressure through bargaining; participants aim to reach a rational consensus through argument and dialogue rather than force. These philosophical differences corresponded to three important differences in attitude towards auxiliary intervention.

First, Clegg seemed at points (like Kahn-Freund) to endorse a teleological view of trade union growth. This was reflected in his view that 'trade unions necessarily follow industrialization unless totalitarian methods are used to destroy them'.[14] This can be contrasted with Flanders' view that the growth of collective bargaining in Britain had been limited by a failure to harness the law in a systematic fashion to promote the extension of trade union recognition.[15] For Flanders, the design and implementation of effective auxiliary intervention was a regulatory priority;[16] for Clegg, by contrast, collective bargaining seemed to emerge organically and spontaneously regardless of legal norms.

Secondly, Flanders' deliberative conception was allied with a cautious scepticism towards the use of the strike weapon in the collective bargaining process. As Kelly has demonstrated, Flanders objected to the strike weapon on ethical grounds. The use of industrial brute force entailed power as the arbiter of disagreement.[17] Instead, Flanders placed his faith in 'reason and dialogue as instruments of social change'.[18] By contrast, the oppositional role of trade unions emphasised by Clegg required the availability of social sanctions such as the strike weapon even where 'the differences which they foster may seem stupid and unnecessary'.[19] On this view, even *unreasonable* resistance and opposition by trade unions could instantiate important democratic values.

Finally, Flanders deplored the sectionalism of the interest-group conception of collective bargaining, which reflected the pluralistic assumption that 'collective agreements are made to satisfy the interests of those who are represented in their negotiation'.[20] These assumptions led to a failure to vindicate vital public interests in the results of collective bargaining, such as ensuring appropriate wage restraint. For Flanders, however, it was untenable that 'sectional advantage should never be subordinated to the common good'.[21] While Clegg did not reject entirely the notion of an overarching public interest in the outcomes of collective bargaining,[22] neither did he embrace it as a central element in his theory.[23]

[13] J Cohen, 'Deliberation and Democratic Legitimacy', in J Bohman and W Rehg (eds), *Deliberative Democracy: Essays on Reason and Politics* (Massachusetts, MIT Press, 1997) 67, 69.

[14] Clegg, *Democracy* 117.

[15] Flanders, above n 9, 159–61.

[16] *Ibid*, 178–87.

[17] Kelly, above n 10, 207.

[18] *Ibid.*

[19] Clegg, *Democracy* 28.

[20] Flanders, above n 9, 162.

[21] *Ibid*, 178.

[22] See HA Clegg, *How to Run an Incomes Policy and why we made such a mess of the last one* (London, Heinemann, 1971).

Flanders had famously (if somewhat rashly) concluded that the principle of bargaining freedom 'must now be unreservedly consigned to the rubbish bin of history'.[24] If direct legal support for collective bargaining did entail greater legal regulation and restriction of group autonomy, for example through the enforcement of objective standards of good faith in regulating the parties' bargaining interaction, this was more problematic for Clegg and Kahn-Freund than it was for Flanders himself. This was because good faith criteria presupposed a public measure of legitimacy as an objective yardstick for scrutinising and judging the parties' behaviour. As such, we might expect a more secure position for the idea of a legal duty to bargain within the civic paradigm. When we turn to Flanders' proposals to the Donovan Commission that is precisely what we find.

B Flanders' Evidence to the Donovan Commission: The Proposal for Direct Auxiliary Support[25]

Flanders proposed the establishment of a permanent specialist tribunal, organised on a tripartite basis and empowered to make recommendations in recognition and procedural disputes. The institutional model for this proposed recognition tribunal was the Court of Inquiry.[26] These courts justified their conclusions through the provision of reasoned deliberation in a public forum. The hope was that the court's deliberative assessment would then provide a basis for compromise and settlement between the parties, and in many cases this had indeed proved to be the case. Flanders rejected the idea of a prescriptive legislative template for the recognition tribunal. Instead, he envisaged a wide discretionary remit for the tribunal subject only to broad guidelines and objectives derived from International Labour Organisation Conventions 87 and 98. This would make it clear that the tribunal's aim was the non-neutral one of *promoting* collective bargaining through the method of public enquiry, while also allowing it discretion to develop a working set of principles. Over time, the expectation was that the tribunal would build up a coherent industrial jurisprudence dealing with such matters as the criteria of support necessary for a recognition recommendation, the techniques suitable for gauging such support, the determination of the bargaining unit, the resolution of jurisdictional disputes where there were competing unions, the subjects over which bargaining should take place, and the standards of 'good faith' in the bargaining process itself. Flanders also rejected the use of legal compulsion to enforce the recommendations of the recognition tribunal. In this respect, Flanders had in mind the

[23] Ackers, above n 8.

[24] Flanders, above n 9, 174.

[25] *Ibid*, 178–82.

[26] On Courts of Inquiry and their mode of operation, see KW Wedderburn and PL Davies, *Employment Grievances and Disputes Procedures in Britain* (Berkeley, University of California Press, 1969) 224–32.

positive experience of the Court of Inquiry in achieving voluntary settlements based on its non-binding recommendations: these recommendations might 'provide a fresh basis for negotiation and settlement between the parties and give them an opportunity to adapt them to their own preferences'.[27]

In arguing that his proposed institutional method was better suited to resolving recognition disputes than resort to strike action, Flanders observed that strike action 'is an unnecessarily costly way of deciding a question of this sort, *which turns to a considerable extent on finding out the facts of the situation*—how representative is the union and so on'.[28] Of course, what degree of support exists in the bargaining unit, what is the level of union membership density and so on, are pre-eminently questions of fact. Nevertheless, what level of worker support *should* be sufficient to justify a public recommendation of recognition is a controversial normative issue, not a simple determination of fact. Flanders was of the view that the recognition tribunal should be authorised to arrange for a secret ballot of workers where this was thought appropriate; equally, it should not be compelled to do so.[29] To characterise this as a straightforward factual choice was, with respect, very misleading. Its effect was to bracket a highly controversial political choice amongst competing conceptions of representational legitimacy and repackage it as an innocent factual enquiry for the recognition tribunal. As later events would demonstrate, this normative choice would prove to be intensely controversial.

Flanders' proposals were rather skeletal, for he envisaged that the detail would be filled in as the new tribunal developed its adjudicative experience over time. Nevertheless, it is important not to underestimate the historical significance of Flanders' contribution to the development of auxiliary intervention. While there was a deliberate lack of specificity in respect of the criteria for determining bargaining units, identifying bargaining agents, and the concrete meaning of bargaining good faith, the retreat from group autonomy had now begun in earnest. The definitive contours of these controversial regulatory choices were then left to be made by the Donovan Commission itself.

C Pluralist and Civic Voluntarism within the Donovan Commission

The terms of reference of the Donovan Commission captured perfectly the parameters of the debate between pluralist and civic voluntarists: 'to consider relations between managements and employees and the role of trade unions and employers' associations in promoting the interests of their members *and* in

27 Flanders, above n 9, 182.
28 *Ibid*, 178 (emphasis added).
29 *Ibid*, 179.

accelerating the social and economic advance of the nation'.[30] In other words, what was the appropriate balance between social groups' pursuit of their sectional interests and their civic responsibility to promote the common good? As we have seen, Clegg and Flanders offered very different responses to that question. The Donovan Commission, too, articulated its own response. The Donovan reform agenda was overcome by political events. Despite this, 'all reform projects for the following decade were viewed through the prism of the Royal Commission's diagnosis and prescription for reform, even when those reforms challenged its premises'.[31]

The primary focus will be on the specific proposals for recognition in chapter five of the Report. Nevertheless, it is also important to acknowledge that State regulation of the collective bargaining process can occur in many, less direct ways not involving legal recognition machinery: (i) State registration of trade unions can indirectly steer bargaining conduct where registration entails State intervention in the internal rules and purposes of registered trade unions; (ii) State regulation of managerial and shop steward education and training can shape the attitudes of bargaining parties and their propensity to engage in deliberative modes of engagement; (iii) State restrictions on the parties' use of economic weaponry may also have significant effects on the balance of bargaining power between the parties. In assessing the political trajectory set by Donovan and the balance between pluralist and civic elements in its reform proposals we need a view of the entire legal matrix, so we shall consider these other regulatory modes where appropriate.

It is tempting to view chapter five as a straightforward triumph for Flanders' civic voluntarism. Thus, the Report states that:

> [W]e agree with Mr Flanders on the essentials of his proposals. They offer a method of encouraging the development of collective bargaining on sound lines. Moreover they avoid the difficulty of detailed intervention by the courts in the processes of industrial relations which appears to us to be a consequence of enforcing recognition by law as in the USA.[32]

In many respects, the institutional proposals offered in the Report are a mirror image of those formulated by Flanders in 'Prescription for Change': an 'Industrial Relations Commission' (IRC) staffed by individuals with practical experience in industrial relations, maximisation of the IRC's decisional discretion subject only to broad normative principles to guide its work,[33] rejection of direct civil

[30] *Royal Commission on Trade Unions and Employers' Associations 1965–1968 Report* (Cmnd 3623, 1968) 1 (*Royal Commission*) (emphasis added).

[31] C Howell, *Trade Unions and the State: The Construction of Industrial Relations Institutions in Britain, 1890–2000* (Princeton, Princeton University Press, 2005) 101.

[32] *Royal Commission*, above n 30, para 256, 65.

[33] *Ibid*, para 203, 50.

penalties as a sanction for non-compliance with IRC recommendations,[34] and a reliance on the deliberative method of public scrutiny and measurement in the proposals for public registration of collective agreements for larger companies.[35] Nevertheless, it would be a mistake to take the Report at face value as far as Flanders' influence is concerned. While the Report's proposals on the criteria for allocating bargaining rights refine and develop Flanders' approach, the legal concept of a duty to bargain in *good faith*—so central to Flanders' civic philosophy of collective bargaining—was rejected emphatically by the Commission.[36] We see here in protean form the ambivalent fate of the principle of group autonomy, and with it CLF, across the 1960s and 1970s. On the one hand, the progressive displacement of group autonomy in respect of bargaining units and bargaining agents; on the other hand, the resilience of group autonomy in respect of the collective bargaining process itself.

(i) Criteria of Union Representativity: The Determination of Bargaining Agents

As we have seen, there was ambiguity in Flanders' specification of criteria of union representativity. This theoretical agnosticism had problematical practical implications, for example when ascertaining what weight to accord to workers' collective consent in the public determination of the union's recognition claim. It was envisaged that this tension would be resolved incrementally as Flanders' tribunal developed its own working principles over time. When we compare the Donovan Commission's proposals for the IRC, however, we find a much higher degree of normative specificity than in Flanders' account. The governing general principles were first, 'that collective bargaining is the best method of conducting industrial relations', and secondly, 'whether the union or unions in question can reasonably be expected to develop and sustain adequate representation for the purpose of collective bargaining'.[37] These general normative principles were elaborated in two distinct ways.

Under the influence of Bain's research on the growth of white collar unionism, the Commission deployed a highly sophisticated conception of workers' consent. This emphasised the *endogenous* character of workers' preferences in this context. In other words, workers' current preferences were often shaped by environmental factors such as past deprivations or constrained future opportunities.[38] One concrete manifestation of this preference endogeneity was the

[34] *Ibid*, para 204, 51; though there was a proposal for the remedy of unilateral compulsory arbitration in the event of a refusal of recognition or where an employer engaged in 'sham' bargaining—see para 273, 69.

[35] *Ibid*, para 192, 47.

[36] *Ibid*, para 317, 82.

[37] *Ibid*, para 203, 50, principles 1 and 2.

[38] For a theoretical account of adaptive preferences, see C Sunstein, 'Legal Interference with Private Preferences' (1986) 53 *University of Chicago Law Review* 1129.

virtuous circle effect identified by Bain's research.[39] Bain found that union membership tended to follow union recognition because workers' preferences adapted to their positive experience of collective bargaining and the sense that the employer was supportive of trade unionism; conversely, if workers had no experience of collective bargaining, or anticipated employer hostility towards unionisation, their preferences might be adaptive to the non-union environment. Either way, it was unsound to confer a privileged status on citizens' currently held preferences, especially if these preferences were adaptive to an unjust status quo. From the civic perspective, the point was rather to scrutinise and transform such 'adaptive' preferences through a dialogical process of deliberation, not simply to aggregate those preferences and treat them as sovereign.[40] Since the IRC was bound under its first guiding principle to exercise its discretion so as to promote the extension of collective bargaining, an insistence on *current* majority support gauged through a public ballot mechanism as a prelude to allocating bargaining rights was not defensible. As the Commission put it, 'the fixing of a figure in this way might set up an impassable barrier to a union which would if only it were granted recognition organise a majority and represent them successfully'.[41] A better approach would be for the IRC to use its industrial relations expertise and judgement to assess how workers' preferences might be expected to develop once recognition had been awarded to the particular union.[42]

(ii) The Regulation of the Collective Bargaining Process

If the IRC's envisaged approach to the allocation of bargaining rights could be characterised as refining and developing Flanders' civic philosophy, the Commission's proposals on the legal concept of 'good faith' bargaining marked a continuation of the pluralist voluntarist paradigm. It is worth recalling Flanders' view that the pluralist commitment to free collective bargaining should be 'unreservedly consigned to the rubbish bin of history'.[43] One corollary of the civic repudiation of free collective bargaining was a growing legitimacy for the State's role in regulating the bargaining process. This meant, for example, that the legal enforcement of good faith standards in the bargaining process was a legitimate regulatory activity where this steered bargaining outcomes in accordance with publicly determined social and economic goals. Despite the Commission's assertion that it had adopted wholesale Flanders' set of proposals, this was not the case with respect to the legal concept of good faith bargaining, which had been a central component of Flanders' proposals. The Commission observed that 'the major difficulty is not a lack of good faith but disagreement as to what

[39] GS Bain, *The Growth of White-Collar Unionism* (Oxford, Oxford University Press, 1970) ch VIII.
[40] Sunstein, above n 4.
[41] *Royal Commission*, para 254, 64.
[42] Although *cf* para 198, 48 where reference is made to 'substantial membership' as a possible criterion of union recognition.
[43] Flanders, above n 24.

would constitute a reasonable bargain. The tribunal would in effect be asked to define an area marking out the limits of reasonable negotiation'.[44] The Commission concluded that this exercise should not even be attempted, although there was no sustained argument or evidence to support this conclusion.

What *was* clear from this conclusion, however, was that the pluralist voluntarist theory of collective bargaining was alive and well in the Committee's deliberations. If the sole metric of reasonableness was each party's calculation of how to maximise its own self-interest in the bargaining process (along the lines of the pluralist voluntarist philosophy of collective bargaining), then the Commission was correct in its suggestion that disagreement over what constituted a reasonable bargain was ineradicable. Beyond blatant refusals to negotiate with the other party, the IRC would have no rational basis for concluding that either party's stance was objectively unreasonable. To enable the IRC to undertake this richer adjudicative role would necessitate an agency of the State engaging in a controversial judgement concerning the parties' own determination of their respective goods and interests. This would have been incompatible with the anti-paternalism underpinning the pluralist voluntarist philosophy. This perceived absence of a publicly defensible metric to scrutinise the parties' bargaining conduct was probably the real reason why 'trade union negotiators have the skill to parry almost indefinitely allegations that they are not acting in good faith'.[45] The point has been well made by Langille and Macklem in their theoretical analysis of the legal concept of good faith:

> The assumption is one of 'self-interested rational action'. Each party is deemed to know what is best for them. The point becomes tautological and definitional. Whatever one decides is by definition one's self-interest. Since self-interest is the name of the game, whatever is decided, goes.[46]

In this respect, at least, Flanders had certainly been premature in concluding that the pluralist theory of free collective bargaining had been consigned to the dustbin of history; and the Donovan Commission had been somewhat misleading in claiming a straightforward adoption of Flanders' institutional proposals as its own. To complete the picture, we also identified three other ways in which the State might steer the collective bargaining process other than through the medium of legal recognition machinery. It is to these steering mechanisms that we now turn.

First, schemes for State registration of trade unions might potentially have significant steering effects on bargaining conduct. The nature and intensity of these effects depend upon a range of variables, for example, whether registration was voluntary or compulsory, whether State control of internal union affairs

44 *Royal Commission*, para 317, 82.
45 Para 317, 82.
46 B Langille and P Macklem, 'Beyond Belief: Labour Law's Duty to Bargain' (1988) 13 *Queens Law Journal* 62, 70.

extended beyond financial 'housekeeping', to encapsulate matters such as the union's procedures for calling strike action, the legitimate purposes of strike action and so on. Thus, registration was a normative technique that was compatible with a range of political ideologies, depending upon the precise degree of State intervention in the union's internal affairs entailed by registration.[47] The Donovan Commission proposed a scheme of compulsory State registration for trade unions so that all of them would have corporate status.[48] However, the envisaged public controls on internal trade union affairs entailed by registration were exiguous, going little beyond the nominal administrative restrictions imposed by the Trade Union Act 1871. In this respect, any steering of unions' bargaining activities was likely to be minimal.

Secondly, civic education is another important technique whereby citizens can be encouraged to engage with each other more deliberatively.[49] This occurs through the inculcation of civic virtues, encouraging citizens to acquire the habits and practices of good citizenship. In an important contribution to the debate about the civic role of trade unions, Phelps Brown argued that educating the *dispositions* and *attitudes* of trade unionists was likely to be more effective in restraining the abuse of industrial power than using coercive legal sanctions as a technique of restraint.[50] This would be facilitated by State-led civic education of trade unionists. The Commission acknowledged that the need for shop steward training was 'immense'.[51] However, its proposals were strikingly tentative. The proposals envisaged that the principal responsibility for the provision of education for trade unionists lay with the trade union movement itself. The Commission acknowledged that 'there is no general agreement on what should be taught'.[52] However, it did not propose that the State should take an active role in leading the development of a civic curriculum for trade unionists or employers, and any indirect steering effects on the bargaining process were likely to be minimal.

Finally, State regulation of social sanctions may also steer the process and outcomes of collective bargaining. As we have seen, Flanders displayed a sceptical attitude towards the use of social sanctions as a method of resolving industrial disagreements. He perceived an inherent incompatibility between coercive sanctions and deliberative reason, and expressed a firm preference for the latter. Suffice it to say that the relation between social sanctions and

[47] Davies and Freedland, above n 1, 250–51.

[48] *Royal Commission*, para 792, 212.

[49] On the relationship between citizenship and civic education, see A Gutmann, *Democratic Education* (Princeton, Princeton University Press, 1987).

[50] H Phelps Brown, *The Origins of Trade Union Power* (Oxford, Oxford University Press, 1983) 299–302. The entire question of trade union education, and the State's involvement in its provision, was a site of intense ideological conflict. For an excellent discussion, see J McIlroy, 'Making Trade Unionists: The Politics of Pedagogy, 1945–1979', in Alan Campbell, Nina Fishman and John McIlroy (eds), *British Trade Unions and Industrial Politics: The Post-War Compromise, 1945–64* (Aldershot, Ashgate, 1999) 37.

[51] *Royal Commission*, para 712, 190.

[52] *Ibid*, para 712, 191.

deliberative democracy is more complex than Flanders' scepticism might imply. Deliberative theorists have defended the right to strike as an essential means of ensuring that the parties are able to deliberate on a basis of equality; where the parties were demonstrably unequal, for example if unions were deprived of all resort to social sanctions, deliberation was likely to be a sham.[53] The point of regulation in this context, from the civic perspective, was very perceptively articulated by Phelps Brown:

> Policy therefore should not be directed simply towards the strengthening or weakening of trade unions: it is the uses of the trade union power, rather than the power itself, that should form the object of policy.[54]

This required very difficult regulatory choices, but it certainly set itself against an unrefined policy of legal restraint against strike action as such.[55] The Commission proposed no significant changes to the current law on strike action, concluding that voluntary reform of bargaining structures was likely to resolve many of the problems that were being experienced with unofficial and unconstitutional strike action.

Does the Donovan Report stand out more for its continuity or its discontinuity with the past? Probably both aspects contain an element of truth. As Davies and Freedland have pointed out, the Donovan Commission's attitude certainly marked a greater readiness on the part of the State to contemplate using legal techniques to pursue its reform objectives.[56] Certainly this was reflected in the Commission's proposals to develop public criteria for the designation of bargaining agents. However, Crouch was also correct in emphasising the continuing dominant influence of a liberal ideology, and this was reflected in the Commission's strong rejection of legal controls on collective bargaining.[57] More specific examples of this tendency can be seen in its rejection of legal good faith bargaining duties, the minimalist approach to union registration, and the caution in articulating a positive role for the State in the provision of civic education for trade unionists and employers. On balance, the civic voluntarism of Allan Flanders fared worse under Donovan than the pluralist status quo represented by Clegg's work. However, the Donovan compromise did provide a way out of the juridification dilemma for the pluralist voluntarists. By giving the IRC a role to promote the extension of union recognition and collective bargaining, while at the same time insulating the bargaining process from public scrutiny, this opened up the possibility of legal support *without* extensive legal control, at least as far as

[53] See ch 7 for a discussion of the relationship between deliberative democracy and the right to strike.

[54] Phelps Brown, above n 50, 293.

[55] *Ibid*, 294.

[56] Davies and Freedland, above n 1, 264. Also, see Howell, above n 31, 107.

[57] C Crouch, *Class Conflict and the Industrial Relations Crisis: Compromise and Corporatism in the Policies of the British State* (London, Heinemann, 1977) 161.

the collective bargaining process itself (as opposed to bargaining units and agents) was concerned.

The next section will explore three distinctive phases in the development of direct auxiliary intervention: the voluntary phase between 1969 and 1971 represented in the work of the Commission on Industrial Relations (CIR I); the juridified phase represented in the IRA 1971 framework between 1971 and 1974 administered by the reconstituted CIR (CIR II); and the social contract phase between 1974 and 1979, administered by the Advisory, Conciliation and Arbitration Service (ACAS) (along with the ordinary courts through judicial review proceedings). In each of these phases, we will examine the fate of CLF's principle of group autonomy as British legislators experimented with different techniques of direct intervention in the bargaining activities of social groups.

III THREE EXPERIMENTS IN DIRECT AUXILIARY INTERVENTION: THE ECLIPSE OF CLF?

A The Legal Duty to Bargain I: The Commission on Industrial Relations 1969–1971

The Labour Government's response to the Donovan Report was set out in the ill-fated White Paper, *In Place of Strife*.[58] It proposed that a Commission on Industrial Relations (CIR I) be set up with immediate effect, along the lines suggested in the Donovan Report.[59] Accordingly, the CIR was established by Royal Warrant on 1 March 1969, with an Industrial Relations Bill putting the CIR I on a permanent statutory footing to follow. The CIR I counted Allan Flanders as one of its commissioners. Of course, the Industrial Relations Bill set out in the White Paper never did follow because Labour lost the 1970 general election. As such, CIR I's curious 31 month interlude is difficult to assess because it ended up operating in a radically different regulatory context to that which had been envisaged for it by the Government, given the TUC's unrelenting hostility to Labour's Industrial Relations Bill. It was, in this respect, an institution severed from its legal matrix at its inception. Accordingly, a judicious assessment of the

[58] *In Place of Strife: A Policy for Industrial Relations* (Cmnd. 3888 1969) (*Strife*).
[59] *Ibid*, paras 33–8, 13–14.

CIR I's work must take place alongside a consideration of the legislative proposals in the White Paper.

(i) Bargaining Units and Bargaining Agents: The Eclipse of Group Autonomy?

In quantitative terms, CIR I dealt with relatively few recognition references, 13 in all; it recommended recognition in 10 of these cases.[60] Nevertheless, its published reports give a fascinating insight into the operation of the first British experiment with third party resolution of recognition disputes. Unsurprisingly given Flanders' pivotal presence as a commissioner, the CIR I was responsive to many of the insights and concerns of the civic voluntarist tradition. First, the CIR I was explicit in its rejection of neutrality towards collective bargaining. Instead, it considered its legitimate role was to promote the extension of collective bargaining wherever possible.[61] Accordingly, the CIR I would recommend recognition whenever it took the view that '"adequate collective bargaining" could be maintained' by the union concerned.[62] Secondly, the CIR I was acutely sensitive to the civic consequences of bargaining unit determination. As Lewis and Latta observed, trade unions often bargained in a manner that was inattentive to the common good because bargaining units had evolved in an unstructured, fragmented and chaotic fashion.[63] This incentivised competitive and sectional bargaining behaviour which undermined important public interests. Conversely, trade unions might bargain with greater civic responsibility where bargaining units were conducive to this. In *Medical Research Council,* for example, CIR I placed significant weight on the need for a unified bargaining unit to include three distinct grades of worker, despite occupational and attitudinal differences between these grades.[64] This single unit would ensure a 'strong and uniform system of representation'.[65] CIR I also sought to shape its bargaining units to reflect existing or potential union support where this was consistent with other criteria, so as to maximise the chances of a positive recognition recommendation.[66]

[60] In the sections that follow on the work of the CIR I and CIR II, I am indebted to the work of Kessler and Palmer. Their thorough assessment of every aspect of the CIR's work on recognition is unrivalled. See S Kessler and G Palmer, 'The Commission on Industrial Relations in Britain 1969–74: A retrospective and prospective evaluation' (1996) 18 *Employee Relations* 6, 45.

[61] *Ibid*, 37–8.

[62] *Ibid*, 38.

[63] R Lewis and G Latta, 'Bargaining Units and Bargaining Agents' (1972) 10 *British Journal of Industrial Relations* 84, 85.

[64] CIR, Report No 12, *Medical Research Council* (Cmnd. 4531, 1970).

[65] Lewis and Latta, above n 63, 89.

[66] S Kessler, 'Trade union recognition: CIR and ACAS experience' (1995) 17 *Employee Relations* 52.

Thirdly, CIR I deployed a civic approach to the allocation of bargaining rights. Kessler and Palmer's thorough analysis of CIR I decision-making disclosed an evolving approach.[67] CIR I placed increasing emphasis on 'potential' rather than 'actual' support, as gauged through systematic and exhaustive attitudinal enquiries of the bargaining unit constituents. Given the significance of 'potential' support in allocating bargaining rights, CIR I never used the ballot as an investigative technique. Once this endogenous view of preferences was endorsed, it made little sense to accord a privileged status to citizens' current preferences, as the ballot mechanism inevitably did. This approach 'greatly increased the CIR's scope for flexible assessment. In every case but three, support was found to be adequate even when membership was low'.[68] CIR I also sought to harness the virtuous circle effect through its flexible use of recommendations. Thus, even where the union had insufficient current or potential support to justify full recognition, CIR I recommended representational or consultative rights as a way of providing an organisational foothold for the union in the bargaining unit.[69] If workers' preferences adapted endogenously, it might be expected that CIR I's 'staged' approach to recognition would stimulate attitudinal changes amongst workers over time.

Overall, CIR I's direct impact on the extension of union recognition was quantitatively small. According to Kessler and Palmer, CIR I published 13 reports on recognition and it recommended recognition in 10 cases.[70] Employers rejected the recommendation in five of those cases. This was not an impressive record, particularly since the pool of cases for CIR I was itself selective: only the Secretary of State could refer a case to CIR I and it was the Secretary of State's practice only to refer a case where all of the parties were agreeable to this.[71] However, CIR I had undoubtedly established itself as a respected agency in the recognition context. Its sensitive encroachment upon group autonomy in respect of bargaining unit and bargaining agent designation can be seen as responsive to many of the insights of Flanders' civic voluntarism. This is unsurprising given Flanders' presence on the staff of the CIR I.

(ii) The Legal Duty to Bargain: The Resilience of Group Autonomy?

There is a departure from this pattern once we consider the enforcement of good faith bargaining standards. Thus, Kessler and Palmer concluded that

> The CIR tried to limit its role to that of advising whether or not a union should be granted negotiating rights. It kept clear of matters of substance and usually argued that

[67] Kessler and Palmer, above n 60, 41–4.

[68] *Ibid*, 43.

[69] See, eg, CIR, Report No 2, *General Accident* (Cmnd. 4247, 1969); CIR, Report No 24, *British Home Stores* (Cmnd. 4791, 1971); CIR, Report No 21, *Electric Windings* (Cmnd. 4730, 1971).

[70] Kessler and Palmer, above n 60, 45.

[71] *Ibid*, 19.

> the procedural details, after recognition was granted, should be sorted out by the parties involved.[72]

This enabled the pluralist State both to promote the extension of collective bargaining while simultaneously shielding the parties' bargaining autonomy from State interference. However, it is important to reiterate the point that CIR I was forced to operate in a radically different legal matrix than had been envisaged by its framers. Once we examine the other steering mechanisms proposed as part of the abortive Industrial Relations Bill, the overall package of reforms envisaged a highly interventionist role for the State despite CIR I's reticence in articulating good faith bargaining standards.

In Place of Strife defended the view that 'Governments should intervene ... if it could be shown that certain important economic or social objectives were not sufficiently furthered or were frustrated by collective bargaining.'[73] It articulated a much more pronounced role for the State and reform through juridification than had been envisaged in the Donovan Report.[74] In relation to (i) it was proposed that trade unions and employers' associations should be required to register with a new Registrar of Trade Unions and Employers' Associations, with refusals to register punished by the imposition of a financial penalty.[75] The regulatory consequences of registration went beyond exiguous scrutiny of financial housekeeping, to specify substantive standards of good administration. Unions would be required to formulate clear and comprehensive rules on matters such as admission and discipline of members, strike ballots and the constitutional position of shop stewards. It marked a decisive step in the utilisation of registration as a regulatory technique for steering bargaining conduct to promote public responsibility in the bargaining process.

In relation to (ii), and the technique of civic education, the radicalism of the Government's approach was more evident still. Two novel initiatives were proposed. First, there was a proposal to place employers under a legal duty of disclosure to the trade union in respect of information for collective bargaining purposes. This was justified in deliberative terms. Negotiation without proper information 'encourages an early retreat to entrenched position, and thus damages industrial relations'.[76] By contrast, an unimpeded flow of information between the parties enabled reasoned dialogue and informed scrutiny of competing arguments. This involved a shift away from the assumption of self-interested strategic action upon which the interest-group pluralist model of collective bargaining was based. On that model, taking strategic advantage of informational asymmetry was simply a way of making best use of one's superior bargaining position. On the deliberative conception, by contrast, full and

72 *Ibid*, 45.
73 *Strife* para 6, 6.
74 Davies and Freedland, above n 1, 269; Crouch, above n 57, 163.
75 *Strife* paras 107–13, 32–3.
76 *Ibid*, para 47, 16.

accurate information was a precursor to the process of rational dialogue and the search for a reasoned consensus. Secondly, there was a proposal to set up a 'Trade Union Development Scheme', administered by the CIR, so that State financial support could be used to promote 'the expansion of training for union officials including shop stewards, the development of unions' often inadequate research facilities … and the employment of management consultants'.[77] The Government was cognisant of the potential breach of voluntarism that this radical initiative entailed, articulating the hope that unions 'will share its belief that such help will contribute to greater trade union effectiveness without compromising trade union independence'.[78]

In respect of (iii), the Government also proposed the so-called 'penal clauses' to regulate the use of economic weaponry. This encapsulated two specific proposals. First, the granting of a discretionary reserve power to the Secretary of State to secure a conciliation pause where the strike was in breach of agreed procedure or adequate joint discussions had not otherwise preceded the strike, and the public effects of the strike were likely to be serious.[79] Secondly, the selective imposition of strike ballots where strikes posed a 'serious threat to the … public interest' and there were doubts over members' support of the strike action.[80] So intense was the trade union hostility towards these legal measures that the proposals never had a chance of enactment. In retrospect, however, these proposals did not form part of a strategy of legal restriction of unions' social power, and they were not an unjustified attack on independent trade unionism. The aim was to modulate the use of social sanctions to promote deliberation, rather than to weaken the social power base of unions. They were theoretically defensible attempts to promote a more civic orientation amongst actors in industrial civil society by discouraging genuine abuses of the strike weapon. Where there was a possibility of deliberative resolution through reasoned dialogue, it was not inappropriate for the State to encourage this through the selective use of conciliation pauses and ballots. With the benefit of hindsight, it is difficult to resist the conclusion that *In Place of Strife* was a missed opportunity for the British labour movement. However, the intensity of trade union hostility indicated how sacrosanct the principle of group autonomy was from the perspective of the main players in industrial civil society.

[77] *Ibid*, paras 71–5, 23–4.
[78] *Ibid*, para 74, 24.
[79] *Ibid*, paras 93–6, 28–9.
[80] *Ibid*, paras 97–8, 29–30.

B The Legal Duty to Bargain II: The Industrial Relations Act 1971 and CIR II

The Conservative Party had been developing its own set of responses to the Donovan Commission's deliberations while in opposition. Indeed, it had crafted a comprehensive set of reform proposals even before the Donovan Commission had issued its final report. These were set out in the Conservative Political Centre's report, *Fair Deal at Work (Fair Deal)*.[81] Its political frame of reference was driven by the widely held perception of a serious civic deficit in industrial civil society: 'The concept of freedom under the law is fundamental, but if that freedom is abused by irresponsible elements to the detriment of the nation or to the basic rights of individuals, government has the duty to step in.'[82] This diagnosis was hardly novel. What was distinctive was the proposed solution. This was to be based upon *total* juridification of the industrial relations system through the enactment of a comprehensive Industrial Relations Act. Every aspect of industrial life—the closed shop, collective bargaining, the use of the strike weapon, and the conduct of internal trade union affairs—was to be embedded in a scheme of legal regulation setting out the parties' legal rights and responsibilities precisely and exhaustively.[83] This strategy of control through juridification was intended to be instrumental in promoting a more civic orientation at the bargaining table.

The IRA 1971 scheme was committed to 'the principle of collective bargaining freely conducted on behalf of workers and employers and with due regard to the general interests of the community'.[84] This was simply a restatement of the political problem that the Donovan Commission and the previous Labour Government had been grappling with. The devil lay in the detail: what were the outer limits of bargaining freedom? What constituted 'due regard'? And what was meant by the community's 'general interest'? The specific answers provided by the IRA scheme would not prove tolerable to the main actors in industrial civil society. Most TUC-affiliated unions refused to register under the IRA framework, and this strategy of conscientious resistance proved fatal to the Act and, ultimately, to the Conservative Government. This makes any assessment of the IRA's experiment in total juridification an especially challenging exercise.

The proposals on union recognition in *Fair Deal* were brief, in comparison with the extended discussion of matters such as the legal regulation of strike action. As a way of solving recognition disputes more peaceably, *Fair Deal* proposed the enactment of a legal duty to recognise and negotiate with registered trade unions. This would be administered by officials of the Ministry of Labour, who

[81] Conservative Political Centre, *Fair Deal at Work: The Conservative approach to modern industrial relations* (CPC 400, 1968) (*Fair Deal*).
[82] *Ibid*, 10.
[83] *Ibid*, 17.
[84] IRA 1971 s 1(1)(a).

would conduct ballots to gauge the level of worker support, and any complaints of a refusal to negotiate would be adjudicated by the newly proposed Industrial Court. Where a registered union enjoyed reasonable support, defined as majority support in the ballot, it would be entitled to a legal order to compel recognition. The remedy was an award of binding unilateral arbitration on terms and conditions of employment.[85] Beyond this broad endorsement of the principle of majority rule, the precise details of the scheme were very sketchy. There was no specific guidance on the determination of the bargaining unit or the enforcement of good faith standards in the bargaining process. One element that was precisely defined, however, was the qualifying criterion for trade unions permitted to utilise the legal procedure. The legal procedure was confined to *registered* trade unions. This captured in microcosm the entire regulatory strategy of the IRA. In submitting to State registration, and the full panoply of State controls over the purposes and methods of collective action, *registered* unions would (in theory) be *responsible* unions. In turn, only responsible unions acting in the public interest would be able to take full advantage of auxiliary State support.

The procedure finally enacted in the IRA, and supplemented by the accompanying Code of Practice on Industrial Relations, took its comparative inspiration from the US statutory recognition procedure.[86] Under section 45, the newly constituted CIR II was empowered to make a determination of the correct bargaining unit and the appropriate bargaining agent, following a reference from the National Industrial Relations Court (NIRC). In turn, applications could be made to the NIRC by registered trade unions, employers or the Secretary of State. Where the CIR II, following a NIRC reference, had recommended recognition of a registered trade union, this could be made the subject of a legally enforceable order administered by NIRC if the union achieved majority support in a ballot.[87] Legal compulsion was, however, a last resort. It was intended that most disputes would be amenable to a conciliated voluntary resolution and the legislative framework made explicit provision for this in its specification of the NIRC's discretion to make a reference to the CIR II.[88] In the event of a ballot and a NIRC order, the employer was then under a legal duty 'to take all such action by way of or with a view to carrying on collective bargaining as might reasonably be expected to be taken by an employer ready and willing to carry on such collective bargaining'.[89] This was enforceable by an award of compulsory unilateral arbitration administered by the Industrial Arbitration Board.[90]

[85] *Fair Deal*, 43–5.

[86] See, eg, WB Gould, 'Taft-Hartley comes to Britain: Observations on the Industrial Relations Act of 1971' (1972) 81 *Yale Law Journal* 1421.

[87] S 49.

[88] S 46(1)(b): NIRC could only refer where it was satisfied that the prospects for a conciliated voluntary settlement were exhausted.

[89] S 55(1)(b).

[90] S 105(5).

Additionally, registered unions could also achieve a kind of partial recognition through the new legal protections for freedom of association. Thus section 5 was interpreted as guaranteeing an individual right for members of *registered* trade unions to participate in trade union activities at an appropriate time on the employer's property,[91] and a corresponding right not to be discriminated against on such grounds.[92] Where there was a 'substantial disparity' in facilities provision between different unions this would constitute unlawful discrimination, even where one of those unions was unrecognised for collective bargaining purposes.[93] This extended to an individual right for members of registered but unrecognised trade unions to be represented by their chosen union in grievance procedures.[94] In effect, this was tantamount to a form of 'members only' collective bargaining, operating alongside the majoritarian recognition procedure in section 45.

(i) Bargaining Units and Bargaining Agents: State Neutrality or State Partiality?

Scholarly characterisation and evaluation of the IRA framework has been diverse. For Mellish and Dickens, there was a disjunction between the Government's rhetorical commitment to promoting collective bargaining, and the reality of the legal recognition procedures. The IRA 'aims not to promote union growth as such but the growth of "responsible" unions. It is equivocal even on their growth.'[95] Such equivocation was characteristic of a stance of State neutrality towards the institution of collective bargaining. More recently, Ruth Dukes has emphasised the continuities between the activities of CIR I as a Royal Commission, and the activities of the reconstituted CIR II in administering the statutory procedure under the IRA. According to Dukes, 'like the non-statutory procedure in place before it, the 1971 recognition procedure was intended to secure the growth of collective bargaining', while ensuring greater order and responsibility in the bargaining process.[96] In this way, the State engaged in active promotion of collective bargaining.

What are we to make of this divergence? I want to suggest that each emphasises an important but partial truth about the IRA's design and operation, depending upon which part of the overall picture is emphasised. In part, this was based on the schizophrenic nature of the statutory drafting itself, reflecting the

[91] S 5(1)(c).
[92] S 5(2)(b).
[93] *Post Office v Union of Post Office Workers* [1974] ICR 378, HL. For an interesting account of the tensions between the NIRC, on the one hand, and the Court of Appeal and House of Lords on the other, in relation to the intersection of individual rights and collective bargaining structures, see AWJ Thomson and SR Engleman, *The Industrial Relations Act: A Review and Analysis* (London, Martin Robertson, 1975) 61–5.
[94] *Howle v GEC Power Engineering Ltd*, [1974] ICR 13, NIRC.
[95] M Mellish and L Dickens, 'Recognition Problems under the Industrial Relations Act' (1972) 1 *Industrial Law Journal* 229, 240.
[96] R Dukes, 'The Statutory Recognition Procedure 1999: No Bias in Favour of Recognition' (2008) 37 *Industrial Law Journal* 236, 242.

influences of Wedderburn's 'two phantom draftsmen': on the one hand, the civil service 'organization man' obsessed with tidiness and ordered bargaining units and, on the other hand, the Conservative lawyer driven by a common law philosophy of 'extreme individualism'.[97] Mainly, however, it was rooted in the layering of overlapping and distinct political frameworks. The Government was certainly pursuing its own political vision with fundamentalist zeal, and this was reflected in the detail of the statutory framework and Code of Practice. However, within the interstices of that statutory framework, the CIR II, NIRC, and even the trade unions were following their own distinctive political trajectories. These trajectories were not necessarily convergent with the Government's agenda, or indeed with each other. It is therefore important to tease these layers apart in order to understand the full political significance of the IRA.

(a) Legislative Ideology and Governmental Neutrality Let us begin with the political theory of the IRA statutory framework as envisaged by its framers. I want to suggest that the most accurate characterisation of its political character is based in a model of liberal neutrality. Liberal rights were predicated on the guarantee of effective agency so that individuals could exercise their autonomy and make their own determinations of the good, free from interference or restraint. The flipside to this commitment to rights-based individual autonomy was the liberal commitment to State neutrality. Only where the State was neutral on controversial matters of value would citizens be unimpeded in choosing their own conception of the good. The most obvious manifestation of this liberal-individualist turn was the IRA's attack on union security arrangements. Section 5 conferred a right to join a registered trade union and to participate in its activities, along with a parallel right to refrain from joining any union, registered or otherwise. This was protected by a range of unfair industrial practices proscribing various forms of industrial pressure that might vitiate the individual worker's freedom to choose. Pre-entry closed shops were declared void.[98] The legislative framework permitted only two forms of union security arrangement for registered trade unions, both of which required legitimating through a public ballot administered by the CIR II on a reference from the NIRC. Legitimacy depended upon the achievement of a super-majority threshold: either a majority of the constituency entitled to vote, or two thirds of those voting.

What is the connection between liberal neutrality and the IRA's conception of freedom of association? An influential account of the structure of liberal rights, and the relationship of that structure to liberal neutrality, has been provided by Michael Sandel.[99] According to Sandel, the neutral State was an inseparable

[97] Lord Wedderburn, *Employment Rights in Britain and Europe: Selected Papers in Labour Law* (London, Lawrence & Wishart, 1991)144–5.

[98] S 7.

[99] MJ Sandel, *Democracy's Discontent: American in Search of a Public Philosophy* (Cambridge Massachusetts, Harvard University Press, 1996) ch 1.

corollary of the liberal rights-based approach to citizenship. This inseparability was based upon

> its central idea … that government should be neutral toward the moral and religious views its citizens espouse. Since people disagree about the best way to live, government should not affirm in law any particular vision of the good life. Instead, it should provide a framework of rights that respects persons as free and independent selves, capable of choosing their own values and ends.[100]

Where freedom of association asserted the moral priority of union membership over non-membership, the legal framework was (arguably) affirming in law a particular vision of the good life. In so doing, the law was violating its commitment to neutrality, and this would constitute a failure to respect worker-citizens as 'free and independent selves, capable of choosing their own values and ends'.[101]

The implications of liberal neutrality radiated far beyond the legality of closed shop arrangements. They also tended to undermine the legitimacy of any form of auxiliary State intervention where the purpose was to promote collective bargaining. Such legislation would be, in Sandel's terms, 'affirming in law a particular vision of the good life'. In the light of this, it is possible to interpret the recognition procedure in sections 45–50 as a coherent liberal package along with the legal provisions restricting union security. The choice of comparative basis for the IRA framework in the US Taft-Hartley Act reinforces this neutrality characterisation, as James Gross' authoritative historical analysis of US labour relations policy makes clear.[102] The Taft-Hartley Act precipitated a shift *away* from a non-neutral conception of the State's role as promoting the extension of collective bargaining, as specified in the Wagner Act of 1935, and towards a liberal conception based on State neutrality. Taft-Hartley expressly protected employees' right to reject collective bargaining, alongside their right to choose it. This symmetry was allied with a concept 'of the federal government as a *neutral guarantor* of employee free choice between individual and collective bargaining, and indifferent to the choice made'.[103] It underpinned the 'balanced' approach to the design of legal techniques in the Taft-Hartley framework: the positing of union 'unfair practices' alongside employer 'unfair practices', the express protection of employer 'free speech' rights in the conduct of recognition ballots, symmetrical provision for derecognition ballots as a mirror of the recognition procedures, and the enactment of statutory restrictions on the closed shop.[104] As such, the Taft-Hartley framework was a quintessentially liberal framework of law.

[100] *Ibid*, 4.
[101] *Ibid*, 12.
[102] JA Gross, *Broken Promise: The Subversion of US Labor Relations Policy* (Philadelphia, Temple University Press, 1995).
[103] *Ibid*, 272.
[104] *Ibid*, 4.

The IRA recognition procedure, while certainly not identical to Taft-Hartley, integrated many of its liberal features. Its exclusive reliance on a ballot procedure as a mandatory precondition of legal enforcement marked a paradigm shift.[105] The centrality of the ballot procedure under the IRA recognition procedure was perfectly fitted to the liberal aspiration to neutrality. The exclusive reliance on a ballot confined the State's role to the neutral enterprise of enforcing fair (democratic) procedures rather than using the legislation to promote substantive ends. This symmetry was reinforced by the inclusion of a parallel ballot procedure to facilitate withdrawal of recognition, as an exact mirror of the recognition procedure.[106] Along with the parallelism of section 5 in respect of membership and non-membership, and the prescribed ballot procedures for approving and terminating lawful union and closed shop arrangements, Mellish and Dickens' 'neutrality' characterisation of the recognition procedure seems closest to the liberal-individualist spirit of the legislation.

(b) CIR II and State Partiality As an account of the CIR II's interstitial role in administering the recognition procedure, however, Dukes' partiality characterisation is more persuasive. CIR II was reconstituted as a statutory body by virtue of section 120 of the IRA. In common with other institutions operating under the Act, CIR II was directed by section 1(2)(a) to have regard to the general normative principles set out in section 1(1)(a)–(d). These included 'the principle of collective bargaining freely conducted', 'the principle of free association of workers in independent trade unions', and 'the principle of freedom and security for workers'. As Simpson and Wood observed in an influential commentary of the time, the 'generality and ambiguity of the section 1 principles' limited their ability to provide concrete and specific guidance.[107] This normative generality gave CIR II very substantial room for manoeuvre in exercising its discretion under the Act. It did not compel a pro-collective bargaining agenda but neither did it preclude it. This allowed the CIR II sufficient normative space to pursue a political agenda that was very much at odds with that of the legislator.

Both Kessler and Palmer's exhaustive study of the CIR and James and Pleasance's *CIR Study 5, Trade Union Recognition: CIR Experience*[108] points to the significant continuity of approach between CIR I and CIR II. In many ways, this continuity was surprising given the major legislative changes that had occurred. These changes affected the CIR II's constitution and operation in important ways. Thus, CIR II could now receive recognition references from the NIRC in addition to the Secretary of State, and its discretion in relation to bargaining units and bargaining agents was guided both by explicit statutory criteria and the accompanying Code of Practice on Industrial Relations published by the

105 RC Simpson and J Wood, *Industrial Relations and the 1971 Act* (London, Pitman, 1973) 116.
106 S 50–53.
107 *Ibid*, 71.
108 *CIR Study 5, Trade Union Recognition: CIR Experience* (*CIR Study 5*) (London, HMSO, 1974).

Department of Employment and brought into effect in 1972. More importantly, perhaps, the personal profile of the CIR II Commissioners altered radically. This was largely due to the TUC's policy of non-cooperation with the IRA and its institutions, although notably Allan Flanders had also decided to step down due to illness. Given these tumultuous changes, how was the transition from CIR I to CIR II so seamless? According to Kessler and Palmer, this was largely due to the retention of the same operational staffing at the Commission 'who were still imbued with the Donovan approach, despite the Industrial Relations Act 1971'.[109]

CIR II thus continued the civic approach that had been developed by CIR I. This was manifest in three ways. First, CIR II continued to exercise its discretion so as to promote collective bargaining wherever possible.[110] This was evident in its determination of bargaining units, where CIR II 'was inclined to define units around groups of people who favoured collective bargaining, who were union members or supporters, and who therefore would be able to maintain negotiating machinery'.[111] Secondly, CIR II continued to shape bargaining units with a view to promoting the 'civic accountability' of bargaining agents. The only nominate statutory criterion guiding the CIR II in the task of unit determination was the 'common interest' of employees, having regard in particular to the 'nature of the work' and 'training, experience and professional or other qualifications'.[112] This was supplemented by a range of discretionary factors in the accompanying Code of Practice. According to Lewis and Latta, the statutory criterion appeared to encourage fragmentation of the bargaining process leading to the severance of white collar from blue collar workers, craft workers from manufacturing workers, and severance of distinct craft groups, thereby serving to 'institutionalize sectional groupings'.[113] In certain respects, this tendency was compatible with the liberal character of the legislation in maximising the right to self-determination of minority groups in the workplace.[114] However, it also cut against the civic need for ordered bargaining structures and processes operating with 'due regard to the general interests of the community'.[115] CIR II mitigated the dangers of sectionalism in its bargaining unit determinations. Thus, in *C A Parsons & Co* the CIR II resisted the attempts of the professional association United Kingdom Association of Professional Engineers (UKAPE) to carve out discrete bargaining units based on professional qualifications.[116] CIR II favoured maintaining the

[109] Kessler and Palmer, above n 60, 31; also, *ibid*, para 18, 6–7.
[110] *CIR Study 5*, above n 108, paras 26–7, 9: the CIR was a public body 'with a commitment to the orderly development of collective bargaining'.
[111] Kessler and Palmer, above n 60, 52; *CIR Study 5*, above n 108, paras 99–132, 28–35.
[112] S 48 (3).
[113] Lewis and Latta, above n 63, 100.
[114] *Ibid*, 101.
[115] S 1(1)(a).
[116] CIR Report No 32, (London, HMSO, 1972).

integrity of the more encompassing bargaining unit represented by the TUC-affiliated Technical, Administrative and Supervisory Section (TASS). In this way, CIR II worked to ensure that bargaining units were as encompassing as possible, and this often overrode the right to self-determination of discrete workgroups.

Thirdly, CIR II continued to build upon the work of CIR I in developing criteria for allocating bargaining rights. In respect of worker support, the interaction between the CIR II's 'endogenous' theory of preference measurement and the legislative endorsement of current majority rule measured through a public ballot, was a potential flashpoint. CIR II viewed the measurement of worker support as a dynamic process extending to a predictive assessment of workers' preference changes even *after* recognition had been awarded;[117] by contrast, the ballot mechanism was focused on crystallising current preferences and measuring them at the discrete moment they were registered. Once again, Kessler and Palmer concluded that 'the CIR did not fundamentally change the way it measured and judged the support an organization had among a group of employees'.[118] The only change that the authors identified was the utilisation of systematic attitudinal surveys of the entire bargaining unit, rather than its previous reliance on sampling in its voluntary phase; this was because of the ever-present possibility that its recommendations might be tested in a ballot.

This general continuity in CIR II's approach was also confirmed by *CIR Study 5*, which pointed to the continuing relevance of 'potential' worker support post-recognition—a core feature of CIR I's endogenous theory of worker preferences—in CIR II's interpretation of 'substantial' support under the Act.[119] Furthermore, CIR II continued to recommend the allocation of representational rights to unions that lacked sufficient support to justify full recognition, thereby harnessing the virtuous circle effects to promote a gradual extension of the union's influence in the workplace.[120] Ultimately, the ballot proved to be a peripheral feature of the recognition procedure in practice, despite its centrality in the statutory edifice. There were only two section 49 ballots: one supported the CIR II's recommendation, the other rejected it.[121]

Whether we focus upon legislative ideology or CIR II practice, the designation of bargaining units and bargaining agents during this period marked a decisive retreat from the principle of group autonomy. Nevertheless, the different directions of retreat represented by the legislator and CIR II are perhaps more interesting still. For CIR II there was continuity with the civic approach that had been developed by its institutional predecessor, CIR I, during its voluntary phase.

[117] *CIR Study 5*, above n 108, para 183, 46–7.

[118] Kessler and Palmer, above n 60, 57.

[119] CIR Study 5, above n 108, para 219, 57. See also para 264, 68: 'The act of recognition thus tends to bring about a significant change in employee attitudes.'

[120] Kessler and Palmer, above n 60, 59.

[121] *Ibid*, 57.

This was manifest in its pro-attitude towards the extension of collective bargaining, its approach to bargaining unit determination, and its flexible interpretation of sufficient worker support. For the legislator, however, the ideology of liberal neutrality and the correlative principle of majority rule measured through a democratic ballot marked a new and radical departure in British industrial relations. Whereas pluralist and civic voluntarists had converged on the policy commitment to collective bargaining as a public good that warranted State support (while differing on the choice of appropriate strategies to achieve this end), the liberal ideology of the IRA framework rejected this political consensus in favour of State neutrality. This corresponded to an approach that countenanced the allocation of bargaining rights to unions only where the neutral aggregation of workers' preferences indicated majority support in the bargaining unit.

(ii) The Legal Duty to Bargain: The Resilience of Group Autonomy?

Like CIR I, CIR II did not intrude on the autonomy of the bargaining process itself through the enforcement of good faith standards.[122] The focus of its work remained on developing methodologies and criteria for determining bargaining units and allocating bargaining rights to appropriate bargaining agents. In large measure, this simply reflected the voluntarist preferences of the parties: once the CIR II had made its voluntary recommendation following a reference from NIRC, in only two cases did the parties seek a legally enforceable order.[123] At a deeper level, however, this also reflected a certain normative reticence where the parties' bargaining autonomy was concerned. Overall, the CIR II's specific legacy was a positive one. During the statutory phase CIR II published 27 reports on recognition issues: in 18 of these reports CIR II recommended recognition. Employers refused to accept the CIR II's recommendations in only four cases. This can be compared favourably to CIR I's employer refusal rate of five out of 10 recognition recommendations.[124]

If the CIR II can be accused of normative reticence in not developing good faith standards, this was not an accusation that could be levelled at either the IRA framework or its framers. The IRA deployed a full range of regulatory modes in order to steer the bargaining process decisively in preferred directions. It was the paradigm case of a strategy of public control through juridification. It is in this respect that Clark and Wedderburn's famous identification of the 'policy of restriction' is most pertinent.[125] On this approach, the pathway to 'responsible' trade unionism was through the reduction of unions' social power. This

122 *Ibid*, 60.
123 *Ibid.*
124 Kessler, above n 66.
125 J Clark and Lord Wedderburn, 'Modern Labour Law: Problems, Functions and Policies', in Lord Wedderburn, R Lewis, and J Clark (eds), *Labour Law and Industrial Relations: Building on Kahn-Freund* (Oxford, Oxford University Press, 1983) 127.

tactic of 'responsibility through disempowerment' was particularly evident in relation to the techniques of union registration and regulation of economic weaponry.

In relation to State registration, this was central to the IRA's regulatory approach. Only registered organisations were able to take advantage of the IRA's positive rights, such as the recognition procedure or lawful industrial action, because State registration entailed the alignment of the union's methods and purposes with the public interest. Registered unions were required to bring their constitutions and rules into conformity with guiding normative principles set out in Part IV of the Act, and enforceable by the NIRC and the Registrar of Trade Unions. As Davies and Freedland have argued, the accent of these normative principles was on constraining 'irresponsible' strike action: union members could not be lawfully disciplined by their union for refusing to participate in 'unlawful' industrial action (with those parameters set publicly through the IRA's 'unfair industrial practices'), while unions themselves were required to delineate clearly the locus of legitimate internal decision-making authority for the calling of strikes.[126] This fitted with the 'restrictive' characterisation of Clark and Wedderburn.

In relation to civic education of the bargaining parties, the IRA contained some limited measures concerning the provision of information for collective bargaining purposes. Thus, section 56 placed employers under a legal duty to provide such information without which the union representative would be impeded to a material extent in the conduct of collective bargaining, and where this provision would accord with good industrial relations practice. As Simpson and Wood observed, this informational duty was so hedged and circumscribed with limitations and employer defences to disclosure (in section 158(1)) that it was likely to be nugatory in practice.[127] Furthermore, the IRA took a quiescent approach to facilities and training provision for shop stewards and trade unionists. The Code of Practice simply indicated that this was to be a matter for voluntary agreement between the parties.[128]

This quiescence was perhaps a reflection of the legislator's political investment in the third technique for steering bargaining conduct, the policy of regulating and restricting unions' economic weaponry. The political investment was very evident in the IRA's elaborate and complex web of legal regulation restricting unions' deployment of social sanctions. This web of regulation constituted the very backbone of the Act. Even industrial action within the reformulated 'industrial dispute' formula was subject to a battery of substantive and procedural restrictions, backed by 'unfair industrial practices'. Some of these restrictions were not necessarily incompatible with the deliberative ideal, in form at least. Thus the emergency procedures set out in sections 138–145, which made

[126] Davies and Freedland, above n 1, 298–301.
[127] Simpson and Wood, above n 105, 131–2.
[128] Para 118.

provision for compulsory cooling off periods and ballots in relation to serious industrial disputes, *could* be rationalised as a valid deliberative technique for promoting reasoned dialogue between the parties. However, other provisions were less ambivalent in their restrictive purposes and their intended cumulative effects. It was variously an 'unfair industrial practice' for registered trade unions to organise industrial action to enforce closed shop arrangements, to disrupt the operation of the legal recognition procedure, or to act in breach of legally binding procedure agreements, to engage in 'sympathetic' strike action in furtherance of other actions constituting 'unfair industrial practices', and all other forms of 'secondary' industrial action.[129] In the final analysis, these measures were effectively neutralised by the TUC's policy of non-registration and the final collapse of the Heath Government. Nevertheless, they exemplified very clearly the increasing elision of the distinction between trade unions' civic responsibility and the policy of restriction in public discourse.

C The Legal Duty to Bargain III: ACAS and the 'Social Contract' Era

The legislative initiatives of the social contract era constituted a bold and radical attempt to restore bargaining autonomy to the system of industrial relations, while simultaneously harnessing State power to promote the democratisation of industrial civil society. At its inception, it was conceived as 'a radical strategy to transform the structure of power and wealth in Britain'.[130] In part, this was to be implemented through the restoration of collective autonomy in industrial relations, and a return to free collective bargaining. This corresponded to the first phase of legislative activity; the repeal of the IRA 1971 and the restoration of statutory immunities, and the abolition of State registration of trade unions.[131] However, State intervention was also envisaged as a necessary complement to free collective bargaining, in order to promote opportunities for democratic participation in all aspects of social and economic policy. This corresponded to the second phase of legislative activity, which in the sphere of collective labour law centred on the positive legal rights enacted in the Employment Protection Act 1975. This included the introduction of a new legal experiment in statutory recognition, legal measures to enrich the quality and scope of collective bargaining, and the construction of a 'collective' right to associate out of the building blocks of individual rights to union membership and union activities.[132]

129 For a full analysis of this labyrinthine web of restrictions, see Simpson and Wood, above n 105, ch 10.

130 Clark and Wedderburn, above n 125, 195.

131 Trade Union and Labour Relations Act 1974, s 1.

132 Davies and Freedland, above n 1, 376–424.

The recognition procedure in section 11 of the Employment Protection Act 1975 (EPA) was, according to Wedderburn, 'the richest plum in the E.P.A. pie'.[133] The EPA framework was notable for the wide margin of discretion it conferred on ACAS. This allowed ACAS to develop its own methods and techniques for designating bargaining representatives within a statutory structure that expressly mandated the extension of collective bargaining.[134] Once ACAS received a recognition reference from an independent trade union, or a request for 'further recognition' from an already recognised independent union, it was directed to 'examine the issue, consult all the parties who it considers will be affected by the outcome of the reference and make such inquiries as it thinks fit'.[135] During the process of inquiry, ACAS was also directed to 'ascertain the opinions of workers to whom the issue relates by any means it thinks fit'.[136] The legislation was not prescriptive concerning the techniques for ascertaining such opinions, although if ACAS opted to hold a formal ballot then various statutory requirements were set out. The legal remedy for a failure to comply with an ACAS recommendation was unilateral compulsory arbitration, administered by the Central Arbitration Committee (CAC).

(i) Bargaining Units and Bargaining Agents: The Eclipse of Group Autonomy?

The IRA's reliance on the statutory ballot mechanism was reflective of the legislator's commitment to liberal neutrality, majority rule through preference aggregation, and the primacy of citizens' freedom of choice in conferring legitimacy on bargaining agents. This was aligned with a symmetrical conception of freedom of association, reflected in the repudiation of union security and closed shop arrangements. By contrast, ACAS was directed to promote the extension of collective bargaining as an element in its more general duty to promote the improvement of industrial relations.[137] This shaped its discretionary formulation of criteria for ascertaining workers' opinions and awarding recognition.[138] It also shaped ACAS's approach to bargaining unit determination, with Dickens observing that unit boundaries were often drawn around concentrations of worker support for collective bargaining, even at the risk of creating fragmented bargaining arrangements.[139] ACAS therefore rejected a narrow procedural approach premised upon majority rule through balloting procedures,

[133] Lord Wedderburn, 'Employment Protection Act 1975: Collective Aspects' (1976) 39 *Modern Law Review* 169, 180.

[134] For a fine account of ACAS's work, see S Wood, 'Learning through ACAS: the case of union recognition', in B Towers and W Brown, *Employment Relations in Britain: 25 years of the Advisory, Conciliation and Arbitration Service* (Oxford, Blackwell, 2000) 123.

[135] S 12 (1).

[136] S 14 (1).

[137] S 1 (2).

[138] L Dickens, 'ACAS and the Union Recognition Procedure' (1978) 7 *Industrial Law Journal* 160, 170–71.

[139] *Ibid*, 169.

broadening its enquiries to embrace 'the level of support for collective bargaining and the level of support for representation by the referring union as well as the potential union membership in the event of recognition'.[140] As such, ACAS recommended recognition in a significant number of cases where there was minority support for recognition.[141]

This was also coupled with an asymmetrical structure for freedom of association. The renewed legitimacy of union security arrangements required certain changes to the unfair dismissal provisions otherwise such agreements would have been difficult to enforce. Consequently, statutory reforms provided that the dismissal of non-unionists was deemed fair except where the worker objected to union membership on grounds of religious belief.[142] In according moral priority to union members over non-members this was further evidence of the legal framework's rejection of liberal neutrality. As with the recognition procedure, the law's prioritisation of union membership over non-membership represented an attempt to affirm in the law a preferred vision of the good: collective bargaining through independent trade unions. Nevertheless, it is also important to remember that legislative agendas can be effectively subverted by the independent actions of other institutions and social actors. On this occasion, it was the ordinary courts, through the medium of judicial review proceedings, which were most prominent in subverting the statutory framework. The flashpoint between ACAS and the courts concerned the choice of criteria for allocating bargaining rights.

(a) ACAS and the Civic Approach to Allocating Bargaining Rights ACAS relied primarily on questionnaires and attitudinal surveys rather than formal ballots, and it deployed a flexible approach to preference measurement.[143] In this vein, ACAS adjusted its measurement of preferences in the light of past-oriented and future-oriented considerations. In respect of past-oriented adjustments, ACAS was attentive to the formative effects of employer hostility or lack of union access to the workforce on the formation of workers' preferences. This adjustment of support thresholds was particularly important in the light of the failure to legislate directly against employer coercion and restraint of workers' freedom of choice, for example through the use of an 'unfair labour practice' technique. Thus in the *Playboy* reference ACAS took the view that 'it was necessary to interpret the expressed support for the union, which was low, in the light of the company's actions and decided to recommend the TGWU be recognised'.[144]

In respect of future-oriented adjustments, ACAS continued to stress the importance of the virtuous circle effects of union recognition upon union

[140] *Ibid*, 170.

[141] L Dickens and GS Bain, 'A Duty to Bargain? Union Recognition and Information Disclosure' in R Lewis (ed), *Labour Law in Britain* (Oxford, Blackwell, 1986) 80, 88.

[142] EPA s 53 (b).

[143] Wood, above n 134, 126–8.

[144] Discussed in Dickens, above n 138, 168.

recruitment, in addition to current levels of union membership. Consequently, in 46 cases where union support was below 50 per cent ACAS still made a recommendation of recognition.[145] As Wood has pointed out, 'the emphasis given to potential support for representation and bargaining by the referring union when assessing employees' orientations was consistent with ACAS's statutory obligation to promote collective bargaining'.[146] Conversely, ACAS was also prepared to override majority preferences in situations where it adjudged that 'good industrial relations' might be undermined by a recognition recommendation.

(b) The Courts and the Liberal Approach to Allocating Bargaining Rights The first clash between ACAS and the courts occurred in *Powley v ACAS*.[147] On one level, this centred upon a technical disagreement over the appropriate design of inquiry questionnaires in multi-union situations. ASTMS had made a recognition reference under section 11 in respect of a bargaining unit that overlapped with the jurisdictional claims of a staff association. Both organisations had members within the bargaining unit, although only the ASTMS had a certificate of independence. ACAS consulted with the staff association, as it was required to do by the legislation, though the staff association alleged that the final version of the ACAS questionnaire was biased against it. This was because only ASTMS had been specifically mentioned by name on the questionnaire. In this way, the very act of measuring workers' preferences distorted them in favour of the ASTMS and against the staff association. Beneath the technical surface of the dispute over polling techniques, *Powley* represented a clash between irreconcilable political philosophies. For Browne-Wilkinson J, it was vital that ACAS's powers were construed strictly so as to ensure that bargaining agents were legitimated by democratic consent. This required that 'every effort should be made to obtain as accurate a view as possible of the true opinions of the employees' in an unbiased manner.[148] This demanded symmetry in ACAS's (and the questionnaire's) treatment of ASTMS and the staff association, even though only ASTMS could be recommended for recognition under section 11. By contrast, the lack of symmetry disclosed a wrongful exercise of discretion since ACAS would be unable to ascertain workers' 'true' opinions.

Browne-Wilkinson J's endorsement of 'symmetry' and the need to gauge workers' 'true' preferences was aligned with a liberal political philosophy. Symmetry denoted impartial treatment of each organisation, and this would ensure State neutrality towards the competing jurisdictional claims of ASTMS and the staff association. Insisting on the aggregation of workers' 'true' preferences would promote genuine (collective) freedom of choice and ensure that

145 Wood, above n 134, 127.
146 *Ibid.*
147 [1978] ICR 123.
148 *Ibid*, 136A.

bargaining agents acquired their legitimacy through a valid exercise of collective worker consent. This ran counter to the political ethos of the legislative framework and ACAS's discretionary remit within that framework. First, the section 11 procedure was predicated on a rejection of State neutrality as was evident from ACAS's general duty to promote the extension of collective bargaining. From this perspective, asymmetric treatment of competing organisations (where one of those organisations was a non-independent staff association) would be a legitimate exercise of discretion by ACAS, where this facilitated the recognition of an independent organisation capable of effective bargaining.

Secondly, Browne-Wilkinson J's faith in the distillation of 'true' or 'objective' preferences reflected a liberal view of citizens' preferences as fixed, exogenous entities capable of isolation and aggregative measurement. This stood in sharp opposition to the endogenous view of preferences prominent in the civic political tradition. On this endogenous view, it was important to be attentive to the environmental constraints on their formation, and how they might be expected to develop in the light of fresh information and newly experienced opportunities. This matched precisely ACAS's discretionary approach in gauging worker support across an expanded timeframe, adjusting support thresholds to reflect the dampening effects of employer hostility on workers' preferences and the anticipated surge in support for the union once recognition was established. The liberal quest for 'true' preferences was futile and illusory. It was better to use regulatory tools to shape citizens' preferences in ways that enhanced their welfare and promoted valuable forms of life.

This specific clash was emblematic of the political tension between ACAS and the courts. It was further reflected in the judgments in *Grunwick* and then *UKAPE*. In *Grunwick*,[149] APEX referred its recognition claim to ACAS under the section 11 procedure in the face of bitter employer resistance to unionisation. ACAS elicited the opinions of those workers who were members of APEX; it could not elicit the opinions of the other two thirds of the workforce because the employer refused to cooperate with ACAS and provide a list of their names. APEX members who participated in the process voted overwhelmingly (91 to 17) in favour of APEX's recognition. In the face of employer intransigence, ACAS made a recommendation of recognition on that basis since there was no realistic prospect of gaining access to the remaining workers.

The employer appealed successfully against Lord Widgery CJ's upholding of ACAS's original determination, and the House of Lords upheld the Court of Appeal judgment. Even where the employer rendered ACAS's task practically impossible due to a refusal of cooperation, this did not discharge ACAS's legal duty to ascertain the opinions of the entire workforce. In the Court of Appeal,

[149] *Grunwick Processing Laboratories Ltd v ACAS and another* [1978] ICR 231.

Lord Denning drew attention to the potential interference with individual contractual liberty entailed by the legal remedy of compulsory unilateral arbitration:

> Such an interference of individual liberty could hardly be tolerated in a free society unless there were safeguards against abuse. So I would construe these safeguards in favour of the individual and not in favour of the trade union.[150]

Since a majority of the workforce had been deprived of an opportunity to vote in the formal ballot held by ACAS, Lord Denning took the view that the recommendation was ultra vires and should be set aside. It was irrelevant that this deprivation had been procured by the employer. Individual liberty required each worker's preference to be elicited and considered by ACAS. If preferences could not be aggregated in this way, then ACAS could not make a recommendation. This attracted the concurrence of Geoffrey Lane LJ and Browne LJ in the Court of Appeal, and it was upheld by the House of Lords. In the House of Lords, Lord Salmon's speech was the most strident in its defence of individual liberty. In Lord Salmon's view:

> If there was a very narrow majority one way or the other there might be special circumstances in which Acas could properly adopt the view of the minority. There is nothing in the Act which expressly provides that the view of the majority shall prevail, but it is, in my view, implicit that it shall, save perhaps in very exceptional circumstances.[151]

On this view, not only could the reviewing court determine the scope of ACAS's inquiry, it could also specify narrowly the circumstances—the 'democratic' principle of majority rule based on workers' 'genuine' opinions—in which it would be proper for ACAS to make a recommendation for recognition.[152]

Finally, in *UKAPE* the courts reviewed ACAS's decision not to recommend recognition where a putative bargaining agent enjoyed majority support.[153] This decision was in accordance with the views of the relevant employers' association (EEF) and union confederation (CSEU), both of which had emphasised the risk of UKAPE's recognition disrupting established national bargaining arrangements. ACAS's decision to override majority consent in order to promote countervailing values was normatively controversial terrain for the courts. Given the dominant liberal ideology articulated in both *Powley* and *Grunwick*, the shoe was likely to pinch tightest for ACAS where it defied the right to self-determination of a majority in the union's proposed bargaining unit. May J's conclusion that ACAS had acted unlawfully and that its report was a nullity was upheld by the Court of Appeal. The pitting of David, in the guise of UKAPE,

150 *Ibid*, 237H.
151 *Ibid*, 270C.
152 *Cf* the more measured tone of Lord Diplock's speech, *ibid* at 263F–G.
153 *United Kingdom Association of Professional Engineers and Another v ACAS* [1979] ICR 303.

against a collection of industrial Goliaths, was ripe territory for Lord Denning's individualistic liberalism.

In subordinating UKAPE's claim to the entrenched institutional interests of the 'big battalions', ACAS had unlawfully subordinated its duty to promote the extension of collective bargaining to its more general duty to promote the improvement of industrial relations. It had been reduced, in Lord Denning's words, to a 'lackey' for powerful established organisations.[154] ACAS had thereby ignored individual citizens' fundamental right to be represented by their chosen union. In a controversial statement of principle, Lord Denning invoked Lord Salmon's speech in *Grunwick* to defend the democratic principle: 'this right of free association is part of English law. When the great majority of workers in a particular group wish to be represented by a union of their choice—and not to be represented by a rival union—Acas should normally give effect to their wishes.'[155] This was the most strongly liberal of the speeches, but Lawton and Brandon LJJ concurred in the result that ACAS's report was void because it had failed to address itself to questions that required addressing, such as whether the engineers formed an appropriate bargaining unit.

In each of these three judgments, the normative flashpoint centred on the legitimacy of criteria for allocating bargaining rights. The liberal-individualist approach of the judiciary emphasised State neutrality, majority rule through preference aggregation, and individual freedom of choice. The civic approach of ACAS emphasised State perfectionism, the transformative interplay between union recognition and workers' preferences, and the need to ensure that bargaining units and structures were compatible with the common good. In his authoritative analysis of the judicial review of ACAS, Simpson drew attention to the 'individualist' tenor of many of the judgments, reflecting a perceived need 'vigilantly to protect individual rights against erosion or displacement by other interests'.[156] This was a natural enough perspective for the ordinary courts to adopt, informed perhaps by common law principles governing the relations between principals and agents. Yet it resurrected a tension that had existed under the IRA framework in respect of CIR II's role: was ACAS to use its expertise and discretionary judgement to promote collective bargaining, or was it to function predominantly as a balloting agency charged with implementing the democratic will of the majority in a bargaining unit? According to Simpson, the judicial curtailment of ACAS's discretion threatened a situation where 'its role in the recognition procedure would in effect be reduced to that of a glorified balloting agency'.[157] This transformation of ACAS's role into a 'glorified balloting agency' was never realised fully, and ACAS continued to emphasise the importance of 'potential support' and other general industrial relations considerations in its

[154] *Ibid*, 314D–E.
[155] *Ibid*, 317D.
[156] RC Simpson, 'Judicial Control of ACAS' (1979) 8 *Industrial Law Journal* 69, 78.
[157] *Ibid*, 82.

deliberations. Nevertheless, it pointed to a public policy problem of real practical significance. Given the retreat from the principle of group autonomy in this context, which criteria were to replace it? The seesaw oscillation between civic and liberal-individualist theories of representational legitimacy was prominent under both the IRA and EPA frameworks, and it generated considerable friction between and even within the institutions charged with administering those frameworks. It was a tension that was never fully resolved.

(ii) The Legal Duty to Bargain: The Resilience of Group Autonomy?

Once the union had been designated as bargaining agent, the employer was under a legal duty to take 'such action … as might reasonably be expected to be taken by an employer ready and willing to carry on such negotiations as are envisaged by the recommendation'.[158] This formulation was ambivalent in respect of good faith bargaining. According to Wedderburn, this provision indicated that 'British labour law has almost adopted a duty to "bargain in good faith" of the kind found in the United States'.[159] Elsewhere, Wedderburn posed the question thus, 'Any American observer would tell us that we have here introduced a "duty to bargain in good faith"; and would he be wrong?'[160] In the event, it transpired that the hypothetical American observer would have been wrong. In this respect even if not in others, group autonomy continued to exercise a tenacious grip on the administration of the statutory procedure.

First, Doyle's analysis of the CAC's remedial jurisdiction under the EPA recognition procedure indicated that in every case where the CAC was called upon to adjudicate a breach of section 15 (2), these were easy cases involving blanket refusals by the employer to have any dealings with the union concerned.[161] These constituted the hardcore of employers who were implacably opposed to collective bargaining. For this reason, the CAC never had an opportunity to develop good faith principles. The most plausible explanation for this was the strong preference of social actors to keep their bargaining autonomy shielded from public scrutiny. Furthermore, Doyle took the plausible view that even if the CAC's remedial role had expanded, 'its concern would have been to ensure formal compliance with the recognition recommendation rather than to promote the collective agreement'.[162] This reflected a generally cautious attitude by third party institutions where substantive adjudication on the parties' bargaining interactions was required.

[158] S 15 (2).

[159] Lord Wedderburn, 'The New Structure of Labour Law in Britain' (1978) 13 *Israel Law Review* 435, 453.

[160] Wedderburn, above n 133, 182.

[161] B Doyle, 'A Substitute for Collective Bargaining? The Central Arbitration Committee's Approach to Section 16 of the Employment Protection Act 1975' (1980) 9 *Industrial Law Journal* 154, 155–6.

[162] *Ibid*, 157.

Secondly, the legal framework placed a heavy premium on voluntary conciliation as the preferred mode of resolving disputes, a traditional tactic of CLF. This preference even extended to the resolution of disputes once ACAS had made a recognition recommendation. Thus, ACAS was required to conciliate on failures to bargain as a necessary step before CAC was prepared to entertain a claim for unilateral arbitration.[163] In Weekes' view, conciliation was 'the core of the Employment Protection Act recognition procedures'.[164] The nature of ACAS as an institution, and the nature of conciliation as a mode of dispute resolution, served to reinforce the autonomy of the bargaining process from State scrutiny and control. In contrast to techniques such as mediation, conciliation was 'low-key, impartial, and essentially passive … it facilitates agreements which emanate from management and trade unions and the agency should have no predetermined views as to the "right" solution to any issue.'[165] The effect of this was to validate and entrench the autonomy of the bargaining parties from State scrutiny. If there were no 'right' solutions to collective disputes, then how could a third party agency determine when parties were behaving 'reasonably' at the bargaining table?

What about indirect modes of steering bargaining conduct? In respect of union registration, there was a clear reversal of the IRA's use of registration as a technique for steering and controlling unions' bargaining conduct. As such, registration of trade unions was abolished by the Trade Unions and Labour Relations Act 1974 (TULRA), restoring the traditional position in British labour law. Certain regulatory functions were given to the newly created position of Certification Officer (CO), who was charged with the task of maintaining the list of unions and employers' associations, and certifying the 'independence' of trade unions. This countenanced no more than purely exiguous controls over the internal affairs of trade unions, however. In this respect, it involved a retrenchment of the law strongly in favour of group autonomy. In respect of civic education, by contrast, the legal framework set out a series of dynamic measures to enrich the deliberative quality of the participants and the bargaining process itself. This was consistent with the democratic radicalism of the 'social contract' settlement. In relation to the deliberative quality of the participants, section 57 of the EPA posited a right for officials of recognised independent trade unions to take *paid* time off to carry out industrial relations duties and to undergo training relevant to those duties in a union/TUC-approved course. While the content of training was determined autonomously by the trade union movement itself, this constituted a bold step forward in terms of State facilitation of civic education.

In respect of the bargaining process, EPA section 17 imposed a legal obligation upon employers to disclose information to a recognised independent trade union for collective bargaining purposes. In important respects, this

[163] B Weekes, 'ACAS—An Alternative to Law?' (1979) 8 *Industrial Law Journal* 147, 154.
[164] *Ibid*.
[165] *Ibid*, 152.

mirrored the informational duty that had been set out in the IRA framework. As with that earlier formulation, the section 17 duty was hedged with hurdles and limitations. It was confined by the current scope of employer recognition, and the 'material impediment' test erected a high threshold for disclosure that focused upon 'whether bargaining can take place at all without disclosure', rather than the qualitative enrichment of bargaining that might occur through disclosure.[166] This no doubt reflected a deeper tentativeness in the intrusion of legal norms into the heart of the bargaining process that was characteristic of the entire legal strategy.[167] The deliberative enrichment of the industrial democratic process could also be seen in proposals for board level representation,[168] and the provisions for 'further recognition' in the statutory recognition mechanism.[169] In relation to this latter mechanism, Bercusson suggested that it might be used to transform radically the frontiers of joint regulation, extending its reach to include matters such as corporate strategy and restructuring, technological innovation, and workplace equality.[170] This legal potential was never realised in practice. The 'further recognition' provisions were only used in a 'handful' of cases that were all withdrawn before the report stage.[171] This was perhaps reflective of the tentativeness of the social actors who were involved in using the legal procedures, as much as the tentativeness of those who had drafted it.

In relation to the regulation of economic weaponry, there was a complete volte-face on the IRA's policy of 'restriction'. TULRA 1974 restored the robust political neutrality of the traditional 'immunities' technique, taking the opportunity to extend the statutory immunity to encapsulate the newly emerging economic torts; and bolstering legal neutrality through restrictions on the scope of unfair dismissal protection for striking employees. This constituted a very strong re-affirmation of a 'laissez-faire' policy in relation to industrial conflict.[172] This was significant because in rhetorical terms it marked a break with the IRA's public equation of trade unions' civic responsibility and trade union restriction. Nevertheless, it was also a missed opportunity to engage in a civic reformist realignment of strike law, along the lines suggested subsequently by Phelps Brown.[173] Thus, the use of legal techniques to steer collective bargaining towards more deliberative modes of engagement—for example, through the use of conciliation pauses or compulsory mediation—were not explored. Given the

[166] Dickens and Bain, above n 141, 98; H Gospel, 'Trade Unions and the Legal Obligation to Bargain: An American, Swedish and British Comparison' (1983) 21 *British Journal of Industrial Relations* 343, 349–56.

[167] Davies and Freedland, above n 1, 387.

[168] See B Bercusson, 'Workers, Corporate Enterprise and the Law' in R Lewis (ed), *Labour Law in Britain* (Oxford, Blackwell, 1986) 134.

[169] EPA 1975, s 11(1) and (3).

[170] B Bercusson, *The EPA 1975 with annotations by Brian Bercusson* (London, Sweet & Maxwell, 1976), cited in Wood, above n 134, 132.

[171] Dickens and Bain, above n 141, 90–91.

[172] Davies and Freedland, above n 1, 376.

[173] Phelps Brown, above n 50.

social contract's unedifying collapse in the so-called winter of discontent, the Labour Government paid the highest political price for this missed opportunity.

IV CONCLUSION

One of the major theoretical frameworks through which legislative development in the 1960s and 1970s has been analysed is the discourse of 'juridification'. This was deployed most systematically in the labour law context by Simitis.[174] In broad terms, juridification was identified as a universal and progressive process, attendant on industrialisation, whereby the autonomy of social actors was progressively curtailed and supplanted by an activist State utilising various steering mechanisms to promote the realisation of publicly determined social and economic goals. The British case was of particular importance because CLF, with its commitment to the principle of group autonomy, seemed to be inconsistent with the universality of the juridification thesis. The dynamic was explained by Simitis in the following way: 'the very rules that permit them to codetermine the employee relationship and that grant their agreements a maximum of effectiveness force them to conform to a system of organization and negotiation laid down by the legislature and the courts'.[175] For Simitis, the process was progressive, it was irreversible by the social actors whose autonomy was being restricted, and it 'climaxed' rather than reversed under the social contract phase.[176] The emergence of direct auxiliary intervention during the period under review might seem to be unequivocal confirmation of Simitis' juridification thesis. Legal bargaining duties were interventions 'designed to restrict the autonomy of one of the actors in collective bargaining' by removing at least one option (that is non-recognition) from employers in particular circumstances.[177] However, this chapter supports Clark and Wedderburn's more nuanced thesis that the British case displays features that are 'much more contradictory, complex and open than suggested' by Simitis' simple picture of an undisturbed linear progression of juridification.[178]

Broadly speaking, the principle of group autonomy led a double life under the various experiments in direct auxiliary intervention. In respect of bargaining units and bargaining agents determined under the auspices of the various procedures, the direction of travel was very much away from the *gesellschaft* model that had underpinned the various modes of indirect auxiliary intervention characteristic of British industrial relations. Two conceptions of representational

[174] S Simitis, 'Juridification of Labor Relations', in G Teubner (ed), *Juridification of Social Spheres* (Berlin, de Gruyter, 1987) 113.

[175] *Ibid*, 136.

[176] *Ibid*, 140.

[177] Davies and Freedland, above n 1, 415.

[178] J Clark and Lord Wedderburn, 'Juridification—a Universal Trend? The British Experience in Labor Law', in G Teubner (ed), *Juridification of Social Spheres* (Berlin, de Gruyter, 1987) 163, 164.

legitimacy competed for ascendancy to replace this *gesellschaft* model. On the one hand, the civic conception pointed to the fact that citizens' preferences were often socially constructed and adaptive to opportunity constraints in their formation. This corresponded to a flexible interpretation of the relationship between worker support and representational legitimacy. On this view, it was sometimes appropriate to allocate bargaining rights to unions where there was less than majority support, on the understanding that support for the union was likely to rise once recognition had been awarded. Since collective bargaining was a public good, it was appropriate to design regulatory environments in order to shape workers' preferences in ways that favoured the extension of collective bargaining. On the other hand, the liberal conception insisted on the principle of current majority support, measured through a public ballot procedure, as a precursor to the allocation of bargaining rights. This corresponded to a commitment to State neutrality in respect of collective bargaining. Whereas the civic conception characterised the general approach of third party industrial relations agencies (CIR I, CIR II, ACAS) across all three phases, the liberal conception was dominant in the legislative ideology of the IRA and the attitudes of the judiciary in judicial review proceedings under the EPA.

In respect of the duty to bargain, however, group autonomy remained fixed in the British industrial relations firmament. This was reflected most prominently in the failure of good faith bargaining standards to take root. During each of the three phases, the general approach of the third party agencies (CIR I, CIR II, ACAS and CAC) was to respect voluntarist strictures in avoiding intensive scrutiny of the parties' bargaining conduct. Although the picture is more complicated in relation to the State's utilisation of other steering techniques—union registration, civic education, and regulation of economic weaponry—it seems true as a very general point that there was persistent tentativeness in the full-blooded deployment of these techniques. Even when juridification reached its zenith during the Heath Government, and when this tentativeness was least evident, the resulting backlash by social actors in vindicating their autonomy successfully against State incursion precipitated a crisis of constitutional proportions in respect of industrial governance.[179] Thus, the ideology of CLF was more resilient than it has perhaps been credited with in labour law histories of the period. Whether this resilience was a virtue of our industrial relations system must be doubtful. Increasingly the normative appeal of group autonomy as a political ideal, of freedom for social groups for freedom's own sake, seemed increasingly hollow. The very difficult questions that Allan Flanders had posed to the pluralist voluntarists in the early post-war period still had not been answered, and the need for answers to those questions had become ever more pressing.

[179] M Moran, *The Politics of Industrial Relations* (London, Macmillan, 1977).

Part 2:

Two Conceptions of Third Way Labour Law: Liberals and Civic Republicans

3

The Third Way and Liberal Labour Law

I INTRODUCTION

ONE MIGHT BE forgiven for concluding that liberalism is the bête-noire of labour law. In the US, critical labour law scholars have criticised the extent to which labour law doctrine is beset by the contradictions and limits of liberal political philosophy. To pick one notable example, Karl Klare's brilliant critique of Supreme Court jurisprudence in US labour law takes as its liberal target the following theoretical axioms: that values are arbitrary and subjectively derived from individual desires; that liberal ethical discourse is 'instrumental' in nature; that liberals view society as 'an artificial aggregation of autonomous individuals'; that public and private spheres are distinct; and a commitment to formal over substantive justice.[1] We might join with Klare in rejecting such an ideology as bleak, even nightmarish. The problem for this radical critique, however, is that most modern liberals—Rawls, Dworkin, Raz, and Kymlicka—have never argued for so bleak a political creed. Each of these modern liberals, in different ways, defends a position that repudiates all of the axioms ascribed by Klare to liberalism. Amongst British labour lawyers, the public image of liberalism has fared little better. Here, however, the deepest opprobrium is reserved for *neo*-liberalism, and the Hayekian defence of 'free' labour markets. Once again, however, we should not make the mistake of assuming that neo-liberalism exhausts the possibilities of the liberal tradition. While freedom through atomistic forms of market exchange is a central motif of the neo-liberal tradition, the same is not true of the egalitarian liberal tradition represented by Rawls and Dworkin. In this vein, it is important to remember that liberalism is a broad and pluralistic tradition that cannot be reduced down to a parsimonious set of unifying principles.

This chapter takes another look at liberalism in the context of labour law by revisiting New Labour's reforms of collective labour law since 1997. These reforms have been criticised from many perspectives. One of the major critiques is that New Labour has been guided by a 'neo-liberal' ideology in its approach to trade union rights. The chapter takes the 'neo-liberal' critique as its point of departure. The first section points to the important potential role of incompletely

[1] KE Klare, 'Judicial Deradicalization of the Wagner Act and the Origins of Modern Legal Consciousness, 1937–1941' (1978) 62 *Minnesota Law Review* 265, 276 n 38.

theorised agreements in labour law. In particular, it argues that there are many policy positions—such as the illegitimacy of the closed shop or the mandating of internal trade union democracy—which different kinds of liberal might support, albeit for different justifying reasons. As such, there is a plea for caution in the ideological characterisation of legislative programmes. We cannot assume that particular policy positions are compatible with only one kind of justificatory argument. For this reason, I argue that the popular 'neo-liberal' characterisation of New Labour's labour law reforms is less straightforward than has perhaps been assumed.

Instead, New Labour's legal relationship with the trade unions is best characterised as based on a State neutrality model of the State–trade union relationship. This is reflected in the structure of the Schedule A1 recognition procedure, which was designed with the aim of ensuring a level playing field between trade unions and employers. This is coupled with a limited conception of the State's role, which is confined to the aggregation of workers' preferences. The State is not permitted any positive role in promoting union recognition and collective bargaining as a public good. This neutrality characterisation is also supported by New Labour's position on the closed shop, which is based upon a liberal conception of rights as augmenting each citizen's fundamental right to choose whether or not to associate.

I then set out the main elements of the well-known civic critique of liberal neutrality, deployed most influentially by Michael Sandel. In essence, this is the claim that liberalism and State neutrality systematically devalue the importance of community because liberalism is based on atomistic foundations. While I have some sympathy with this critique, the chapter explores three possible alternative forms of liberal strategy for promoting the value of community, elucidating their regulatory implications in the trade union context: Will Kymlicka's 'cultural marketplace' argument; Stuart White's 'liberal egalitarian' argument; and Joseph Raz's perfectionist liberalism. Each of these strategies indicates the considerable intellectual resources at liberalism's disposal to respond to the allegation that liberalism is based on an asocial individualism that neglects the good of community. This indicates the possibility and plausibility of an alternative liberal reform agenda that is more supportive of trade union rights and less vulnerable to Sandel's civic critique than New Labour's approach to collective labour law reform thus far.

II NEW LABOUR'S APPROACH TO COLLECTIVE LABOUR LAW: NEO-LIBERAL OR LIBERAL?

Some prominent critics have urged that New Labour's industrial relations settlement is based on a liberal political philosophy. More specifically, they have characterised it as embodying a variant of *neo-liberalism*. Thus, Smith and Morton contend that 'Neoliberalism is embedded within New Labour's view of the labour market and the discourse of the "third way"'.[2] In a similar vein, Fredman concludes that 'behind the Third Way rhetoric, neoliberalism has, by stealth, become the dominant ideology'.[3] Both of these important critiques demonstrate a particular approach to the task of ideological characterisation. In particular, the critiques point to New Labour's deliberate retention of many of the previous Conservative government's reforms of collective labour law. On this basis, they conclude that these legislative continuities betray ideological continuities. Two examples will suffice.

First, New Labour was firm in its hostility to closed shop arrangements, because of the value of individual freedom of choice for workers. Workers should be free to choose to join a union.[4] Equally, they should be free not to join a union. Consequently, the Conservative Government's restrictions on the enforceability of closed shop agreements were retained by New Labour. Secondly, the Conservative Government introduced a battery of legal measures mandating democratic procedures in the internal affairs of trade unions. Such matters as the election of union officers, the administration of political funds and the calling of strike action, were all subject to prescriptive democratic templates.[5] In addition, trade unionists were granted important new rights that placed substantive restrictions on union discipline and expulsion, including a right not to be disciplined for refusing to participate in lawful strike action.[6] Once again, New Labour deliberately retained these legal measures. The overarching concern in respect of both contexts was the protection of individual freedom of choice for workers and trade union members. On this basis, the 'neo-liberal' critique takes the following form. The Conservative legislative reforms were inspired by a neo-liberal ideology that identified individual freedom as an important political value. This ideology was used to justify various measures such as the attack on the closed shop, or the democratisation of trade unions' internal affairs, in the name of individual freedom. Since New Labour has adopted these measures as its own, New Labour is ideologically neo-liberal. From this characterisation, various specific criticisms of neo-liberalism's normative flaws can be levelled at New Labour's reforms.

The logic seems impeccable. Nevertheless, I want to suggest that the approach of the neo-liberal critique is flawed. First, the critique seems to assume that neo-liberalism displays certain characteristics that are distinguishing and peculiar features of neo-liberalism, and that these features provide a definitive boundary

[2] P Smith and G Morton, 'Nine Years of New Labour: Neoliberalism and Workers' Rights' (2006) 44 *British Journal of Industrial Relations* 401.

[3] S Fredman, 'The Ideology of New Labour Law', in C Barnard, S Deakin, and G Morris (eds), *The Future of Labour Law* (Oxford, Hart Publishing, 2004) 9.

[4] *Fairness at Work* (Cm 3968, 1998) para 4.8.

[5] For a general overview of the terrain post-1997, see T Novitz and P Skidmore, *Fairness at Work: A Critical Analysis of the Employment Relations Act 1999 and its Treatment of Collective Rights* (Oxford, Hart Publishing, 2001) ch 3.

[6] TULRCA 1992 s 64–5.

rendering it easily distinguishable from other forms of liberalism. In other words, once we define neo-liberalism then it should be easy enough to spot it. Drawing on Waldron's work, I want to suggest that political traditions are better understood as 'family resemblance' concepts. We should not expect to find well-defined and crisp ideological boundaries within the liberal family. Instead, we should expect to find a complex network of similarities and differences between different members of the liberal family. This gives us a reason to be cautious when engaging in the task of ideological characterisation.

Secondly, the neo-liberal critique has underestimated the important potential role of incompletely theorised agreements in this context.[7] An agreement is incompletely theorised where there is agreement on the particulars of what ought to be done in a given case, but there is no agreement on the underlying justifications for that course of action. Such agreements are common currency in law and politics. They enable legislators (and judges and citizens) in pluralistic societies to transcend the paralysis that would otherwise obtain if agreement on abstract foundations was necessary as a prelude to social action. To demonstrate the point, Sunstein uses the example of public policy on trade unions.[8] A utilitarian legislator may vote for supportive legislation because she considers that trade unions are a good thing from the perspective of overall utility; others may vote because they believe trade unions protect workers' basic rights more vigorously than a labour inspectorate; still others because trade unions contribute to economic efficiency. Agreement only becomes possible where the legislators move from the abstract to the particular. This gives us an extra reason to be cautious when inferring agreement on underlying justifications for policies from agreement on the policies themselves, because particular policies can often be justified in diverse ways. They might be potentially consistent with a wide range of ideologies.

A Varieties of Liberalism

What is it that makes neo-liberalism sufficiently similar to liberalism to justify its inclusion in the liberal family, yet sufficiently distinct to justify its prefix? The task of pinning down neo-liberalism is fraught with difficulties. Ideological boundaries are porous, and the cross-pollination of ideas across political traditions is frequent. Political ideologies rarely exert successful monopolistic claims over specific principles. According to Waldron, 'it is fruitless, not only to look for a core of *common* characteristics, but also to think that we can find *distinguishing* or *peculiar* characteristics which differentiate views in one tradition from views in

[7] C Sunstein, 'Incompletely Theorized Agreements' (1995) 108 *Harvard Law Review* 1733.
[8] *Ibid*, 1736.

another'.[9] We should instead expect to find, in Wittgeinstein's memorable formulation, 'a complicated network of similarities overlapping and criss-crossing ... sometimes overall similarities, sometimes similarities of detail',[10] both within and across political traditions. Nevertheless, even if positions such as 'liberal' or 'neo-liberal' cannot be reduced to a pithy set of definitional criteria, neither are they labels devoid of content.

Liberals of all persuasions broadly endorse the political value of enabling all citizens to lead an autonomous life. One important division within the liberal family is between egalitarian liberalism and neo-liberalism. The divergence between egalitarian liberals and neo-liberals centres upon the extent to which economic liberties, such as private property and contract, are considered integral to the autonomous life. For egalitarian liberals, economic liberties play an important but subordinate role in the realisation of autonomy.[11] In contrast to command economies, market institutions respect citizens' free choice between occupations, while simultaneously ensuring that citizens are responsible for the costs of their preferences between, for example, work and leisure. Market institutions are also superior in achieving efficient allocation of productive resources, which can have the egalitarian effect of enhancing the life prospects of the least advantaged through the creation of social wealth. Consequently, there is an unavoidable egalitarian role for some scheme of property and contract rights. Nevertheless, egalitarian liberals also acknowledge the egalitarian limitations of market institutions. While markets are responsibility-sensitive, which is an egalitarian virtue, they are also endowment-sensitive, which is not. Success in the marketplace is often based on morally arbitrary endowments such as natural talent, intelligence and social class. The resulting inequalities can have a devastating effect on the opportunities for the least advantaged to lead a worthwhile, autonomous life. For this reason, economic liberties are, in Rawls' terminology, 'non-basic', and egalitarian liberals would countenance, amongst other things, 'health and safety laws regulating working conditions, product safety provisions, minimum wage laws, and laws requiring overtime for more than a 40-hour week'.[12]

For neo-liberals, economic liberties and market institutions play a critical role in the realisation of individual freedom. However, there are also significant points of divergence within the neo-liberal tradition. For neo-liberals such as Nozick, the centrality of the free market to individual freedom flows from inherent natural rights to property, life and liberty in the state of nature.[13] For

[9] J Waldron, 'Theoretical Foundations of Liberalism' (1987) 37 *Philosophical Quarterly* 127, 128 (italics in original).

[10] L Wittgenstein, *Philosophical Investigations* (Oxford, Blackwell, 1953) 66.

[11] The best general account of theories of egalitarian liberalism can be found in W Kymlicka, *Contemporary Political Philosophy*, 2nd edn (Oxford, Oxford University Press, 2002) ch 3.

[12] S Freeman, *Rawls* (Abingdon, Routledge, 2007) 57.

[13] R Nozick, *Anarchy, State, and Utopia* (Oxford, Blackwell, 1974).

neo-liberals such as Hayek,[14] however, the idea of natural rights, even a natural right to private property,[15] was anathema to his anti-rationalist philosophy. Individual freedom, and the citizen's creative exploration of preferences and values, could only be realised in the spontaneous order of a free market under the rule of law. This necessitated a strong yet limited State committed to entrenching market institutions. Consequently, a scheme of property and contract rights provided an essential framework for the emergence of *catallaxy*: 'a special kind of spontaneous order produced by the market through people acting within the rules of the law of property, tort and contract'.[16] Market freedom under the rule of law minimised the potential for arbitrary coercion through State intervention, while simultaneously harnessing the epistemic advantages of market institutions in assimilating and transmitting widely dispersed and fragmented knowledge in society.[17]

What this demonstrates is the sheer variety of political positions within the liberal family. Even within the tradition identified (loosely) as neo-liberal, there are significant differences between the theories of Nozick and Hayek. On this basis, ideological characterisation and critique in labour law needs to proceed cautiously. However, caution is not only warranted through an appreciation of the subtle differences within the liberal family. It is also warranted on account of the similarities. All liberals endorse the value of personal autonomy. Now there are vigorous disagreements between liberals on what that means and what it entails for the State's duties towards its citizens. Nevertheless, we should also expect a degree of convergence between different kinds of liberalism on policies that engage questions of personal freedom. We should expect, that is, incompletely theorised agreements.

B The Role of Incompletely Theorised Agreements

According to Smith and Morton, 'it is in this stress upon the role and value of individuals' decisions that New Labour's acceptance of a neoclassical economic framework is apparent'.[18] They then equate neo-liberalism with a commitment to a neoclassical economic framework. For Fredman, too, the fact that individual

[14] The literature of and on Hayek is vast. The most accessible introduction to the general themes in Hayek's work can be found in FA Hayek, *The Constitution of Liberty* (London, Routledge, 1960) (*Constitution*). A fine critical overview of Hayek's work can be found in A Gamble, *Hayek: The Iron Cage of Liberty* (Cambridge, Polity 1996).

[15] As Hayek observed of property rights and their demarcation, 'Precisely where those boundaries are most effectively drawn is a very difficult question to which we certainly have not found all the final answers. The conception of property certainly did not fall ready made from heaven.' See FA Hayek, *Law, Legislation and Liberty Vol 1, Rules and Order* (London, Routledge, 1982) 109.

[16] FA Hayek, *Law, Legislation and Liberty Vol II, The Mirage of Social Justice* (London, Routledge, 1982) 107–109.

[17] On the epistemic dimension of Hayek's defence of the market order, see S Deakin and F Wilkinson, *The Law of the Labour Market* (Oxford, Oxford University Press, 2005) 278–84.

[18] Smith and Morton, above n 2, 404.

choice is a 'key principle' in New Labour's reform of collective labour law is indicative of its neo-liberal alignment.[19] This might help in explaining, for example, New Labour's avowal that there would be no return to the closed shop. During the 1980s, the gradual legal extinction of all enforceable union security arrangements in the interests of individual liberty took on the guise of a fundamentalist crusade undoubtedly fired by Hayekian neo-liberalism.[20] Is this deliberate adoption of the Conservative legal reforms on closed shops indicative of New Labour's neo-liberalism? The 'neo-liberal' critique appears to assume, without more, that it is so indicative. However, I want to suggest that this assumption is flawed because it ignores the possibility of an incompletely theorised agreement on the illegitimacy of the closed shop. Egalitarian liberals might join with neo-liberals in condemning the closed shop, but they might do so for different reasons. Worse still for the 'neo-liberal' critique, not all neo-liberals are hostile to the closed shop. Closed shop arrangements are completely legitimate from the perspective of Nozick's neo-liberalism, even if they are anathema to Hayek. Consequently, New Labour's policy on the closed shop is not necessarily neo-liberal because hostility to the closed shop is neither exclusively nor distinctively a neo-liberal position. We shall also see that there is considerable scope for incompletely theorised agreement on the question of regulating for internal union democracy.

(i) Incompletely Theorised Agreements I: The Case of the Closed Shop

The closed shop institution straddles both the egalitarian liberal concern for citizens' freedom of association and liberty of conscience, and the neo-liberal preoccupation with economic liberties and unrestricted market freedom. As such, there is every reason to think that liberal attitudes towards the closed shop, and radically different variants of liberalism at that, might converge on an incompletely theorised agreement on this particular issue.

Hayekian neo-liberalism is implacably hostile towards the closed shop. For Hayek, closed shops, like mass picketing, represented the prime institutional technique through which unions deployed coercion against workers to entrench their privileged position: 'the chief factor which enables unions to coerce individual workers is the sanction by both legislation and jurisdiction of the closed or union shop and its varieties'.[21] This coercive distortion of the market order was criticised for depressing real wages, stifling productivity, increasing unemployment, and imperilling the very foundations of a free society under the

[19] Fredman, above n 3, 26.

[20] Lord Wedderburn, 'Freedom of Association and Philosophies of Labour Law', in Lord Wedderburn, *Employment Rights in Britain and Europe* (London, Lawrence & Wishart, 1991) 198, 210–11.

[21] Hayek, *Constitution* 275.

rule of law.[22] For Hayek, the only remedy was the immediate repeal of unions' statutory immunity from restraint of trade doctrine. Since all closed shop arrangements were *ipso facto* in restraint of trade, restoration of the common law's general rules of just conduct would have the effect of depriving unions of their coercive powers. While Hayek is concerned to stress a liberal concern for 'true' freedom of association, and the individual's right to disassociate, the accent in Hayek's work rests much more heavily upon the neo-liberal concern to restrict unions' coercive interference with the market order.

However, egalitarian liberals might also join with Hayek in condemning the closed shop, albeit for different reasons.[23] They can participate, that is, in an incompletely theorised agreement with neo-liberals. The basic liberties of egalitarian liberalism are predicated on the priority of citizens' interests in leading their lives in accordance with their own conceptions of value. If citizens are forced to associate with groups that are antithetical to their fundamental religious or ideological commitments, their most elemental interests in leading a good life are impaired.[24] Compelled association through the closed shop, and the resulting curtailment of exit rights from particular associations, may be as noxious to egalitarian liberals as to Hayekian neo-liberals for reasons quite unconnected to the latter's concern to foster undistorted labour markets.

The difficulties with the 'neo-liberal' critique are compounded once it is appreciated that incompletely theorised agreement on the illegitimacy of the closed shop cannot attract the assent of all who would properly describe themselves as neo-liberal. Neo-liberalism as a blanket label has a tendency to distort rather than illuminate important nuances within the right-wing liberal tradition. As Gamble has observed, for example, the theoretical differences between Hayek and Nozick are considerable.[25] In particular, there is no theoretical space for a doctrine of restraint of trade in Nozick's liberalism: all voluntary exchanges are to be enforced except in circumstances disclosing a violation of natural rights to property and bodily integrity.[26] As such, closed shop arrangements are a perfectly legitimate exercise of the parties' contracting powers.[27] For Nozick, natural rights impose fixed limits on what the State can legitimately do to its citizens. Whatever pattern of distribution emerges once voluntary exchange has been unleashed is just, even if this includes a strong web of closed shop

[22] FA Hayek, *1980's Unemployment and the Unions* (London, IEA, 1981) 51–9.

[23] Of course, they might not! For a subtle liberal egalitarian defence of the closed shop, see S White, 'Trade Unionism in a Liberal State', in A Gutmann (ed), *Freedom of Association* (Princeton, Princeton University Press, 1998) 330, 334–47. See also V Mantouvalou, 'Is there a human right not to be a trade union member? Labour rights under the ECHR', *LSE Legal Studies Working Paper* No 8/2007.

[24] W Kymlicka, *Liberalism, Community, and Culture* (Oxford, Oxford University Press, 1989) 59.

[25] Gamble, above n 14, 111.

[26] RA Epstein, *Skepticism and Freedom: A Modern Case for Classical Liberalism* (Chicago, University of Chicago Press, 2003) 131–2.

[27] On the differences between Hayek and Nozick concerning the closed shop, see C Kukathas, *Hayek and Modern Liberalism* (Oxford, Oxford University Press, 1989) 163.

practices. For Hayek, by contrast, the very idea of fixed limits on the State in the form of natural rights is a pernicious rationalist error.[28] The Hayekian State's limits are correspondingly more fluid and pragmatic in nature, as are the conventional parameters of property rights and freedom of contract, since strong intervention (in accordance with general rules of just conduct) is sometimes necessary to preserve the free institutions of the market order. Thus, distinct strands within neo-liberalism can lead to radically divergent prescriptions on important policy issues, even where some egalitarian and neo-liberals can come together on those same issues in incompletely theorised agreement.

(ii) Incompletely Theorised Agreements II: The Case of Internal Union Democracy

The Conservative Government introduced a battery of legal measures imposing prescriptive obligations on unions, leading to the progressive substitution of internal union autonomy by legislatively imposed democratic templates. These included pre-strike postal ballots, postal ballots for the election of specified trade union offices and committees, periodic ballots to re-legitimate union funds for political objects, and statutory restrictions on the legitimate scope of justifiable discipline and exclusion from membership. New Labour adopted this broad regulatory canvas as its own, albeit with some minor adjustments. For Smith and Morton, this adoption provided a telling indication of New Labour's neo-liberalism.[29] For the Conservative Government, as for New Labour, trade unions were special organisations that warranted special regulatory treatment. This justified the imposition of legal rules to ensure internal democracy and the protection of individual members from arbitrary treatment by the group. As with the closed shop, regulatory continuities denoted ideological identity. Once again, however, very different justificatory arguments are compatible with this notion that trade unions are special organisations warranting special regulatory treatment.

Critics of Conservative policy on internal union regulation were astute to observe the umbilical cord linking this pattern of legal intervention with Hayekian neo-liberalism.[30] For Hayek, trade unions were indeed 'unique' associations warranting special regulatory attention, quite unlike churches or corporations or environmental groups, since they threatened the ethical preconditions of the only freedom possible in advanced societies—freedom through market exchange. The instincts fostered by trade unions—such as solidarity and altruism—were a socialistic atavism in the changed circumstances of an impersonal market order.[31] These instincts were antithetical to market freedom and so needed to be unlearned. The logic of trade unionism was so dangerous to

[28] A Gamble, 'The Political Economy of Freedom', in R Levitas (ed), *The Ideology of the New Right* (Cambridge, Polity 1986) 25, 45–6.

[29] Smith and Morton, above n 2, 404.

[30] Wedderburn, above n 20, 216–19.

[31] FA Hayek, *Law, Legislation and Liberty Vol III, The Political Order of a Free People* (London, Routledge, 1982) 165–76.

Hayekian neo-liberalism precisely because it was structured around these allegedly atavistic virtues of solidarity and altruism. The prescriptive democratic models imposed upon trade unions during the Thatcher years—described by Fredman as 'essentially individualistic' and based on 'a highly atomistic form' of democracy—can be understood as a regulatory strategy designed to challenge that solidaristic logic,[32] harnessing democratic norms to stifle the instincts that threatened the market order. For Hayekian neo-liberals, trade unions are special because they inculcate habits and dispositions that undermine the market order. This is problematic because the market order is, according to Hayek, the only institutional framework capable of safeguarding liberty against totalitarian encroachment.

However, egalitarian liberals might agree that trade unions are special organisations and that regulation of their internal procedures to promote democratic values is justified from a liberal egalitarian perspective. In this vein, Stuart White has argued that trade union internal procedures should be legally regulated to ensure they are fair and democratic.[33] Internal union democracy ensures greater congruity between the private lives of trade unions and the public life of the liberal egalitarian State. This 'logic of congruence' cannot be pressed to its fullest extent against all associations without serious injustice resulting. The liberal State must respect the rights of certain associations, like religious groups or social clubs, to reject liberal values in their internal affairs. But unions are unlike these associations in ways that render the 'logic of congruence' more apt for them. Unions function characteristically as instrumental rather than expressive associations. They are not concerned with the propagation of a controversial ideological or religious form of life, but in the distribution of 'primary social goods' such as income and wealth, equal opportunities at work, and the social bases of self-respect. According to White, legal measures to promote internal democratic procedures are unlikely to violate citizens' capacity to pursue a good life because trade unions generally have only instrumental significance in the lives of trade union members.[34] Thus, the reasons *against* congruence are less weighty than they might otherwise be for religious or expressive associations.

In addition, instrumental associations such as trade unions have a major impact on the economic, social and political opportunities available to many citizens through their bargaining practices. This is because collective bargaining is primarily a distributive mechanism for allocating primary goods such as income and job security amongst workers. As such, collective bargaining practices can have significant distributive effects on different groups of workers in the labour market. For example, where collective bargaining is decentralised and

[32] S Fredman, 'The New Rights: Labour Law and Ideology in the Thatcher Years' (1992) 12 *Oxford Journal of Legal Studies* 24, 29.
[33] White, above n 23, 347–50.
[34] *Ibid.*

occurring on a firm or sector basis, it can have potentially inegalitarian consequences for groups of workers who are not unionised, as the costs of products and services increase in order to subsidise pay rises extracted by unionised workers with greater bargaining strength.[35] Thus, there are strong reasons *in favour* of congruence to ensure the distribution of social and economic advantages through collective bargaining conforms to egalitarian principles.

Thus, trade unions are special groups from the perspectives of neo-liberalism and egalitarian liberalism albeit for very different reasons. For Hayekian neo-liberals, trade unions should be subjected to special restrictions because of the damage they do to free markets. For egalitarian liberals such as White, trade unions should be subjected to special restrictions because of the good they can do in rectifying the inegalitarian consequences of free markets. Yet many of the specific democratic reforms of trade union internal affairs—for example, pre-strike ballots—could be justified on either basis. And there is nothing in Smith and Morton's work to indicate why we should prefer the neo-liberal to the egalitarian liberal characterisation of New Labour's regulatory choices.

The conclusions thus far are modest. I have pointed to *possible* alternative justificatory arguments for some of New Labour's policy choices, and I have emphasised the fact that these alternative justificatory arguments are explicable in terms other than neo-liberalism. It may be the case that the 'neo-liberal' critique is ultimately correct in its perception of New Labour's ideology. However, much more work is needed before this conclusion can be sustained.[36]

C The Impossibility of Incompletely Theorised Agreement: The Case of Trade Union Recognition

The most puzzling feature of the 'neo-liberal' critique is its indictment of the statutory recognition procedure as emblematic of New Labour's neo-liberalism.[37] The procedure gives independent trade unions a right to make a legal claim for recognition for collective bargaining purposes against single employers. The procedure is administered by the Central Arbitration Committee (CAC). Bargaining rights are allocated to the union where it is able to demonstrate majority support, either through majority membership or majority support in a ballot of the bargaining unit. According to Smith and Morton, it 'has been a

[35] For an egalitarian critique of collective bargaining on this basis, see DM Beatty, 'Ideology, Politics and Unionism', in K Swan and K Swinton (eds), *Studies in Labour Law* (Toronto, Butterworths, 1983) 299.

[36] *Cf* Kilpatrick's close interrogation of particular justifying factors for some of New Labour's legislative activities, in C Kilpatrick, 'Has New Labour Reconfigured Employment Legislation?' (2003) 32 *Industrial Law Journal* 135.

[37] TULRCA 1992 Schedule A1.

diversion for trade unions. It enshrines their illegitimacy'.[38] For Smith and Morton, the multitude of design weaknesses stem from the fact that 'the statutory union-recognition procedure is not designed to promote collective organization'.[39] In other words, the recognition procedure is neutral towards collective bargaining, and this neutrality is reflective of underlying neo-liberal commitments. This equation between State neutrality and neo-liberalism is, however, mistaken. While legal measures on the closed shop and internal union democracy can form the basis of incompletely theorised agreement between egalitarian and neo-liberals, laws designed to facilitate union recognition (even neutrally) cannot.

If we take Hayekian neo-liberalism, the legal implications for trade unions are stark: 'There can be no salvation for Britain until the special privileges granted to the trade unions three-quarters of a century ago are revoked.'[40] Trade unions may continue to exist since 'in a free society much that is undesirable has to be tolerated'.[41] They can be encouraged to perform worthwhile 'friendly society' pursuits such as mutual insurance, or to assist employers in the administration of wage structures and differentials.[42] But neither must they be permitted 'to force up wages by coercive action'.[43] The facilitation of collective bargaining through 'social' legislation contributes to the destruction of 'the characteristic attribute of universal rules of conduct, the equality of all under the same rules'.[44] The very idea of neo-liberal recognition machinery is a political oxymoron. For egalitarian liberals, by contrast, free markets perform an important but auxiliary role in promoting autonomy: contractual freedoms are 'non-basic' and their curtailment is more easily justified. It is thus perfectly intelligible for the egalitarian liberal to defend a neutral procedural framework to facilitate workers' freedom to associate for collective bargaining purposes. Any contraction in 'non-basic' individual contractual liberty implied by collective bargaining is of less concern than the corresponding enhancement of workers' 'basic' liberty to associate.

III NEW LABOUR'S LIBERALISM AND THE CIVIC REPUBLICAN CRITIQUE

> The political philosophy by which we live is a certain vision of liberal political theory. Its central idea is that government should be neutral toward the moral and religious views its citizens espouse. Since people disagree about the best way to live, government

[38] Smith and Morton, above n 2, 414. For Fredman, too (above n 3), 'Third Way rhetoric is frequently used to produce neoliberal solutions' in New Labour's approach to union recognition (at 34).

[39] Smith and Morton, above n 2, 409.

[40] Hayek, above n 22, 58.

[41] Hayek, *Constitution* 275.

[42] *Ibid*, 276–7.

[43] *Ibid*, 276.

[44] Hayek, above n 15, 142.

> should not affirm in law any particular vision of the good life. Instead, it should provide a framework of rights that respect persons as free and independent selves, capable of choosing their own values and ends ... this liberalism asserts the priority of fair procedures over particular ends.[45]

Sandel's characterisation is addressed to the constitutional and economic structures of the US, but it also neatly encapsulates the liberal character of British labour law's recent trajectory. This character is reflected in two mutually reinforcing features of the law—liberal neutrality and respect for citizens' capacities for autonomous choice. As Sandel argues, liberal neutrality is the flipside of the liberal account of personhood. This conceives of persons as unencumbered by attachments, roles and obligations that are not the object of autonomous choice—what matters most is that we are 'free and independent selves, unbound by prior moral ties, capable of choosing our ends for ourselves'.[46] Since it is this capacity that counts above all, rather than the worth of the ends that are chosen, the neutral State is its natural counterpart. The neutral State rejects any preference for particular goods or virtues in its public framework of laws. The public designation of worthwhile forms of life would constitute a failure to do justice to citizens' fundamental moral powers to shape their own lives. Instead, its role is strictly confined to ensuring citizens have the necessary rights and resources to 'secure their equal right to live the lives they choose',[47] hence 'the priority of fair procedures over particular ends'.

New Labour's policy on the illegitimacy of the closed shop embodies these procedural liberal tenets in a particularly strong form. It is a policy that reflects clearly the White Paper commitment to 'the rights of the individual, whether exercised on their own or with others, as a matter of their choice'.[48] It is the worker's capacity to choose whether or not to associate that is paramount, and the State must be neutral with respect to that choice. The new statutory recognition procedure also reflects the liberal priority of 'fair procedures over particular ends'. In this respect, it does not seek to embody in law a controversial conception of the good. Instead, it creates a neutral procedural framework enabling workers to choose to be (or, equally importantly, to choose *not* to be) represented collectively by a particular trade union. As Ruth Dukes has argued, this aspiration to neutrality was defended explicitly during the passage of the legislation.[49] The Government was keen to emphasise that Schedule A1 would display no bias in favour of collective bargaining, and this was reflected in the refusal to place the CAC under a general duty to promote the extension of collective bargaining in executing its functions under the procedure. It was also

[45] M Sandel, *Democracy's Discontent* (Cambridge Massachusetts, Harvard University Press, 1996) 4.

[46] *Ibid*, 12.

[47] *Ibid*, 13.

[48] *Fairness at Work*, above n 4.

[49] R Dukes, 'The Statutory Recognition Procedure 1999: No Bias in Favour of Recognition?' (2008) 37 *Industrial Law Journal* 236, 246–51.

reflected in the centrality of majority rule, gauged either through union membership or more usually through a ballot procedure, as the governing principle for allocating bargaining rights. And, finally, it was also reflected in the symmetrical provision for a statutory derecognition procedure as a mirror of the recognition procedure. These features underscored the limited nature of the State's role under the statutory procedure. It was required to aggregate workers' revealed preferences through democratic procedures, and to ensure that trade unions and employers enjoyed reasonably balanced rights to influence the worker's vote. However, the State had no legitimate standing to scrutinise, judge, censor or otherwise shape workers' preferences. That would constitute a denial of respect to workers' fundamental moral capacities to choose their own ends.

The model of liberal neutrality has been subjected to a powerful civic republican critique. First, republicans such as Sandel allege that liberal neutrality 'devalues, neglects, and/or undermines community'.[50] This is undesirable because community is 'a fundamental and irreplaceable ingredient in the good life for human beings'.[51] Secondly, republicans allege that liberalism postulates a defective conception of the self. Whereas liberals endorse the idea that persons are essentially separate from their ends, republicans point to the importance of constitutive obligations that seem to encumber the lives of conscientious citizens, such as obligations of loyalty to one's family or nation.[52] These obligations penetrate the very identities of citizens and seem not to be mere objects of choice, yet according to its republican critics, liberalism cannot offer an adequate account of these unchosen constitutive obligations. Consequently, liberal States are unable to take the kinds of action needed to ensure that citizens can lead their lives in ways that are bound up with the good of their constituent communities.

As will be clear from the next chapter, I have some sympathy with this civic critique of liberalism. Nevertheless, it is important not to underestimate the richness and diversity of the liberal tradition. This civic critique of liberalism has stimulated a renewed and vigorous interest among liberal thinkers in the relationship between community and individual autonomy.[53] And there has been a tendency, in labour law as elsewhere, to be hasty in making reductive assumptions about the 'asocial individualism' of liberalism.[54] Many liberals explicitly reject the allegation that liberalism is linked to excessive individualism either in theory or in practice. In this vein, Buchanan has argued that liberals 'can embrace an expanded psychology and a richer theory of the good and can admit not only autonomy but also community is of fundamental importance'.[55]

[50] AE Buchanan, 'Assessing the Communitarian Critique of Liberalism' (1989) 99 *Ethics* 852.
[51] *Ibid.*
[52] W Kymlicka, 'Liberalism and Communitarianism' (1988) 18 *Canadian Journal of Philosophy* 181.
[53] See, eg, A Gutmann, 'Communitarian Critics of Liberalism' (1985) 14 *Philosophy and Public Affairs* 308.
[54] S Mulhall and A Swift, *Liberals and Communitarians*, 2nd edn (Oxford, Blackwell, 1996) 13–18.
[55] Buchanan, above n 50, 878.

The next section sets out three liberal arguments that are self-consciously supportive of the claims of community, and it suggests some promising legal reforms that might flow from these alternative liberal arguments in the trade union context. These three liberal positions might be termed (i) the 'cultural marketplace' argument; (ii) the 'liberal egalitarian argument'; and (iii) the 'perfectionist liberal' argument. It shall be argued that each of these liberal positions is less vulnerable to the charge of atomistic and asocial individualism levelled at liberalism by its republican critics. However, despite New Labour's frequent invocation of community in its political rhetoric,[56] these liberal alternatives to New Labour's current 'State neutrality' model of the State-trade union relationship remain unexplored as blueprints for legislative reform.

IV LIBERALISM, COMMUNITY AND LABOUR LAW: THREE LIBERAL POSITIONS

A Liberal Neutrality: The State, Trade Unions and the Cultural Marketplace

Will Kymlicka has argued that liberal commitments to State neutrality and individual rights provide the best political strategy for promoting the good of community in the lives of citizens.[57] Kymlicka thus denies that there is any inherent connection between liberal neutrality and asocial individualism. On the contrary, the basic liberties are fundamental to liberals precisely because they enable citizens to deliberate about what is valuable. This framework creates what Kymlicka has described as a 'cultural marketplace':

> freedom of speech and association allow different groups to pursue and advertise their way of life … Since individuals are free to choose between competing visions of the good life, civil liberties have non-neutral consequences—they create a marketplace of ideas, as it were, and how well a way of life does in this market depends on the kinds of goods it can offer to prospective adherents.[58]

According to Kymlicka, communal forms of life are likely to prosper in the cultural marketplace precisely because lives go better in communion with others than they might do in solitude. When citizens have the freedoms and resources to deliberate properly, valuable forms of life will prosper in the cultural marketplace while valueless forms of life will wither away. If republicans are correct in their claim that citizens are social beings, then it is difficult to see why communal forms of life would wither under conditions of liberal freedom and State neutrality.

[56] See S Driver and L Martell, *New Labour: Politics After Thatcherism* (Cambridge, Polity, 1998) 28.
[57] W Kymlicka, 'Liberal Individualism and Liberal Neutrality' (1989) 99 *Ethics* 883.
[58] *Ibid*, 884.

This positive endorsement of the beneficial effects of the cultural marketplace is matched by scepticism concerning the merits of perfectionist State intervention to interfere with the invisible hand of the cultural marketplace. According to Kymlicka, State perfectionism distorts the ordinary processes of deliberation through the threats and inducements of coercive State power, and it exacerbates the power imbalance between culturally dominant and subordinate groups in civil society. By contrast, the cultural marketplace 'gives culturally disadvantaged groups a greater ability to choose the time and place in which they will confront majority sensitivities and to choose an audience with whom they are most comfortable' such that 'the costs of that imbalance for subordinate groups are minimized'.[59] On this view, the disagreement between liberals and republicans is often strategic rather than principled. Liberals do not deny the great intrinsic worth of communal forms of life. Indeed, the best case for State neutrality lies in its superior ability to allow those communal forms of life to prosper:

> neutrality requires a certain faith in the operation of nonstate forums and processes for individual judgment and cultural development, and a distrust of the operation of state forums and processes for evaluating the good.[60]

In many respects, the Schedule A1 recognition procedure can be understood as a cultural marketplace technique of the kind endorsed by Kymlicka. The State provides a neutral procedural framework within which trade unions and employers compete for the support of workers in the bargaining unit. If the union is successful in persuading workers either to join in sufficient numbers or support it in a ballot, the State will compel the employer to recognise it. If the employer is successful in persuading workers not to support the union, then recognition will not be ordered. The State's role is confined to aggregating workers' preferences either through measuring the level of union membership or through the ballot procedure. The allocation of bargaining rights adjusts to the collective preferences of the bargaining unit, tracking a liberal conception of the common good

> the process of combining individual preferences into a social choice function is often said to determine the common good for a liberal society … the common good is adjusted to fit the pattern of preferences and conceptions of the good held by individuals.[61]

Does the operation of Schedule A1 justify Kymlicka's faith in 'non-state forums and processes' as a strategy for supporting valuable collective forms of life? Before we can answer that question, we must distinguish between two different conceptions of State neutrality. On one view, State neutrality equates with 'status quo neutrality'.[62] The common law establishes a baseline of rights and

[59] *Ibid*, 901.
[60] *Ibid*, 899.
[61] Kymlicka, above n 24, 76–7.
[62] C Sunstein, *The Partial Constitution* (Cambridge Massachusetts, Harvard University Press, 1993) ch 3.

entitlements allocated through the rules of contract, tort and property. When the State enforces the pattern of entitlements established by the common law baseline it is neutral; however, if the State disrupts this baseline by modifying the pattern of entitlements 'it is said to be violating its obligation of neutrality, by taking from one group for the benefit of another.'[63] If this is what neutrality means, the liberal faith in non-State forums seems misplaced. The liberal rationale for the cultural marketplace is that it minimises the organisational costs for disadvantaged groups: it reduces the risks of deliberative distortion by the State's coercive power, and it enables groups to choose 'the time and place in which they will confront majority sensibilities'.[64] If liberal neutrality is 'status quo neutrality', however, this common law baseline entrenches the union's disadvantage in the cultural marketplace. 'Neutral' enforcement of property rights mean that unions can be excluded from the employer's property, while the employer can campaign to a 'captive audience' workforce at any time during the working day. 'Neutral' enforcement of freedom of contract means that workers can be dismissed with impunity for choosing to support the union.

'Status quo' neutrality has been subjected to a powerful critique. The fallacy of 'status quo' neutrality is its underlying assumption that the common law represents a natural, pre-political baseline from which State intervention can then be measured.[65] But the common law is itself a conventional legal construct embodying specific regulatory choices by the State. If the State enforces existing entitlements this is neither more nor less neutral than if the State modified those entitlements by redefining property rights or limiting the latitude for contractual freedom. The legal invisibility of the State in supporting existing patterns of distribution is illusory. As Kimel has argued

> contractual activity is pursued within a framework which is largely created, and the boundaries of which are largely defined, by the state ... by defining the framework in a way which enables a certain 'strong' party to capitalise on the vulnerability of a certain 'weak' party, the state—the law—does not merely fail to help the latter: it plays an active role in creating the conditions for its fall.[66]

A more plausible interpretation of liberal neutrality, defended by Stuart White, is a 'power-adjusted' conception of neutrality.[67] Where common law entitlements place individuals or groups at an unjust disadvantage in the cultural marketplace, the common law baseline should be redefined to ensure a level playing field for disadvantaged groups. Kymlicka defends a similar idea, that the liberal State may

[63] *Ibid*, 40; Epstein has defended this sense of neutrality in R Epstein, 'A Common Law for Labor Relations: a Critique of the New Deal Labor Legislation' (1983) 92 *Yale Law Journal* 1357.

[64] Kymlicka, above n 57, 893–905.

[65] Sunstein, above n 62, 68–92. Karl Klare has been particularly prominent in deploying a similar kind of critique in labour law: see, eg, K Klare, 'Workplace Democracy and Market Reconstruction: An Agenda for Legal Reform' (1988) 38 *Catholic University Law Review* 1.

[66] D Kimel, *From Promise to Contract: Towards a Liberal Theory of Contract* (Oxford, Hart Publishing, 2003) 125.

[67] White, above n 23, 337.

legitimately deploy its regulatory power 'to counteract biases against minority values … not because of a general principle of perfectionism, but because of a general principle of redressing biases against disadvantaged groups'.[68] Once groups enjoy a fair opportunity to access the cultural marketplace, the State then remains neutral as to the outcome of the cultural contest that ensues.

This provides a framework for evaluating the Schedule A1 recognition procedure as an instance of the cultural marketplace in operation. Given the superiority of the 'power-adjusted' over the 'status quo' conception of State neutrality, the defensibility of Schedule A1 depends upon how closely it incorporates the 'power-adjusted' conception in its regulatory design. The more closely Schedule A1 approximates to the 'power-adjusted' conception, the better it is from a liberal cultural marketplace perspective. We can measure the degree of approximation along two axes. According to Kymlicka, the cultural marketplace is to be preferred for two reasons. First, it avoids the deliberative distortions brought about by perfectionist State coercion, and it simultaneously minimises the potential costs of coercive State action taken against unpopular forms of life. Secondly, it allows disadvantaged groups the freedom to choose when and how they will advertise their way of life in the cultural marketplace. Since each argument provides a distinct rationale for preferring the cultural marketplace, we should evaluate the operation of Schedule A1 through both lenses in order to determine which conception of neutrality has been deployed in the legal framework.

(i) Evaluating the Cultural Marketplace I: The Problem of Deliberative Distortion

'Status quo' neutrality would ensure wide latitude for employers to impede unionisation. Employers would be at liberty to dismiss union activists, to threaten closure or relocation as a sanction against unionisation, and even to close the business as a way of avoiding union recognition. As White has argued, this 'can be expected to have a severe chilling effect upon union formation and collective action … [this] looks less like a strategy of neutrality than a strategy for indirectly discouraging unionism.'[69] The legal framework has placed some legal limits on employer freedom to resist unionisation. Individuals are protected from dismissal and detriment on a range of proscribed grounds, both generally in relation to an individual's union membership and activities and more specifically in connection with campaigning activities under Schedule A1 itself.[70] Moreover, employers (and unions) are under a duty to refrain from various enumerated 'unfair practices' once a ballot has been ordered under Schedule A1, including the broad

[68] Kymlicka, above n 57, 902.

[69] White, above n 23, 337.

[70] For the general protections of trade union membership and participation in trade union activities, see TULRCA 1992, ss 145A, 146, 152; for the ballot-specific protections of workers, see TULRCA 1992, Schedule A1 paras 156–65.

proscription of 'undue influence' deployed with the purpose and effect of influencing the outcome of the ballot and individual workers' voting intentions.[71] The US experience is a powerful reminder that it is not sufficient to evaluate the dynamics of the cultural marketplace solely by reference to the law-in-the-books. Where employers resort to blatantly unlawful tactics with relative impunity because of weak remedies and ineffective enforcement,[72] such as routine dismissal of union supporters, the law-in-action is also relevant to any assessment of the prevalence of deliberative distortion in non-State forums. It is therefore important to evaluate the legal rules, the corresponding remedies, and their overall social effects.

While there has been a rejection of pure 'status quo' neutrality, the regulatory framework falls short of 'power-adjusted' neutrality in two main ways. First, the timeframe of the 'unfair practice' provisions is limited to the ballot procedure. This leaves wide scope for employers to deploy various anti-union strategies before the ballot has been ordered. Thus, threats of closure or relocation addressed to the entire workforce in the early stages of a recognition claim might have a devastating effect on union organising, but are completely lawful.[73] 'Power-adjusted' neutrality would require that 'unfair practice' provisions operate as free-standing legal protections independent of the narrow timeframe specified in Schedule A1.[74]

Secondly, the CAC has adopted a cautious interpretive approach to the 'unfair practice' jurisdiction. There have now been (only) seven 'unfair practice' complaints, one of which was withdrawn before the CAC had an opportunity to give a decision. None of the complaints have yet been upheld. The early signs suggest that the CAC has set a very high evidential bar for successful claims, particularly in relation to the statutory requirement that the unfair practice changed, or was likely to change, the voting intention or voting behaviour of a worker entitled to vote in the ballot. Thus, in *Unite—the Union and Kettle Foods Ltd* the union alleged that the employer had sought to exercise 'undue influence' over workers in the bargaining unit.[75] Many of the workers in the bargaining unit were vulnerable migrant workers from Poland. The union alleged that the employer's tactics had consisted in, amongst other things, captive audience meetings and the provision of misleading information about workers' forced participation in strikes if the union won its recognition claim. In dismissing the complaint, the CAC took the

[71] TULRCA 1992, Schedule A1 para 27A.

[72] Human Rights Watch, *Unfair Advantage: Workers' Freedom of Association in the United States under International Human Rights Standards* (New York, Human Rights Watch, 2000) 18.

[73] See, eg, J Kelly and V Badigannavar, 'Union organizing', in J Kelly and P Willman (eds), *Union Organization and Activity* (London, Routledge, 2004) 32, 44 where the authors draw attention to the employer's very effective counter-mobilisation strategy during an organisational campaign at Amazon, the bookseller.

[74] As Dukes has pointed out, the International Labour Organisation's Committee of Experts has been critical of this aspect of Schedule A1: see Dukes, above n 49, 262.

[75] TUR1/557/2007.

view that the union had provided no credible evidence that such actions were likely to change a voting intention. Although there is no indication of what would constitute credible evidence of this, the CAC has emphasised elsewhere that anonymous letters from workers would not suffice.[76] This creates obvious evidential difficulties for trade unions, particularly given the potentially coercive backdrop in disputed 'unfair practice' cases. Perversely, the more cowed and terrified the workforce, the less likely individual workers would be prepared to provide evidence to the CAC against their employer. Consequently, the unfair practice remedy might be unavailable in those cases where it is most needed.

The most recent statistics from the CAC indicate that unions are winning more recognition ballots than they are losing. In 2007–2008 unions won 70 per cent of recognition ballots.[77] This had risen slightly from a historical average of 63 per cent. While some scholars have pointed to the prevalence of anti-union tactics in cases where the union did not achieve recognition,[78] the picture painted by the CAC suggests that unions are faring relatively well within the narrow confines of the Schedule A1 cultural marketplace. This narrow focus may, however, be misleading. It is just as important to consider the pool of potential recognition cases that do not make it into the statutory recognition procedure because of hostile employer tactics and that are consequently beyond the reach of the tight timeframe of the 'unfair practice' provision. There is evidence that voluntary recognition deals are less prevalent now than in the early years of Schedule A1, so unions are faring less well in the broader cultural marketplace operating in the shadow of the legislation.[79] One explanation for this is that the pool of easy cases, with supportive or neutral employers targeted, has now been exhausted; and trade unions are now facing the prospect of coordinating organisational campaigns in a more hostile workplace environment. This decline in new voluntary recognition deals supports the argument that there are problems of 'deliberative distortion' in civil society, and this is supported by some recent studies that draw attention to the activities of US-style 'union busting' consultants.[80] As such, 'power-adjusted' neutrality is only likely to be achieved once the unfair practice provisions are detached from Schedule A1 and operate as freestanding legal protections.

[76] *CWU and Cable and Wireless Services UK Ltd* TUR1/570/2007 para 26.

[77] *CAC Annual Report 2007–08*, 8.

[78] S Moore, 'Union mobilization and employer counter-mobilization in the statutory recognition process', in J Kelly and P Willman (eds), *Union Organization and Activity* (London, Routledge, 2004) 7, 20.

[79] G Gall, 'Trade Union Recognition in Britain: An Emerging Crisis for Trade Unions?' (2007) 28 *Economic and Industrial Democracy* 78.

[80] J Logan, *US Anti-Union Consultants: A Threat to the Rights of British Workers* (TUC 2008).

(ii) Evaluating the Cultural Marketplace II: Choosing the Time and Place of Organisational Activity

The cultural marketplace is also justified on the basis that it 'gives culturally disadvantaged groups a greater ability to choose the time and place in which they will confront majority sensitivities and to choose an audience with whom they are most comfortable'.[81] Once again, 'status quo' neutrality embodies a style of reasoning 'that seeks to protect as much as possible a pre-existing set of common law private property entitlements from legislative incursion. Private property rights are the norm, and statutory rights are the exception.'[82] On this view, the State is neutral to the extent that it upholds an employer's right to exclude union organisational activity from its property. It is difficult to see how such a cultural marketplace would give unions a fair opportunity to succeed. In respect of 'time' and 'place', it would enable the employer to engage in unlimited campaigning on its premises even during working time, perhaps through the medium of large 'captive audience' meetings or one-to-one interviews with senior managers. By contrast, the trade union would be confined to campaigning outside the workplace, perhaps in local halls or on grass verges by public highways, and outside working time. Property rights thus confer a kind of sovereignty on the employer, allowing it to control the union's access to the cultural marketplace.[83]

The British regulatory framework has steered a mid-way course between 'status quo' and 'power-adjusted' neutrality. Even before Schedule A1 was enacted, the courts indicated that employers should be prepared to tolerate employees' union activities on their property where this involved only 'minor infringements of their strict legal rights which do not require the employer to incur expense or cause substantial inconvenience'.[84] This was an element of the employer's legal duty to permit employees to participate in the activities of an independent trade union at an appropriate time. This right was limited in important respects. In particular, it did not permit access to the employer's property for professional union organisers who were not employed by the employer. Often, the presence of trained organisers can be critical where unorganised workgroups have little or no experience of union activities. Schedule A1 took the radical step of placing the employer under a legal duty to allow the union 'reasonable access' to the employer's property once the CAC has ordered a recognition ballot.[85] The accompanying Code of Practice on union access articulates a principle of parity of campaign access between unions and employers, with the employer's access arrangements for campaigning purposes

[81] Kymlicka, above n 57, 901.
[82] P Macklem, 'Property, Status and Workplace Organizing' (1990) 40 *University of Toronto Law Journal* 74, 81.
[83] In the US context, see CL Estlund, 'Labor, Property, and Sovereignty after Lechmere' (1994) 46 *Stanford Law Review* 305.
[84] *Post Office v Union of Post Office Workers* [1974] ICR 378, 400 (Lord Reid).
[85] TULRCA 1992, Schedule A1, para 26(3).

during the ballot period providing the benchmark for determining the union's access rights.[86] This aspect of the procedure has proved to be surprisingly non-contentious. In the vast majority of cases, employers and unions have negotiated access agreements regulating campaign activity during the ballot period. The CAC has only issued formal decisions on the employer's duty to grant reasonable access on six occasions in the first five years of the Schedule's operation.[87] In particular, the CAC has proved to be particularly receptive to ordering access for full-time union officials during the access period.[88] The presence of full-time union officials with organisational expertise is crucial in ensuring that the union has a fair opportunity to succeed in the ballot contest.

Nevertheless the framework falls short of 'power-adjusted' neutrality in respect of the timing of access. The access period falls within the narrow time frame between the CAC's ballot order and the holding of the ballot. Prior to the ballot order the union enjoys no right of organisational access; the employer's property rights remain sovereign, and 'status quo' neutrality is thus the normal default mode for union organisational activity on the employer's property. The Employment Relations Act 2004 posited a right for unions to distribute written communications to the constituent workforce in the initial period between acceptance and ballot order through an intermediate 'qualified independent person'.[89] However, this is unlikely to offset the employer's competitive advantage in situations of incipient unionisation, where the employer enjoys unrestricted access to a 'captive audience' workforce. Furthermore, it does nothing for a union seeking to achieve membership and support in non-union workplaces as a precursor to bringing an admissible statutory claim under Schedule A1. In order for the claim to be admissible, the union must demonstrate 10 per cent membership in the bargaining unit, and that a majority of the constituents would be likely to favour recognition of the applicant union.[90] This establishes a vicious circle. Without property access the union is less likely to surmount the preliminary admissibility thresholds; without surmounting those thresholds the union cannot get into a position to secure a legal right of access to the bargaining unit. Consequently, despite a modest departure from 'status quo' neutrality during the statutory access period, the cultural marketplace remains skewed against the union beyond the narrow limits of Schedule A1's sphere of operation.

In summary, the British framework is stuck somewhere along the spectrum between 'status quo' and 'power-adjusted' neutrality. New Labour's reforms have eased the barriers hindering trade unions' opportunities to prosper in the cultural marketplace, although some barriers undoubtedly still remain. The principal

[86] DTI, *Code of Practice: Access and unfair practices during recognition and derecognition ballots* (Department of Trade and Industry, 2005).

[87] *CAC Annual Report 2004–2005*, 17.

[88] See, eg, *TGWU and King Asia Foods Ltd* TUR1/111/2001 and *TGWU and TVR Engineering Ltd* TUR1/371/2004.

[89] TULRCA 1992, Schedule A1 paras 19C–19F.

[90] *Ibid*, Schedule A1 para 36.

issue is one of timing. In relation to deliberative distortion, the unfair practice provisions should be operative beyond the limits of the statutory ballot procedure. In relation to union access to the employer's property, professional union organisers should be able to gain access to non-recognised workplaces subject to reasonable 'time, place, and manner' restrictions. This should be the focus of liberal reforms that endorse the position that the liberal State should be neutral towards trade unions.

However, the very idea of an aspiration to State neutrality in this context might itself be flawed in the light of the UK's international obligations. As Dukes has reminded us, ILO Convention 98 places States under an obligation to *promote* the development and utilisation of voluntary collective bargaining machinery.[91] For this reason, it is necessary to establish whether it is possible for the liberal State to go beyond neutrality, and to promote trade unionism and collective bargaining. The final two sections suggest two ways in which it might be legitimate for liberals to reject a policy of neutrality in this context, without violating liberal principles.

B Beyond Liberal Neutrality: The State, Trade Unions and Liberal Justice

It is often assumed that the defining mark of liberalism is its commitment to State neutrality. This liberal ideal of State neutrality is also sometimes equated with a doctrine of limited government. Such a connection is mistaken. For egalitarian liberals, the State has a legitimate role in promoting economic justice as well as securing basic liberties. Certain inequalities, such as those linked to morally arbitrary endowments like race, gender, intelligence or social position, are unjust from the egalitarian perspective. The aim of liberal justice is the rectification of these morally arbitrary inequalities. It is an aspiration famously captured in John Rawls' commitment to fair equality of opportunity and the difference principle.[92] Fair equality of opportunity demands that social disadvantages be corrected through education and the limiting of undue concentrations of wealth, so that citizens with similar latent abilities can compete on the basis of equal starting points. The difference principle holds that inequalities are permitted only to the extent that this benefits the least advantaged group in society. Similarly, Dworkin articulates an egalitarian form of liberal justice that is 'endowment-insensitive' and 'choice-sensitive': citizens should not have their life chances hindered by arbitrary misfortune in the distribution of endowments, yet their

[91] Dukes, above n 49, 261.

[92] J Rawls, *A Theory of Justice*, revised edn (Cambridge Massachusetts, Harvard University Press, 1999).

ultimate fate should be sensitive to the choices they make.[93] As such, the egalitarian liberal State must eschew neutrality where the justice of society's social and economic arrangements is concerned.[94] Exploring this perspective is particularly appropriate since Dworkin has suggested that egalitarian liberalism is at the heart of the third way political project.[95]

In a powerful analysis from an egalitarian liberal perspective, Stuart White has argued against State neutrality in the trade union context.[96] *If* trade unions are indispensable components in a scheme of just institutions, then the liberal egalitarian State should adopt a promotional stance towards them. Unions are not primarily expressive associations tied to a controversial conception of the good, like religious associations. Instead, they are instrumental associations in that their 'primary purpose is to secure for . . . members improved access to strategic goods, such as income and wealth, the possession of which is important from the standpoint of more or less any conception of the good life.'[97] The liberal model of State neutrality is certainly appropriate for expressive associations. If the State promotes an expressive association it also promotes a specific conception of the good, and this would fail to treat citizens with equal concern and respect. State neutrality can be dispensed with, however, where instrumental associations are concerned. The strategic goods that unions secure, such as employment, education, training, income and job security, are primary goods that enable different citizens to pursue a diverse range of options. Consequently, to promote instrumental associations is not to foist a specific and determinate conception of the good on citizens. More positively, insofar as unions contribute to a more egalitarian distribution of primary goods, the liberal State should promote them as part of its more general duty to secure justice for its citizens. This promotional stance might include, amongst other things, the inclusion of trade unions in structures of public governance such as skills forums or wage settlement through national incomes policies. This strategy of inclusion in public governance 'directly promotes union influence, enhances the public utility of unions, and may also thereby enhance the legitimacy of unions in the eyes of the wider citizenry, so encouraging union growth'.[98]

It is important to note that there is a conditional clause in White's argument for a promotional State stance:

[93] R Dworkin, *Sovereign Virtue: The Theory and Practice of Equality*, revised edn (Cambridge Massachusetts, Harvard University Press, 2000).

[94] W Kymlicka, 'Liberal Egalitarianism and Civic Republicanism: Friends or Enemies?' in AL Allen and MC Regan, *Debating Democracy's Discontent* (Oxford, Oxford University Press, 1998) 131.

[95] R Dworkin, 'Does Equality Matter?', in A Giddens (ed), *The Global Third Way Debate* (Cambridge, Polity, 2001) 172.

[96] White, above n 23.

[97] *Ibid*, 335.

[98] *Ibid*, 338.

> If a liberal state is unable to promote unionism in a form that can be reliably expected to promote liberal ends, then the liberal argument for the promotional stance obviously fails.[99]

This is significant, because collective bargaining and trade unionism have been subjected to a powerful left-liberal critique. The first version of this critique argues that collective bargaining is unjust from an egalitarian perspective. The second version argues that trade unions are now operating from such a position of social weakness that they are largely irrelevant in ensuring egalitarian outcomes. If this left-liberal critique in either of its guises is compelling then White's argument for a promotional stance fails, and New Labour's endorsement of the 'State neutrality' model of State-trade union relations is more defensible.

David Beatty has been prominent in formulating the first version of the left-liberal critique.[100] Liberal egalitarians advocate the rectification of inequalities arising out of morally arbitrary endowments. Collective bargaining, however, 'will distribute its goods and bads more or less consistently with the natural distribution of inherited endowments'.[101] Workers who constitute the elite of the labour market, with superior skills and abilities, will generally have greater bargaining power. By contrast, unskilled workers in secondary labour markets will continue to extract low wages even through collective bargaining 'either because of the nature of the demand for their labour or because of its inexhaustible supply'.[102] In this way, collective bargaining as a redistributive mechanism does not rectify morally arbitrary endowments. It simply mirrors them in its distributive patterns. More seriously, redistribution to advantaged groups can occur *at the expense of* the most disadvantaged citizens in industrial society. As collective elites extract enhanced material gains through collective bargaining, this is subsidised by weaker groups as costs are transmitted through higher prices for goods and services. Moreover, to the extent that wage settlements translate into reduced hiring of labour in these elite conclaves of the labour market, displaced workers increase the supply of labour in secondary labour markets. This reduces the bargaining strength of disadvantaged workers still further.

The second kind of left-liberal critique focuses on the relative social weakness of trade unions. Stuart White has argued that egalitarian trade unions might recast themselves as 'human capital agencies' using their regulatory capacities to promote their members' acquisition of skills thereby enhancing their employability. They might do this in a variety of ways: 'they can contribute, through the political process, to the fixing of public goals in the area of education and training; to the establishment of managerial structures at national and local levels, incorporating an ongoing union input, to oversee the pursuit of such

[99] *Ibid*, 340.
[100] Beatty, above n 35.
[101] *Ibid*, 313.
[102] *Ibid*, 310.

goals'.[103] This strategy constitutes a form of 'asset-based egalitarianism', ensuring that citizens are enabled to participate fully in an increasingly highly skilled knowledge economy.[104] A potential problem is that trade unions' impact on the low-skill equilibrium in Britain appears to have been minimal. Thus, Davies and Freedland have suggested that the combined impact of newly created Sector Skills Councils and provision for 'union learning representatives' in the Employment Act 2002 have been slight, resulting in a situation of 'uncoordinated employers … left to make most of the running … with consequently little improvement overall in the skill levels of the workforce'.[105] Moreover, in Moore, McKay and Bewley's Department of Trade and Industry (DTI) study of new voluntary recognition arrangements between 1998 and 2002, they found that in only a minority of cases was discussion over training characterised by the employer as involving 'negotiation'. In a third of cases, training was specifically excluded from the ambit of negotiations in written procedures.[106]

As White has emphasised, it is only where trade unions are encompassing and authoritative institutions that they will be well placed to promote egalitarian objectives in labour market governance. However, the left-liberal critique points to the fact that trade unions and bargaining structures, in the US and the UK at least, are neither authoritative nor encompassing. Trade unions are bargaining from a position of social weakness which undermines their authoritativeness. Furthermore, decentralised bargaining structures militate against encompassing bargaining behaviour. This is because the decentralised nature of collective bargaining undermines its ability to transcend the assurance and collective action problems associated with the egalitarian provision of public goods. Adopting Joel Rogers' influential typology of bargaining systems, the structure of collective bargaining in the UK approximates to a 'low density decentralized case' as opposed to a 'high density centralized case'.[107] Such a decentralised environment is 'dense with incentives for collectively irrational conflict'.[108] These institutional features determine the pathways of rational action open to social actors within the institutional framework. Both employers and trade unions are under powerful

[103] *Ibid*, 342.

[104] See S White, 'The Ambiguities of the Third Way', in S White (ed), *New Labour: The Progressive Future?* (Basingstoke, Palgrave, 2001) 3, 10, where White defines asset-based egalitarianism as 'concerted action to change the initial distribution of assets and productive endowments, such as skills, which people bring to the market in the first place'.

[105] P Davies and M Freedland, *Towards a Flexible Labour Market* (Oxford, Oxford University Press, 2007) 216.

[106] S Moore, S McKay and H Bewley, *The content of new voluntary trade union recognition agreements 1998–2002 Volume 2* (Department of Trade and Industry, Employment Relations Research Series No 43, 2005) 48–9.

[107] J Rogers, 'Divide and Conquer: Further "Reflections on the Distinctive Character of American Labor Laws"' (1990) *Wisconsin Law Review* 1.

[108] J Cohen and J Rogers, *Associations and Democracy* (London, Verso, 1995) 80.

incentives to behave in narrowly particularistic ways that are individually rational but impede the realisation of egalitarian objectives in the labour market as a whole.

Does this mean that White's argument for a promotional stance fails? Only if we assume that bargaining institutions are 'a product of nature, or culture, or some other unalterable substrate of a country's political life'.[109] An alternative approach holds that associational life is 'artifactual'.[110] This means that the behaviour of groups is shaped significantly by laws, institutions and the political economy of the State. Since group actions are 'a product of opportunities and incentives that are induced by the structure of political institutions and the substance of political choices',[111] this entails that associational patterns can be *reshaped* through a modification of the regulatory framework that creates those opportunities and incentives. Often the regulatory question has been posed in an unhelpful way: *if* trade unions contribute to egalitarian bargaining outcomes then the liberal egalitarian State *ought* to promote them. According to the left-liberal critique, since they do not so contribute then they ought not to be promoted. *However, bargaining institutions and regulatory environments are so enmeshed and mutually reinforcing that States are invariably implicated in the inegalitarian consequences of particular institutional forms.* Consequently, it is impossible to disentangle the State from the egalitarian shortcomings of a decentralised system of collective bargaining.

Accordingly, the liberal egalitarian State ought to promote encompassing and authoritative bargaining institutions that are well placed to realise egalitarian ends. The major flaw with New Labour's general regulatory approach is its rejection of the 'artifactual' view of regulation. According to New Labour, legal norms may reflect a change in associational culture, but they cannot of themselves bring about such a change.[112] This regulatory quiescence has contributed to three important features of the current framework that militate against egalitarian outcomes in collective bargaining by entrenching a defective set of bargaining institutions and structures.

First, decentralised bargaining practices have been reinforced by Schedule A1's confinement to recognition claims against single employers. The Government has so far resisted proposals to extend the recognition procedure to multi-employer bargaining.[113] Given the 'artifactual' nature of associations, however, such reform would be a vital stimulus to encourage more encompassing bargaining arrangements. Decentralised bargaining structures are 'locked in' by Schedule A1's legal model of single employer bargaining and other legal

[109] *Ibid*, 46.
[110] *Ibid*, 46.
[111] *Ibid*, 46–7.
[112] *Fairness at Work*, above n 4, Foreword.
[113] DTI, *Review of the Employment Relations Act 1999: Response to Public Consultation* (Department of Trade and Industry, 2003) 12–13.

doctrines such as the bar on secondary industrial action. To the extent that decentralised bargaining institutions militate against encompassing bargaining behaviour, the State must share the responsibility for having created a regulatory environment that has entrenched a sub-optimal bargaining pattern.

Secondly, the Government has been very reticent in rediscovering its historic 'institution-building' role in industrial relations. As Ewing has argued, this mode of intervention was crucial in ensuring encompassing industry-wide bargaining structures in the UK at the height of British trade unions' prestige and influence.[114] In his more recent work, Ewing has highlighted the extent to which this 'regulatory' model of collective bargaining is no longer supported by the State, and it is increasingly ill-fitted to the legal framework.[115] It remains to be seen whether the Warwick accord of 2004, with its proposals for tripartite sectoral forums in industries where low pay and low skills are concentrated, will bear institutional fruit.[116] At a minimum, the re-enactment of extension machinery to underwrite the regulatory effects of industry-wide bargaining would seem to be critical in ensuring more encompassing bargaining practices are supported by the legal framework.[117]

Thirdly, the narrow range of subject-matter in the legal duty to bargain (confined to 'pay, hours, and holidays') has been justified by reference to prevalent social bargaining practices. Thus, in its review of the recognition procedure, the DTI indicated that it would not expand the legally mandated bargaining agenda to include topics such as pensions, equality or training, until this was reflected in voluntary bargaining practices.[118] On this view, the law should mirror rather than shape social practices. The 'artifactual' perspective defended by Cohen and Rogers rejects this understanding of the relation between legal norms and social practices. Social practices might themselves be shaped and constrained by legal norms, and there is increasing evidence that voluntary bargaining practices are reflecting the rather limited version of bargaining promoted by the statutory framework rather than vice versa.[119] If this is so, it is circular to invoke social practices as a way of justifying existing legal norms. Instead, changes in the regulatory environment should be implemented with a view to encouraging more egalitarian forms of bargaining practice. In this

[114] KD Ewing, 'The State and Industrial Relations: "Collective Laissez-Faire" Revisited' (1998) 5 *Historical Studies in Industrial Relations* 1.

[115] KD Ewing, 'The Function of Trade Unions' (2005) 34 *Industrial Law Journal* 1, 14.

[116] *Ibid*, 21.

[117] For analysis of historical antecedents, see G Latta, 'The Legal Extension of Collective Bargaining: A Study of Section 8 of the Terms and Conditions of Employment Act 1959' (1974) 3 *Industrial Law Journal* 218; P Wood, 'The CAC's Approach to Schedule 11 to the Employment Protection Act 1975 and the Fair Wages Resolution 1946' (1978) 7 *Industrial Law Journal* 65.

[118] *DTI Review of the Employment Relations Act 1999* (Department of Trade and Industry, 2003) 41–3.

[119] On the influence of legal norms upon voluntary bargaining practices, see S Moore, 'The relationship between legislation and industrial practice: A study of the outcome of trade union recognition' (2006) 28 *Employee Relations* 363.

context, this would necessitate extending legal duties to bargain to cover equality policies, training, and pension provision. This contains only the briefest sketch of pro-egalitarian regulation that might be undertaken by the liberal State as part of its positive duty to promote egalitarian justice. As long as New Labour continues to endorse the view that legal norms should mirror rather than shape bargaining practices, the prospects for an egalitarian reform agenda are not encouraging.

C Beyond Liberal Neutrality: Autonomy, Community and Perfectionist Liberalism

Liberal perfectionists such as Joseph Raz have rejected the liberal tenets of State neutrality and rights-based individualism.[120] On this perfectionist approach, personal autonomy is not an individualistic ideal at all. It necessitates a particular kind of cultural structure that provides a rich and pluralistic range of valuable social forms from which individuals can choose. Worthwhile autonomy is dependent upon a supportive framework of socially constituted options. This public culture gives social shape to the contours, norms and expectations of different forms of life, such as occupational pursuits, hobbies, leisure activities and personal relationships. Given this dependence of autonomy on social forms, there is no essential conflict between individual freedom and community. Rather, since personal autonomy necessitates a viable social framework of collective goods, 'the notion of an inherent general conflict between individual freedom and the needs of others is illusory'.[121] This also leads Raz to reject liberal neutrality on the grounds that it is self-defeating. If the social forms upon which autonomy depends are liable to wither and perish without perfectionist support, then a liberal State committed to promoting autonomy must also reject neutrality. Instead, it must make judgements about which forms of life are worth supporting as part of its autonomy-based duty to ensure an adequate range of valuable options from which citizens might choose.[122]

This generates an alternative liberal account of rights that is non-individualistic in nature. Raz's work on rights points to the gap between the strength of a right and the corresponding strength of the right-holder's underlying interest. Free political expression, while a prized aspect of our liberal political culture, seems to be rather peripheral in many citizens' daily lives. Should not this prompt us to reassess its moral centrality in public culture, since it is simply inert for the politically inactive? Only if we fall prey to the individualist fallacy, that liberal rights are *just* about serving individual interests. The moral gap is bridged once we understand that rights also—indeed primarily—protect common goods. Freedom of expression is prized because it contributes to an open

[120] J Raz, *The Morality of Freedom* (Oxford, Oxford University Press, 1986).
[121] *Ibid*, 250.
[122] *Ibid*, 162.

and tolerant society based on democracy, and this is a common good for all citizens whether or not politically active;[123] the right to vote is prized because it supports democratic government, and this is a common good even for those who choose not to vote; freedom of religion is prized even in predominantly secular societies, because it fosters a public culture that is respectful of citizens' deeply held beliefs and convictions. As such, liberal rights are neither essentially individualistic nor essentially confrontational. Instead, they demarcate a juridical boundary where both individual interests and the common good come together to justify certain rights as central aspects of liberal political culture.[124]

Raz's discussion of freedom of religion is particularly instructive in illustrating the interdependence of individual interest and the common good: 'thus, while religious freedom was usually conceived of in terms of the interest of individuals, that interest and the ability to serve it rested in practice on the secure existence of a public good …Without the public good the right would not have had the significance it did have.'[125] As such, freedom of religion was just as important in facilitating the ways of life of religious communities, as it was concerned with individuals' religious choices. Without vibrant and strong religious communities, the latter was an empty shell. A non-individualistic conception of freedom of association would share these features. Freedom of association is concerned, at least in part, with facilitating the associational choices of individual citizens. However, it also derives its salience from the existence of valuable groups in civil society, such as trade unions, that enable citizens to have meaningful choices to exercise in this particular domain. It is not surprising that constitutional provisions guaranteeing freedom of association often refer explicitly to 'trade unions', suggesting their centrality to the right's particular significance in liberal democracies.[126] This common good seems based on a range of mutually supportive arguments: (1) unions are a source of political empowerment for disenfranchised citizens in the democratic process and in the workplace;[127] (2) unions embody a valuable form of shared good in that the 'benefit for people depends on people enjoying the good together and thereby contributing to each other's good'—and 'one particularly important type of common good is the cultivation of a culture and a social ambience which makes possible … a variety of forms of social association of intrinsic merit';[128] (3) unions provide the possibility for social relations between workers of great intrinsic value, akin to the good of friendship: shared histories of struggle and solidarity, civic pride, duties of loyalty and

[123] See, generally, J Raz, 'Free Expression and Personal Identification', in J Raz, *Ethics in the Public Domain*, revised edn (Oxford, Oxford University Press, 1994) 146.

[124] J Raz, 'Rights and Politics' (1995) 31 *Indiana Law Journal* 27, 31–40.

[125] Raz, above n 120, 251.

[126] See, eg, Art 11(1) of the European Convention on Human Rights: 'Everyone has the right to freedom of peaceful assembly and to freedom of association with others, *including the right to form and to join trade unions for the protection of his interests.'* (emphasis added).

[127] Raz, above n 124, 42.

[128] *Ibid*, 35–6.

self-sacrifice, concern for one's fellows, and the self-respect that goes with securing material achievements through collective bargaining. We shall now examine some possible regulatory implications of liberal perfectionism in two areas of contemporary legal controversy: the 'normative' effect of collective agreements; and the law's treatment of dissentient trade union members.

(i) Perfectionist Liberalism and the Compulsory Normative Effect of Collective Agreements

It is 'an almost unique feature of British law' that employers and workers may lawfully contract out of the collective agreement such is the dominance of individual freedom of contract from a comparative perspective.[129] This has been particularly controversial in light of the *Wilson and Palmer* litigation.[130] Here the employers used financial incentives to induce workers to forgo collective bargaining and to sign new 'personal' contracts. The House of Lords concluded that this practice was lawful, since withholding pay increases from workers who preferred to have their terms and conditions of employment collectively determined did not constitute 'action short of dismissal' against them on the grounds of their trade union membership. Following the judgment in *Wilson v UK*, which found that this position was incompatible with Article 11, the UK government reformed the statutory framework in the Employment Relations Act 2004. Notably, these reforms demonstrate a continuing concern to preserve wide latitude for individual freedom of contract even where there is a collective agreement in place, and it is doubtful that the current law has remedied the incompatibility identified by the European Court of Human Rights.[131] As Davies and Freedland observe, the major impediment to reform has been that 'the government did not want any reform to imperil the traditional principle of British labour law that the terms of a collective agreement do not automatically and compulsorily become part of the contracts of the workers covered by the agreement'.[132]

This reluctance to restrict individual freedom of contract might seem to evince a laudable respect for personal autonomy. After all, does it not follow that 'to prevent people from voluntarily undertaking obligations or to fail to acknowledge the binding force of such obligations is to show disrespect for their autonomy'?[133] On closer analysis, however, the asserted connection between personal autonomy and freedom of contract is unpersuasive. Indeed, as Kimel has persuasively

[129] PL Davies and MR Freedland (eds), *Kahn-Freund's Labour and the Law*, 3rd edn (London, Stevens & Sons, 1983) 177. See *Hulland v Saunders & Co* [1945] KB 78, CA.

[130] *Associated Newspapers Ltd v Wilson; Associated British Ports v Palmer and Others* [1995] 2 All ER 100, HL. This culminated in the ECtHR judgment in *Wilson v UK* [2002] IRLR 128, where the Court found that UK law was not compatible with Art 11.

[131] TULRCA 1992 s 145B; for analysis, see AL Bogg, 'Employment Relations Act 2004: Another False Dawn for Collectivism?' (2005) 34 *Industrial Law Journal* 72, 72–5.

[132] Davies and Freedland, above n 105, 115.

[133] Kimel, above n 66, 126.

argued, respect for personal autonomy might sometimes be properly invoked as a valid justification for *restricting* individual freedom of contract.[134]

This argument from personal autonomy might play out in two ways in this particular context. First, in situations where the employer uses its contracting power to 'sell' less favourable terms to vulnerable workers in the bargaining unit, so driving them below the collectively bargained minima, respecting vulnerable workers' own personal autonomy seems to justify restricting their freedom of contract. Preventing the employer's deployment of bargaining power to induce workers to forgo superior terms in the collective agreement might be justified as a way of protecting those workers' *future* autonomy.[135] Secondly, and more problematic, is the situation where workers are offered more favourable terms than the collective agreement as was the situation in *Wilson and Palmer* itself. Superficially, at least, it seems difficult to justify restriction of the individual worker's freedom of contract on the basis of respect for his autonomy; after all, he is being prevented from entering a more advantageous bargain than the collective agreement itself can provide. However, it is not just *this* individual worker's autonomy that is at stake. The aggregate effect of individually advantageous 'bargains' may be the erosion of the collective agreement for all workers, displacing the collective security of a stable collective agreement in favour of short-term financial advantages for discrete individuals. In this respect, it actually seems easier to invoke an autonomy-based justification for restriction since citizens should enjoy less freedom to sacrifice the well-being of others than they do to sacrifice their own well-being.

Another line of argument draws upon Raz's work on *nonconvertible* rights.[136] His reflections on the right to vote are illustrative of the point. The right to vote is nonconvertible—it cannot be exchanged in the marketplace for other goods, it cannot be extinguished by voluntary consent, its use cannot be bought or sold to the highest bidder. In short, the choice to vote may only be exercised within strictly confined parameters. It cannot be converted because 'it is grounded in a common good of a distinctive kind which would be undermined were the right convertible'.[137] The reason is clear enough. While the free market itself is a public good of importance, it is only so within permissible limits. Certain transactions lie beyond the spectrum of obligations it is legitimate to permit and enforce. In the words of Raz, while many goods could be the subject of value-enhancing transactions, 'citizenship was not up for sale'.[138] Allowing citizens to trade votes in the marketplace would destroy the public good of a civic democratic space where citizens engage deliberatively in a political process

[134] See D Kimel, 'Neutrality, Autonomy, and Freedom of Contract' (2001) 21 *Oxford Journal of Legal Studies* 473.

[135] *Ibid*, 485–7.

[136] Raz, above n 124, 34.

[137] *Ibid.*

[138] Raz, above n 120, 252.

uncorrupted by fraud or bribery. Might this kind of argument justify a restriction on individual contracting out of collective agreements?

As a first step, it is useful to identify a labour right that *is* generally treated as nonconvertible in most legal systems. Generally speaking, it is unlawful to stipulate that a worker may not be a union member as a condition of employment. Historically, such contracts were known as 'yellow dog' contracts in the US. For Epstein, the restriction is puzzling. From this libertarian perspective, yellow dog contracts should be respected as legitimate exercises of contractual liberty and enforced as such. As Epstein has argued

> any worker who accepts a yellow dog contract will demand some compensation for giving up the possibility of the gains of union membership. One has to assume an enormous degree of incompetence or ignorance by workers to ban the yellow dog contract on paternalistic grounds.[139]

Moreover, any subsequent decline in employment conditions and compensation could be met by the employee terminating her contract, perhaps in coordination with other employees, and joining the union in order to subject the employer to industrial pressure. If trade unions are justified by the material advantages that accrue from collective bargaining, and if employers are prepared to match or better those material advantages in a contractual bargain that involves signing a yellow dog contract, then where is the justification for restricting that contractual option? From Epstein's perspective, the elimination of the contractual option makes employees worse off than they might otherwise be. Furthermore, there only seems to be a difference of degree between yellow dog employers and employers who use sophisticated human resources techniques and enhanced compensation packages in order to convince their employees that unionisation is unnecessary. Yet no-one is seriously arguing that this latter group of employers should face legal restriction.

In fact, it seems plausible that the yellow dog contract is singled out for special legal opprobrium because it is treating what is widely regarded as a nonconvertible right as just another object of market exchange. Even the popular historical label for this type of contract was revealing. In signing the contract the worker so demeaned himself in ceding his industrial enfranchisement that he was no better than a yellow dog; it was a relinquishment of dignity in exchange for a price. This involved putting citizenship up for sale in a way that was analogous to the sale of political votes in the marketplace. Epstein's argument completely fails to address the possibility that there might be ethical limits on the scope of market exchange, or that particular kinds of contractual transaction might have such powerful symbolic significance that it renders them ethically impermissible. Interestingly, it is also an 'unfair practice' for employers (or unions) to use financial incentives to persuade workers to vote in a particular way during the

[139] Epstein, above n 63, 1382.

recognition ballot process under the British recognition procedure.[140] Once again, it is impermissible to buy and sell votes in the process of instituting collective bargaining in the workplace.

This leads us to the question of 'contracting out' of the collective agreement. Under ERA 2004 section 145B, employers can make financial offers to induce union members to sell their right to collective representation with impunity, provided that it is not the employer's 'sole or main purpose' that the workers' conditions of employment will no longer be determined by a collective agreement. Just as workers cannot sell their union membership, it seems invidious to permit the worker's right to collective representation to be traded in this way. There seems to be no discernible moral difference between these two facets of industrial citizenship, so both should be treated as nonconvertible rights. The sale of the worker's right to collective representation erodes the collective good upon which collective bargaining is based, and it treats what should be a nonconvertible right as one that is convertible in the marketplace.

A radical overhaul of the current law is therefore necessary. There are two options for reform that would be more consonant with the perfectionist liberal argument set out here. First, one possibility would be to tighten up the definitional elements in section 145B. This would necessitate giving the trade union itself a legal remedy in situations where the solidarity of the bargaining unit was threatened by financial inducements, bringing UK law into line with the European Court of Human Right's judgment in *Wilson v UK*.[141] The liability test could also be made more stringent by affixing liability where the employer simply has an unlawful *purpose*, namely that the workers' terms of employment will no longer be determined by collective agreement. The current 'sole or main purpose' test leaves employers with wide latitude to operate with impunity where they can point to other lawful purposes such as ensuring flexibility or rewarding performance. A more radical step still would be to delineate clearly a narrow range of *lawful* purposes (for example, a demonstrable need to increase the pay of particular workers due to a pressing need for retention), coupled with strict scrutiny of the necessity of the employer's means. Where the employer could not demonstrate a lawful purpose and necessity of means it would be liable under the statutory provision.

Secondly, a more radical reform strategy would be to enact a strong form of 'inderogability' along the lines of the US concept of bargaining exclusivity, such that collectively agreed terms constitute both a floor and a ceiling to the terms set in the individual contract.[142] Preventing individual contracts from derogating with terms 'less favourable' than the applicable collective agreement is common in European legal cultures. The idea of the collective agreement as a normative

[140] TULRCA 1992, Schedule A1 para 27A(2)(a) –(b).

[141] The ECtHR considered that the trade union's rights under Art 11 had been violated, quite apart from the individual workers' rights under Art 11.

[142] Lord Wedderburn, *Labour Law and Freedom* (1995) 212–36.

ceiling, while unusual in European terms, is integral to some legal systems with decentralised collective bargaining structures. In the US, for example, the Supreme Court characterised all forms of individual bargaining as an 'unfair labor practice' once the union had been designated as bargaining agent for the constituent bargaining unit.[143] This principle of collective exclusivity, with its preclusion of individual bargaining, was designed to bolster the bargaining authority of the union:

> The practice and philosophy of collective bargaining looks with suspicion on such individual advantages … They are a fruitful way of interfering with organization and choice of representatives; increased compensation, if individually deserved, is often earned at the cost of breaking down some other standard thought to be for the welfare of the group, and always creates the suspicion of being paid at the long-range expense of the group as a whole.[144]

This restriction of individual contract is normatively attractive once we endorse the non-individualistic conception of liberal rights defended by Raz.

(ii) Perfectionist Liberalism and the Problem of Union Discipline of Individual Dissentients

The second area of controversy relates to the authority of the union to discipline strike breakers who contravene disciplinary clauses in the contract of membership. The union may not lawfully discipline or expel members who refuse to participate in industrial action, even where such discipline would be permitted by the contract of membership.[145] Moreover, it is irrelevant that the industrial action was supported in a democratic ballot by a majority of those voting and was legally compliant with the complicated statutory rules on strike action. The individual trade unionist's choice takes absolute precedence over the union's interest in determining and enforcing norms of solidarity. Is this not to take personal autonomy seriously, protecting individual choices from a stifling collective autocracy? Only if we understand personal autonomy in narrowly individualistic terms. Once we endorse the non-individualistic account of liberal rights, however, there are three powerful objections to the statutory framework. First, the image that underlies the statutory framework draws its inspiration from a 'confrontational' view of individual rights, setting the individual at odds with the group. Given the dependence of personal autonomy on social forms, however, this 'confrontational' perspective is misguided. As Fredman has argued:

> The central image of conflict between the individual and the collective underpins the legal endorsement of individual rights … the importance given to such individual

[143] *J I Case Co v NLRB* 321 US 332 (1944).
[144] *Ibid*, 337–9.
[145] TULRCA 1992 s 64.

> rights within this legislative matrix is based on a denial of any possibility that the collective could enhance individual fulfilment.[146]

Secondly, a certain understanding of duties as fetters on liberty seems to underlie the legislator's concern to uphold the individual's freedom of choice as an indefeasible value. On the conventional view, duties 'restrict people's ability to do as they wish. Restrictions cannot be good in themselves … Hence duties cannot have intrinsic or ultimate value.'[147] However, duties can also be constitutive of intrinsically valuable options. Without the duties of friendship, friendship would not be the intrinsically valuable option that it is. Those duties are constitutive of the good of friendship, and without them our range of valuable options, and so our personal autonomy, would be diminished. The same is also true of the trade unionist's participation in the corporate life of the trade union. The intrinsic value of this form of life is constituted by socially defined pattern of duties and expectations—duties of loyalty and fidelity to the good of one's fellows. The statutory technique effectively overrides the contractual duties contained in the contract of membership. In doing so, it disrupts the socially defined pattern of duties and expectations that shape the contract of membership. This undermines valuable autonomy by eroding the intrinsically valuable option of trade union membership.

Thirdly, unions are voluntary associations based on the contract of membership: at the inception of this relationship contractual duties are voluntarily incurred, and individuals can exit the group at any time. In this situation honouring the parties' contractual freedom to shape their relationship *respects* personal autonomy. More importantly, there is no countervailing autonomy-based reason to restrict the parties' freedom of contract. The possibility of exit from the union ensures this is not a situation of bargaining inequality, and the duty to abide by the democratic will of the union certainly 'falls within the spectrum of obligations that it is judged to be morally desirable or at any rate *permissible* for people to have or be able to assume'.[148] Indeed, it is good to permit members to assume such duties because they are then able to participate fully in an intrinsically valuable form of life.

V CONCLUSION

When New Labour swept to power in 1997, it attempted to set out a distinctive ideological orientation based on a commitment to community and civic responsibility, as political counterweights to individual autonomy and individual

[146] Fredman, above n 32, 37.

[147] See J Raz, 'Liberating Duties', in J Raz, *Ethics in the Public Domain*, revised edn (Oxford, Oxford University Press, 1994) 31, setting out the view he then convincingly demolishes.

[148] Kimel, above n 66, 128.

rights.[149] Given this civic rhetoric, it was perhaps surprising that its reforms of collective labour law settled upon a liberal 'State neutrality' model of the State–trade union relationship. While this seemed to diverge from the neo-liberal agenda that had dominated labour law between 1979 and 1997, it was ill-suited to realising New Labour's self-avowed communitarian goals. Nevertheless, there has perhaps been a tendency to dismiss liberalism too quickly as a normative reference point for reconfiguring and revitalising a labour law that is sensitive to collective interests and purposes. There is no doubt that so-called 'critical' orientations in legal theory have derived their appeal, at least in part, from the rather stark political possibilities offered by Hayekian liberalism or unrefined State neutrality. However, liberalism is a dynamic political tradition that is far richer than this pair of stark alternatives would suggest. Modern liberalism has displayed an almost inexhaustible capacity to re-imagine itself in ways that are responsive to the civic and communitarian critiques of the last 30 years. Regrettably, New Labour's liberal imagination in the sphere of collective labour law has been, so far at least, needlessly moribund.

[149] See Driver and Martell, above n 56. See also Fredman, above n 3.

4

The Third Way and Republican Labour Law

I INTRODUCTION

THE LONG POLITICAL exile of Labour prompted a radical ethical and intellectual retrenchment of the democratic socialist tradition. For Marquand, the failure of the post-war democratic socialist consensus was rooted in its liberal political foundations.[1] The success of democratic socialist policy depended upon a shared sense of community and a willingness on the part of citizens to subordinate their private interests to the pursuit of a common good. Yet (for Marquand as for other republicans) liberalism could not provide the normative resources to underwrite the democratic socialist project. It eschewed any talk of a common good, shared purposes articulated through deliberative politics, or civic duty. Instead, the public political philosophy of liberalism rested upon a set of alternative assumptions, emphasising a society 'made up of separate, sovereign, atomistic individuals. The obligations which these individuals owe to their society derive ultimately from the fact that it can be shown that it is to their advantage to belong to it. They follow their own purposes, which they choose for themselves.'[2] While the previous chapter suggested that liberalism was not without its own replies to this critique, nevertheless Marquand's arguments were powerful against some dominant strands within liberal thought. In many respects, David Marquand's *The Unprincipled Society* was an important staging post in the development of third way ideas, every bit as significant as Hutton's or Giddens' contributions to the left's intellectual and electoral renewal.[3]

In philosophical terms, the leading critic and exponent of this civic alternative to liberalism has been Michael Sandel. According to Sandel, the liberal promise of the 'free personality' and the free choice of ends is distorting of our moral experience, in its failure to acknowledge the ethical importance of obligations of solidarity arising out of communal membership.[4] Liberal political commitments, with their emphasis on State neutrality, individual choice and rights, were unable

[1] See, generally, D Marquand, *The Unprincipled Society: New Demands and Old Politics* (London, Jonathan Cape, 1988).

[2] *Ibid*, 214.

[3] See S Driver and L Martell, *New Labour: Politics After Thatcherism* (Cambridge, Polity, 1998) 11.

[4] See, generally, M Sandel, *Democracy's Discontent* (Cambridge Massachusetts, Harvard Univeristy Press, 1996).

to sustain the goods of community and collective self-government, and their attendant civic virtues. As such, Sandel argues for the retrieval of a civic republican understanding of freedom and politics. On this view, freedom consists in political participation in a self-governing community, rather than in the liberal understanding of freedom as 'the capacity of persons to choose their values and ends'.[5] For Philip Pettit, on the other hand, republican freedom is best understood as 'the absence of dependency upon the will of another and the absence of vulnerability to interference at the will of that other: it requires the absence of mastery or domination by any other'.[6] This recent resurgence of interest in civic republican political thought has generated a rich seam of scholarship with the ability to provide a viable alternative to the liberal policy agenda in labour law.

A striking feature of the New Labour project has been the extent to which its rhetoric has drawn upon civic republican themes. Thus, Sandra Fredman's powerful critique of 'third way' labour law has pointed to the pervasive influence of civic values of community, democracy, and civic responsibility in New Labour's ideological rhetoric.[7] The break with liberalism is clearly set out in Tony Blair's embrace of community and civic responsibility as New Labour's guiding values:

> In the 1960s the pendulum swung towards a more individualistic ethos. For a generation or more, the dominant model of human behaviour on Left and Right was highly individualistic. This was true in the liberation of private life and in intellectual debate. The Left was captivated by the elegance and power of Professor John Rawls' *Theory of Justice*. His manifesto for an egalitarian society is … derived from a highly individualistic view of the world … But there is also an alternative view gaining currency … For myself, I start from a simple belief that people are not separate economic actors competing in the marketplace of life. They are citizens of a community. We are social beings, nurtured in families and communities and human only because we develop the moral power of personal responsibility for ourselves and each other.[8]

This chapter will draw upon the political theory of civic republicanism to offer a normative defence of a republican labour law. Civic republican citizenship is aligned with three important values: community, collective self-government, and non-domination. Each of these values will be explored, and their legal implications set out. What emerges most strikingly from this chapter is the yawning chasm between New Labour's civic rhetoric and New Labour's liberal legal

[5] *Ibid*, 5.

[6] P Pettit, 'Reworking Sandel's Republicanism', in AL Allen and MC Regan (eds), *Debating Democracy's Discontent* (Oxford, Oxford University Press, 1998) 40, 49; see generally P Pettit, *Republicanism: A Theory of Freedom and Government* (Oxford, Oxford University Press, 1997).

[7] See S Fredman, 'The Ideology of New Labour Law' in C Barnard, S Deakin, and GS Morris (eds), *The Future of Labour Law* (Oxford, Hart Publishing, 2004) 9.

[8] T Blair, 'The Stakeholder Society', in T Blair, *New Britain: My Vision of a Young Country* (London, Fourth Estate, 1996) 297, 299–300. The civic republican orientation of New Labour is described in F Klug, *Values for a Godless Age* (London, Penguin, 2000) 50–66.

reform agenda. There has been an almost total failure to translate civic rhetoric into concrete legal reforms. In this respect, it supports Fredman's systematic critique of New Labour's double life: on the one hand, its life lived out in lofty proclamations of values and ideology; and on the other hand, the rather stunted reality of its specific legal reforms.

II THE GOOD OF COMMUNITY

A Community in Civic Republican Thought

The intrinsic value of community is central to republican thought. This is based on a view of citizens as social beings encumbered by obligations of solidarity to their communities of belonging, obligations that they have not voluntarily incurred and that they cannot simply discard at will. These include 'those loyalties and responsibilities whose moral force consists partly in the fact that living by them is inseparable from understanding ourselves as the particular persons we are—as members of this family or city or nation or people, as bearers of that history, as citizens of this republic'.[9] The important point about such communities is they are constitutive of the very identities of their members. As such, it is one of the republican State's primary responsibilities to nurture and protect such communities, and to enable citizens to experience their lives as bound up with the good of the communities of which they form part. By contrast, where citizens are detached from the corporate lives of their constitutive communities, they often suffer from what Daniel Bell has described as 'damaged human personhood', a stunted form of life consisting in moral disorientation and an inability to experience deep personal attachments.[10] These 'strong' constitutive communities—communities of place such as one's city of birth, communities of memory such as the nation state, one's family, one's religious community—resist translation into the idiom of liberal politics based on individual choice, with obligations and ties voluntarily incurred and voluntarily severable. Once such groups are recast as liberal associations, based on a mere convergence of individuals tied together by mutual consent in order to pursue their own private purposes,[11] their significance in the lives of citizens is distorted.

Communities are also valued by republicans because of the crucial role they play in the inculcation of *civic virtues* amongst citizens. Civic virtue involves the 'disposition to further public over private good in action and deliberation'.[12] In

[9] Sandel, above n 4, 14.

[10] D Bell, *Communitarianism and its Critics* (Oxford, Oxford University Press, 1993) 103.

[11] R Dagger, *Civic Virtues: Rights, Citizenship, and Republican Liberalism* (Oxford, Oxford University Press, 1997) 49.

[12] S Burtt, 'The Good Citizen's Psyche: On the Psychology of Civic Virtue' (1990) *Polity* 23, cited in Dagger, *ibid*, 14.

emphasising citizens' civic responsibilities to defend and promote the common good of the political community, it stands in opposition to liberal accounts of citizenship that legitimise the individual pursuit of self-interest in the political realm. For republicans, this would be to confuse the public realm of the forum with the private realm of the market, and it would lead to the vice of corruption in public life. In the republican tradition, corruption is the unrelenting pursuit of one's own self-interest at the expense of the common good. Adrian Oldfield's influential interpretation of the republican tradition describes the republican antithesis of corruption as 'civic friendship':

> It is to seek the good of others at the same time as, and sometimes in neglect of, one's own good. It is to approach social relationships in an Aristotelian spirit of 'concord'. It is this that creates the sense of community; and it is this that creates citizens.[13]

This corresponds to a range of more specific civic virtues: (i) fair play and reciprocity, so that citizens are disposed 'to bear a fair share of the burdens of a cooperative enterprise *and* to insist that others bear their share as well';[14] (ii) civic skills such as the capacity to empathise imaginatively across difference, political advocacy, the ability to make concessions and achieve principled compromise;[15] (iii) the virtue of public deliberative discourse, encompassing 'the willingness to engage in a conversation: to listen as well as to speak, to seek to understand what others say, and to respond respectfully to the views of others, so as to continue the conversation'.[16]

It has been a commonplace of republican thought that these civic virtues, the dispositions and habits of good citizenship, are learned and transmitted in the constitutive communities that operate below the level of the nation State, in the realm of civil society. Richard Dagger has drawn attention to the importance of small, stable communities in inculcating the civic disposition of fair play in citizens. One of the most corrosive solvents of civic community is the practice of free-riding, where citizens take advantage of public goods supplied by cooperative practices without undertaking their share of the burden in producing them. In large scale communities such as the nation state, free riding is difficult to detect and easy to do without attracting the censure of fellow citizens. However, as Dagger's argument demonstrates, in smaller communities that are stable over time, it is possible to make reliable judgements about the reliability and trustworthiness of other group members. Defection is easier to detect, the loss of reputation for citizens more likely to evoke powerful feelings of shame. This ensures that well-motivated citizens can contribute their fair share of the

13 A Oldfield, *Citizenship and Community: Civic Republicanism and the Modern World* (London, Routledge, 1990) 173.

14 Dagger, above n 11, 197.

15 C Estlund, *Working Together: How Workplace Bonds Strengthen a Diverse Democracy* (Oxford, Oxford University Press, 2005) 106.

16 W Kymlicka, *Contemporary Political Philosophy*, 2nd edn (Oxford, Oxford University Press, 2001) 289.

productive effort, assured that they will not be taken advantage of by civic free-riders. For Dagger, this is why smaller communities are more effective in inculcating the disposition to play fairly.[17]

Republicans have focused on many sites of civic engagement as a way of supporting the nation State's formative project of creating citizens. For Tocqueville, federalism and the regional dispersal of sovereign power multiplied the opportunities for civic participation.[18] The self-governing, independent township was the ideal forum to enable citizens to attend to the tasks of democratic governance within a strongly rooted sense of place. For Sandel, too, 'local attachments can serve self-government by engaging citizens in a common life beyond their private pursuits, by forming the habit of attending to public things ... Civic capacities first awakened in neighbourhoods and town halls, churches and synagogues . . . find broader expression.'[19] The question naturally arises to what extent the sphere of work is an appropriate site of civic engagement. In many ways, the workplace might seem to be an unpromising candidate. Historically, republicans were vehemently critical of the degrading and dehumanising effects of the factory system on the civic character of wage labourers.[20] Furthermore, the growth of capitalism and the intensifying division of labour led to the erosion of traditional communities.[21]

Nevertheless, it is testament to the ingenuity of republican thought that a virtue was made out of necessity. Durkheim had famously argued that the new division of labour might itself sow its own seeds of communal renewal, with new patterns of social solidarity based on the division of function in the economy.[22] Drawing upon Durkheimian sociology, Raymond Plant has argued that it is participation and membership in these functional communities that provides the best hope for civic community in the modern world. It is meaningful to describe these functional groups as communities, for members are bound together by shared values, possess a common identity arising out of their functional ties, and are subject to a common source of authority.[23] This makes the sphere of work important as a potential site of community, social solidarity and civic friendship.

[17] This is also supported by Robert Putnam's very influential work on 'social capital': see RD Putnam, *Making Democracy Work: Civic Traditions in Modern Italy* (Princeton, Princeton University Press, 1993) 167. Putnam's work explored the relationship between economic and democratic institutional performance, and civic culture, in different regions of Italy. Less civic regions, mainly located in the South, tended to perform less well than the more civic regions in the North. On this basis, Putnam argued that 'civic community', one characterised by 'high levels of cooperation, trust, reciprocity, civic engagement and collective well-being', was a crucial condition of both economic prosperity and the successful functioning of democratic institutions: see Putnam, *ibid*, 177.

[18] The classic text is A de Tocqueville, *Democracy in America* (London, Harper and Row, 1966).

[19] Sandel, above n 4, 314.

[20] *Ibid*, 150–54.

[21] R Plant, *Community and Ideology: an essay in applied sociology* (London, Routledge, 1974) 16–19.

[22] Durkheim's thought is subjected to a stimulating analysis, placed in historical context, in Estlund, above n 15, 110–11.

[23] Plant, above n 21, 42–3.

The most recent and systematic exploration of the workplace as a site of civic engagement has been offered by Cynthia Estlund.[24] While acknowledging that the workplace is unlike many other voluntary associations in civil society, Estlund argues that these distinctive features give the workplace special salience in a scheme of republican regulation. First, the workplace is much more susceptible to legal regulation when compared with other kinds of voluntary association. One aspect of this in the US has been the deep penetration of anti-discrimination law into the American workplace. This has ensured that workplaces are more likely to be racially diverse than, say, neighbourhood groups or churches. This is particularly important in diverse and pluralistic societies, in helping to 'build connections, trust, and norms of reciprocity and cooperation across lines of social division and enable people to cooperate for the good of diverse collectives'.[25] Secondly, the authority structure in workplaces acts as a stimulus to deliberation and communicative interaction across cultural cleavages in a manner that is not replicated in most other settings. In short, the need to get the job done, and the use of sanctions and rewards to promote efficient collaboration between co-workers, ensures that worker-citizens are exposed to a diverse mix of others rapidly and effectively.

Estlund's work provides a rich exploration of these themes, setting out both the regulatory possibilities and limits of a civic agenda in the workplace. Ultimately, however, she acknowledges the inescapable limit on the workplace as a site of civic engagement: 'the problems of hierarchy and class inequality would seem to stand as major hurdles to the admission of the workplace into the realm of civil society and the overlapping realm of public discourse'.[26] Even if workers can transcend racial, religious, age, or sex-based cleavages in the workplace, they cannot transcend the barriers imposed by class. Indeed, the very structure of the employment relation is constitutive of that form of pervasive inequality. A more promising possibility for functional civic community, then, is the trade union. Like employers, trade unions are generally susceptible to the full range of anti-discrimination measures so they at least have the potential to bring together a diverse mix of differently situated citizens united in a common cause; yet they also avoid the problems of capitalistic subordination characteristic of the workplace. In this way, trade unions emerge as plausible sites of civic engagement. In fact, both Sandel[27] and Kohler[28] are explicit in their focus on trade unions as seedbeds where the virtues and practices of good citizenship can be learned and transmitted.

[24] Estlund, above n 15.

[25] *Ibid*, 107.

[26] *Ibid*, 131.

[27] Sandel, above n 4, 185–200.

[28] See TC Kohler, 'Individualism and Communitarianism at Work' (1993) *Brigham Young University Law Review* 727.

The next step is to consider the law's conceptualisation of trade unions as forms of community. As we shall see, New Labour's ideological rhetoric concerning the importance of community and civic responsibility has not translated into corresponding legal reforms. On the contrary, we find a highly attenuated vision of community encoded in the law and this ultimately degrades the role that trade unions can play as sites of civic engagement. This is reflected in the law's approach to four issues in collective labour law: (i) the closed shop; (ii) the position of dissentient trade union members who refuse to participate in industrial action; (iii) the treatment of secondary industrial action; (iv) the protection of trade union organisational activity.

B Freedom of Association and Civic Community

(i) Civic Community and the Closed Shop

New Labour's policy on the illegitimacy of the closed shop reflects the view that trade unions should be conceived as purely voluntary communities based on the consent of workers. For the republican, however, this narrow fixation on free choice signifies an impoverished public discourse that precludes other attractive possibilities. Closed shops do abrogate individual choice, but they also provide a powerful institutional arrangement for inculcating and reinforcing the habits and practices of solidarity and reciprocity, and the enforcement of social norms against free riding. Legal toleration of the closed shop constitutes a public affirmation 'of the special responsibilities that flow from the particular communities I inhabit … such as obligations of solidarity'.[29] Encouraging these virtues and habits of good citizenship, and promoting individual participation in the lives of communities, is a legitimate aim of civic governance even where this involves the curtailment of individual choice in certain contexts. For republicans, 'the meaning of our membership resists redescription in contractarian terms'.[30] Yet this contractarian redescription is now so deeply ingrained in political discourse on union membership it is difficult to imagine a public conversation conducted in any other terms.

It should be noted that this republican defence of the closed shop is distinctive in invoking a moral justification. Kahn-Freund famously declared that the question of the closed shop and its enforcement was a matter of pure social expediency, and that the matter could not be settled one way or another as a matter of general ethical sentiment.[31] McCarthy was also sceptical of the

[29] Sandel, above n 4, 15.

[30] *Ibid.*

[31] PL Davies and MR Freedland (eds), *Kahn-Freund's Labour and the Law*, 3rd edn (London, Stevens & Sons, 1983) 244.

standard 'common obligation' moral argument generally offered by trade unionists for the closed shop.[32] This argument was based in the moral intuition that 'no man or woman is entitled to benefit from the work of trade unions without acceptance of the obligations of trade union membership'.[33] Certainly, we might join with McCarthy in being sceptical as to whether considerations of fair play and the fair distribution of benefits and burdens justify a moral obligation to join the union. It is one thing for the non-member *willingly to accept* the benefits of unionisation while rejecting the burdens of collective action. Yet many of the goods supplied by collective bargaining are akin to nonexcludable public goods—safe workplace practices, equal opportunities policies, childcare facilities—so non-members might argue that they cannot avoid the benefits of unionisation except by resigning their employment. In these circumstances, the non-member might argue that there can be no moral obligation where the benefits are foisted upon them. The republican argument from fair play, however, avoids these difficulties. What matters for the republican is that institutions inculcate the virtuous dispositions and habits of good citizenship. One of the most important civic virtues is the virtue of fair play and reciprocity. Where citizens participate fully in the cooperative endeavour of collective bargaining, they learn to shoulder the burdens and partake of the benefits in fellowship with other trade unionists. In so doing, they learn the virtues of fair play and reciprocity. In this way, the closed shop is valued principally for its educative effects in the civic lessons it teaches to citizens. The hope is that worker-citizens will carry those same virtuous dispositions and habits into the wider polity.

The liberal might respond in the following way. If republicans are correct in their claim that experiencing our lives as bound up with the destinies of our communities is most faithful to our nature as encumbered selves, then communities will prosper naturally under conditions of free association.[34] However, republicans would reject such an assumption. Adrian Oldfield has argued that 'civic republicanism is a hard school of thought. There is no cosy warmth in life in such a community. Citizens are called to stern and important tasks which have to do with the very sustaining of their identity.'[35] Since civic citizenship is a demanding form of life, civic torpor and problems of civic motivation are commonplace. As such, one of the main tasks of civic public policy is to place constraints on easy escape from those 'stern and important tasks'. Where disassociation from the union is made more costly, as under closed shop arrangements, citizens might be more inclined to circumspection before severing

[32] WEJ McCarthy, *The Closed Shop in Britain* (Berkeley, University of California Press, 1964) 179–84.

[33] *Ibid*, 179.

[34] For a version of this argument, see W Kymlicka, 'Liberal Individualism and Liberal Neutrality' (1989) 99 *Ethics* 883; and for a powerful critical rejoinder, see S Caney, 'Consequentialist Defences of Liberal Neutrality' (1991) 41 *Philosophical Quarterly* 457.

[35] Oldfield, above n 13, 5.

their ties to the fate of the community.[36] Furthermore, McCarthy's seminal study suggested that unwilling workers who were initially compelled into association often went on to acquire a very strong and active attachment to the collective good of the union.[37] These individuals discovered an enriched (and encumbered) form of life that would otherwise have been missed without the constraining effects of social norms.

(ii) Civic Community and the Trade Unionist Conscientious Objector

The law's current attitude towards dissentient union members also discloses a tangible shift away from a civic conception of community. The nature of this shift can be discerned in the contrast between statutory and judicial techniques concerning the trade union's disciplining of union members who have refused to participate in industrial action. The statutory technique, in sections 64–65 TULRCA 1992, confers a right on the union member not to be unjustifiably disciplined by her trade union for failure to participate in a strike or other industrial action. This protection applies regardless of whether the industrial action achieved majority support in a valid ballot, or whether the discipline was authorised by the union rules. Its enactment was justified explicitly on the basis of the right of the individual to choose to go to work as an 'essential freedom'.[38]

An example of the judicial technique is provided by the famous case of *Esterman v NALGO*.[39] Louise Esterman had defied a union instruction not to assist returning officers in local government elections and was given notice of a disciplinary charge that this rendered her 'unfit for membership' of the union. She successfully sought an interlocutory injunction to restrain disciplinary proceedings against her, Templeman J deciding that no reasonable tribunal could conclude her conscientious refusal to follow the instruction constituted unfitness for membership. Now at first sight these techniques appear very similar in justification and outcome. In both cases, the individual dissentient's objections are elevated above the union's claim to allegiance in collective action. The statutory technique has been derided for according 'absolute supremacy to the individual over the collective';[40] and in a similar vein, *Esterman* is criticised for establishing a principle of 'potentially staggering width … Each of the members

[36] Analogies with civic positions on the family are instructive in this context. For example, Daniel Bell has suggested that it is not 'implausible to suggest that the easy availability of legal marriage dissolution reduces the probability of a successful long-term marriage, for such availability is likely to affect the expectations brought to the marriage'. He has argued that divorce might be made more time-consuming, to force the parties to engage in 'a certain period of reflection before the knot is permanently untied': Bell, above n 10, 183.

[37] McCarthy, above n 32, 86.

[38] *Trade Unions and their Members* (Cm 95, 1987).

[39] [1974] ICR 625.

[40] S Deakin and G Morris, *Labour Law*, 4th edn (Oxford, Hart Publishing, 2005) 1085.

could effectively decide for themselves what the union interests require.'[41] Despite these surface similarities, however, these techniques are rooted in radically distinct political theories. Only the judicial technique contains elements hospitable to civic thought. The dominant statutory technique is, by contrast, a brash embodiment of procedural liberalism.

The characterisation of the statutory technique as liberal seems to have an air of paradox. After all, the statutory right effectively overrides the contractual stipulations freely entered into by the union member. Is this statutory displacement of voluntary contractual obligations not better characterised as illiberal, a thinly disguised attack on union solidarity owing more to visceral hostility towards trade unions than liberal principle? Though the identified tension is real enough, the statutory technique is in fact readily explicable in terms of procedural liberalism. The liberal significance of the statutory technique lies in its tendency to loosen 'the relation between the self and its roles; it makes … roles easier to shed and relaxes the obligations that attach to them'.[42] If persons are essentially unencumbered, and if identities are simply the product of a creative exercise of will by an antecedent self, then this loosening of roles and their attendant obligations is a legitimate expression of liberal citizenship. When citizens exercise choice in shedding or acquiring their roles, they are exercising their highest order moral capacity to be self-originating. And this is precisely the significance of the statutory technique—the individual's choice to shed the loyalties and obligations of union membership (without, of course, shedding the union card itself) is paramount. The intrinsic value in fulfilling the role-morality of the loyal trade unionist disappears from view in the legislative schema.

The technique deployed in *Esterman* is very different. The case arose out of an industrial dispute concerning the quantum of the London weighting allowance for public sector staff. The Secretary of State for Employment had refused to authorise a pay settlement secured by National Association of Local Government Officers (NALGO) because it exceeded the norms specified in the government's counter-inflation policy. In response to this refusal, and against the advice of the TUC, NALGO instructed its members to withdraw voluntary cooperation with returning officers in the forthcoming local elections. This escalation of industrial action had been ordered without recourse to a ballot. Despite this, Louise Esterman assisted in the local elections because she felt it dishonourable to resile from her promise to assist the returning officer, to be complicit in the disruption of the electoral process, and to undermine the common good of the counter-inflation policy. In short, to obey the instruction would violate her deeply held conscientious objections. The language used by Templeman J to justify the injunction is very revealing. The conscientious trade unionist might conclude that

[41] P Elias and K Ewing, *Trade union democracy, members' rights, and the law* (London, Mansell, 1987) 207.

[42] Sandel, above n 4, 112. Sandel is discussing the tendency of role relaxation within the context of divorce law, although his observations retain their salience in this context too.

this was an order 'which, as a person—*a loyal member of NALGO*—acting in its best interests, *he felt bound to disobey*'.[43] And again, 'a member was entitled to take the view that this was an order which he might be under a *positive duty to disobey*'.[44] Or again, this was an order that 'in all the extraordinary background of this case, he *could not* conscientiously accept'.[45] Now what is at stake here is not the union member's right to make a choice, as with the statutory technique, but the right to be guided by one's sense of duty as a loyal trade unionist. The decisive point for Templeman J was that Louise Esterman was *constrained by the encumbrances of conscience*—she could not rather than would not obey. The judgment is thus a legal interpretation of the role-morality of a 'loyal member', rather than a repudiation of it. In this way, *Esterman* rejects the voluntaristic logic that underpins the statutory schema, and its related ideal of the unencumbered citizen. To reconfigure Louise Esterman's dilemma as the exercise of a choice is to misunderstand its moral significance. Instead, this trade unionist felt, for good reasons, that she was encumbered by duties of citizenship that necessarily entailed disobedience to the union order. In this way, the eclipse in practical significance of the judicial technique, and the corresponding ascendancy of procedural liberal assumptions in the statutory technique, is a regrettable civic loss.

(iii) Civic Community and Secondary Industrial Action

Civic republicanism offers a fresh perspective on the legitimacy of secondary industrial action. Secondary industrial action occurs where there is inducement of industrial action, and the employer is not a party to the industrial dispute. It often arises in the form of 'sympathy' action, where a group of workers strikes in order to demonstrate solidarity with the plight of other workers who are in dispute with their own employer. Secondary industrial action was rendered unlawful, by restricting the scope of the statutory immunities.[46] This formed part of a strategy of 'enterprise confinement' of collective activity, initiated in earnest by the Thatcher Government, and consisting in

> an attack on expressions of solidaristic behaviour by trade unions and workers, and the encouragement of individualistic attitudes … by fostering patterns of behaviour which would isolate trade unions and workgroups from each other, and which would cause individual workers to define their own interests against participating in industrial action.[47]

[43] 633D (Templeman J) (emphasis added).
[44] 634A (Templeman J) (emphasis added).
[45] 633G (Templeman J) (emphasis added).
[46] TULRCA 1992, ss 219(4), 224(1).
[47] PL Davies and MR Freedland, *Labour Legislation and Public Policy* (Oxford, Oxford University Press, 1993) 428.

This policy of individualism sits uneasily with republican thought. Solidarity is an integral aspect of republican citizenship. Given that secondary industrial action is often an expression of the republican virtues of fair play and reciprocity, it can perform a valuable role in strengthening civic bonds. For this reason, a republican State would be more inclined to adopt a policy of legal toleration, in the interests of fostering solidarity and norms of reciprocity between industrial citizens. As an example of the significance of political perspective in the interpretation of events, the mass secondary picketing during the infamous Grunwick recognition dispute is instructive.[48] What was from one perspective a harmful and imminent threat to the Rule of Law and public order in the local community, from the civic perspective was a powerful forging of civic bonds across racial difference (since many of Grunwick's employees were Asian migrant workers).

(iv) Civic Community and the Right to Organise

An attenuated perception of community also underlies the law's conceptualisation of the trade union member's relationship with her trade union in respect of freedom of association rights. On the one hand, the courts have stressed the distinctness of individual activities from those of their group. In *Carrington v Therm-A-Stor Ltd* the employer responded to a union's request for recognition by selecting 20 employees for dismissal on the ground of redundancy.[49] The question arose whether they had been dismissed by reason of their union membership or participation in union activities. The Court of Appeal, explicitly rejecting the communal basis of union activities, held that they had not. The statutory protection was accorded to employees as individuals; protection only extended to their *individual* membership or activities. Since the employer's reason for acting was based on the union's request for recognition, and not the membership or activities of any specific individual, the employees' claims failed. The union was accordingly treated as a severable entity from the aggregate activities of individual union members, thereby rejecting the employees' argument that union activities had an essentially plural base.

On the other hand, recent legislative reforms have stressed the distinctness of the group from its individual members. The new 'unfair practice' jurisdiction, introduced in the Employment Relations Act 2004 and inserted into TULRCA 1992 Schedule A1, proscribes certain modes of interference with worker free choice during the ballot procedure.[50] The provision envisages a collective enforcement mechanism, so that the complaint must be made by either the employer or union: the provision does not confer any rights on workers

48 See J Rogaly, *Grunwick* (Harmondsworth, Penguin, 1977).

49 *Carrington v Therm-A-Stor Ltd* [1983] ICR 208.

50 TULRCA 1992, Schedule A1 para 27A. See, generally, AL Bogg, 'Employment Relations Act 2004: Another False Dawn for Collectivism?' (2005) 34 *Industrial Law Journal* 72, 78–81.

themselves. The collective enforcement mechanism is also correlative to a collective remedy. If the Central Arbitration Committee (CAC) finds that the complaint is 'well-founded', then it *must* make a declaration to that effect and it *may* order the party to take action to mitigate the effects of the unfair practice. The tactic used in *Carrington* itself would now constitute an 'unfair practice' on this basis (provided it took place during the relevant timeframe of the ballot procedure). However, workers themselves would continue to have no legal redress as individuals since the remedy is confined to the union rather than its members.

As such, the law displays a distorted perception of the relation between individuals and their communities, oscillating between exclusively individual and exclusively collective modes of protection. This reflects a distorted understanding of community and its significance for individuals, conceiving it in narrowly contractarian terms. On this view, communities are 'mere associations' of individuals who join together in pursuit of 'cooperation for mutual advantage'.[51] Individuals are ontologically prior to the associations of which they form part, such that it is meaningful to perceive individuals as severable from their constituent groups. Individuals are individuals, and remain so even when they participate in communal life; groups are groups, and remain so even when they are constituted by the participation of individuals. This reflects the law's current bipolar structuring of freedom of association.

The civic understanding of community rejects this bipolar approach as too reductive, because individuals and their communities cannot always be neatly separated in this way. Communities may be constitutive in nature, engaging the identity of the participants; this encompasses 'loyalties and convictions whose moral force consists partly in the fact that living by them is inseparable from understanding ourselves as the particular persons we are'.[52] This civic understanding, defended most eloquently by Kohler, rejects the bipolar view of persons and their communal attachments:

> [C]ommunities and associations exist only for the individual. Yet, the social good is prior to—stands at a higher level than—the individual good, because without it, the good for discrete individual persons could not exist. In short, perspective requires binocular vision.[53]

[51] S Avineri and A de-Shalit, 'Introduction', in S Avineri and A de-Shalit (eds), *Communitarianism and Individualism* (Oxford, Oxford University Press, 1992) 4–5.

[52] M Sandel, 'The Procedural Republic and the Unencumbered Self', in S Avineri and A de-Shalit (eds), *Communitarianism and Individualism* (Oxford, Oxford University Press,1992) 12, 23.

[53] TC Kohler, 'Civic Virtue at Work: Unions as Seedbeds of the Civic Virtues', in MA Glendon and D Blankenhorn (eds), *Seedbeds of Virtue: Sources of Competence, Character and Citizenship in American Society* (London, Madison, 1995) 147. For a rare judicial adoption of this binocular vision, see *Shipside (Ruthin) Ltd v TGWU* [1973] ICR 503, 506 (*per* Sir John Donaldson): 'From the union's point of view the dismissal involves far more than unfairness to the employee. It is a blow aimed at the union itself, particularly in the case of dismissal of a union official. As the union sees the situation the whole prestige and credibility of the union is at stake. Monetary compensation for the employee … is an inadequate remedy.'

What is needed is a synthesis of individual and collective modes of protection. Consistent with this 'binocular' vision of constitutive attachments, the employer's wrong in *Carrington* necessitates a remedy for both individuals *and* their union. To attack either the individual or the group is to attack both simultaneously.[54]

III THE GOOD OF COLLECTIVE SELF-GOVERNMENT

A Freedom as Collective Self-Government as a Political Ideal

For many republicans, active participation in self-government is intrinsically related to the freedom of citizens:

> [L]iberty is understood as a consequence of self-government. I am free insofar as I am a member of a political community that controls its own fate, and a participant in the decisions that govern its affairs.[55]

From this perspective, liberal citizenship holds out a false promise of effective agency. Liberal rights augment an inviolate moral space where individual citizens are free to choose their values and ends; liberal neutrality ensures the State will not trespass on each individual's sovereign domain. Yet republicans such as Sandel point to the disjunction between this liberating vision of freely choosing selves and the sense of political disempowerment often experienced by citizens in the liberal polity. As citizens retreat from the public sphere into private enclaves of individual autonomy, their collective agency is correspondingly diminished. Personal autonomy and self-mastery is illusory when citizens are buffeted by social and economic forces that lie beyond each individual's sovereign control.

As Sandel has observed, 'the liberal self-image and the actual organization of modern social and economic life are sharply at odds. Even as we think and act as freely choosing, independent selves, we confront a world governed by impersonal structures of power that defy our understanding and control.'[56] These forces can only be tamed and brought under collective control in a civic republic of self-governing citizens, for it is only 'together we can take charge of the social conditions that we collectively create, that would otherwise constrain our individual lives as alien powers'.[57] The idea here is simple and powerful. Our personal autonomy is shaped and constrained to a large degree by the structures

[54] See also the requirement in TULRCA 1992 s 146 that workers be subjected to relevant trade union detriment 'as an individual'. This was designed to ensure that detrimental action taken against the union, such as a withdrawal of recognition, was not treated *ipso facto* as detrimental action against individual trade union members. Again, this rests upon a monocular vision of the individual's relationship to her community in treating the individual as essentially severable from the fate of her community.

[55] Sandel, above n 4, 26.

[56] *Ibid*, 323.

[57] HF Pitkin, *Fortune is a Woman: Gender and Politics in the Thought of Niccolo Machiavelli* (Berkeley, University of California Press, 1984) 325.

and practices of the socially determined collective context, including such matters as which options are worth pursuing or which opportunities are effectively closed off. Participating in collective self-government enables citizens to take some control over the social framework that provides the setting for their autonomous choices.[58]

The cause of republican freedom necessitates what Sandel has called a 'formative' political project. The republican State seeks to inculcate the virtues and habits of citizenship as self-government, while also creating opportunities for self-government in multiple spheres of social life. For liberals, citizenship is a status rather than a practice, and that status consists in the unconditional allocation of liberal rights. These rights protect each citizen's capacity 'to pursue private affairs without interference from society or from other citizens'.[59] For republicans, political participation is a duty, and its performance 'means deliberating with fellow citizens about the common good and helping to shape the destiny of the political community'.[60] Accordingly, republican citizenship 'is a practice, not a status; active, not passive; public not private ... Carrying out the practice entails performing duties associated with it—notably, the duties of honouring, defending and sharing in the government' of the civic polity.[61] 'Formative' governance rejects value neutrality. Instead, the State must take an active part in shaping a virtuous citizenry equipped for deliberative participation in the public realm.

As Marquand reminds us, citizenship as self-government is 'a demanding practice, requiring commitment and self-discipline. Citizens are made, not born'.[62] How can the practices of citizenship be nurtured and sustained? One strategy is through a public policy supportive of the institutions of civil society. For republicans, a central locus of civic formation is in the intermediate communities of civil society: 'trade unions, reform movements, and local government all offer examples of practices that have at times served to educate people in the exercise of citizenship by cultivating the habits of membership and orienting people to common goods beyond their private ends'.[63] The republican State cannot be neutral to the fate of such communities, because it cannot be neutral to the demise of citizenship as self-government: their fates are intertwined. The dispersion of power across multiple sites of civic engagement, empowering citizens to take charge of their collective fates, gives citizens the opportunity to learn the practices of deliberative governance. Only then can the promise of effective political agency be fulfilled.

58 I Honohan, *Civic Republicanism* (London, Routledge, 2002) 188.

59 D Marquand, 'Reinventing Civic Republicanism', in D Marquand, *The New Reckoning: Capitalism, States and Citizens* (Cambridge, Polity, 1997) 37, 45.

60 Sandel, above n 4, 5.

61 Marquand, above n 59, 46.

62 *Ibid.*

63 Sandel, above n 4, 117.

B Freedom as Collective Self-Government and Collective Bargaining

Citizenship as self-government prompts searching questions of the workplace as a site of civic significance. What does it mean for wage labour to be free in this strong republican sense? Is industrial servitude based on contractual exchange inimical to civic freedom, or does free contract legitimate subordination? From a liberal perspective and consistent with its vision of sovereign freely choosing selves, the exchange of labour for wages is free if it is the outcome of a bargain embodying voluntary consent. The meaning of contractual freedom has been a matter of great controversy amongst liberals. For laissez-faire liberals, individual contracts were freely entered into provided that the taint of duress or fraud was absent; for left liberals, however, true freedom of contract necessitated collective bargaining through unions as a way of perfecting consent to subordination.[64] From a republican perspective, this pair of possibilities signified an impoverished set of political concepts. According to Sandel, free labour is 'labor carried out under conditions likely to cultivate the qualities of character that suit citizens to self-government'.[65] On this view, it does not matter that I have consented to forfeit my civic responsibility to participate in self-government, whether through individual or collective agreement. The loss of democratic control over economic forces, and the corresponding erosion of civic virtue, is too great a cost to civic freedom. These distinct understandings of industrial freedom have shaped the labour movement's understanding of industrial democracy at different periods, with the republican understanding now very much eclipsed.

Sandel's fascinating historical study of American trade unionism has demonstrated how civic freedom was emblematic of the nascent union movement in North America, embodied particularly in the aspirations of the 'Knights of Labor'. According to the Knights, the servility of wage labour was incompatible with civic freedom. Citizenship as self-rule could only be achieved through radical democratisation of the industrial sphere. This was captured in their vision of a 'cooperative commonwealth, in which producers and consumers would organize cooperative factories, mines, banks, farms and stores'.[66] To be citizens in the workplace, to be free in the republican sense, workers needed to rule themselves. Only then could the disempowering servility of wage labour be transcended. Furthermore, these civic aspirations were best realised through the autonomous striving of workers themselves. As Sandel points out, 'this emphasis on collective self-help was essential to the formative, edifying, character-building aspiration of the movement'.[67] Over time the civic ideal waned. As the 'Knights'

[64] *Ibid*, n 4, 184.

[65] *Ibid*, 169.

[66] *Ibid*, 186. For Sandel's full treatment of the historical development of civic freedom in the workplace context, see *ibid*, ch 6.

[67] *Ibid*, 187.

died and the American Federation of Labor was born, civic freedom was eclipsed as a guiding ideal, to be replaced by the competing liberal conception. On this liberal conception, freedom lay in the equalisation of bargaining strength through collective bargaining. This allowed for true freedom of contract between workers and their employer, but it sacrificed the larger understanding of freedom that had animated the visions and practices of the Knights.

Clegg's theorisation of industrial democracy traced a similar trajectory in the British context. Early proponents of industrial democracy, such as the 'guild socialists', argued that industrial self-government would lead to workers being 'free, not slaves to their boss and their weekly wage. They would be able to fashion co-operative relationships of good fellowship at work which would make work a pleasure.'[68] Over time, this gave way to a conception of 'industrial democracy by consent'.[69] The union's democratic role was to stand as an oppositional and countervailing power against management; to share in management would compromise its democratic credentials. The republican vision of democratic self-rule was just that—a vision—but 'visions are not tough, nor practical, nor empirical ... Now we think we know better.'[70] Citizenship as self-rule was substituted by narrower material concerns such as extracting higher wages and better conditions of employment. The effect of this was to make servility more comfortable, not to displace servility itself. The democratic limits of collective bargaining were reached when 'recognition of unions moved capital-labor relations one step beyond "industrial despotism" to a kind of "constitutional monarchy" that at least limited the "employer's formerly autocratic power"'.[71]

Clegg's portrayal of the civic aspiration as naïve and idealistic should be resisted. If we take seriously the civic image of self-determining citizens in work and politics, this leads to a radical democratic vocation for labour law. Taking his inspiration from this radical democratic tradition, Karl Klare has argued for a reform agenda based on systematic democratisation of working life that republicans would find attractive: 'the workplace should provide opportunities to live adulthood as a continuous, developmental experience'.[72] In this way, 'democratic involvement in employment also contributes to civic democracy by enhancing peoples' inherent capacities to participate in politics'.[73]

Statutory recognition procedures are integral to the success of democratic self-rule in the workplace. These procedures structure the processes of collective organisation prior to the allocation of bargaining rights, and set limits on the democratic reach of collective bargaining once bargaining rights have been

[68] HA Clegg, *A New Approach to Industrial Democracy* (Oxford, Blackwell, 1960) 5.
[69] *Ibid*, 131.
[70] *Ibid*, 29.
[71] Sandel, above n 4, 213.
[72] KE Klare, 'Workplace Democracy and Market Reconstruction: An Agenda for Legal Reform' (1989) 38 *Catholic University Law Review* 1, 8.
[73] *Ibid*.

allocated. In both of these respects, the Schedule A1 recognition procedure falls far short of the civic ideal. In both phases of the procedure, the statutory framework is predicated on an interest group pluralist model of democracy. On this view, the point of democracy is simply to aggregate citizens' preferences through ballot procedures and, once bargaining rights have been allocated, to foster a notion of collective bargaining as interest-group bargaining. Citizenship as self-rule, however, rejects the aggregative and interest-group pluralist models as a blueprint for democratic renewal. Instead, democracy is conceived in deliberative terms.

(i) Pluralist and Deliberative Democracy: Allocating Bargaining Rights

Democratic ballot procedures are central to the Anglo-American model of statutory recognition. Bargaining rights are then allocated to the union where it has attracted majority support in the bargaining unit.[74] The interpretive issue seems straightforward enough: how to measure majority preferences for union recognition. However, the gauging of preferences is fraught with theoretical controversy.[75] Liberal conceptions of politics take preference aggregation as their guiding ideal. Whatever preferences are expressed by citizens should simply be respected. When citizens get what they want through satisfaction of their existing preferences then welfare is maximised. A repudiation of this liberal commitment to preference aggregation appears to lie at the thin end of the political wedge; alternative political approaches envisaging a paternalist role for the State in scrutinising, shaping or censoring private preferences 'tend to be treated as at best misguided and more likely tyrannical'.[76]

By contrast, civic conceptions of politics reject the ideal of maximising satisfaction of current preferences. Certain kinds of preference seem to be driven by external constraints rather than being autonomously endorsed by citizens. This is captured in the metaphor of 'sour grapes'.[77] If citizens are faced with opportunity constraints in the pursuit of certain goods, their preferences often 'adapt' to those constraints. To reduce cognitive dissonance, citizens are apt to conclude on the basis of 'sour grapes' that they did not want the good anyway. As a corollary of this there is a tendency for preferences to adapt to the pattern of

74 Significantly, of course, Schedule A1 makes provision for the allocation of bargaining rights in a situation where the union has demonstrated majority membership in the bargaining unit *and* none of the qualifying conditions for a recognition ballot has been met. This has significant advantages over exclusive reliance on a statutory ballot procedure. However, it does not deviate from the 'preference aggregation' model that is characteristic of the Schedule A1 mechanism. It just provides another route for aggregating preferences.

75 See, eg, CR Sunstein, 'Preferences and Politics' (1991) 20 *Philosophy and Public Affairs* 3.

76 CR Sunstein, 'Legal Interference with Private Preferences' (1986) 53 *University of Chicago Law Review* 1129.

77 J Elster, 'The Market and the Forum: Three Varieties of Political Theory', in J Bohman and W Rehg (eds), *Deliberative Democracy: Essays on Reason and Politics* (Cambridge Massachusetts, MIT Press, 1999) 3, 8.

current entitlements. This has been characterised as the 'endowment effect'.[78] Furthermore, if citizens were encouraged to experience the previously deprived opportunity so that the endowment is shifted, they might come to value it very highly. Whereas liberal accounts of preferences take them as a 'given' to be respected whatever, the civic perspective treats preferences as a socially constructed phenomenon. Where preferences are 'adaptive' to unjust social and economic constraints in their formation, respecting such preferences has a pallid democratic legitimacy. Accordingly, republicans are certainly hospitable to the idea that such distorted preferences should be overridden in certain circumstances in order to improve the welfare of citizens.[79] This will be particularly attractive where overriding such preferences leads to citizens being exposed to practices that engage them in the practices of democratic self-rule.

In the light of this, a recognition procedure inspired by civic values would seek to ameliorate adaptive preferences. For civic republicans, the principal remedial technique is through deliberative transformation of distorted preferences. When citizens deliberate together, insulated from the distorting effects of power and coercion, preferences can be subjected to critical scrutiny and 'laundered' through public dialogue. Adaptive preferences can then be identified and transformed in the deliberative process.[80] This stands in contrast to the liberal concern to aggregate private preferences, regardless of the social constraints shaping their formation. Deliberative democracy certainly requires the maximisation of union opportunities to deliberate with workers about the prospect of unionisation. However, this should not lead us to endorse the centrality of democratic ballot procedures based on majority rule, with employers and unions accorded equal opportunity to shape workers' preferences. First, ballot procedures in the workplace can have the effect of entrenching adaptive preferences. The dilatoriness of ballot procedures, coupled with the increased scope for employers to utilise non-deliberative tactics in the recognition campaign, constitute serious adaptive constraints on preference formation.[81] The anticipation of legal delay and the prospect of employer retaliation against union adherents may lead workers to conclude that unionisation is not a realistically available option.[82] The Canadian experience is instructive in this regard. By eliminating the recognition campaign, either through expedited ballots subject to strict statutory time limits or reliance on other evidence of union support such as signed authorisation cards, Canadian unions have been more successful in securing bargaining rights than their US counterparts.[83]

[78] For discussion, see C Sunstein, 'Switching the Default Rule' (2002) 77 *New York University Law Review* 106.

[79] For an argument along these lines, see Honohan, above n 58, 201–203.

[80] See Elster, above n 77.

[81] On the American experience in this regard, see PC Weiler, *Governing the Workplace* (Cambridge Massachusetts, Harvard University Press, 1993) ch 6.

[82] *Ibid*, 279.

[83] *Ibid*, 254–5.

Secondly, elimination of adaptive constraints might still be insufficient to give the union option a fair chance of success. As Sunstein points out, there is a danger that citizens 'will not take advantage of an opportunity which, because of previous deprivation, they no longer value'.[84] In this situation, shifting the endowment position from non-union to union allows citizens to experience the previously deprived option. When the endowment shifts in this way, preferences are likely to follow. One such endowment-shifting technique is 'staged recognition'.[85] This would give the union some representational rights with less than majority support allowing a much broader class of workers to experience some form of union representation. Another possibility is permitting discretionary adjustment of requisite support thresholds for the allocation of bargaining rights. It is more difficult to achieve majority support in the expectation of union recognition than it is once recognition has been awarded. Preferences tend to track rather than precipitate endowment shifts. A more future-oriented perspective, allocating bargaining rights on the basis of *potential* majority support post-recognition, would therefore be warranted.[86]

Thirdly, the notion of statutory recognition as establishing a neutral procedural framework as between unions and employers is a natural corollary of State neutrality towards workers' preferences. The liberal recognition procedure provides 'a framework of rights that respects persons as free and independent selves, capable of choosing their own values and ends. Since this liberalism asserts the priority of fair procedures over particular ends, the public life it informs might be called the procedural republic.'[87] However, the republican State eschews proceduralism and value neutrality. It may legitimately discourage practices that 'promote privatized, materialistic habits, enervate civic virtue, and induce a selfish disregard for the public good'.[88] Conversely, it has a political duty to promote institutions that inculcate civic virtues and provide forums for shared deliberation. From the republican perspective, unions are the embodiment of civic values. When workers join together collectively to exercise democratic influence over their working lives they are acting as *citizens*; unions are 'seedbeds' of civic virtue, civic communities providing 'a forum for serious deliberation and self-directed action' while reducing 'the fragmentation and isolation that dissolves community and undermines the possibility of authentic self-rule'.[89] The essence

[84] Sunstein, above n 76, 1149.

[85] For a recent restatement of 'staged recognition' as a preferred regulatory option, see PL Davies and C Kilpatrick, 'UK Worker Representation After Single Channel' (2004) 33 *Industrial Law Journal* 121.

[86] Such was the approach taken by both the CIR and ACAS in discharging their respective functions under recognition machinery in the 1970s. For discussion, see B Simpson, 'Trade Union Recognition and the Law, A New Approach—Pts I and II of Schedule A1 to TULRCA 1992' (2000) 29 *Industrial Law Journal* 193, 203.

[87] Sandel, above n 4, 4.

[88] M Sandel, 'Reply to Critics', in AL Allen and MC Regan (eds), *Debating Democracy's Discontent* (Oxford, Oxford University Press, 1998) 329.

[89] Kohler, above n 53, 152–3.

of republicanism's formative project is that forms of life *can* and *should* be ranked as better or worse. It is better to live as an actively engaged citizen, in community with others and engaged in the practice of deliberative self-rule; and it is right that the State should encourage this. There is nothing illegitimate in tilting the legal framework to favour collective bargaining as a desired outcome.

(ii) Pluralist and Deliberative Democracy: The Duty to Bargain

Disagreement over the democratic nature of collective bargaining reflects a continuing tension between pluralist and deliberative conceptions of democracy. On the one hand, industrial relations pluralism has traditionally emphasised the pluralist aspect of collective bargaining. Collective bargaining mirrors political bargaining between interest groups in the polity. In essence, both involve 'a process of competitive bargaining between different interest-groups, which involves no attempt to evaluate the propriety of any of the interests represented'.[90] In certain respects, this seems rooted in attractive ideals of freedom and equality. It is anti-paternalist, leaving workers themselves free to define their own interests and promote them through voluntary association. Moreover, equality is seemingly honoured, in that interest group bargaining 'gives equal weight to the interests of citizens in part by enabling them to present and advance their interests'.[91]

On the other hand, pluralist democracy has been challenged in democratic theory by the proponents of deliberative democracy; and deliberative democracy has been central to the civic republican revival in political thought. Deliberative democracy rejects the pluralist creed that democratic citizenship consists in the rational pursuit of self-interest through bargaining. Instead, freedom and equality are better realised where citizens deliberate together for the sake of the common good. Deliberation necessitates reasoned dialogue and the search for consensus. Collective decisions are to be justified on the basis of reasons that all citizens could reasonably accept. This furnishes a more attractive basis for democratic legitimacy. For deliberative democrats, 'outcomes are democratically legitimate if and only if they could be the object of a free and reasoned agreement among equals'.[92] Threats and prudential strategising give way to reasons and reciprocity:

[90] P Pettit, 'Reworking Sandel's Republicanism', in AL Allen and MC Regan (eds), *Debating Democracy's Discontent* (Oxford, Oxford University Press, 1998) 40, 44.

[91] J Cohen, 'Procedure and Substance in Deliberative Democracy', in J Bohman and W Rehg (eds), *Deliberative Democracy* (Cambridge Massachusetts, MIT Press, 1997) 407, 411.

[92] J Cohen, 'Deliberation and Democratic Legitimacy', in J Bohman and W Rehg (eds), *Deliberative Democracy* (Cambridge Massachusetts, MIT Press, 1997) 67, 73.

> Prudence aims at only a modus vivendi whereby self-interested citizens can deal with their disagreements through various forms of bargaining. Reciprocity aims at deliberative agreement, whereby citizens are motivated to justify their claims to those with whom they must cooperate.[93]

The choice between pluralist and deliberative conceptions of democracy shapes the choices between different regulatory frameworks for collective bargaining: what form should the duty to bargain take? Should collective bargaining assume a centralised or decentralised pattern? How far should the democratic reach of joint regulation extend into areas of unilateral managerial prerogative? Each of these regulatory problems will be addressed in turn.

(a) The Legal Duty to Bargain: Passive or Active? Theoretical accounts of the legal duty to bargain have pointed to an important distinction between passive and active conceptions of the legal duty.[94] The passive duty was a natural corollary of the interest group pluralist conception. It served a narrow, recognitional function. Employers were legally compelled to bargain with representative unions, but beyond this the State would not intrude on their contractual autonomy. Bargaining outcomes would reflect relative bargaining strength, and 'hard' bargaining was democratically legitimate. As such, stronger parties could press their bargaining advantages resolutely in their own self-interest. By contrast, the active duty to bargain was aligned with a deliberative conception. It moved beyond the recognitional function, enjoining the parties to 'explain their respective positions, listen to reasoned arguments, and pursue the search for agreement with sincerity and in genuine good faith'.[95] This countenanced much greater State involvement in the collective bargaining process. To ensure compliance with the active duty, the State might need to scrutinise the reasonableness of bargaining practices, even extending to evaluation of whether the parties had adopted reasonable substantive positions or made reasonable concessions during the collective bargaining process. The passive duty, with its contractualist underpinning, has exercised a tenacious hold on specification of bargaining duties in Anglo–American labour law. In the US the passive duty has been defended vigorously by the Supreme Court, safeguarding the bargaining process against State intrusion.[96]

In the UK, Schedule A1 has been designed to ensure collective bargaining retains its 'voluntary' character once bargaining rights have been allocated; every effort is made to steer collective bargaining beyond the public scrutiny and oversight of the CAC and the courts. There is a pious hope that voluntary

[93] A Gutmann and D Thompson, *Democracy and Disagreement* (Cambridge Massachusetts, Harvard University Press, 1996) 54.

[94] For the classical theoretical analysis of the legal duty to bargain deploying this framework, see H Wellington, 'Freedom of Contract and the Collective Bargaining Agreement' (1964) 112 *University of Pennsylvania Law Review* 467.

[95] *Ibid*, 472.

[96] *NLRB v Insurance Agents' Union* 361 US 477, 488–9 (1960).

bargaining will assume a more deliberative character, but the State has no direct role in encouraging this through the enforcement of 'active' good faith duties.[97] As we saw in chapter two, this is entirely in keeping with a long tradition of 'passive' duties to bargain in British labour. Under both the Industrial Relations Act and the Employment Protection Act (EPA) legal recognition procedures, bargaining autonomy was insulated from extensive State control. Republicans are much less concerned with the need to insulate bargaining autonomy in this way. Consequently, there is much greater space for the implementation of 'active' good faith duties in a scheme of republican labour law.

(b) Bargaining Structure: The Perils of Excessive Decentralisation The civic perspective also defends the need for a multi-layered bargaining structure to facilitate deliberative governance. In certain respects, the decentralised character of Anglo-American collective bargaining seems to fit nicely with civic values. As Kohler argues from a civic perspective, the organisational norm of subsidiarity 'teaches that social institutions of every description should be ordered so that decision making and the responsibility for acting remain at the lowest capable level'.[98] However, decentralised communities may not be public-regarding in their orientation, and decentralised bargaining can easily become detached from the common good of the political community. More seriously, it is vital that the scale of democratic control is matched precisely to the scale of economic and social forces over which democratic mastery is to be achieved. In this vein, Sandel has pointed to the massive forces unleashed by globalisation, with its concomitant effects on the possibilities for democratic control. According to Sandel

> self-government today . . . requires a politics that plays itself out in a multiplicity of settings, from neighbourhoods to nations to the world as a whole. Such a politics requires citizens who can think and act as multiply situated selves.[99]

What is needed is comprehensive public action to integrate multiple levels of democratic governance: transnational bargaining, national bargaining, industry bargaining, regional bargaining, and company and plant-level bargaining. Centralised deliberation forces participants to argue their case transparently and publicly, and share public responsibility for the ultimate decisions. As groups become more encompassing in their constituencies, the incentives for factional betrayal of the common good are reduced. In this way, 'proliferating sites of civic activity and political power can serve self-government by cultivating virtue … and generating loyalties to larger political wholes'.[100] This also aligns self-government with the scale of economic life. Self-rule through decentralised

[97] R Rideout, 'What shall we do with the CAC?' (2002) 31 *Industrial Law Journal* 1, 31.
[98] Kohler, above n 53, 155.
[99] Sandel, above n 4, 350.
[100] *Ibid*, 348.

bargaining leaves workers confronting 'a world governed by impersonal structures of power that defy … understanding and control'.[101] The dispersion of decisional sovereignty across different levels of economic organisation is necessary to achieve civic freedom in the industrial sphere, bringing economic forces within the reach of workers' democratic self-rule.

The Anglo-American experience of decentralised bargaining, entrenched by the structure of the recognition procedure itself, is a salutary lesson in the civic dangers of excessive devolution.[102] According to Rogers, the institutional incentives associated with 'low density decentralized' structures have inhibited the emergence of coordinated deliberation. Faced with the economic costs of unionisation and the prospect of competition with non-union firms, rational employers strive to stay non-union through hostile deployment of union suppression strategies. In turn, unions are driven into particularistic strategies of 'militant economism', rejecting cooperation in an attempt to maintain the material incentives for workers to stay unionised. The effect of this is to reinforce the narrow and short-term-oriented representation of interests in the bargaining process. Legal procedures reinforce this dysfunctional logic by reflecting and encouraging bargaining decentralisation.[103] The result is a fragmented and sectionalised pattern of union organisation that leaves unions increasingly vulnerable to escalating employer resistance.

By contrast, Rogers' typology also points to the 'high density centralized' structures that increase the incentives for deliberative cooperation and the supply of public goods.[104] Encompassing structures enable coordination and resolve the collective action problems that beset decentralised bargaining by reducing the incentives for opportunistic free-riding and short-term gain strategies. Take the example of training. Inter-firm bargaining structures 'can powerfully discourage even temptations to defection, making the consideration of cooperation more familiar, extending and securing its reach, and lowering monitoring costs … a strong employer's association, especially one "kept honest" by a strong union, can provide a powerful boost to the quality and extent of firm training efforts.'[105] Without this overarching coordination, however, plant level bargaining cannot insulate individual firms from the corrosive effects of civic free-riding, and the vicious circle of distrust and hostility continues to reinforce itself. Space precludes a systematic exploration of the possibilities and pitfalls in achieving an integrated structure of industrial governance, although both Cohen and Rogers and

[101] *Ibid*, 323.

[102] See J Rogers, 'Divide and Conquer: Further "Reflections on the Distinctive Character of American Labor Laws"' (1990) *Wisconsin Law Review* 1.

[103] For example, the Schedule A1 procedure is confined to recognition claims addressed to *single* employers. There is no provision for legal support for multi-employer bargaining, nor has there been much evidence of the British State engaging in an 'institution-building' role to support the emergence and operation of multiple sites of civic engagement in the industrial sphere.

[104] Rogers, above n 102, 34.

[105] J Cohen and J Rogers, *Associations and Democracy* (London, Verso, 1995) 85.

Marquand have done important work in elucidating the design of regulatory frameworks, and the need for constitutional reform,[106] to encourage multi-level industrial governance.

(c) Towards a Civic Bargaining Agenda? The commitment to civic freedom also has implications for the democratic scope of the duty to bargain. The contrast between civic and liberal freedom is reflected in differing accounts of the legitimate democratic reach of collective bargaining. Liberal freedom conceives of collective bargaining in instrumental terms. It is a means to ensure true consent based on bargaining equality, promoting distributive justice in the allocation of basic goods such as income. The democratic reach of collective bargaining is correspondingly narrow, confined to wages, hours and conditions of employment. Civic freedom conceives of collective bargaining as a forum of democratic self-rule in industry. On this view, the material achievements of collective bargaining are less significant than the provision of an effective voice in industrial governance. The democratic reach of collective bargaining is far broader, encapsulating 'any topic relevant to the strategic future of the enterprise or to employee job security'.[107]

This tension plays out in the distinction between mandatory and permissive subjects of bargaining in the US. Mandatory subjects of bargaining, within the legal scope of the good faith bargaining duty, are encapsulated in the statutory phrase in section 8(d) of the Wagner Act framework, 'wages, hours, and other terms and conditions of employment'. In *First National Maintenance Corporation v NLRB* the Supreme Court was faced with the question of whether partial plant closure fell within the scope of mandatory bargaining.[108] The court decided that it was not. Such decisions fell within 'a core of entrepreneurial control' insulated from democratic influence. It would violate the neutral purposes of the statutory procedure for the State to encroach on this proprietary core of managerial prerogative, which was left intact by the supervening statutory duty to bargain. Furthermore, voluntary bargaining practices extended to these kinds of decision only rarely. As such, the law should mirror these social practices in determining the scope of mandatory bargaining. In effect, this created a situation where, along the spectrum of managerial decisions, 'roughly speaking, the least significant are subject to bargaining; the most important—those involving basic changes in the scope of the enterprise and many jobs—are not'.[109] Collective bargaining was conceived as instrumental to the achievement of material advantages for workers; the civic understanding of citizenship as self-rule, giving workers democratic influence over fundamental decisions relating to the basic

[106] Marquand, above n 1, ch 8.
[107] Klare, above n 72, 50.
[108] *First National Maintenance Corporation v NLRB* 452 US 666 (1981).
[109] CL Estlund, 'Economic Rationality and Union Avoidance: Misunderstanding the National Labor Relations Act' (1993) 71 *Texas Law Review* 921, 944.

scope of the enterprise, was eclipsed by the court's striking deference to subsisting employer property rights and inherent managerial prerogatives.

The legal scope of the 'default procedure agreement' under Schedule A1 is similarly constrained. The duty to bargain extends only to a narrow range of subjects: 'pay, hours and holidays'.[110] Although 'pay' was interpreted expansively in *UNIFI and Union Bank of Nigeria* to include pensions,[111] the CAC relied upon social practices to justify its conclusion. The CAC reasoned that since voluntary bargaining often included pensions within its scope, it was appropriate for the legal duty to reflect this social practice. The corollary of this reasoning was that legal norms should not overreach social practices. It was on this basis that the Government reversed the CAC's decision in *Union Bank of Nigeria* in the Employment Relations Act 2004, restricting the scope of the legal duty to exclude pensions.[112] The Government shared the CAC's perception that legal and voluntary modes of bargaining should be congruent. Nevertheless, and contrary to the CAC's assumption, empirical evidence suggested that pensions did not tend to figure in voluntary bargaining. As such, it was important that the legally binding 'default procedure agreement' did not become 'more comprehensive in scope than voluntary bargaining arrangements'.[113]

The civic perspective proceeds from a fundamentally different premise to the current law: not how to secure a proprietary exclusion zone of unilateral employer control or to mirror social practices, but to ask which economic arrangements are most hospitable to the virtues and practices of citizenship as self-rule? The notion articulated in *First National Maintenance*, of private property rights insulating a core of entrepreneurial control from democratic encroachment, is deeply suspect. The particular contours of private property embody a regulatory choice to prioritise certain values. Managerial prerogative 'is not inherent in the concept of private property, much less in the nature of things. Managerial prerogative is a social convention. It can and should be altered and redefined.'[114] Judicial enforcement of the 'core of entrepreneurial control' is neither more nor less neutral than if the court had extended the reach of employees' democratic influence through a broader statutory interpretation. It represents an active regulatory choice to prioritise an absolutist conception of private property over citizenship as self-rule. But property can be *redefined* in the image of industrial self-government.

Similarly, the understanding of law as a 'mirror' of social practices is problematic from the civic perspective. Preferences and social practices are often a function of legal rules. What we want is sometimes shaped by what we already

[110] TULRCA 1992, Schedule A1, para 168; The Trade Union Recognition (Method of Collective Bargaining) Order 2000, SI 2000/1300.

[111] *UNIFI and Union Bank of Nigeria* [2001] IRLR 712.

[112] DTI, *Review of the Employment Relations Act 1999* (Department of Trade and Industry, 2003) 42–3.

[113] *Ibid*, 43 para 2.56.

[114] Klare, above n 72, 50.

have (the endowment effect) and what we think we can realistically get (adaptive preferences); in turn, this is shaped by the allocation of entitlements and opportunities through legal norms. As such, it is disingenuous and circular to argue that legal norms should simply reflect social practices, as if social practices were wholly autonomous of the law. Legal rules and social practices must be defended in terms of the values or policies they embody. If a social practice is unjust or undemocratic then it should not be bolstered through supportive legal norms. Instead, the law should be harnessed to mould social practices so that they better reflect democratic values.

This also provides an answer to Davies and Wedderburn's historical observation that workers might not be prepared to contemplate the possibility of industrial action, with its certain, immediate costs, in respect of longer-term, more strategic entrepreneurial decision-making in the enterprise.[115] If workers are not prepared to contemplate strike action, perhaps because their preferences are confined to the achievement of short term material improvements, then the proper response of the law might be simply to defer to those preferences. However, the civic perspective teaches that legal norms can shape preferences by framing perceptions of available opportunities. If the legal duty to bargain is limited to 'pay, hours and holidays', and if the trade dispute defence is not expansive enough to confer immunity on organisers of industrial action for objectives related to corporate strategy, it seems dubious then to argue that workers' preferences legitimate the legal status quo. It is hardly surprising that workers 'prefer' not to risk dismissal by participating in unlawful industrial action. Expanding the scope of the legal duty to bargain, and with it the definition of legitimate purposes in the trade dispute defence, might galvanise workers' sense of entitlement to participate in a richer range of bargaining subjects. In any case, if preferences are a product of legal rules allocating entitlements and opportunities, those preferences provide a weak justification for the legal rules themselves.[116] As Sunstein argues:

> [W]orkers seem not to be willing to trade much in the way of money for self-government. But that preference may be a product of a belief that self-government in the workplace is unavailable. Were the option to be one that workers thought conventionally available, the option might be highly valued.[117]

The civic conception of collective bargaining would accordingly dispense with artificial *a priori* limits on its scope; 'unions would have the right to seek to influence management policy in *any* area—including such matters as investment

[115] PL Davies and Lord Wedderburn, 'The Land of Industrial Democracy' (1977) 6 *Industrial Law Journal* 197, 206.

[116] See K Klare, 'Countervailing workers' power as a regulatory strategy', in H Collins, PL Davies, and R Rideout (eds), *Legal Regulation of the Employment Relation* (London, Kluwer, 2000) 63, 64 fn 9.

[117] Sunstein, above n 76 , 1148.

decisions, rates of profit, management salaries and so on'.[118] This civic conception acknowledges the complex intersection of different influences on the terms of the wage–work bargain. Wage settlements cannot be compartmentalised (without deliberative distortion) from broader corporate objectives such as technological innovation, work organisation, marketing and pricing policies, product development and the exploitation of new product markets. Without this expansion of the frontiers of joint regulation, citizenship as self-rule is illusory. If corporate strategies lie outside the scope of collective bargaining, then workers will remain at the mercy of economic forces that lie beyond their control. Furthermore, trusting cooperation depends upon an expanded bargaining agenda. Multiplying the range of bargaining subjects might increase the possibilities for conflict, but it simultaneously increases the potential for management and unions to achieve novel and imaginative deliberative solutions to pressing problems. As Dryzek argues:

> [D]eliberation can multiply dimensions and options, and so it would seem to add to the complexity of choice. But complexity should not be equated with intractability, for this proliferation increases the possibilities for stable and non-arbitrary agreement.[119]

IV THE GOOD OF NON-DOMINATION

A Non-Domination as a Political Ideal

The concept of freedom admits of a variety of competing interpretations. Liberals have often been aligned with a negative conception of freedom as non-interference.[120] On this view, freedom is defined as an absence of intentional interference by others. I am free insofar as my choices are not subjected to coercion, interference or restraint by other agents. This fits well with the kind of freedom implicated in liberal citizenship, and the concomitant emphasis on liberal rights. These rights are conceived as negative constraints on interference by other agents, thereby protecting individual choice. Civic republicans such as Philip Pettit have rejected the negative conception of freedom as non-interference as inadequate. In response to the weaknesses of the negative conception, the republican tradition has articulated a richer account of freedom, defined in terms of security from domination. It is this conception of freedom, rather than the negative one, that provides the inspiration for civic republican citizenship.

[118] WEJ McCarthy and ND Ellis, *Management by Agreement* (London, Hutchinson, 1973) 97.

[119] JS Dryzek, *Deliberative Democracy and Beyond* (Oxford, Oxford University Press, 2000) 41.

[120] For the classical statement of liberal freedom, see I Berlin, *Two Concepts of Liberty* (Oxford, Oxford University Press, 1958). See also P Pettit, *Republicanism: A Theory of Freedom and Government* (Oxford, Oxford University Press, 1997) 17–50.

The moral case for a conception of freedom as non-domination emerges out of an appreciation of the limitations of negative liberty. First, freedom as non-interference fails to convey all that is problematic about relationships of subordination. Negative freedom stigmatises interference. But it is possible to be subordinate even in the absence of interference. The essence of subordination is that 'someone lives at the mercy of others. That person is dominated by those others in the sense that even if the others don't interfere in his or her life, they have an arbitrary power of doing so: there are few restraints or costs to inhibit them'.[121] Relationships of subordination are both *demeaning* and *insecure*. In order to avoid arbitrary interference, subordinates might resort to developing 'strategies of placating and anticipating the powerful'.[122] This reinforces the inferior social standing of the subordinate citizen, for there will often be a shared awareness that 'one is weaker than the other, vulnerable to the other, and to that extent subordinate to the other'.[123]

Secondly, negative freedom stigmatises all forms of interference. It fails to discriminate between arbitrary and non-arbitrary interference.[124] No distinction is drawn between, on the one hand, a State that coerces citizens in accordance with constitutional and democratic constraints and in a manner responsive to their avowed interests and, on the other hand, coercion and manipulation practised without reference to those interests. Yet these distinctions are constitutionally and morally significant. Given its inability to convey the significance of these distinctions, negative freedom seems too blunt conceptually to provide a useful tool for thinking about citizenship.

In the light of these limitations, Pettit offers an alternative account of freedom as non-domination. Domination exists where one party enjoys the capacity to interfere on an arbitrary basis in the choices of another.[125] Freedom consists in the status of being securely protected from domination. On this view, I am free to the extent that any exercise of power is forced to track my avowable interests; if interference is forced to track my interests I am not dominated by the interfering party. Conversely, I am in a state of subordination to the extent that another party has the capacity to interfere arbitrarily, even if through grace or favour that other party does not in fact interfere. This provides a more robust and resilient foundation to civic freedom than the negative conception. The status of citizen is constituted by a framework of laws and constitutional constraints which permit the State an active and legitimate role in eliminating domination in civil society, while preventing the State itself from becoming a dominating presence in the lives of its citizens.

[121] P Pettit, *A Theory of Freedom: From the Psychology to the Politics of Agency* (Cambridge, Polity, 2001) 137.
[122] Pettit, above n 120, 87.
[123] *Ibid*, 88.
[124] Pettit, above n 121, 34–136.
[125] Pettit, above n 120, 52.

(B) Non-Domination as a Labour Law Ideal

The employment relationship has been of particular concern to civic republicans concerned with non-domination.[126] As Pettit observes:

> [T]he image of workers as wage slaves casts them as dependent on the grace and mercy of their employer, and as required to court paths of caution in dealing, individually or collectively, with their bosses. If that image is to serve as a way of showing what is objectionable in the condition of workers, then it is premised on the appeal of its opposite: on the appeal of the idea that workers should not be exposed to the possibility of arbitrary interference, that they should enjoy freedom as non-domination.[127]

Accordingly, the civic republican agenda for labour law will be concerned with the relief of the status of subordination in the industrial sphere, to ensure that the capacity of employers to wield power over their workforce on an arbitrary basis is eliminated.

The characterisation of unrestrained managerial prerogative as a form of stigmatised *dominium* is not unfamiliar to labour lawyers. In his seminal analysis of the nature and value of collective bargaining, Flanders argued that 'the value of a trade union to its members lies less in its economic achievements than in its capacity to protect their dignity'.[128] It is striking how Flanders' understanding of workers' dignity reflects the republican understanding of freedom as non-domination; as a form of joint regulation within the industrial sphere, collective bargaining protects workers' dignity by defining 'their rights, and consequently their status and security, and *so liberates them from dependence on chance and the arbitrary will of others*'.[129] It is precisely in 'diminishing a degrading dependence on market forces and arbitrary treatment' that the republican virtue of unionisation lies.[130] Similar concerns with *dominium* shaped Kahn-Freund's canonical reflections on law and power in the industrial sphere. Although sometimes and perhaps misleadingly couched in terms of inequality of bargaining strength, it was the *status* of subordination inherent in the employment relation that gave pluralist labour law its distinctive vocation. Given the perennial divergence of interest inherent in the employment relation, the scope for dominating arbitrary interference by powerful employers in a manner unresponsive to workers' interests is particularly acute. For Kahn-Freund, freedom of contract in the sphere of labour relations had an air of paradox; it equated with 'not more than the freedom to

[126] For a recent engagement with Pettit's account of freedom as non-domination in the labour law context, see the excellent piece by V Mantouvalou, 'Life After Work: Privacy and Dismissal' *LSE Legal Studies Working Paper* No 5/2008.

[127] Pettit, above n 120, 141. See also P Pettit, 'Reworking Sandel's Republicanism' in AL Allen and MC Regan (eds), *Debating Democracy's Discontent* (Oxford, Oxford University Press, 1998) 40, 57–58; Sandel, above n 4, 168–200.

[128] A Flanders, 'Collective Bargaining: A Theoretical Analysis' (1968) 6 *British Journal of Industrial Relations* 1, 26.

[129] *Ibid*, 26 (emphasis added).

[130] *Ibid*, 17.

restrict or to give up one's freedom. Conversely, to restrain a person's freedom of contract may be necessary to protect his freedom.'[131] The apparent paradox dissolves when it is refracted through the lens of freedom as non-domination. Freely entered contractual relations might nevertheless give rise to an ongoing relationship of domination and subordination. When this occurs 'the free contract cannot serve the role of automatic legitimator—even prima facie legitimator—of what happens under the terms of the contract. The idea of free contract loses the authorizing capacity that it was given in the classical liberal tradition.'[132]

C Freedom as Non-Domination in the Workplace: Welfare Capitalism or Collective Bargaining?

What are the appropriate regulatory means to the realisation of freedom as non-domination in the workplace? We can identify two regulatory possibilities: welfare capitalism through the medium of 'modern companies', and countervailing power through collective bargaining. Beginning with welfare capitalism, Freedland has identified this as a central thread running through the shape and structure of New Labour's post-1997 settlement in labour law.[133] It is manifest in the eulogy to 'modern companies' in chapter two of the white paper *Fairness at Work*.[134] Competitive success is achieved through trust and flexibility in the workplace, based on a sense of partnership between workers and employers; unions may perform a complementary role in partnership arrangements, but this is counterbalanced by the observation that 'each business should choose the form of relationship that suits it best'.[135] In many cases, however, unions will be otiose in the modern company. Instead, loyalty is engendered through the paternalistic adoption of good employment practices by the best organisations, harnessing 'the talents of their employees in a relationship based on fairness'.[136] These paternalistic tenets infuse the structure of Schedule A1. In particular, the statutory priority of voluntary recognition, based as it is on the principle of employer consent, gives employers considerable latitude to shape representational arrangements in accordance with their preferences. Where the employer confers voluntary recognition on a union, perhaps in the interests of cooperative partnership, this is sufficient to block the statutory procedure even where the anointed union has no organisational strength or is non-independent, and even

131 Davies and Freedland, above n 31, 25.
132 Pettit, above n 120, 164.
133 MR Freedland, 'Modern companies and modern manors—placing statutory trade union recognition in context' (1998) 20 *Comparative Labor Law and Policy Journal* 3.
134 *Fairness at Work* (Cmnd 3968, 1998).
135 *Ibid*, 12 para 2.6.
136 *Ibid*, 11 para 2.2.

where there is a competing independent union with substantial worker support.[137] In effect, there is a right of paternalistic override of workers' choices, exercisable by employers and inscribed into the statutory procedure.

From the civic republican perspective the technique of welfare capitalism, entrusting workers' welfare to the benevolent paternalism of good employers, is anathema to freedom as non-domination. This is not to deny that the best employers might treat their workers very well, or even that the majority of employers can be characterised as modern companies, wisely guided by a long-term view of their economic interests. What it does deny is that this kind of benevolent paternalism is consistent with workers' non-domination. As Freedland observes, 'welfare capitalism prioritizes capitalism over welfare when the going gets tough'.[138] Workers' reliance on an employer's benevolent paternalism is too insecure and uncertain a basis to satisfy the exacting demands of freedom as non-domination. After all, *kindly* masters are still *masters*: 'economic rationality may have argued for gentleness among their masters, but it remained objectionable from the socialist point of view that workers lived in subjection to those masters: that their employers were, precisely, masters'.[139] Welfare capitalism relies upon the discretionary indulgence of employers in treating the workforce in accordance with workers' perceived interests in fairness and security. However, what matters for civic republicans is not that workers are treated well by employers in a manner responsive to workers' interests, but that employers are *forced* to track those interests through robust and effective institutional mechanisms allowing for democratic contestation of employer decision-making. In this respect, welfare capitalism is as much a form of *dominium* as capitalism without welfare.

The civic limitations of welfare capitalism bring the corresponding strengths of collective bargaining as a technique for neutralising employer domination into clearer perspective. For Pettit, the primary safeguard against domination is through effective democratic contestation of political decision-making.[140] This republican model of contestatory democracy has two dimensions. First, its authorial aspect emphasises that citizens should be able, through the institutions of representative democracy, to shape and influence political decision-making. However, the authorial aspect alone is insufficient to prevent domination. Majorities can still tyrannise minorities even where authorship has been exercised democratically. For this reason, republican democracy requires a second, contestatory dimension. This necessitates ensuring that citizens subject to political decision-making are empowered, through the provision of an audible and powerful voice, to contest political decisions where they do not track the

[137] See *R (On the application of NUJ) v CAC* [2006] ICR 1.
[138] Freedland, above n 133, 8.
[139] Pettit, above n 120, 141.
[140] See P Pettit, 'Republican freedom and contestatory democratization', in I Shapiro and C Hacker-Cordon (eds), *Democracy's Value* (Cambridge, Cambridge University Press, 1999) 163.

perceived interests of citizens. It is this contestatory dimension, and the provision of oppositional voice, that forces political decision-making to track the common interests of citizens thereby safeguarding against political domination. When citizens are empowered to voice their concerns through the medium of associations in civil society, and to impress upon decision-makers their own perceptions of where their interests lie, the capacity to exercise power on an arbitrary basis is tamed. For this reason, contestatory procedures are an important bulwark against arbitrary *dominium* in republican political philosophy.

Given the republican emphasis on democratic modes of contestation, the value of independent trade unionism in republican thought is obvious. For Pettit, the surest means of guaranteeing citizenship as non-domination in the workplace is the technique of reciprocal power.[141] Thus, 'the trade union movement almost certainly advanced the non-domination of workers in the industrial world of the nineteenth century. And that movement increased workers' non-domination precisely by giving them collective powers with which to confront the powers of employers.'[142] For this reason, freedom as non-domination provides a powerful republican justification for the right to strike.[143] Without the opportunity of effective recourse to collective action, employer decision-making can proceed without any heed being paid to workers' interests. Collective action through autonomous trade unions provides collective countervailing power in the workplace. This collective equalisation of social power redresses the power disparity in the individual employment relationship. It also provides the basis of a system of democratic contestation in the workplace. Collective bargaining provides an effective procedural check on managerial decision-making. The process provides a democratic forum whereby workers can collectively articulate their self-avowed interests, and monitor managerial decision-making. This safeguards the workforce against domination. While individual employment rights can assist in this regard, the republican tradition places much greater emphasis on the secure and resilient protection offered by collective organisation in industrial civil society, since 'freedom as non-domination of industrial workers was surely more effectively furthered by the power they developed as a result of unionization than it was by the recognition of workers' rights'.[144]

[141] Pettit, above n 120, 95.

[142] *Ibid.*

[143] *Ibid*, 142: 'The ideal of freedom as non-interference has always been invoked, usually in the context of free contracts of employment, to make a case against collective industrial action by workers. Such action is a form of interference, of course, since it involves coercion or active obstruction … The ideal of freedom as non-domination gives a very different cast to collective action … It may be the only way of giving the workers sufficient power to enable them to be able to stand up, individually, to their employer.'

[144] *Ibid*, 304.

D The Civic Limitations of New Labour's Conception of 'Social Partnership'

Freedom as non-domination generates a critical perspective on New Labour's ideology of social partnership. The critical work of Novitz, along with that of Smith and Morton, has been very important in this regard. For Novitz, New Labour's ideology is essentially individualistic and unitaristic in its denial of a preferred role for contestatory collective bargaining to mediate conflicts of interest in the employment relation. As translated into specific legal reforms, legislative initiatives 'fail to pay attention to the crucial imbalance of power in the employment relationship'.[145] This has been manifest in a preference for cooperative modes of interaction, such as consultation methods, that bypass independent trade unions. Where trade unions exist, these should function as domesticated appendages in the promotion of managerial objectives by signing 'partnership' arrangements with employers. For Smith and Morton, too, the traditional sensitivity to power imbalance is absent from New Labour's ideology of social partnership with predictable regulatory consequences:

> The power imbalance inherent in the employment relationship ... is rejected ... the case for autonomous workers' collective organization . . . is diluted, and other forms of representation and communication are deemed adequate.[146]

If freedom as non-domination is central to the modern republican tradition, it has failed to appear at all on New Labour's republican radar. This has had problematic regulatory implications. Two specific examples will suffice. First, the increasing preference for consultative voice mechanisms that bypass independent trade unions; secondly, the preference for 'voluntary' recognition arrangements that legitimates the emergence of non-independent voice mechanisms in the workplace.

(i) The Civic Limitations of Consultation

In recent years, there has been an increasing policy preference for the use of non-union consultation representatives. If we focus on the Information and Consultation of Employees Regulations 2004, there is no priority rule for trade unions—even recognised trade unions. Part VIII of the Regulations follows a familiar pattern in setting out a framework of protections and entitlements for designated representatives. Paragraphs 27 and 28 provide for a right to reasonable paid time off for the discharge of representative functions. Paragraphs 30 and 32 provide protection from dismissal and detriment in respect of the

[145] T Novitz, 'A Revised Role for Trade Unions as Designed by New Labour: The Representation Pyramid and "Partnership"' (2002) 29 *Journal of Law and Society* 487, 493.

[146] P Smith and G Morton, 'Nine Years of New Labour: Neoliberalism and Workers' Rights' (2006) 44 *British Journal of Industrial Relations* 401, 403.

discharge of representative functions. Is this sufficient to ensure the independence of representatives? That depends upon which political conception of freedom we find most appealing. From the perspective of freedom as non-interference, what matters is that there is no actual interference with the activities of the representative. If there is interference then that is problematic, if there is no interference then there is no problem. From the perspective of freedom as non-domination, however, we might be more circumspect. Non-domination stigmatises not only arbitrary interference but also the *liability to arbitrary interference* (even if no such interference actually occurs in practice). This would require altogether more searching scrutiny of the protective insulation of representatives from employer interference and control. Interestingly, legal criteria of trade union 'independence' focus on the question not only of actual employer interference, but also whether the union 'is *exposed to the risk of interference* tending towards such control'.[147] There is no comparable legal technique for scrutinising the resilience of non-union consultation representatives to withstand the employer's dominating control.

(ii) The Civic Limitations of Voluntary Recognition: The Need for a Company Union Ban

Secondly, the preference for 'voluntary' bargaining arrangements under Schedule A1 also discloses an approach that fails to incorporate a concern for freedom as non-domination. The recognition procedure is based on the priority of voluntary recognition; in turn, voluntary recognition is predicated upon employer rather than worker consent. The employer is entitled to confer recognition on a non-independent union under employer domination or control, so blocking a statutory claim by an independent union.[148] Although Schedule A1 provides for cumbersome de-recognition machinery in this situation, in most cases the status quo is unlikely to be displaced by the independent union given the high thresholds required for an order of de-recognition.[149] Alternatively, the employer can confer voluntary recognition on a 'sweetheart' independent union that has no organisational support in the bargaining unit; in this situation, there is no possibility of statutory de-recognition.[150] The priority of employer consent, inscribed into the admissibility criteria of the statutory procedure, deliberately gives the employer considerable latitude to shape representational arrangements.

Its effect is to legitimate the emergence of so-called 'company unions' as an alternative to collective bargaining through independent *and* sufficiently representative trade unions. In historical terms, the 'company union' device was characteristic of welfare capitalism. 'Company unionism' encompassed a rich

[147] Deakin and Morris, above n 40, 758 (emphasis added).

[148] TULRCA 1992, Schedule A1 para 35(4); see KD Ewing, 'Trade Union Recognition and Staff Associations—A Breach of International Labour Standards?' (2000) 29 *Industrial Law Journal* 267.

[149] TULRCA 1992, Schedule A1 Pt VI.

[150] *R (On the application of NUJ) v CAC* [2006] ICR 1.

variety of representational forms: quality circles, job enrichment initiatives, autonomous work teams with devolved responsibility for task design and execution, and management sponsored 'shop committees'. Despite this variety, the unifying theme of company unionism is the provision of a paternalistic mechanism whereby 'employee acceptance and cooperation in securing management's goals' can be secured,[151] without the need for employers to relinquish unilateral control of the enterprise. In essence, such participatory schemes are under the 'domination' of employers. Given the centrality of trusting cooperation to social partnership, the 'integrative' vision implicit in company unionism might seem attractive when set against the adversarial character of arms-length collective bargaining with independent unions.

The US provides an illuminating comparison in assessing the threat posed to independent unionism by 'company unions'. The most striking feature of the US pattern of worker representation is its repudiation of welfare capitalism. This is reflected in one of the cornerstones of the statutory edifice, the section 8(a)(2) ban on 'company unions'. Thus, it is an 'unfair labor practice' for an employer to 'dominate or interfere with the formation of any labor organization, or contribute any financial or other support to it'. At the time of its enactment, section 8(a)(2) was considered an inseparable counterpart of the statutory guarantee of employee free choice of bargaining representative. During the inter-war period 'the company union had become firmly established as an alternative to collective bargaining with self-organized employee associations'.[152] These employer-dominated entities proved highly durable and effective devices of union substitution, offering the promise of collective voice within the enterprise but without the 'costs and risks associated with collective bargaining. Consequently, they hold an allure against which it is difficult, if not impossible, for conventional unions to compete.'[153] Recent research lends further empirical weight to these historical concerns with union substitution by 'company unions'; Freeman and Rogers' wide-ranging analysis of worker preferences demonstrates that 'employee involvement' schemes significantly 'reduce interest in unions by giving workers more say at the workplace outside the union venue'.[154] Accordingly section 8(a)(2) was critical in eliminating anti-union employers' weapon of choice against workers' right to self-organisation. In so doing, section 8(a)(2) sealed the fate of 'company unionism' as a viable pattern of worker representation, embodying instead a preference 'for the private ordering of the employment relationship that is based on collective bargaining through self-organized and autonomous employee associations'.[155]

[151] TC Kohler, 'Models of Worker Participation: The Uncertain Significance of Section 8(a)(2)' (1986) 27 *Boston College Law Review* 499, 516.

[152] *Ibid*, 523.

[153] Note, 'Collective Bargaining as an Industrial System: An Argument against Judicial Revision of section 8(a)(2) of the National Labor Relations Act' (1983) 96 *Harvard Law Review* 1664, 1679.

[154] RB Freeman and J Rogers, *What Workers Want* (Ithaca, ILR Press, 1999) 113.

[155] Kohler, above n 151, 533.

The normative choice whether or not to outlaw company unions depends upon our underlying conception of political freedom. From the liberal perspective of negative freedom as non-interference, the ban on company unions seems an illegitimate restriction on the parties' freedom to choose their own representational arrangements. In implementing a ban on employer-dominated entities, the State has curtailed the parties' available options and in so doing they are less free than if the 'company union' option had been permitted; since intentional restrictions on choice are an evil to be avoided, this might lead us to endorse the less restrictive regulatory scheme in Schedule A1. This conclusion is bolstered by the fact that the structure of Schedule A1 is often sensitive to workers' preferences. In situations of worker dissatisfaction the ballot procedures can be triggered and the non-independent union de-recognised if the statutory support thresholds are reached. Similar concerns have shaped the US courts of appeals' rather controversial specification of criteria for identifying employer domination of labour organisations under section 8(a)(2). Where employees willingly assent to representation through non-independent unions the courts have been scrupulous in respecting employee free choice, with evidence of employee satisfaction negating a finding that the labour organisation is under employer domination.[156] This interpretive approach seems similarly informed by a conception of political freedom as non-interference. After all, if employers and workers both get what they want then there seems little justification for the law to interfere and frustrate the satisfaction of their preferences.

The debate takes a different turn when refracted through the lens of freedom as non-domination. Civic republicanism does not stigmatise the non-arbitrary exercise of State power, particularly if State power is being harnessed in support of non-domination. If workers are consenting to their own subjugation in submitting themselves to representational arrangements that are under employer domination, there is no reason for the republican State to defer to that consent. It can legitimately interfere and prevent domination without itself being a dominating presence. In so doing, freedom (understood as non-domination) is promoted rather than restricted. Such a republican understanding of freedom lay at the base of the legislator's justification for the proscription of company unions in section 8(a)(2), and it makes sense of Senator Wagner's statement that 'to argue that freedom of organization for the worker must embrace the right to select a form of organization that is not free is a contradiction in terms'.[157]

Where organisations are not free from employer domination then effective democratic contestation cannot occur. It is as if the employer is sat on both sides of the bargaining table, with the contestatory voice of workers filtered through the medium of the dominating employer. By contrast, independent unions provide an effective mode of democratic contestation. As Kohler argues, 'it is

[156] *Hertzka & Knowles v NLRB* 503 F. 2d 625 (9th circuit 1974).
[157] Cited in Kohler, above n 151, 533.

through this association that workers are afforded the means to voice and protect their own interests and, thereby, to achieve effective participation in the ordering' of the employment relation.[158] Since independent unions are built upon grass roots self-organisation they are uniquely suited to the articulation of workers' interests; organisational strength ensures that voice is audible and powerful. Civic republicans are keenly aware of the importance of voluntary associations in civil society in the promotion of non-domination as a political ideal. Widespread civility enables the realisation of democratic contestation, and the vigilant monitoring of private power, by actuating the self-organising capacities of associations in civil society. As Pettit points out, civically oriented citizens 'display a form of civility which leads them to work at organizing the group and at articulating shared grievances; in their disposition to approval and action, they embody norms of fidelity and attachment to that group'.[159] The republican State will therefore be keen to support the independent associations of civil society, such as autonomous trade unions, in encouraging the spread of such civility. As such, robust enforcement of a 'company union' ban designed to ensure the institutional autonomy of bargaining parties is critical to the realisation of freedom as non-domination; this should operate regardless of parties' preferences for representative arrangements tainted by domination.

V CONCLUSION

Civic republican citizenship offers an attractive foundation for a radical new third way in labour law. Guided by the values of community, collective self-government, and non-domination, collective bargaining assumes a central place in a civic republican industrial relations settlement. Civic republican values have figured prominently in the political rhetoric of the third way. Time and again, the republican slogans of community, civic responsibility, and democratic renewal lay at the heart of New Labour's stirring invocation of a new political era. Unfortunately, this stirring republican rhetoric failed to leave its imprint on the detailed design of New Labour's legislative programme in labour law. In respect of *community*, New Labour's reforms continued to treat unions as mere associations of individuals rather than constitutive communities of great intrinsic significance in the public realm. In respect of *democratic self-government*, the statutory recognition procedure was shaped by pluralist rather than deliberative democratic values. This has led to a public conception of collective bargaining that is democratically impoverished and ill-suited to enabling workers to regain democratic control over their working lives. In respect of *non-domination*, New Labour's conception of social partnership totally marginalises any acknowledgment of the imbalance of power between employers and workers. This has led to

158 *Ibid*, 514.
159 Pettit, above n 120, 247.

a concept of worker representation that legitimises the emergence of voice mechanisms tainted by employer domination and control. When we look at the historical development of auxiliary State intervention in Britain, set out in chapter two, this prompts an unerring sense of déjà-vu. At crucial junctures in labour law's historical development, legislators have appealed to civic rhetoric in justifying their respective programmes for reform. Then, as now, the political opportunity was missed, with the liberal centre of gravity exercising a powerful hold over legal reform agendas.

Part 3:

Evaluating the Schedule A1 Recognition Procedure

5

The Political Theory of Union Recognition Campaigns I: Liberal Neutrality and the Cultural Marketplace

I INTRODUCTION

SCHEDULE A1 embodies a democratic commitment to preference aggregation. Bargaining rights are allocated on the basis of workers' majority preferences, either through membership evidence or ballot procedures. This idea of democracy as preference aggregation fits the liberal basis of New Labour's project in collective labour law, for the 'political and economic processes by which individual preferences are combined into a social choice function are liberal modes of determining the common good'.[1] These democratic procedures create a kind of cultural marketplace for unions. The success of trade unions depends upon their attractiveness to potential adherents in the constituent workforce, and this is reflected in their ability to secure majority support.

Nevertheless, the legitimacy of the cultural marketplace depends upon unions and employers enjoying fair equality of opportunity to compete in the democratic process. From a liberal perspective, the task for regulation is to 'create a level playing field for the transmission of arguments for and against recognition'.[2] As Ruth Dukes has pointed out, this liberal task is not an easy one in the workplace:

> In a situation of unequal power, decisions that are, on the face of them, unbiased will, in reality, function to benefit the stronger party.[3]

We have already encountered similar concerns in Will Kymlicka's liberal defence of the cultural marketplace. For Kymlicka, the legitimacy of the cultural marketplace depends upon the adoption of a 'power-adjusted' notion of liberal neutrality as part of a general principle of redressing group disadvantage in civil

[1] W Kymlicka, *Contemporary Political Philosophy*, 2nd edn (Oxford, Oxford University Press, 2002) 220.

[2] S Moore, S Wood and P Davies, 'Recognition of Trade Unions—Consultation over the Access Code and Method of Bargaining' (2000) 29 *Industrial Law Journal* 406, 410.

[3] R Dukes, 'The Statutory Recognition Procedure 1999: No Bias in Favour of Recognition?' (2008) 37 *Industrial Law Journal* 236, 257.

society.[4] This chapter will assess whether the legislator, courts and Central Arbitration Committee (CAC) have done enough to ensure parity between employers and unions in the cultural marketplace that Schedule A1 creates.

Given the influence of the North American legal model on the design of the Schedule A1 recognition procedure,[5] analysis will be placed in this comparative context. Two regulatory aspects will be assessed from this comparative perspective. First, there is the question of the lawfulness of the parties' tactics during the recognition campaign. It is widely accepted that the US recognition procedure has failed because it has been unable to deal effectively with employer unfair practices. The regulatory failings of the US 'unfair practice' technique will be outlined. The most significant regulatory flaw is the problem of legal delay engendered by circuitous legal procedures. This will provide a framework for scrutinising the structure of ballot regulation in Schedule A1. While Schedule A1 avoids many of the design flaws identified in the US system, it still falls short of ensuring genuine parity. The possibility of by-passing the ballot procedure in situations of majority union membership will also be considered. Although Schedule A1 makes provision for ballot orders even where the union enjoys majority membership in the bargaining unit in three specific situations, the CAC has interpreted these exceptions restrictively. This has ensured that Schedule A1 has integrated many of the best features of the Canadian legal model by minimising the regulatory problem of legal delay.

Secondly, there is the question of union organisational access to the workforce. In the US, the statutory procedure adopts a rigid and absolutist conception of the employer's property rights. The employer enjoys an almost unfettered right to exclude union organisers from its property. By contrast, the British procedure facilitates union access to the workforce by placing the employer under a duty to grant reasonable access to the union during the ballot process. While this avoids many of the most serious regulatory failings of the US system, the British framework still falls short of achieving a level playing field in the recognition procedure.

Overall, Schedule A1 approximates more closely to the liberal ideal of a fair cultural marketplace than the US legal procedure. Nevertheless, favourable comparison with the failing US system should not breed complacency. Schedule A1 still falls short of parity in significant ways, and these regulatory failings require urgent reform if the liberal aspiration is to be realised fully. Of course, the liberal aspiration itself remains open to the civic republican critique set out and defended in chapter four. Consequently, the conclusion ends by setting out a civic challenge to the cultural marketplace model, and suggesting some regulatory implications of this endorsement of civic republican values.

[4] See ch 3.

[5] See B Towers, *Developing Recognition and Representation in the UK: How Useful is the US Model?* (London, Institute of Employment Rights, 1999).

II REGULATING THE CULTURAL MARKETPLACE I: THE PROBLEM OF UNFAIR PRACTICES

A The North American Model of 'Unfair Labor Practices'

The choice of comparative inspiration for the British recognition procedure was a curious one. The US procedure in particular is not generally regarded as having created a cultural marketplace that gives trade unions a fair opportunity to succeed. As Godard has observed, 'by the late 1950s, the US labor movement had begun what was to be a steady long term decline, with density gradually dropping to its present day levels of 13 per cent overall and 8.5 per cent in the private sector'.[6] It is now almost universally acknowledged that US employers routinely coerce and intimidate workers during recognition campaigns, and that there are insufficient legal safeguards to prevent this. According to a recent influential study of the US system:

> As of the late 1980s, one in every four elections involved unlawful dismissal of workers for union activities, an increase from one in 20 in the early 1950s. Based on NLRB [National Labor Relations Board] records, it has been estimated that, as of the mid-1990s, one out of every eighteen employees involved in union election campaigns was subjected to discharge or other discrimination intended to discourage union representation.[7]

The US procedure provides two modes for protecting worker freedom of choice from interference or restraint during the ballot procedure. First, there are a series of 'unfair labor practices' which it is illegal for employers (and unions) to engage in. The statutory framework utilised broad language in this regard, with section 8(a)(1) of the US statutory procedure declaring it illegal 'to interfere with, restrain, or coerce employees in the exercise of' employees' rights to self-organisation, to select a bargaining representative and so on. Although there was some statutory amplification of specific unfair labour practices—for example, employer discrimination to encourage or discourage union membership—the scope of unfair labour practices has been largely developed incrementally through adjudication by the labour board and appellate courts. Moreover, the Taft-Hartley amendments in 1947 entrenched employers' free speech rights, with section 8(c) declaring that 'the expressing of any views, argument, or opinion, or the dissemination thereof, whether in written, printed, graphic, or visual form, shall not constitute or be evidence of an unfair labor practice under any of the provisions of this Act, if such expression contains no threat of reprisal or force or promise of benefit'. Consequently, only expressive activity during a campaign

[6] J Godard, *Trade Union Recognition: statutory unfair labour practice regimes in the USA and Canada* (Department of Trade and Industry, Employment Relations Research Series No 29, 2004) 6.

[7] *Ibid*, 25.

that constitutes either 'threat of reprisal or force', or 'promise of benefit', can constitute an unfair labour practice. This has ensured a wide zone of legality for vigorous employer campaigning against unionisation.

Secondly, even if campaign activity does not constitute an unfair labour practice due to the employer's free speech protections, it may still be challenged through the *General Shoe Corporation* doctrine.[8] Where conduct 'creates an atmosphere which renders improbable a free choice' then the board may set aside the ballot and order a rerun ballot, because 'in election proceedings, it is the Board's function to provide a laboratory in which an experiment may be conducted, under conditions as nearly ideal as possible, to determine the uninhibited desires of the employees'.[9] In this way, the scope of substantive proscription is generally broader than under the unfair labour practice jurisdiction. Nevertheless, the remedies are also correspondingly weaker. Violation of 'laboratory conditions' without the commission of unfair labour practices warrants, at most, a rerun election. The consequent delay in determining the representative status of the union is unlikely to operate to the advantage of the union's claim.

The contrast with the Canadian legal and institutional framework, and the fortunes of Canadian trade unions operating in that distinctive regulatory environment, is striking. Although recognition laws are based predominantly on State rather than federal regulation, it is nevertheless possible to point to a distinctive Canadian 'model' that has important advantages over the US federal procedure. As Godard has pointed out, this is reflected in union success rates of 69 per cent in respect of recognition claims under the Canadian legal procedures (as compared with 48 per cent under the US procedure), with the level of unfair practice complaints against Canadian employers from one fourth to one tenth of the comparable US rate.[10] Godard has made a persuasive argument that these differences are rooted in three salient legal-institutional differences between the US and Canadian procedures. First, most of the Canadian jurisdictions permit the demonstration of majority support on the basis of membership evidence rather than insisting on a mandatory ballot procedure in all cases where the employer contests the union's support in the bargaining unit. As Godard points out, this 'effectively eliminates the problem of time delays and hence precludes employers from engaging in practices designed to undermine employee choice'.[11] Even where ballots are held these are generally subject to strict time limits.

Secondly, the regulation of employer free speech in Canada comes closer to insisting on employer neutrality towards unionisation.[12] This is reflected in the perception that all forms of employer speech have an inherently coercive

[8] *General Shoe Corporation* 77 (1948) NLRB 124.
[9] *Ibid*, 127.
[10] Godard, above n 6, 37.
[11] *Ibid*, 33–4.
[12] *Ibid*, 29.

potential given the backdrop of workers' economic dependence and subordination in the workplace. This can be contrasted with the US fixation on protecting employer free speech during the recognition campaign, and its passionate commitment to the employer's democratic right to oppose (and campaign against) unionisation. Finally, Canadian labour boards have recourse to a wider range of effective remedies in situations of egregious employer conduct, and this is coupled with more expeditious procedures to ensure speedy disposition of unfair practice cases. This avoids the problem of procedural delay in the US system, with circuitous appeals often leading to delays of up to three years in many unfair practice cases.[13]

We might add two further points to Godard's perceptive institutional analysis of North American procedures. First, the prevalence of labour board decisions in formulating the relevant standards for scrutinising the effects of employer conduct on worker free choice has incentivised dilatory litigation in the US. Over time, specific doctrines have waxed and waned, often shaped by empirical 'uncertainty concerning the effects of campaign tactics on the election process'.[14] This has generated a complex regulatory web that has been widely condemned by scholars. As Gould accounts for it:

> The problem with legal regulation of this arena is that it is simply impossible to determine the impact of propaganda on workers … Involvement in this area by the Board is at best a wasting asset, at worst, fundamentally counterproductive because of the litigation and consequent delay to the electoral process spawned by it.[15]

It is notable that Canadian statutory frameworks have tended to specify more exhaustively the types of conduct that constitute an unfair practice,[16] and this has contributed to the minimisation of legal delay by minimising the scope for speculative legal arguments.

Secondly, the US experience suggests it is misplaced to invest much intellectual energy in demarcating the elusive boundary between legitimate and illegitimate campaign activity. The principal technique deployed by anti-union employers in the US is the discriminatory discharge of union supporters in the bargaining unit, a blatantly unlawful tactic. It has been suggested that discriminatory discharges took place in one union election out of every three, and that 'one worker was illegally fired for every twenty union voters'.[17] Certainly there is widespread acknowledgement that discriminatory victimisation of union activists

[13] See WB Gould, *Labored Relations* (Cambridge Massachusetts, MIT Press, 2000) ch 13; see also Human Rights Watch, *Unfair Advantage: Workers' Freedom of Association in the United States under International Human Rights Standards* (Human Rights Watch, 2000) 18.

[14] DC Bok, 'The Regulation of Campaign Tactics in Representation Elections under the National Labor Relations Act' (1965) 78 *Harvard Law Review* 38, 41–2.

[15] WB Gould, *Agenda for Reform: Employment Relationships and the Law* (Cambridge Massachusetts, MIT Press, 1993) 157.

[16] Godard, above n 6, viii.

[17] PC Weiler, 'Hard Times for Unions: Challenging Times for Scholars' (1991) 58 *University of Chicago Law Review* 1015, 1020–21.

is 'commonplace' despite its illegality.[18] For this reason, sensible reform proposals have focused on bolstering remedies rather than expanding the doctrinal reach of the regulatory framework, arguing for rapid injunctive relief for discharged workers and the availability of punitive damages as an effective deterrent against egregious employer violations;[19] and on eliminating the opportunities for employers to engage in such activities in the first place by ensuring an expedited legal process subject to strict time limits.

B Unfair Practices and Ballot Regulation under Schedule A1

To what extent has campaign regulation in Schedule A1 been successful in establishing a fair cultural marketplace for trade unions? Compared with the US, union win rates have been relatively high. In the CAC's study of Schedule A1's first five years, the CAC found that recognition had been supported in 70 out of 110 CAC commissioned ballots.[20] In 2006–07 there were 15 ballots, with unions winning just under half of them,[21] and in 2007–08 the union was successful in 70 per cent of ballots.[22] Furthermore, the CAC was awarding recognition without a ballot (where the union had majority membership and no qualifying conditions applied) in a significant proportion of cases.[23] On the other hand, Ewing, Moore and Wood's influential study concluded that in ballots where the union was unsuccessful, employers used two or more unfair practices in nine out of 10 cases.[24] This suggests that unions are not as successful as they might otherwise have been in a well-designed regulatory environment.

In the TUC's evidence to the *DTI Review of the Employment Relations Act 1999* it provided persuasive evidence of employers engaging in a range of unfair tactics designed to subvert workers' freedom of choice. These included 'placing workers under surveillance as they walk past union organisers outside the workplace, issuing threats that they will close or re-locate the business rather than face recognition … packing union access meetings with management personnel, giving workers the option of going home early when there is a meeting organised, dismissing activists or declaring their jobs to be redundant, intimidating workers on a one-to-one basis'.[25] Overt hostility to unionisation was sometimes coupled with so-called 'velvet glove' techniques. These sought to

18 Human Rights Watch, above n 13, 18.

19 For the classic work in this vein, see PC Weiler, 'Promises to Keep: Securing Workers' Rights to Self-Organisation under the NLRA' (1983) 96 *Harvard Law Review* 1769.

20 *CAC Annual Report 2004–2005*.

21 *CAC Annual Report 2006–2007*, 13.

22 *CAC Annual Report 2007–2008*, 8.

23 See, eg, 2007–08 where there were 10 decisions to declare recognition without a ballot, which was 'consistent with the pattern over previous years': *CAC Annual Report 2007–2008*, 8.

24 K Ewing, S Moore and S Wood, *Unfair Labour Practices: Trade Union Recognition and Employer Resistance* (London, Institute of Employment Rights, 2003) 48.

25 TUC, *Modern Rights for Modern Workplaces* (TUC, 2002) para 78.

undermine collective organisation through conferring enhanced pay and benefits during the ballot procedure, spontaneous resolution of long-standing grievances or the implementation of alternative channels for worker participation bypassing independent unions. Other empirical studies of employer responses to union recognition claims supported the TUC's findings.[26]

In the Employment Relations Act (ERA) 2004 the Government introduced radical reform of the ballot procedure. In particular, it enacted a new 'unfair practice' jurisdiction to be administered by the CAC in the period between a ballot order and the holding of the ballot.[27] Prior to this, workers had been protected from detriment on certain specified grounds related to the ballot procedure.[28] The individualist nature of these protective rights undermined their efficacy from a collective perspective. Detriment had to be referable to the specific activities of the individual worker.[29] This placed an employer's response to the union's organisational activities beyond the protective scope of the right, including threats of closure or relocation addressed to a 'captive audience' of the constituent bargaining unit. Furthermore, there was no provision for a collective remedy. If individual victimisation led to the failure of the union's recognition claim, individual compensation was no substitute for joint regulation. The 'unfair practice' provisions were designed to fill this collective lacuna.

The analysis will proceed in three stages. First, we will examine the legal concept of unfair practices under Schedule A1, focusing first upon the definitional structure of the new 'unfair practice' provisions, and thereafter upon the CAC's interpretation of those provisions. Thus far, there have only been seven complaints under the 'unfair practice' jurisdiction (with one of those withdrawn). None of those complaints have been upheld by the CAC. Secondly, the CAC's general supervisory jurisdiction over the ballot procedure (arising independently of the unfair practice provisions) will be examined. In relation to the unfair practice provisions, there are serious problems of definition and interpretation that need to be surmounted before we can be confident that a level playing field has been achieved. In relation to the CAC's general supervisory jurisdiction over the ballot procedure, the CAC has been careful in keeping a tight rein on its power to order re-run ballots. This has been positive from a cultural marketplace perspective in minimising the prospects for procedural delay. Thirdly, we will consider the scope for allocating bargaining rights without a ballot in situations of majority union membership. Generally speaking, the CAC has ensured that the statutory exceptions have not swallowed up the general rule that recognition

[26] See, eg, S Moore, 'Union mobilization and employer counter-mobilization in the statutory recognition process', in J Kelly and P Willman (eds), *Union Organization and Activity* (London, Routledge, 2004) 7.

[27] TULRCA 1992, Schedule A1 para 27A.

[28] TULRCA 1992, Schedule A1 paras 156–65.

[29] *Therm-A-Stor Ltd v Atkins and Carrington* [1983] IRLR 78.

should follow majority membership without the need for a ballot. This has been crucial in avoiding some of the worst regulatory failings of the dilatory US system.

(i) ERA 2004 and the Unfair Practice Regime

(a) Problems of Definition The 'unfair practice' provision is symmetrical, applying to both employers and unions for the duration of the ballot procedure. The substantive definition of 'unfair practice' is articulated in paragraph 27A(2), which provides an exhaustive specification of the different modes of 'unfair practice'. Paragraph 27A(2)(a)–(b) addresses certain 'velvet glove' tactics, such that financial inducements 'in return for the worker's agreement to vote in a particular way or to abstain from voting' and the making of 'outcome-specific' offers related to ballot result now constitute an 'unfair practice'. Paragraph 27A(2)(c)–(f), by contrast, addresses coercive union suppression tactics, covering different forms of individual victimisation; thus, discipline, subjection to detriment and dismissal (or threats thereof) perpetrated 'with a view to influencing the result of the ballot' now constitute unfair practices. Further, coercion (or threats thereof) to elicit disclosure of voting intention is also an unfair practice. Paragraph 27A(2)(g) is a broader, 'catch-all' provision extending the reach of 'unfair practice' to cover use or attempted use of 'undue influence' in order to influence the ballot result. For a complaint to be 'well-founded', the substantive definition of unfair practice is linked to a condition that 'the use of that practice changed or was likely to change' the voting intention or behaviour of a worker entitled to vote in the ballot.[30]

The provision envisages a collective enforcement mechanism, so that the complaint must be made by either the employer or union: the provision does not confer any rights on workers, though this is without prejudice to any individual rights that a worker may have. The collective enforcement mechanism is also correlative to a collective remedy. If the CAC finds that the complaint is 'well-founded', then it *must* make a declaration to that effect and it *may* order the party to take action to mitigate the effects of the unfair practice. The CAC also has an explicit power to cancel or annul a ballot and order a re-run ballot.[31] Ultimately, for certain very serious infringements of the unfair practice provisions or further commission of unfair practices after a CAC declaration or order, the CAC may further order that the party either be recognised or not recognised, depending on the identity of the offending party.

On its face, the substantive coverage is inclusive enough to *potentially* encapsulate many of the employer abuses identified by the TUC. However, there are three important problems with these new unfair practice provisions. First, the timeframe of the unfair practice provision is limited to the ballot procedure. Yet

[30] Schedule A1, para 27B(4)(b).
[31] Schedule A1, para 27C(3)(b).

unfair practices in the lengthy gap between application acceptance and ballot order may be effective in thwarting incipient support for the union. Moreover, the employer may also utilise unfair practices before a recognition application even reaches the Schedule A1 procedure. This might be sufficient to chill support for the union before it is able to secure the necessary preliminary support for an admissible statutory application.

Secondly, a comparative perspective casts doubt on the effectiveness of the remedies for unfair practices. One possibility is a re-run ballot. This raises the spectre of legal delay in the resolution of the recognition claim.[32] Its predictable effect is to expand the opportunities for hostile employers to continue aggressive campaigning against the union. Another possibility is a remedial bargaining order in cases of serious and recurrent employer unfair practices. Evidence from the US on similar remedial 'Gissel' bargaining orders highlights the limited effectiveness of such remedies.[33] Thus, Weiler argues, 'Gissel' bargaining orders contain a 'catch-22' for unions:

> The bargaining order has been issued because the employer's behaviour is thought to have so thoroughly cowed the employees that they cannot express their true desires ... But all the order can do is license the union to bring negotiations to the point at which its leadership must ask those same employees to put their jobs on the line by going on strike.[34]

Substantive remedies such as compulsory unilateral arbitration may be better suited to dealing with serious unfair practices.

Thirdly, the substantive definition of unfair practice falls short of the desired level of legal certainty. In certain respects, the exhaustive specification of particular modes of 'unfair practice' set out in paragraph 27A(2) is to be welcomed. This avoids the dysfunctional US tendency to specify vague statutory standards and then leaving these to be filled out incrementally through adjudication. However, the broad and inclusive category of 'undue influence' in 27A(2)(g) departs from this pattern of clear statutory definition. There is no statutory elaboration of what constitutes 'undue influence', and the recent definitional amplification of 'unfair practice' in the Code of Practice dealing with unfair practices does little to mitigate this uncertainty. This uncertainty is exacerbated by the condition that, in order for the complaint to be 'well-founded', the CAC must be 'satisfied that the use of that practice changed or was likely to change' a worker's voting intention or behaviour. This inevitably draws the CAC into an

32 See D H Pollitt, 'NLRB Re-run Elections: A Study' (1963) 41 *North Carolina Law Review* 209. In Pollitt's valuable study of re-run ballots, he found that a different result was achieved in the re-run ballot in only a minority of cases where the initial ballot had been set aside on the basis of unfair campaign practices. Significant delay in holding the re-run ballot made a different ballot outcome less likely still. On this basis, he concluded (at 223) that 'some employer unfair electioneering practices (plant-closing threats, for example) can seldom be dissipated' in a ballot re-run.

33 *NLRB v Gissel Packing Co* 395 US 575 (1969).

34 Weiler, above n 19, 1794–5.

empirical minefield it is ill-equipped to navigate. For example, in an influential empirical study of individual voting behaviour in representation ballots in the US, the authors concluded that campaign activity had a minimal effect on employee voting patterns.[35] By contrast, other scholars have argued that employer unfair practices do have a tangible and significant impact on voting behaviour.[36] As yet, the debate is inconclusive. Indeed, it may be impossible to formulate any general propositions. As one seasoned observer of the US scene has put it, 'a speech found to be coercive when made by an employer to a South Carolina mill hand may have nothing resembling that impact on a Detroit or Chicago Teamster-affiliated truck driver—indeed the speech may engender militancy rather than produce intimidation'.[37] It is certainly arguable that these definitional problems have had a constraining effect on the CAC's role in interpreting and applying the 'unfair practice' provisions. This has had the effect of diminishing the practical relevance of the 'unfair practices' to vanishing point.

(b) Problems of Interpretation One of the more surprising aspects of the CAC's work has been the sparse incidence of unfair practice complaints. All but one of the complaints has involved a union's complaint against the employer, and in every case the complaint has not been upheld by the CAC. An analysis of CAC decisions indicates that Panels are adopting an extremely cautious interpretive approach. The CAC has stated that there are three necessary criteria that must be satisfied for a complaint to be upheld: (i) the conduct must fall within the action-descriptions set out in paragraph 27 A(2)(a)–(g) (for example, it must be 'undue influence' or an 'outcome-specific' offer); (ii) the conduct must be deployed with a view to influencing the result of the ballot; (iii) the conduct must have changed or be likely to change the voting intention of a worker in the bargaining unit. We might term these three elements *conduct*, *intention*, and *effect*; and each of them has to be satisfied through a strict insistence on specific evidence. While some of the CAC decisions have dealt with insubstantial allegations,[38] other decisions have been less clear-cut and seem to have set the evidential bar for a successful complaint exceptionally high. Let us take each of these elements in turn.

In respect of *conduct*, some of the Panel decisions indicate an unduly strict approach. In *CWU and Cable & Wireless Services UK Ltd*,[39] the CEO had written to workers indicating that they would receive maximum bonus payments following the publication of the company's annual results. In the same email, the CEO had encouraged workers to vote against recognition in the forthcoming ballot. The

[35] JG Getman, SB Goldberg and JB Herman, *Union Representation Elections: Law and Reality* (New York, Russell Sage, 1976).

[36] Weiler, above n 19.

[37] Gould, above n 15, 156–7.

[38] See, eg, the employer's complaint of union unfair practices in *Prospect & PCS and National Maritime Museum* TUR1/529/2006, which seemed insubstantial on the facts.

[39] TUR1/570/2007.

CAC rejected the union's claim that this constituted 'undue influence', setting out its reasoning in the following way:

> The Panel can understand how the Union comes to this view but it cannot agree. For there to be undue influence there would need to be evidence that the employer was threatening or inducing employees by linking the bonus payment to the outcome of the ballot. Apart from being in the same letter the two statements on bonus and the ballot were not connected.[40]

This reasoning is problematic. Insisting on a linkage between bonus payments and ballot outcomes is correct in the context of paragraph 27A (2)(a)–(b) which proscribes financial inducements 'in return for the worker's agreement to vote in a particular way or to abstain from voting' and the making of 'outcome-specific' offers. An 'outcome-specific' offer is an 'offer to pay money or give money's worth which is conditional on the issuing by the CAC of a declaration that the union is entitled to be recognised or is not entitled to be recognised'.[41] However, the union did not allege a breach of these particular paragraphs. Instead, it had alleged 'undue influence' which is a broader concept than either paragraph 27A (2)(a) or (b). Indeed, the Code of Practice states that undue influence encapsulates 'the introduction of higher pay or better conditions in the ballot period … if this is not the normal time for reviewing pay or if there is not some other reason unconnected with the ballot for raising pay'.[42] The importation of a 'linking' requirement between the grant of financial benefits and the outcome of the ballot process in the context of 'undue influence' is unnecessarily stringent.

Another example of undue stringency in respect of 'conduct' can be found in *Unite—the Union and Kettle Foods Ltd.*[43] Here the union alleged that the employer had utilised compulsory 'captive audience' speeches during its campaign. The Panel concluded that 'we do not consider that the Union's *allegations* constitute undue influence under paragraph 27A (2)(g).'[44] So even if the union's factual allegations were found to be substantiated they would not constitute 'undue influence'. While paragraph 61 of the Code of Practice only refers to the importance of *small group meetings* (rather than large meetings of the whole workforce) being voluntary rather than compulsory, it certainly seems to be within the spirit of 'undue influence' that any form of coerced 'captive audience' speech should be proscribed.

Similar interpretive tendencies can also be discerned in *TGWU and Comet Group plc*, where the employer had been assisted by anti-union consultants in the

40 *Ibid*, para 29.

41 DTI, *Code of Practice: Access and unfair practices during recognition and derecognition ballots* (Department of Trade and Industry, 2005) para 53.

42 *Ibid*, para 56.

43 *Unite—the Union and Kettle Foods Ltd* TUR1/557/2007.

44 *Ibid*, para 14.

preparation of campaign material.[45] The employer had not disclosed this assistance in respect of the distributed material. In the Panel's view, the campaign material had not been inappropriately anonymised since it had been signed by company managers, and further 'there is no evidence that the Company asked the consultants to campaign anonymously on the Company's behalf'.[46] Strictly speaking, the Panel's view was in accordance with the Code of Practice. This envisages that consultants should disclose their status when communicating directly with the workforce.[47] It is silent on whether there should be disclosure of the consultant's activities where the consultant is acting in an indirect advisory capacity. Nevertheless, given the highly effective nature of consultants in fending off unionisation,[48] it is certainly arguable that the undisclosed use of consultants to give advice on employer strategy and communication *should* constitute 'undue influence'.

A more general point relates to the normative significance of the Code's central assumption that partisan and vigorous campaigning by the parties is a normal and legitimate activity:

> Campaigning is inherently a partisan activity. Each party is therefore unlikely to put across a completely balanced message to the workforce, and some over-statement or exaggeration may well occur.[49]

This model of competing political parties is a central element in the democratic model upon which the statutory procedure is based, enshrining the legitimacy of the employer's role as an oppositional force to the trade union. This normative theory of legitimate employer activity indicates a closer alignment with the US rather than the Canadian model, since the Canadian model perceives the need for employer neutrality during the recognition process.[50] Its practical effect has been to set a high threshold of toleration for the employer's campaigning activity. Thus, in *Unite—the Union and Kettle Foods Ltd* the CAC invoked the Code of Practice to justify its conclusion that the employer's exaggerated statement to vulnerable migrant workers that the trade union would generate pressure upon them to engage in strike action was simply part of the rough and tumble of partisan democratic politics, and that no unfair practice had been committed.[51] Similarly in *TGWU and Comet Group plc* the CAC pointed to 'the very important point made in paragraph 65 of the *Code of Practice* that "campaigning is inherently a partisan activity"'.[52] Where robust campaign material fell within the 'range of normal campaigning activity' it would not constitute an unfair practice. Legal entrenchment of the employer's democratic right to oppose unionisation

[45] *TGWU and Comet Group plc* TUR1/501/2006.
[46] *Ibid*, para 23.
[47] *Ibid*, para 58.
[48] J Logan, *US Anti-Union Consultants: A Threat to the Rights of British Workers* (TUC, 2008).
[49] DTI, above n 41, para 65.
[50] See Godard, above n 12.
[51] Para 14.
[52] Para 26.

makes the legal protection of employer free speech one of the central objectives of recognition campaign regulation.

In respect of *intention*, identification of the employer's purpose in utilising certain forms of campaign conduct has been similarly problematic. To recap, actions need to be engaged in *with a view to influencing the result of the ballot* to constitute an unfair practice. This particular criterion was analysed by the CAC in *GMB and JF Stone Investments Ltd t/a The American Dry Cleaning Company*.[53] Here a lead union activist in a recognition campaign had had disciplinary proceedings instituted against her. The union alleged that this constituted an unfair practice. The employer argued that the disciplinary proceedings had been brought due to legitimate concerns about the worker's inadequate performance. The CAC concluded that the criterion of intention had not been demonstrated in this case:

> The fact that the Employer kept the proceedings entirely confidential throughout leads us to conclude that the disciplinary and associated action was not done with a view to influencing the ballot since if the balloting constituency were unaware of the action, how would they be influenced? . . . The union was not able to demonstrate or even speculate, other than in the most general and unspecified terms, how the employer was seeking to influence the result of the ballot by its disciplinary action against Ms Lis.[54]

In fairness to the CAC panel, the evidence set out in its written decision was finely balanced. Despite this, its understanding of 'influence' on ballot outcomes seems unduly restrictive. The fact that constituent voters were unaware of the disciplinary proceedings against the activist does not mean that there was no attempt to influence the ballot result. 'Decapitating' the main activists in a campaign through discriminatory victimisation is a powerful technique for stalling the union's organisational momentum. Although the Panel concluded that the activist did not feel 'affected or curtailed in her campaigning activities' that is nothing to the point.[55] What matters under the second criterion is the employer's purpose, *not* the effects of its actions.

In respect of *effects*, the excessive stringency of the statutory test is very pronounced. This hurdle is particularly difficult for the union to overcome in unfair practice proceedings. In *CWU and Cable & Wireless* the Panel noted that 'it cannot take account of anonymous letters from employees forwarded by the Union'.[56] Furthermore, in every case where this criterion has been relevant the complainant has failed to adduce sufficient evidence to demonstrate that the actions changed or were likely to change the voting intention of a worker in the bargaining unit entitled to vote. It seems implicit in the decisions that only direct evidence from workers that their voting intentions were in fact affected would suffice to meet this criterion. In situations where the employer is overtly opposed

[53] *GMB and JF Stone Investments Ltd t/a The American Dry Cleaning Co* TUR1/492/2006.
[54] *Ibid*, para 23.
[55] *Ibid*.
[56] Para 26.

to unionisation, which is likely to be the case in any unfair practice situation, it seems unlikely that workers would be prepared to take the risk of submitting unanonymised statements to the CAC. The statutory wording does not necessitate such a strict approach. It is sufficient if the actions are 'likely' to change a voter's intention. This seems to allow for the possibility of an objective test, with the CAC ascertaining whether a *reasonable* worker might change their voting intention in the circumstances outlined in the complaint. This would bring the British scheme into closer alignment with a positive element of the US framework, which holds that it is sufficient for the Board's General Counsel to demonstrate that the employer's action would *tend* to coerce a *reasonable* employee.[57]

In every case (bar one) where there has been an unfair practice complaint against the employer (none of which have yet been upheld), the trade union has lost the subsequent ballot by a decisive margin. While it is not possible to demonstrate conclusively that this was because of the alleged unfair practices, the pattern nevertheless seems suspiciously revealing; particularly since the CAC must have already concluded in the preliminary stage of the union's application that a majority of the bargaining unit were likely to favour recognition of the union. What conclusions can be gleaned from the very low incidence of successful unfair practice complaints? Does this indicate that they are superfluous legal techniques and that employer interference with worker free choice is comparatively rare in the British context?

There are two possible explanations for the apparent practical insignificance of the unfair practice provisions. First, it is possible that the preference-shaping effects of the 'unfair practice' provisions have been so pronounced that employers have begun to desist from unfair practices in order to avoid unfair practice complaints. This does not seem plausible, particularly in the light of recent evidence of employers' continuing utilisation of union resistance strategies.[58]

Secondly, it should be remembered that the unfair practice provisions are only operative across a very narrow timeframe (the period between the ballot order and the holding of the ballot). Consequently, employers may routinely resort to unfair practices with impunity to stymie unionisation before Schedule A1 becomes a realistic option for the union. This is consistent with the pattern of applications for statutory recognition and the level of voluntary recognition arrangements. Both of these have peaked and now seem to be tailing off, suggesting that the pool of easy cases involving 'soft' employers is starting to dry up, leaving unions exposed to more challenging workplace environments where unfair practices are likely to be more prevalent.[59] Hostile employers therefore

[57] RA Gorman and MW Finkin, *Labor Law: Unionization and Collective Bargaining*, 2nd edn (St Paul Minnesota, Thomson West, 2004) 150.

[58] Logan, above n 48.

[59] On voluntary recognition deals in recent years, see Dukes, above n 3, 260; G Gall, Trade Union Recognition in Britain: An Emerging Crisis for Trade Unions?' (2007) 28 *Economic and Industrial Democracy* 78.

have significant opportunities to *lawfully* prevent unionisation from occurring at the outset of an organisational drive, thereby preventing the union from mustering sufficient initial support to even trigger Schedule A1. If this is occurring, those employers most in need of targeting by an unfair practice provision are least likely to be caught by its sphere of operation. Significantly, the narrow timeframe of the statutory unfair practices has been criticised by the International Labour Organization's (ILO's) Committee of Experts as incompatible with the UK's international obligations under ILO Convention 98 for precisely this reason.[60]

All of this supports the view that urgent reform of the unfair practice provision is necessary to ensure it makes more than a marginal contribution to ensuring genuine freedom of choice for workers.

(ii) The CAC's General Supervisory Jurisdiction over the Ballot Procedure

The CAC also exercises a general supervisory jurisdiction over the ballot procedure, and on this basis it has the power to order a re-run ballot in certain circumstances. In *TGWU and King Asia Foods Ltd* the union won majority support in a postal ballot of the constituent bargaining unit.[61] However, the union failed by three votes to reach the 40 per cent threshold. The union alleged the ballot result had been tainted by a series of administrative errors on the part of the Qualified Independent Person (QIP). Furthermore, the union claimed this had been compounded by the employer's breach of the access order and a 'climate of fear and intimidation which was evident during the ballot.' The CAC found that four workers may not have received ballot papers in adequate time to return them. The allegations relating to the employer's conduct were, however, unsubstantiated. On the basis that not all workers 'had a proper opportunity to cast an effective vote' and that, in consequence, 'the outcome of the ballot was materially affected', the CAC declared the ballot result void and ordered a re-run ballot. The Panel considered this inherent power to be derived from the CAC's general duty under paragraph 171 Schedule A1. This assertion of jurisdiction by the CAC left a number of questions unanswered. What kind of threshold did 'materially affected' envisage? Would it be satisfied if it could be demonstrated that at least one worker had been denied the opportunity to vote? Or did it necessitate demonstration that the overall result of the ballot might have been different? Furthermore, on the facts in *King Asia Foods Ltd* the Panel did not find the union's complaints about the employer's conduct to be well founded. But if they had been, might this have triggered a ballot re-run if the CAC speculated the employer's 'unfair practices' may have materially affected the ballot result?

[60] Dukes, *ibid*, 262.

[61] TUR1/111/2001. There was also a ballot re-run order in *TGWU and Economic Skips Ltd* TUR1/121/2001 as a result of administrative deficiencies on the part of the QIP.

In a carefully reasoned decision the CAC in *GMB & URTU and Ultraframe (UK) Ltd* clarified the basis and limits of its supervisory jurisdiction over the ballot procedure.[62] Here the union had won majority support amongst those voting but fell short of the 40 per cent threshold by four votes. However, five workers had not received ballot papers and had no alternative means for registering their vote. These workers testified that they would have voted in favour of recognition. On these facts the CAC ordered a re-run ballot. The CAC reasoned that its jurisdictional power was derived from paragraph 23 (2) of the Schedule, which sets out the character of ballot it is required to arrange. The statutory ballot has three elements: it must be secret, it must ask the correct question, and it must be addressed to the workers constituting the bargaining unit. The ballot must therefore be defective in one of these three ways before the CAC may then consider whether to invalidate the ballot and order a fresh one. In this case the ballot had not addressed the question to all of the constituent members of the bargaining unit. This was not, however, sufficient to trigger a re-run.

In deciding whether to take this step the CAC must have regard to its overarching duty to promote 'fair and efficient practices' in paragraph 171 of the Schedule. In the context of ballot reruns, this duty required the CAC to balance 'the desirability of giving every worker a fair opportunity to vote' against the danger of 'producing a set of rules for the conduct of postal ballots which make it easy for the losing party opportunistically to seek a re-ballot.'[63] In the circumstances of this case the union needed to demonstrate that the workers who did not receive a ballot paper had no reasonable alternative opportunity to register a vote *and* would have voted for the union had they been given such an opportunity, *and* that this would have affected the overall outcome of the ballot. The reasoning in the Panel decision was upheld by the Court of Appeal, Buxton LJ commenting that 'the CAC, not the courts, is intended to be the decision making body in the specialised area of industrial relations.'[64]

This approach is to be welcomed. It clarifies the uncertainty of the earlier Panel decisions, making it clear that a very high threshold needs to be reached before the CAC will invalidate the ballot result and order a re-run. The standard situation triggering a ballot re-run order will generally involve serious error in the administration of the ballot procedure, as in *King Asia Foods Ltd*, *Ultraframe (UK) Ltd*, and *Economic Skips Ltd*. This will curtail any over-extension of the remedial principle articulated in *King Asia Foods Ltd*. The importance of preserving the exceptional character of the remedy is underscored when tracing the fate of the

[62] TUR1/313/2003.
[63] *Ibid*, para 30.
[64] *R (on the application of Ultraframe (UK) Ltd) v CAC* [2005] EWCA Civ 560, para 16.

union's recognition claim in each of these cases. On the occasions where there has been a re-run ballot, the union has fared significantly worse in the second ballot.[65]

(iii) Minimising Legal Delay: Regulatory and Reconstructive Conceptions of Statutory Recognition

Legal delay (and its avoidance) provides the key to understanding the significance of design differences between the US and Canadian statutory procedures, and this is crucial in understanding the relative success of Canadian unions in invoking their statutory rights. In a controversial reversal of its White Paper commitment to automatic recognition in situations of majority membership,[66] New Labour specified three qualifications to the automatic award of recognition in situations of majority union membership. In this way, Schedule A1 incorporated distinct elements from the US and Canadian statutory models, corresponding to a distinction between 'regulatory' and 'reconstructive' statutory design.[67] The 'regulatory' model is characteristic of the US system. It envisages the allocation of bargaining rights through the exclusive mechanism of a democratic ballot procedure. Employer and union compete in the fashion of political parties to secure the allegiance of a majority within the constituent bargaining unit. The State's role is confined to regulating the parties' campaign tactics, usually through the technique of an unfair labour practice jurisdiction, to ensure workers' freedom of choice is protected from interference or restraint during the ballot process.

'Regulatory' design has been spectacularly unsuccessful. The US system is beset by spiralling employer unfair practices that the law is ill-equipped to stem. The 'reconstructive' model, by contrast, is characteristic of the Canadian approach. 'Reconstructive' statutory design resists the logic of the democratic turn in allocating bargaining rights. Instead, the scope for employer influence is minimised by allocating bargaining rights where there is demonstrated majority support on the basis of union membership cards or expedited ballots subject to strict statutory time limits. Often the union will be certified as bargaining representative before the employer is even aware that organisational activity is afoot. Defenders of the 'reconstructive' model point to the far lower incidence of

[65] In *King Asia Foods Ltd* the union won majority support but failed by three votes to achieve the 40% threshold. In the second ballot 68.8% voted against the union's claim. In *Economic Skips Ltd* the union won majority support in the ballot and 46.7% of those entitled to vote in the bargaining unit supported the union's claim. In a spectacular reversal of fortunes, 88.6% voted against the union in the second ballot. Only 8.5% of those entitled to vote in the bargaining unit voted in favour of the union.

[66] For discussion, see T Novitz and P Skidmore, *Fairness at Work: A Critical Analysis of the Employment Relations Act 1999 and its Treatment of Collective Rights* (Oxford, Hart Publishing, 2001) 92–3.

[67] PC Weiler, *Governing the Workplace* (Cambridge Massachusetts, Harvard University Press, 1993) 241–73.

employer unfair practices and, as a consequence of this, the far greater success of Canadian unions in gaining statutory certification.[68]

One critical question has been the extent to which the balance between the 'reconstructive' and 'regulatory' features of Schedule A1 would be maintained by the CAC. The statutory procedure allows for the allocation of bargaining rights without a ballot where the union has majority membership. This 'reconstructive' mechanism is subject to three qualifying conditions which function as a gateway into the 'regulatory' ballot procedure, and the CAC has been the principal gatekeeper. Analysis of CAC decision-making indicates that it has been scrupulous in ensuring that ballot orders in situations of majority membership remain the exception rather than the rule. Thus has ensured that Schedule A1 has avoided many of the regulatory problems that have plagued the US system of ballot exclusivity, and it has harnessed the best features of the Canadian model.

The CAC's report on the first five years of the Schedule's operation indicated there had been 57 applications for recognition based on majority membership in the bargaining unit,[69] with the CAC awarding recognition without a ballot in two thirds of these cases. More recently, the CAC has continued to treat the exceptions to 'automatic' recognition in situations of majority membership as precisely that: narrowly confined exceptions to the general rule that absent specific relevant evidence, majority membership ordinarily justifies recognition without a ballot.[70] It is fair to say the CAC has adopted a rigorous, evidence-based approach under each of these qualifying conditions. Simple assertions by an employer that a ballot would be desirable have generally been rejected by the CAC, which has instead insisted on specific evidence and arguments that the qualifying conditions apply. This is demonstrated by the CAC's interpretation of paragraphs 22(4)(b) and 22(4)(c). These two qualifying conditions are triggered where there is evidence negating the linkage between union membership and support for collective bargaining. Under 22(4)(b) the CAC must order a ballot if 'the CAC has evidence, which it considers to be credible, from a significant number of the union members within the bargaining unit that they do not want the union (or unions) to conduct collective bargaining on their behalf'; under 22(4)(c) the ballot trigger is that 'membership evidence is produced which leads the CAC to conclude that there are doubts whether a significant number of the union members within the bargaining unit want the union (or unions) to conduct collective bargaining on their behalf'.[71]

[68] *Ibid*, 255.

[69] *CAC Annual Report 2004–2005*, 16.

[70] In 2006–07 the CAC declared recognition without a ballot in 13 cases: see *CAC Annual Report 2006–2007*, 13; in 2007–08 the CAC declared recognition without a ballot in 10 cases: see *CAC Annual Report 2007–2008*, 8.

[71] The concept of 'membership evidence' is amplified in para 22(5). Membership evidence under para 22(4)(c) relates specifically to the circumstances in which workers *became* union members or to the duration of their union membership.

(a) Paragraph 22(4)(c) CAC scrutiny of evidence has been particularly strict under 22(4)(c). Employers have sometimes asserted that workers might join unions for reasons unrelated to union recognition such as individual representation or friendly society functions. The CAC has been forthright in rejecting these speculative assertions.[72] Instead, the CAC has adopted a working presumption that, in the absence of specific evidence to the contrary, workers join unions to achieve collective bargaining. Neither is the CAC easily persuaded that specific countervailing evidence is present. Thus, the practice of offering reduced subscriptions to induce union membership in the absence of recognition has not been found to constitute such evidence.[73] This displays a perceptive understanding of the recruitment difficulties faced by unions in non-recognised workplaces where membership *is* less valuable in virtue of the union's inability to fulfil its regulatory functions prior to recognition. Similarly, allegations of union intimidation and the deployment of aggressive recruitment tactics to induce membership have also been carefully scrutinised by the CAC for an evidential basis. In all of the cases where this has been raised the employer has failed to discharge the burden of providing persuasive evidence.[74]

The CAC has maintained this distinction between assertion and evidence in its more recent decisions. Thus, in *GMB and Vinci Park (UK) Services Ltd* the employer argued that one member had only recently joined the union and that this raised doubts over that member's commitment to collective bargaining.[75] Moreover, the employer drew attention to ambiguities in the union's campaign literature where the union had stated it would negotiate improvements in terms and conditions of employment, whereas the statutory procedure merely conferred a right to bargain about pay, hours, and holidays. Consequently, the employer argued that support for statutory union recognition could not be deduced from trade union membership. The CAC rejected both claims as disclosing no evidence to negate

[72] See *UNIFI and Phillipine National Bank* TUR1/141/2001, where the employer's speculative assertion that workers might join the union for reasons other than recognition did 'not provide *evidence* that members joined the Union for reasons other than recognition' (emphasis added).

[73] *ISTC and Mission Foods* TUR1/256/2003 at para 38; *NUJ and AOL (UK) Ltd* TUR1/424/2005 at para 28. Though compare *AEEU v Huntleigh Healthcare Ltd* TUR1/19/2000, for an early CAC decision where the Panel accepted uncritically the employer's argument that free membership was evidence negating support for recognition. The deferential stance to the employer's position exemplified in *Huntleigh Healthcare Ltd* is rather out of line with the stricter approach taken in later decisions.

[74] In *Amicus and Gledhill Water Storage Ltd* TUR1/342/2004 the evidence related to signed statements by managerial staff that workers had complained about union recruitment tactics. The Panel concluded 'unsupported statements lodged by members of the company's own management team are, by themselves, not persuasive.' See also *NUJ and AOL (UK) Ltd* (above n 52) at para 30. In accordance with the narrow definition of relevant membership evidence under para 22(5) of Schedule A1 the CAC has also rejected evidence that union members changed their mind about supporting recognition during the operation of the statutory procedure. This was not evidence related to the circumstances of their joining or duration of their membership: see *Amicus and Premdor Crosby Ltd* TUR1/343/2004. It might, of course, be relevant evidence under either of the other two qualifying conditions.

[75] *GMB and Vinci Park (UK) Services Ltd* TUR1/496/2006.

the linkage between union membership and collective bargaining. Once again, the CAC was sensitive to the recruitment difficulties faced by non-recognised unions:

> It is well known that workers are often reluctant to join trade unions which do not have recognition rights in relation to them and so that a worker might be reluctant to join a non-recognised union until it was clear that the union had a significant chance of achieving recognition.[76]

This reflects the default position that in the absence of specific evidence to the contrary, referable to particular facts in the specific case, 'membership of a union can be accepted as indicative of that person's likely support for collective bargaining on his or her behalf by that union with his or her employer'.[77] Speculation that individuals might have joined for reasons other than collective bargaining, such as individual representation in disciplinary procedures, did not constitute specific evidence that that was their factual motive for joining the union.[78] Relevant evidence might include 'free membership obtained, other inducements proffered, or membership for personal professional reasons'[79] but it has been rare for employers to adduce such evidence successfully.

(b) Paragraph 22(4)(b) The CAC has also adopted this strict evidence-based approach to the qualifying condition under paragraph 22(4)(b). Under the pre-ERA 2004 definition the CAC was required to hold a ballot where 'a significant number of the union members within the bargaining unit inform the CAC that they do not want the union to conduct collective bargaining on their behalf'. What of the situation where union members so inform the CAC, through the intermediation of their employer, in circumstances raising a suspicion this has been orchestrated and manipulated by an anti-union employer? Could the CAC scrutinise the extent to which the letters were an accurate reflection of freely expressed workers' preferences? In early decisions the CAC tended to adopt a circumscribed remit. If it had been so informed then this, without more, triggered the qualifying condition.[80]

In *TSSA and Gatwick Express* the CAC adopted a far bolder stance.[81] Seven letters had been collected from union members by personnel managers then sent on to the CAC. Each letter was on company-headed notepaper and had been expressed in identical terms. The Panel considered these letters had no evidential weight, seemingly importing a requirement that the letters be received *directly* by

[76] *Ibid*, para 29.

[77] *NUJ and Staffordshire Sentinel Newspapers Ltd* TUR1/506/2006, para 16; see also *NUJ and Newsquest (Essex) Ltd* TUR1/539/2006, para 19.

[78] *AMICUS and Ritrama (UK) Ltd* TUR1/542/2006, para 25; see also *Unite the Union and Flyglobespan* TUR1/610/2007, paras 22–4.

[79] *CWU and Cable & Wireless*, above n 39, para 44.

[80] See *UNIFI and Turkiye Is Bankasi AS* TUR1/90/2001 where, despite union allegations that letters had been sent to the CAC under management pressure, the Panel ordered a ballot.

[81] *TSSA and Gatwick Express* TUR1/261/2003.

the CAC, rather than through the intermediation of the employer. While this was dubious as a matter of statutory construction it was clear enough what concerned the Panel: these letters were tainted by undue influence on the part of the employer and were not an accurate reflection of worker preferences. The High Court quashed the Panel decision, holding that it was not necessary that the CAC be informed directly by workers.[82] Further, and with the agreement of TSSA and Gatwick Express, the court did not remit the decision back to the CAC for a fresh hearing. Instead, and in the face of objections by the CAC itself, the court decided that eight letters was a 'substantial' number and ordered the CAC to give notice to the parties that it intended to arrange a secret ballot.

With respect, the meaning of 'substantial' was not the only point of statutory construction at issue. More germane was the question of whether the revealed preferences were genuinely held or unduly influenced. The court's order precluded the CAC from considering, on the basis of all the available evidence, whether these letters reflected genuine opinions. The reasoning in the High Court judgment was laconic. Nevertheless, the position seemed to be that once the CAC was informed by a substantial number of union members, directly or otherwise, that they did not want the union to conduct collective bargaining on their behalf, then there was nothing left for the CAC to do except mechanistically order the ballot. Certainly, it did not seem to be within the CAC's remit to use its industrial relations expertise and judgement to evaluate the veracity of that evidence. As Simpson has pointed out, the effect of the judgment was 'highly interventionist since it had the effect of substituting the court's judgment on an issue which the legislation reserved to the CAC'.[83] The CAC's surprising decision not to appeal it was probably due to the CAC anticipating that the legal point in *Gatwick Express* would be rendered 'otiose' by impending changes to the statutory definition brought about by the ERA 2004.[84]

It did not take long before the CAC faced a similar problem in *ISTC and Brian Hewitt Construction Ltd*.[85] The employer initiated and co-ordinated the collection of letters from union members communicating to the CAC they did not wish the union to conduct collective bargaining on their behalf. The union alleged the employer had unduly pressurised the signatories into signing. In the light of *Gatwick Express* was it 'open for the Panel to look behind the letters and to take into account their provenance as the union would urge?'[86] On a superficial reading of the Panel's reasoning the answer appears to be no. The Panel felt 'constrained' by the clear statutory wording. The qualifying condition was not couched in terms of the CAC exercising judgement. Rather, Parliament seemed to envisage CAC's task as simply arithmetical in assessing whether a 'substantial'

82 *R (On the application of Gatwick Express) v CAC* [2003] EWHC 2035 Admin.
83 B Simpson, 'Judicial Control of the CAC' (2007) 36 *Industrial Law Journal* 287, 294.
84 *Ibid.*
85 *ISTC and Brian Hewitt Construction Ltd* TUR1/279/2003.
86 *Ibid*, para 25.

number informed the CAC. If so then a ballot order followed inexorably. Significantly, however, the Panel also noted the union's allegations were not substantiated by *evidence* such as individual testimony. The CAC was bound to order the ballot 'given the number of letters, some basic calculations *and in the absence of any evidence to the contrary*'.[87] The implication here seems to be that if there had been specific evidence to the contrary, demonstrating undue influence by the employer, this would have blocked the condition from being triggered.

This also reflects the tenor of the CAC's reasoning in *GMB and Varn International*.[88] Here the union alleged that the employer's petition had been collected against a coercive backdrop of threats of dismissal and small group meetings with US–style union-busting consultants. The union possessed individual statements from union members substantiating these allegations but would not disclose this evidence to the employer for fear that those individuals testifying would be subject to reprisals and victimisation. The CAC would not accept the union's evidence without disclosure. Again, the CAC did not rule out the possibility that given appropriate evidence of undue influence the qualifying condition would not apply. Nevertheless, there was no such evidence in this case.

The position now seems to have been codified in the ERA 2004 statutory reformulation of paragraph 22(4)(b), which makes reference to the need for 'credible' evidence.[89] Thus, where the CAC 'has evidence which it considers to be credible from a significant number of union members in the bargaining unit that they do not want the union to conduct collective bargaining on their behalf', then the CAC is required to hold a ballot. This strict evidence-based approach ensures the balance of tactical advantage lies with the employer, and this is reflected in the fact that employers have enjoyed more success invoking 22(4)(b) as compared with 22(4)(c), both before and after the ERA 2004 changes. Paragraph 22(4)(b) seems to be the weapon of choice for anti-union employers seeking to engender delay through the ballot procedure, particularly where the employer is taking strategic advice from professional consultants.

There have been two recent Panel decisions where a ballot was ordered on the basis of the revised paragraph 22(4)(b). In *Unite the Union and CSI Group Ltd* the employer had orchestrated the collection of letters from workers in the bargaining unit indicating either their hostility to collective bargaining or preference for a ballot, and it passed these sealed letters on to the CAC.[90] In addition, the employer had held a captive audience meeting with the workforce, with the union excluded from it, and afterwards the company manager invited workers to participate in a poll to register their preferences in respect of the union's recognition claim. The poll was not anonymous in that the employer could identify the individual worker's response.

[87] *Ibid*, para 26.
[88] TUR1/355/2004.
[89] Employment Relations Act 2004 s 6.
[90] TUR1/618/2008.

The Panel discounted the poll evidence, pointing to the particular evidential difficulties with employer (as distinct from union) administered polls: 'it seems to us that unions are rarely in the same position to influence workers' decisions through explicit or implicit inducements or threats, if views are expressed or not expressed in a particular way'.[91] Nevertheless, the solicited letters were treated as 'credible' evidence for the purposes of paragraph 22(4)(b), with the Panel pointing to the fact that the letters were sealed and did not appear to be standard form communications. In these circumstances, the Panel concluded that the letters were 'genuine expressions of the workers' opinions' and there was no direct evidence that they had been improperly influenced by the employer.[92] Although the evidence on the record was finely balanced, the general context (captive audience speeches, clear communication of employer hostility to unionisation, the conduct of an employer-administered poll of preferences, orchestration of letter writing campaign) certainly seemed to raise a legitimate doubt that the preferences were freely formed and communicated. In these circumstances, it would seem implausible that a worker would be prepared to go on the record and testify that her letter had not been a genuine expression of opinion.

In *CWU and COLT Telecom Group plc* there had been a similar campaign of employer orchestration of worker communications with the CAC.[93] According to the union, pressure had been placed on individual workers to write to the CAC indicating their hostility to collective bargaining. The Panel took the view that four out of 14 union members had written to the CAC, that this constituted a 'significant' proportion of the total number of union members, and that there was no direct evidence undermining the credibility of the evidence. In both cases, the union lost the subsequent ballot.[94] Of course, it might be argued that this demonstrated that the CAC's decision to order a ballot was therefore justified. Nevertheless, these were cases where the employer was demonstrably hostile to collective bargaining and the union faced an uphill struggle in the ballot procedure despite having achieved majority membership in the absence of union recognition. Moreover, it should not be forgotten that the CAC had earlier concluded that a majority of the bargaining unit was likely to favour recognition in scrutinising the validity and admissibility of the unions' applications.

It would be misleading to give the impression that this qualifying condition succeeds every time it is raised. This is not the case. The CAC has emphasised three constraints on successful invocations of paragraph 22(4)(b). First, the Panel stated in *GMB and Vinci Park (UK) Services Ltd* that there was a continuing requirement that the CAC receive communications from union members, either

91 *Ibid*, para 24.
92 *Ibid*, para 29.
93 TUR1/590/2007.
94 In *United the Union and CSI Group Ltd* the union lost the ballot 32% to 68% against recognition; in *CWU and COLT Telecom Group plc*, the union won the ballot but on a low turnout such that it did not reach the 40% support threshold (21.74% of the bargaining unit voted in favour).

directly from workers themselves or indirectly through the intermediation of the employer, indicating a lack of support for recognition.[95] Circumstantial evidence indicating a lack of support for recognition—for example, a failure to sign a petition in support of collective bargaining—needed to be dealt with through either 22(4)(a) or 22(4)(c) as this was not relevant evidence within the meaning of 22(4)(b).

Secondly, the evidence needed to be 'credible'. So, for example, where an employer adduced the results of a non-confidential straw poll initiated and conducted by the employer suggesting that polled union members did not support recognition, the Panel rejected this evidence on the basis that it was not 'credible'.[96] Moreover, speculative inferences from circumstantial evidence—such as a failure of union members to sign union petitions—have been rejected as not disclosing 'credible' evidence. Thus, in both *GMB and Vinci Park (UK) Services Ltd* and *Unite the Union and Flyglobespan*[97] the employer argued that a failure on the part of union members to sign a union petition indicated that those members did not support collective bargaining. As the Panels indicated in both cases, these were merely speculative assertions rather than credible evidence. A failure to sign was equally consistent with a union member taking the view that their membership and payment of union dues was sufficient evidence of support for recognition.

Finally, the number of union members needs to be 'significant'. In *TGWU and Cardinal Health* the Panel took the view that two out of 77 members was not 'significant',[98] and in *Unite—the Union and Texol Technical Solutions* the Panel concluded that 13 out of 83 union members was not 'significant'. In *CWU and Cable & Wireless*,[99] the Panel took the bold view that 'significance' was to be judged as a proportion of total union membership. Thus, even in a situation of marginal majority membership where a small number of communications might depress membership *below* a majority of the bargaining unit, what mattered was the proportion of dissenting union members when compared with the total number of union members.

Nevertheless, in a situation where the employer successfully orchestrates individually written communications from a substantial proportion of union members to the CAC, perhaps using captive audience meetings or one-to-one interviews with senior management as an inducement, then the employer's invocation of paragraph 22 (4)(b) is likely to be successful in the absence of specific testimony by workers that they have been pressurised into writing letters.

[95] TUR1/496/2006.

[96] *Unite—the Union and Texol Technical Solutions* TUR1/555/2007; a similar non-independent and non-confidential poll was rejected in *Unite the Union and Flyglobespan* TUR1/610/2007.

[97] TUR1/610/2007.

[98] TUR1/514/2006.

[99] TUR1/570/2007 above n 39.

(c) Paragraph 22(4)(a) The most crucial guide to the balance between the 'regulatory' and 'reconstructive' models in Schedule A1 is the qualifying condition based upon a ballot order 'in the interests of good industrial relations'. A broad interpretation of its scope by the CAC would have diminished the 'reconstructive' character of Schedule A1 considerably. This had the potential to undermine the efficacy of the procedure. Predictably this qualifying condition is the one that has been most frequently invoked by employers. However, it has been operative in only a narrow range of cases, and 'has never been viewed by the CAC as an "easy" option for ordering a ballot'.[100] Two main arguments have been offered by employers: we might term these the argument from democratic legitimacy, and the argument from democratic therapy. The argument from democratic legitimacy identifies the secret ballot as the pre-eminently authoritative, democratic arbiter of majority opinion. The seal of democratic legitimacy that a ballot confers on the union's recognition claim dispels any doubts or uncertainty about the extent of support and this lays the foundations for a stable collective bargaining relationship. The argument from democratic therapy identifies the ballot process as an opportunity for both parties to clear the air, to heal the wounds of divisiveness and acrimony, and this enables the parties to conduct trust-based collective bargaining.

On occasion these arguments have persuaded the CAC.[101] Nevertheless, the CAC has generally been unreceptive to generalised assertions based on the democratic imperative of a ballot. Receptiveness to generalised assertion raises the spectre that 'the exception would swallow up the rule' of recognition without a ballot in a situation of majority membership.[102] The CAC has resisted the lure of 'democracy creep' in its reasoning. The democratic argument was rejected in *TSSA and WAGN Rail Ltd*.[103] The CAC did not accept the employer's argument that recognition awarded on the basis of majority membership lacked legitimacy. Indeed, the Panel emphasised the exceptional nature of a ballot order, noting that: 'Parliament has specifically provided that a ballot is not required except in particular circumstances.'[104]

More recently, this important point has been reiterated by the CAC. Thus, in response to the employer's argument that a ballot would be 'fair and equitable', the Panel observed that it could 'only order a ballot if it is satisfied that one or more of the qualifying conditions is met. The Panel cannot take into account whether the holding of a ballot would be "fair or equitable". The legislation

[100] *CAC Report 2004–2005*, 16.

[101] The argument from democratic legitimacy seemed to figure as a justification for ordering a ballot in *GMB and Halo Healthcare* TUR1/259/2003 where the Panel noted 'that a properly conducted independent ballot would be just and equitable'; see also *GMB and The Royal Pigeon Racing Association* TUR1/331/2004. The argument from democratic therapy figured in *GPMU and Red Letter Bradford Ltd* TUR1/12/2000.

[102] *GMB and Oughtred and Harrison (Facilities) Ltd* TUR1/301/2003 para 15.

[103] TUR1/314/2003.

[104] *Ibid*, para 17.

makes no allowance for such considerations.'[105] What are needed are *specific* arguments, pointing to specific factual features of the particular circumstances of the case, which demonstrate how 'good industrial relations' would be furthered by a ballot in the particular context.[106] The proposition that a ballot is generally the most democratically legitimate mechanism for allocating bargaining rights is therefore inconsistent with the structure of the legislation. This has been underpinned by two recurrent lines of argument in CAC decisions.

First, the CAC has tended to emphasise the virtue of collective bargaining, as opposed to the ballot procedure, as the preferred method of facilitating the voluntary resolution of disagreement between the parties. This position was articulated in *NUJ and Newsquest (North East) Ltd* when the CAC declared that 'good industrial relations in the company would be better served by securing the establishment of a bargaining relationship between the parties as soon as possible and that no benefit would accrue from prolonging the present situation by the holding of a secret ballot'.[107] Secondly, the CAC has been sympathetic to union submissions that, in contrast to the democratic therapy argument of employers, ballots tend to exacerbate divisiveness and polarise the bargaining parties, heightening tensions in the workplace, and this risks poisoning any subsequent collective bargaining relationship.[108] This is consistent with the rationale of 'reconstructive' statutory design. As such, the elimination of legal delay through bypassing the ballot procedure has been cemented by the CAC as an important

[105] *United and Independent Union and Wallace Cameron & Co Ltd* TUR1/517/2006, para 16.

[106] *Unite the Union and Victim Support West Yorkshire* TUR1/609/2007, para 20: 'The Panel is conscious that it must not misconstrue the qualifying condition under this paragraph. Parliament has determined that recognition of the union must be awarded where a majority of workers constituting the bargaining unit are members of the Union unless one or more of the qualifying conditions apply. Therefore, whilst a party may take issue with the statutory provision for recognition without the need for a ballot, the Panel must look closely at specific arguments if it is to be persuaded that this qualifying condition applies.' See also *Unite the Union and Kamns Paper Mill Ltd* TUR1/615/2008, para 34: 'It is not sufficient simply to take issue with the statutory provision for recognition without the need for a ballot. Rather, the Panel must examine carefully the specific arguments if it is to be persuaded that this qualifying condition applies.'

[107] TUR1/304/2003. For other expressions of this position, see *ISTC and Palagan Ltd* TUR1/225/2002 at para 16; *NATFHE and Alliance Francaise de Londres (2004) Ltd* TUR1/443/2005 at para 23; *Amicus and Premdor Crosby Ltd* TUR1/343/2004 at para 24; *Amicus and Gledhill Water Storage Ltd* TUR1/342/2004 at para 22; *Unite the Union and Kamns Paper Mill Ltd* TUR1/615/2008, para 35; *Unite the Union and Sutton Bridge Power Station GE II* TUR1/552/2007, para 19.

[108] See *ISTC and Fullarton Computer Industries Ltd* TUR1/29/2000, upheld in *Fullarton Computer Industries Ltd v CAC* [2001] IRLR 752, Ct of Session. In an important exercise of respectful deference, the Court accorded the CAC a large margin of discretion on account of its industrial relations expertise. Lord Johnston suggested, *obiter*, that a ballot order might be appropriate in a situation of marginal majority membership. This prompt does not seem to have constrained the CAC in its later decisions. See, eg, *TSSA and First North Western* TUR1/333/2004 (membership density 52.9%, no ballot order); *Amicus and Premdor Crosby Ltd* TUR1/343/2004 (membership density 51.11%, no ballot order); *GMB and Oughtred and Harrison (Facilities) Ltd* TUR1/301/2003 (membership density 54.76%, no ballot order).

statutory goal.[109] There is strong comparative support for this negative characterisation of the ballot procedure. Adams has vividly described the US ballot procedure as a 'dysfunctional vortex' nurturing 'a climate of distrust and animosity'.[110] In the light of this, the CAC has been rightly cautious in ordering a ballot in a situation of majority membership.

Nevertheless, the CAC has been persuaded on occasions that specific evidence justifying a ballot order under paragraph 22(4)(a) is present. First, where the parties are in agreement that a ballot would be in the interests of good industrial relations, the CAC has deferred to the parties' voluntary agreement.[111] This is to be expected, and it is consistent with the general primacy accorded to the parties' voluntary arrangements under Schedule A1. Secondly, the significant decision in *CWU and Cable & Wireless* also provides a rare example of paragraph 22(4)(a) being invoked successfully by an employer. In order to resist the union's recognition claim, the employer was receiving strategic guidance from 'The Burke Group', a US-style union busting consultancy. The employer had allegedly utilised a wide range of techniques to undermine union support in the bargaining unit: dilatory litigation culminating in an unsuccessful judicial review challenge to the CAC's bargaining unit determination; an orchestrated campaign to encourage workers to write to the CAC to declare their hostility to recognition; expansion of the bargaining unit to dilute membership density; the reinvigoration of an 'employee consultation forum'; and the waging of a hostile campaign by the employer. The CAC decided to order a ballot under paragraph 22(4)(a) because a significant number of workers in the bargaining unit (both members and non-members) had written to the CAC requesting a ballot. The CAC concluded that there was no evidence of undue influence in respect of these employer-orchestrated communications, although short of individual testimony to this effect it is unclear what would constitute sufficient evidence of undue influence.

In these circumstances, the CAC considered that a ballot was imperative in conferring democratic legitimacy on the union's claim:

> What a ballot does, if the union is successful, is to give it legitimacy. Without a ballot, in circumstances where a majority of employees had indicated that they did not want

[109] The union's submission on this point was preferred in *Amicus and J W Froehlich UK Ltd* TUR1/393/2004; *NATFHE and Alliance Francaise de Londres (2004) Ltd* TUR1/443/2005; *ISTC and Capital Coated Steel Ltd* TUR1/285/2003; *GPMU and Newcastle Chronicle and Journal Ltd* TUR1/133/2001; and in *Unite the Union and Kamns Paper Mill Ltd* TUR1/615/2008 the Panel took the view that the delay engendered by a ballot order, coupled with the likelihood that the ballot was likely to be 'combative' rather than 'conciliatory', justified the CAC's decision not to order a ballot 'in the interests of good industrial relations'.

[110] RJ Adams, 'Why statutory union recognition is bad labour policy: the North American experience' (1999) 30 *Industrial Relations Journal* 96, 98.

[111] See, eg, *NUJ and Staffordshire Sentinel Newspapers Ltd* TUR1/506/2006; *Prospect and Rocksavage Power Company Ltd* TUR1/525/2006.

> automatic recognition, there would always be arguments that the union gained recognition without a popular mandate.[112]

It is not surprising that CWU lost the subsequent ballot by a margin of 23.3 per cent to 76.7 per cent, within the context of multiple 'unfair practice' allegations during the ballot process. It is submitted that this was an ill-advised exercise of discretion by the CAC. Where well-resourced employers are operating with the assistance of specialist anti-union consultants, ballots are likely to be irretrievably skewed in the employer's favour and fatal to the union's recognition claim.

To recap, the regulatory framework established under Schedule A1 has avoided some of the weaknesses identified in the US recognition procedure. Most notably, the Schedule A1 procedure envisages the allocation of bargaining rights in situations of majority membership without the need for a ballot. Generally speaking, the CAC has ensured that the exceptions to this 'majority membership' route to recognition have been interpreted restrictively, although employers have enjoyed a degree of success in securing (and winning) ballots under paragraph 22(4)(b). The CAC has also ensured that its general supervisory jurisdiction over the ballot procedure (in *Ultraframe*), and its power to order a re-run ballot, have been kept within tight and well-defined bounds. This has contributed to the minimisation of legal delay. On the other hand, serious weaknesses have been identified in the design and subsequent interpretation of the 'unfair practice' provisions. This raises the prospect that employers can still subvert worker free choice with impunity in many cases, which undermines the procedure's liberal objective of a level playing field.

III REGULATING THE CULTURAL MARKETPLACE II: ENSURING EQUAL CAMPAIGN OPPORTUNITIES

A The Sanctity of Private Property in the US Recognition Procedure

The tension between employers' private property rights and employees' organisational rights is ubiquitous in labour law. As the Supreme Court observed in *NLRB v Babcock and Wilcox Company*, 'accommodation between the two must be obtained with as little destruction of one as is consistent with the maintenance of the other'.[113] That accommodation will be reflective of deeper value judgements ascribing relative weights to these competing rights. The most recent attempt at judicial accommodation in the US reflects the subordination of attenuated organisational rights to an absolutist conception of employer private property

112 Para 51.
113 (1956) 351 US 105, 112.

rights. Thus, in *Lechmere v NLRB*, the Supreme Court erected a virtually unassailable barrier to organisational access to the employer's property by professional union organisers.[114] The scenario in *Lechmere* was typical of many organising campaigns. In an attempt to reach the non-unionised workforce, professional union organisers accessed the car park of a shopping mall open to the general public to distribute promotional material. The organisers were ejected. In subsequent months the organisers attempted to pass out handbills to cars from a grassy strip just beyond the perimeter of the employer's property. The union also resorted to other, less direct forms of communication, including advertisements in local newspapers, and mailings, telephone calls and home visits to about 20 per cent of the workforce whose addresses had been obtained using car licence plates. Not surprisingly, these organisational efforts were ineffective. The NLRB concluded that the employer's denial of access constituted unlawful interference with its employees' right to self-organisation.

The Supreme Court denied enforcement of the NLRB order. The judgment contained a double blow for organised labour, simultaneously affirming the pre-eminence of sovereign property rights while rejecting a collectivist conception of the right to organise. The resulting 'accommodation' was predictably skewed against organisational rights. First, the court's reasoning embodied an extraordinary deference to the employer's property rights. The overriding strength of the employer's property rights was beyond scrutiny. As such, that strength was invariable, regardless of the kind of property at stake or the employer's reason for exclusion. The right to exclude from parking lots, public shopping malls or the factory floor attracted equal protection. Furthermore, if the exclusion was motivated by anti-union animus, this was respected to the same degree as an exclusion motivated by legitimate concerns for health and safety or ensuring continuity of production.

Secondly, the court denied that *unions* enjoyed any organisational rights under the statutory framework. Instead, organisational rights were guaranteed to individual *employees*. The only statutory interest enjoyed by unions was purely derivative, in ensuring that employees received information on the prospect of unionisation. This derivative interest would, in practically all cases, be satisfied without the need of access to the employer's property. No enquiry into the relative effectiveness of different modes of organisational communication would be permitted. On this view, face-to-face dialogue with a union organiser was equivalent to other forms of non-dialogical activity, such as newspaper advertisements or the display of picketing signs, regardless of how diluted the effectiveness of that indirect communication might be. *Lechmere* constitutes 'a general testament to breadth and importance of employer property rights as against federal

[114] (1992) 502 US 527.

labor rights'.[115] Its effect was to place draconian constraints on effective organisational activity in the workplace. The accommodation effectuated by the Supreme Court rests upon seriously flawed assumptions. These flaws have distorted its understanding of both property rights and organisational rights.

(i) The Right to Private Property: Realism and Neutrality

The Supreme Court's conception of private property can be challenged on two bases: the 'realist' critique, and the 'neutrality' critique. With respect to the 'realist' critique, this was inspired by the legal realist deconstruction of private property and the myth of the 'free' market. The realist position emerged in part as a critical response to what has been described as 'a distinctively American property story', one that conceptualised property rights as 'absolute, individual, and exclusive'.[116] This absolutist conception of private property is the unarticulated premise that lies beneath the reasoning in *Lechmere* and legitimates the employer's right to exclude union organisers under any circumstances. This belies the judicial rhetoric of accommodation. Instead, *Lechmere* embodies a style of reasoning 'that seeks to protect as much as possible a pre-existing set of common law private property entitlements from legislative incursion. Private property rights are the norm, and statutory rights are the exception.'[117] Legal realism attacked the 'free market' dogma that legal property rights tracked some natural, pre-conventional baseline of proprietary ownership.[118] Rather, the concept of ownership and its incidents is entirely a construct of legal rules. As such, the legal rules constructing private property should not be treated as axiomatic. Private property is a complex product of specific regulatory choices. Those regulatory choices should stand or fall on their contribution to compelling human values and social policies.

This realist perspective strips property rights 'of their talismanic force and presumptive breadth and generality',[119] and argues for a more subtle and differentiated account of the specific instances in which the employer's right to exclude should have priority. None of this is to deny that property rights *can* augment important values such as privacy, human personality, personal

[115] CL Estlund, 'Labor, Property, and Sovereignty after Lechmere' (1994) 46 *Stanford Law Review* 305, 322.

[116] MA Glendon, *Rights Talk* (New York, Free Press, 1991) 23.

[117] P Macklem, 'Property, Status and Workplace Organizing' (1990) 40 *University of Toronto Law Journal* 74, 81.

[118] See, eg, F Cohen, 'Transcendental Nonsense and the Functional Approach' (1935) 35 *Columbia Law Review* 809; M Cohen, 'Property and Sovereignty' (1927) 13 *Cornell Law Quarterly* 8. For adaptation of realist insights within the context of union organisational activity, see K Klare, 'Workplace Democracy and Market Reconstruction: An Agenda for Legal Reform' (1988) 38 *Catholic University Law Review* 1. J Gresham, 'Still as Strangers: Non-employee Union Organizers on Private Commercial Property' (1983) 62 *Texas Law Review* 111. See also Macklem, *ibid* and Estlund, above n 115.

[119] Estlund, above n 115, 346.

autonomy, political citizenship and economic efficiency. But it is to recognise that this range of values will not be implicated to the same degree on every occasion, and that a just 'accommodation' necessitates interrogation of those underlying values on a case-by-case basis. For example, organisational access to a publicly accessible shopping centre or car park is likely to raise very different issues to organisational access to a small, single-proprietor enterprise.[120] The values of privacy and autonomy might be engaged far less in the former scenario. A union's claim to the use of a staff canteen outside of working hours raises different issues to its claim to use of the factory floor during working time.[121] And an employer's denial of access motivated by hostility to unionisation is very different to a denial of access on the grounds of a legitimate interest in ensuring productive efficiency. Genuine accommodation would, however, start from a radically different premise to the current law: not preservation of the employer's right to exclude to the maximum possible extent, but a conception of private property and the right to exclude that mirrors a humane and democratic vision of political community under the rule of law.[122]

With respect to the 'neutrality' critique, this emerged out of legal realist insights into the incoherent myth of some natural, pre-legal marketplace, and it questions the extent to which the State can disentangle itself from partiality in the enforcement of common law entitlements. The difficulties of tracing the elusive boundary between State neutrality and State partiality are reflected in the contrast, drawn by Cass Sunstein,[123] between *PruneYard Shopping Center v Robins*[124]

[120] NLRB decision-making prior to *Lechmere* reflected this idea that the strength of the private property claim varied with the nature of the property. For critical discussion of *Lechmere* on this basis, see RA Gorman, 'Union Access to Private Property: A Critical Assessment of *Lechmere, Inc v NLRB*' (1991) 9 *Hofstra Labor Law Journal* 1. Its strength was correspondingly diluted where the employer's property was 'widely accessible to the public for purposes of parking, visiting and shopping' (*ibid* at 2). In arguing for a general right of access to private property for expressive activities, Rowbottom makes a similar point: see J Rowbottom, 'Property and Participation: A Right of Access for Expressive Activities' [2005] *European Human Rights Law Review* 186, 194: 'the need to preserve a largely unfettered right to exclude varies with different types of private property'.

[121] In *Republic Aviation Corp v NLRB* 324 US 793 (1945), the Supreme Court drew a distinction between union activity on an employer's property interfering with production or discipline (eg, union solicitation in a working area during working time), and union activity on an employer's property that did not constitute such interference (eg, union solicitation in a non-work area outside of working time). Only in the former scenario could union activity be lawfully prohibited by an employer. This rule still holds good for *employee* organisational activity on an employer's property. As both Gresham (above n 118, 168) and Estlund (above n 115, 348–50) argue cogently, legitimate employer interests in efficient management of the enterprise would be well-served by repeal of *Babcock/Lechmere* and implementation of a free-standing *Republic Aviation* standard applying to both employees *and* professional union organisers.

[122] As Estlund observes (above n 115, 347 fn 245), the conception of private property that emerges from the realist 'demystification' shares much in common with the civic republican tradition, whereby the conventional contours and limits of private property are shaped by the animating ideal of the common good of a political community. On the relation between private property and the common good, see JM Finnis, *Natural Law and Natural Rights* (Oxford, Oxford University Press, 1980) 165–84.

[123] CR Sunstein, *The Partial Constitution* (Cambridge, Harvard University Press, 1993) 72–5.

[124] 447 US 74 (1980).

and *Hudgens v NLRB.*[125] In *PruneYard Shopping Center* the Supreme Court held that the curtailment of state trespass laws to permit expressive activity on certain kinds of private property involved State action attracting constitutional scrutiny. By contrast, in *Hudgens,* enforcement of state trespass law against protesters to prevent expressive activity on the owner's private property did not attract constitutional scrutiny because there was no State action. Sunstein suggests we account for this difference in terms of 'status quo neutrality'.[126] The neutrality/partiality distinction makes sense only if we identify a baseline of measurement. In constitutional terms that baseline is the common law's allocation of proprietary and contractual entitlements. Where the State upholds existing entitlements through enforcing contracts and proprietary entitlements, the State is, in constitutional terms, invisible. Where the State disrupts those entitlements, it intervenes and its constitutional visibility is emblematic of its partiality. This accounts for the scrupulousness of the Supreme Court's efforts in *Babcock* and *Lechmere* to disrupt the employer's proprietary entitlements as little as possible.[127] To do so would violate a stance of State neutrality as between the union and employer. This kind of partiality would be tantamount to illiberal favouritism towards the union and an injustice to the employer.

However, the allure of the common law as a baseline for measuring the continuum between neutrality and partiality dissipates once the cogency of the legal realist insights is acknowledged. Property and contract are legal constructs. Accordingly, it is the State that breathes life into these common law categories and, in the last resort, it is the State that underwrites their enforcement. State enforcement of the common law's pattern of entitlements reinforces the status quo and entrenches the position of those already privileged through proprietary ownership. From the vantage point of organised labour, the neutrality of *Lechmere* is very much 'neutral on the side of the employer'.[128] Respect for this baseline might be defended but not in terms of the neutrality/partiality distinction. In truth, the common law baseline can only be defended by invoking some independent criterion of justice in allocation. Moreover, the principle of liberal neutrality in political philosophy has little, if anything, to do with the ideal of 'status quo' neutrality that underpins *Lechmere.* For example, while Will Kymlicka is committed to liberal neutrality this is perfectly compatible with his simultaneous endorsement of a liberal principle of redressing group disadvantage in the cultural marketplace.[129] The principle of redressing group disadvantage might lead to a large scale reframing of property rights to enable unions to compete more effectively without this involving the liberal State's endorsement of trade unionism as embodying an intrinsically valuable form of life. It is only this latter

[125] 424 US 507 (1976).
[126] Sunstein, above n 123, 71–5.
[127] Estlund, above n 115, 343.
[128] Klare, above n 118, 63.
[129] For discussion see ch 3.

sense of partiality that would violate neutrality from a liberal anti-perfectionist standpoint, certainly not State intervention per se.

(ii) The Union's Right to Organise

The Supreme Court's conception of organisational rights in *Lechmere* is also flawed. This is manifested in two ways. First, the court's interpretation of the right to organise rests on a restrictive understanding of the right's scope. This is reflected in its assertion that the union's interest is wholly derivative of unorganised employees' right to learn about unionisation. Secondly, the court's interpretation of reasonably effective alternative means of communication is based on an impoverished understanding of effective strategies for union mobilisation.

With respect to the first, the court in *Babcock* asserted (without argument) that the distinction between employee and non-employee organisers was one of 'substance'. Non-employee organisers' interests were merely derivative and parasitic upon the core right of employees to be informed about the prospect of unionisation and collective bargaining. This derivative characterisation ensured the union's interest attracted diminished weight in the balance against employer property rights. Quite apart from the interpretive objection that union organisers are themselves 'employees' of the union and therefore within the statutory scope of core section 7 organisational rights,[130] this dilution of the union's organisational stake is based upon a highly distorting separation of the individual and collective dimensions of union activity. Unions are not some kind of alien contraposition set against the working lives of individual workers; they are industrial communities *constituted* by the individual participation of working people. Refracting organisational rights through an individualistic lens, as in *Babcock* and *Lechmere*, sets the law adrift from the realities of collective action. Even then, the precise framing of the union's derivative interest by the court leads to further dilution of its strength against the employer's property right. Thus, as Estlund argues, 'the presence of a large non-union sector in the relevant labor market constrains the leverage that organized employees can exert';[131] consequently, organised employees themselves have a legitimate interest in extending the frontier of union organisation to maintain their bargaining strength, and this is vindicated by the organisational activities of the union itself as their bargaining agent. This dimension has been ignored by the courts in their conceptualisation of the relevant employee interests at stake in an organising drive.

Secondly, *Lechmere* adopted a sanguine attitude towards the relative worth of different avenues of organisational communication in assessing their 'reasonable effectiveness'. Newspaper and radio advertisements, display of picket signs,

[130] On this point see the arguments of Gorman, above n 120, 11 and Estlund, above n 115, 326.
[131] Estlund, above n 115, 327.

mailing, and home visits were all deemed equivalent to face-to-face dialogue between employees and professional union organisers in the workplace. Where those alternatives are available, as in the vast majority of cases, it is not appropriate to encroach on the employer's property rights. However, this communicative equivalence is simply assumed. Moreover, it is an assumption of dubious validity. In theoretical terms the process of worker mobilisation requires the coalescence of individual workers into an industrial community marked by the shared identification of collective interests and a willingness to engage in collective action.[132] This process of mobilisation is best promoted by grass-roots, participatory techniques involving face-to-face dialogue between workers and union organisers within the workplace. This kind of contact best nurtures and sustains the bonds of community upon which resilient collective organisation is predicated.

This has been recognised at different times by the courts,[133] the Board,[134] and a broad consensus of academic opinion.[135] As Gresham observes:

> [T]he employer's premises are the one place where the natural solidarity of employees is immediately felt, where mutual forbearance, trust, and sympathy are directly expressed ... Given that the ultimate question for the workers is whether to organize and, as one, bargain for each, it is fitting and even necessary that this collective decision is made in a social, public, and collective forum.[136]

The unique efficacy of participatory workplace strategies also receives powerful empirical support both in the US context,[137] and within the context of organisational campaigns under Schedule A1.[138]

This eclipse of organisational rights at the perimeter of the employer's property does not provide an attractive blueprint for Schedule A1. The current position of glaring access inequality has been subjected to trenchant and unequivocal criticism from an international human rights perspective. Human Rights Watch has condemned the present 'haphazard' access of union organisers and its striking contrast with the unlimited campaigning opportunities open to employers, particularly the use of captive audience speeches during working

[132] J Kelly, *Rethinking Industrial Relations* (London, Routledge, 1998) 39–65.

[133] See, eg, *NLRB v Magnavox Co* 415 US 322, 323–4 (1974); *Eastex Inc v NLRB* 437 US 556 (1978).

[134] *May Department Stores Co* 136 NLRB 191, at 802 (1962).

[135] Estlund, above n 115, 332; Macklem, above n 117, 77–80.

[136] Gresham, above n 118, 161.

[137] JG Getman, SB Goldberg and JB Herman, *Union Representation Elections: Law and Reality* (New York, Russell Sage, 1976). In their analysis of 31 recognition campaigns under the NLRA procedure, the authors found substantial inequality of opportunity in organizational communication between employers and union. Employer meetings in the workplace during working time attracted a far higher proportion of workers (83%) than union meetings off-site (36%). Moreover, those that attended union meetings were usually already union supporters. Vote switching during the campaign was associated with campaign familiarity. On this basis, the authors concluded (at 157) 'if the union could communicate with more of those not already committed to it, it might do significantly better in the election'.

[138] In Ewing, Moore, and Wood (above n 24), the authors identified 'a significant relationship between the holding of union surgeries in the ballot period and ballot success ... *This highlights the key role of personal contact with workers in determining success or failure*' (at 28, emphasis added).

time.[139] This condemnation is echoed in the ILO Committee on Freedom of Association calling on the US Government to revisit the absolute exclusionary rule posited in *Lechmere*.[140] More pertinent for reform purposes is the litany of proposals that have emerged from the criticisms of the current law. Many of these have called for repeal of the *Lechmere* and the retrieval of the *Republic Aviation* standard applicable to both employees and professional union organisers without distinction.

Put simply, only where the employer can identify a compelling managerial interest, for example in ensuring continuity of production or health and safety, should it be possible to limit union access to its property. Reform along these lines would ensure at the least a basic entitlement of union access for organisational purposes to non-work areas of the employer's property in non-working time.[141] This would be coupled with a commitment to parity of campaign access. It envisages an escalating union access entitlement proportionate to the extent of the employer's campaign activity. The parity principle is a corollary of democratic equality of opportunity for 'it is fundamental to the democratic process that each party should have a roughly equal opportunity to communicate with the electorate'.[142] This achieves a more equitable balance between private property and democratic values, thereby bringing the inescapable partisanship of the State's role in enforcing property rights into clearer view.

B Employer Property Rights and Union Organisational Access under Schedule A1

Schedule A1 posits a duty on employers to grant the union 'such access to the workers constituting the bargaining unit as is reasonable to enable the union (or unions) to inform the workers of the object of the ballot and to seek their support and their opinions on the issues involved'.[143] The parity principle is implicit in the accompanying *Code of Practice on access and unfair practices during recognition and derecognition ballots*.[144] The practical implications of the parity principle are explicitly traced out in three ways. First, the employer's methods of communication constitute the benchmark standard in determining the methods of communication open to the union during the access period. Thus if the employer resorts to large-scale meetings, then the union ought to be entitled to use meetings of a similar scale. Conversely, if the employer uses small meetings for campaign

139 Human Rights Watch, above n 13, 20–21.

140 See JA Gross, 'Applying human rights standards to employment rights in the USA: the Human Rights Watch Report 2000' (2002) 33 *Industrial Relations Journal* 182, 189–90.

141 Human Rights Watch , above n 13, 20.

142 Getman, Goldberg and Herman, above n 137, 157.

143 TULRCA 1992, Schedule A1, para 26(3).

144 This version of the Code of Practice, which came into force on 1 October 2005, superseded the original Code of Practice on union access.

communication, then the union's entitlement should correspond to this method.[145] Secondly, in deciding the timing of meetings and other campaign activities, 'the union and the employer should be guided by the employer's custom and practice when communicating with his workforce'.[146] So if the employer organises meetings during working time, then this facility ought to be open to the union. Thirdly, the extent of permitted campaign access for the union ought to be quantitatively equivalent to the employer's campaign access, subject to a basic union entitlement to one large-scale meeting of at least 30 minutes for every 10 days of the access period.[147] This ensures that, where campaign activity exceeds the level of basic entitlement, the number of campaign meetings and their duration are equivalent as between the parties.[148]

In other respects, the Code falls short of the parity principle. Moore, Wood and Davies outline three potential limitations. First, drawing upon the TUC's concerns about employer campaign activity outside the workplace, the authors speculate as to whether the CAC ought to take account of this in assessing the extent of the union's workplace access entitlement. Given the potentially efficacious nature of this employer campaign activity it would be desirable for the CAC to take such activity into account. Secondly, the authors highlight the fact that 'the union's right of access is triggered only when the parties are informed of the arrangements for the ballot and not at any earlier stage'.[149] This position certainly diverges from the North American proposals offered by Getman, Goldberg and Herman, who advocated employer commencement of campaign activity as the trigger for union access rights. Thirdly, the authors point to the lack of basic entitlement to union surgeries in working time, reflecting a dilution in basic entitlement from the draft Code to the final version. Of more concern is the apparent dilution of the parity principle, since the fact that the employer resorts to one-to-one meetings as a campaign tactic is not of itself determinative of the issue of union entitlement to one-to-one meetings.

Despite these limitations in the Code, the application and enforcement of union access rights by the CAC has been remarkably successful. The principal technique for determining the scope of union access has been through agreement between the parties. Voluntary agreements, sometimes reached with the assistance of the CAC, have been achieved in the vast majority of cases. In at least some of these cases, the parameters of the voluntary access agreement have reflected the principles set out in the Code of Practice.[150] The CAC has issued

[145] *Ibid*, para 28.

[146] *Ibid*, para 29.

[147] The minimum permitted duration of such a meeting increases to 45 minutes in the absence of union surgeries.

[148] *Ibid*, para 30.

[149] Moore, Wood and Davies, above n 2, 413.

[150] I am extremely grateful to Steph Marston, of the union *Connect*, who provided two specimen copies of sample voluntary access agreements (on file with author). A more systematic study of voluntary access agreements was not possible, regrettably.

formal decisions on the employer's duty to grant reasonable access only rarely.[151] Those formal CAC decisions disclose an approach that does not simply genuflect to the claims of private property and managerial rights. Instead, the CAC has struck a pragmatic accommodation between the legitimate interests of management and organised labour.

First, while the parity principle along with the detailed guidance in the Code of Practice has largely shaped the detail of formal access orders,[152] the CAC has not permitted the employer to use the parity principle to diminish the union's access entitlement below the basic threshold specified in the Code. Thus, in *Amicus and South Marston Distribution Centre Ltd* the employer refused to allow the union any mass meetings during working time to avoid any disruption to its production commitments.[153] The employer justified this refusal on the basis of parity in that it would not be conducting similar meetings. The Panel concluded that 'the Employer's usual methods of communication with workers are insufficient to use as a benchmark for the union's access to the workers during the forthcoming ballot'.[154] Accordingly, the CAC ordered six on-site mass meetings (one per shift per site), each to last 30 minutes, during working time. This tracked the basic threshold requirement specified in the Code of Practice.

Secondly, the CAC has been generally unreceptive to employer attempts to deny union surgeries despite the absence of basic entitlement to union surgeries in the Code of Practice. In *TGWU and King Asia Foods Ltd* the employer invoked its interest in maintaining continuity of production as a justification for denying on-site union surgeries in working time.[155] This argument was rejected by the CAC which ordered the employer to make provision for each worker to have the opportunity to attend two on-site union surgeries of 15 minutes duration each during the access period.[156] This is likely to be critical to the union's organisational strategy since there is now compelling empirical evidence that union surgeries are strongly linked to union success rates in the ensuing ballot.[157]

Thirdly, the CAC has not been reticent in ordering access for full-time union officials as part of the access arrangements.[158] The presence of full-time union officials with organisational expertise is often crucial in ensuring the union has a fair opportunity to succeed in the ballot contest. This mitigates the rigours of the strict exclusionary rule posited in *Lechmere*. Fourthly, the CAC has generally ensured that union meetings take place during working time with attendance

[151] Only six times in the first five years of Schedule A1's operation: see *CAC Report 2004–2005*, 17.

[152] See, eg, *TGWU and TVR Engineering Ltd* TUR1/371/2004 at App 2 ('If the company decides to hold large scale meetings, it will do so on the same basis as the Union').

[153] TUR1/361/2004.

[154] *Ibid*, para 13.

[155] TUR1/111/2001.

[156] Union surgeries were also ordered in *TSSA and Culina Logistics* TUR1/236/2002, *TGWU and King Asia Foods Ltd* TUR1/111/2001 and *TGWU and TVR Engineering Ltd*.

[157] Ewing, Moore and Wood, above n 24, 28.

[158] See *TGWU and King Asia Foods Ltd* and *TGWU and TVR Engineering Ltd*, above n 156.

paid for by the employer thereby maximising democratic participation of the workforce.[159] This goes further than even the boldest reform proposals emerging out of the US context, since most of those stop short of permitting organisational activity on the employer's property *during* working time.

The approach taken by the CAC interpreting the employer's access duty in Schedule A1 provides a striking contrast to that taken by the US Supreme Court. The double helix of property and managerial rights, corresponding to the twin axes of the employee/professional union organiser and working time/non-working time distinction, has not had the same tenacious hold on the CAC's juridical imagination. The CAC has routinely ordered the employer to permit organisational access to full-time union officers during working time on the employer's property during the access period. It is difficult to resist the conclusion that this divergence is a function of institutional factors. In the US the ordinary courts are very much in the interpretive driving seat. Should we then be surprised that property and managerial rights have maintained such a tight grip on the limits of legitimate organisational activity? After all, the ideology of the common law 'is hostile to workers' combination and collective action, leading judges to interpret restrictively all legislation which has provided … ever-shrinking immunities from certain wrongs'.[160] The CAC is not laden with the same ideological baggage. Furthermore, it has not been subjected to the same degree of judicial scrutiny as the NLRB.[161]

For all that, the CAC's remit is bound tightly by the statutory framework. The incursion on inherent common law rights may only occur during the access period once the ballot has been ordered. Prior to the ballot order the common law status quo remains untouched, and union organisers have no right of access to the employer's property. This generates predictably limiting effects on workers' right to organise. As such, the narrow timeframe for access envisaged by Schedule A1 gives the CAC very limited scope for reordering common law entitlements in the image of democratic values. The access duty is a modest step towards genuine parity but there is still a long road left to travel.[162] In particular, there is still little scope for organisational access for unions to achieve the necessary initial support thresholds (10 per cent membership and a majority likely to support recognition) for the purposes of a valid and admissible application under Schedule A1.[163]

[159] See *TGWU and TVR Engineering Ltd*, above n 156.

[160] Lord Wedderburn, *Labour Law and Freedom* (London, Lawrence & Wishart, 1995) 111.

[161] As Gresham (above n 118) observes in the US context, the NLRB has tended to adopt a less absolutist view of employer property rights, as compared with the interpretive approach of appellate courts.

[162] The Government has now introduced an entitlement in the Employment Relations Act 2004 for a union to distribute written communications to the constituent workforce in the initial period between acceptance and ballot order through an intermediate QIP, inserted into Schedule A1, paras 19C–19F.

[163] Two very modest exceptions to this general position should be noted. First, workers may participate in trade union activities in non-working time on their employer's property if they would

IV CONCLUSION

The quest for a level playing field in the cultural marketplace has been an elusive one. While Schedule A1 has mitigated some of the disadvantages faced by unions in the cultural marketplace, the field of play still slopes decisively in the employer's favour: the practical effects of the new 'unfair practice' jurisdiction are as yet uncertain, and their confinement to the narrow time frame of the ballot procedure undermines their utility; the 'reconstructive' elements in the procedure remain very dependent upon sympathetic CAC interpretation; and employer property rights remain sovereign and absolute outside the narrow confines of the statutory ballot procedure. The ambiguities of liberal neutrality in the workplace have been subjected to a devastating critique by Stone:

> If there is a structural inequality of power between management and labor based upon the incidents of private property as the law has defined it, then no procedural solutions will create true industrial democracy. In that case, the law must intervene actively to alter the definitions of property rights in order to create true equality.[164]

Despite many improvements on the US model, true equality has yet to be achieved under Schedule A1. One reform strategy might be to leave the underlying normative model of the cultural marketplace untouched. Even on this modest approach to legislative reform, and as we have seen through the course of this chapter, there are many specific adjustments that might be made to the current law to promote democratic parity between employers and unions. A more interesting strategy still would be to attack the normative foundations of the liberal cultural marketplace model itself. The civic republican tradition provides a powerful political basis to provoke a systematic rethinking of ballot regulation.

If we take first the question of campaign tactics and employer free speech, the legal protection of employer free speech rights has been a dominant theme in both the US and British statutory models. It has set the normative tone for ballot regulation, the effect of which has been to entrench toleration for the employer's democratic right to campaign vigorously against unionisation. This betrays a distinctively liberal understanding of the nature of free speech and its underlying value. Michael Sandel has offered a powerful critique of the liberal assumptions that pervade contemporary discourse concerning the legal protection of free

otherwise be permitted to be there (eg, during lunch breaks). This principle was enunciated by the House of Lords in *Post Office v Union of Post Office Workers* [1974] ICR 378, which required the employer to tolerate minor infringements of property rights. Secondly, workers now have a right under sections 10–15 of the Employment Relations Act 1999 to bring a companion to disciplinary and grievance hearings. This includes trade union officials even if there is no recognised trade union in the workplace.

164 K Stone, 'The Post-War Paradigm in American Labor Law' (1981) 90 *Yale Law Journal* 1509, 1579–80.

speech.[165] On this liberal view, it is illegitimate for the State to articulate any moral judgement on the content of speech. This would entail a violation of liberal neutrality. Instead, the State must eschew controversial evaluation of the worth of particular instances of expression, and be even-handed towards all of the participants in the marketplace of ideas. This is linked to the liberal foundation of the right to protect individual acts of autonomous self-fulfilment and expression.

According to Sandel, this whole approach leads to a characterisation of 'freedom of speech as a particular case of a more general principle of respect for persons as independent selves, capable of choosing their values for themselves'.[166] On this liberal approach, the sanctity of employer free speech is natural enough. It would be illegitimate for the law to evince partiality since this would be to embody a controversial view of the good life in the law. As such, arguments *against* unionisation are no less entitled to respect than arguments *for* unionisation. The law must be even-handed and allow free traffic in ideas, tastes, values and ideologies. To do otherwise would be to disrespect the autonomy of employers and workers who might be hostile to unionisation.

From the civic republican perspective, by contrast, free speech is valued for its contribution to the realisation of important civic goods such as community or self-government.[167] On this alternative approach, there is no space for value neutrality in determining the protective scope of the right. Where speech is germane to the virtues and practices of self-government, it will be safeguarded scrupulously. By contrast, where speech does not augment those virtues and practices then it will attract diminished protection. This has important implications in the context of employer free speech during recognition campaigns. If collective bargaining instantiates a valuable form of life for worker-citizens—for example, by encouraging the civic virtues of solidarity and loyalty, by promoting the practice of self-government in the industrial sphere or by ensuring the enjoyment of freedom as non-domination in the workplace—then the deployment of campaign tactics to suppress collective bargaining would strike at the very goods that a civic conception of freedom of speech would aim to protect. Employer free speech of this nature would not be protected, while union campaign speech would fall squarely within the right's protective scope. Such asymmetry would be intolerable for the liberal who defends neutrality. However, it is reasonable from the republican perspective on the simple ground that employer speech is an attack on civic values whereas union speech promotes them. This would justify a system of campaign regulation that insists on

[165] MJ Sandel, *Democracy's Discontent* (Cambridge Massachusetts, Harvard University Press, 1996) 71–90.

[166] *Ibid*, 80.

[167] *Ibid*, 79.

complete employer neutrality towards unionisation during the process for determining recognition, while allowing significant scope for union organisational access.

If we take the question of union access to the employer's private property, the civic perspective on property rights asks which pattern of entitlements would support the virtues and practices of citizenship as self-rule. As the history of republican thought demonstrates, the relation between private property and citizenship has been keenly contested.[168] For early republicans, freehold property was conceived as an essential bulwark against the corruption of civic virtue.[169] It fostered the resilient independence needed for citizens to deliberate for the sake of the common good. As a reaction to the emergence of industrial capitalism, later republican thought came to emphasise the barriers to citizenship erected by unequal proprietary distributions. Property became emblematic of servility rather than independence. As Sunstein argues, 'because of the republican emphasis on social construction of property rights, republicans are hardly hostile to redistribution or to collective efforts to reassess the existing distribution of wealth and entitlements'.[170]

As we have seen, the US insistence on an absolutist conception of employer property rights which reached its zenith in the Supreme Court decision in *Lechmere* has erected significant barriers to union organisational activities. While the British scheme has countenanced some fetters on the employer's right to exclude union organisers from its property, the proprietary barriers remain largely impenetrable outside of the narrow timeframe of the ballot procedure. A republican conception of property rights would lead to a radical rethinking of our current assumptions about private property and union organisation. First, atomistic alternative modes of communication such as newspaper advertising or telephone calls would not be treated as equivalent to participatory, face-to-face communication between workers and unions. The individual choice to unionise 'is ultimately a decision to trust the group and act collectively. The workplace thus serves a unique forum for discussion about unionization because it is the one place where all employees … gather as a group.'[171] Citizenship cannot occur in solitude; it is a practice that can only take place in communion with others.

Secondly, property rights are only as vital as the specific values they serve. Employers might have legitimate interests in maintaining safety or ensuring continuity of production, but the bare invocation of proprietary sovereignty should carry no weight. This would erect a strong presumption in favour of union access to company property subject to 'reasonable "time, place and

[168] PP Craig, *Public Law and Democracy in the UK and the USA* (Oxford, Oxford University Press, 1991) 318–28.

[169] Sandel, above n 165, 123–67.

[170] C Sunstein, 'Beyond the Republican Revival' (1988) 97 *Yale Law Journal* 1539, 1551.

[171] Estlund, above n 115, 332.

manner" restrictions'.[172] From a liberal perspective, this seems like a partisan betrayal of employers, taking from their bundle of property rights in order to confer special privileges on favoured interest groups. From a republican perspective, this seeming betrayal of neutrality is not to be regretted. The civic conception of property rights would justify reshaping the legal contours of property and its incidents in a manner more faithful to underlying values of citizenship as self-rule, community, and non-domination. Certainly, the absolute and unfettered right to exclude union organisers from the employer's property is difficult to justify once we endorse the republican view that property rights stand or fall in their contribution to the virtues and practices of republican citizenship.

[172] Klare, above n 118, 48.

6

The Political Theory of Union Recognition Campaigns II: The Problem of Adaptive Preferences

I INTRODUCTION

THE PREVIOUS CHAPTER explored the range of techniques for insulating workers' preferences from improper interference during the ballot procedure. It did not, however, challenge the underlying premise of Anglo-American recognition procedures: that tracking freely expressed private preferences furnishes the legitimate, democratic basis for allocating bargaining rights. The allocation of bargaining rights in the statutory recognition procedure is based on a simple idea rooted in a pluralist conception of politics: that an award of union recognition should track what workers want. This simple idea is intuitively appealing. In respecting their preferences, and in formulating legal responses that are preference-sensitive, we also seem to respect each worker's standing as a free and equal citizen.

This chapter will argue against preference-sensitivity as the touchstone for allocating bargaining rights. More specifically, preference-sensitive conceptions of politics are often insensitive to a range of distorting factors that affect the formation of preferences. Sometimes what we want may be constrained by perceptions of what we think we can get. Or we might discount the value of options we have never experienced, favouring instead to stick with the status quo. These adaptive preference effects undermine the legitimacy of preference-sensitive legal mechanisms. This adaptive critique of preference-sensitivity is often associated with a civic republican political philosophy. After tracing the pervasive influence of adaptive constraints within the context of union recognition, the chapter then evaluates five strategies for countering adaptive preference effects. While these strategies have as yet been realised only imperfectly, they indicate that the current legal framework has important civic resources at its disposal. In terms of future development, legal reforms should focus on enhancing these civic elements as a response to the problem of adaptive preferences.

II MODELS OF POLITICAL AND INDUSTRIAL DEMOCRACY: DEMOCRACY AS PREFERENCE AGGREGATION AND THE PROBLEM OF DISTORTED PREFERENCES

The Anglo-American model of statutory recognition is liberal in aspiration. This is reflected in the centrality of democratic ballot procedures designed to aggregate workers' preferences, allocating bargaining rights on the basis of majority rule; and this is precisely what we should expect from liberal legislation, for the 'political and economic processes by which individual preferences are combined into a social choice function are liberal modes of determining the common good'.[1] Pluralist democratic models of social choice embody an aura of moral legitimacy. Liberal ideals of liberty and equality seem to lie at their heart. This is reflected in the notion that individual preferences should be sovereign and entitled to presumptive respect by the State, and the utilitarian assumption that individual preferences should count equally in the process of aggregation. A repudiation of these democratic commitments appears to lie at the thin end of the political wedge; alternative political approaches envisaging a paternalist role for the State in scrutinising, shaping or censoring private preferences 'tend to be treated as at best misguided and more likely tyrannical',[2]

Civic conceptions of politics, by contrast, argue that consumer sovereignty provides a tenuous democratic legitimacy. Certain kinds of preference seem to be driven by external constraints rather than being endorsed autonomously by citizens. For example, preferences may be affected by the phenomenon of 'sour grapes' and so 'shaped by adaptation to what is possible',[3] such that if the opportunity were available preferences would then shift. A related distortion is the endowment effect. Citizens tend to ascribe higher value to those goods they currently have rather than those they lack. Consequently, preferences have a tendency to 'adapt' to the status quo. In the marketplace, 'the notion of consumer sovereignty is acceptable because, and to the extent that, the consumer chooses between courses of action that differ only in the way they affect him'.[4] In politics, however, citizens vie for influence over decisions that affect the community as a whole. This point is particularly vivid in union representation ballots: a vote against collective bargaining undermines the prospects for collective representation for the whole bargaining unit; it is simply not akin to a private consumer choice to forgo an individual right to trade union representation. The political community can therefore legitimately expect that preferences figuring in

[1] W Kymlicka, *Contemporary Political Philosophy*, 2nd edn (Oxford, Oxford University Press, 2002) 220.

[2] CR Sunstein, 'Legal Interference with Private Preferences' (1986) 53 *University of Chicago Law Review* 1129.

[3] J Elster, 'The Market and the Forum: Three Varieties of Political Theory', in J Bohman and W Rehg (eds), *Deliberative Democracy* (Cambridge Massachusetts, MIT Press, 1997) 3, 9. See also J Elster, *Sour Grapes: Studies in the Subversion of Rationality* (Cambridge, Cambridge University Press, 1983).

[4] Elster, *ibid*, 10.

the political decisions that affect its citizens are undistorted. This looks towards a civic conception of politics, such that citizens 'achieve a measure of critical distance from prevailing desires and practices, subjecting these desires and practices to scrutiny and review'.[5] One of the central objectives of civic politics is the identification and transformation of such distorted preferences. As the next two sections will demonstrate, the problem of preference distortion is particularly acute in the union recognition context.

A Adaptive Preferences and Collective Bargaining

Adaptive preferences arise out of a perception that opportunities are unavailable or too costly to realise. Preferences tend to track the range of feasible options, so reducing citizens' sense of frustration and 'cognitive dissonance' associated with unfulfilled aspirations. On the basis of 'sour grapes', citizens often conclude they did not want those unavailable opportunities anyway. The range of feasible options is in turn framed by legal norms allocating entitlements and opportunities. In the context of statutory recognition the question of adaptive preferences might seem misplaced. Indeed, the whole point of the legal framework, specifying democratic procedures whereby the constituent bargaining unit can choose to institute collective bargaining, is to provide workers with this opportunity. In this way, statutory recognition mechanisms 'displace the private market, generating a certain amount of worker control of the workplace even if the market would not provide it'.[6] This might appear to eliminate the potential for an adaptive preference effect; the opportunity for joint regulation through collective bargaining is facilitated by legal procedures permitting designation of bargaining representatives through workers' free choice. The adaptive preference effect is only present when legal norms are constitutive of opportunity deprivation, not opportunity provision. This understanding of statutory recognition as opportunity provision, and the consequent elimination of adaptive preferences, may however rest upon an unduly optimistic assessment of the nature and practical impact of statutory recognition.[7]

If we take the US statutory procedure, the phenomenon of adaptive preferences is particularly acute for two reasons: legal delay and employer hostility. First, layered institutional structures culminating in a prominent role for appellate courts entail dilatory statutory procedures for the resolution of recognition disputes. In contested cases involving discriminatory discharge of union supporters, for example, it may take more than four years for an employer to pursue

[5] CR Sunstein, 'Beyond the Republican Revival' (1988) 98 *Yale Law Journal* 1539, 1549.

[6] Sunstein, above n 2, 1149 fn 76.

[7] PC Weiler, *Governing the Workplace* (Cambridge Massachusetts, Harvard University Press, 1993) 117.

appeals through the federal courts.[8] Such legal delays can be fatal to the union's organisational base.[9] Secondly, the intensity of employer hostility to unionisation is manifested in routine and flagrant violation of fundamental labour rights. Unlawful discriminatory victimisation of union activists is commonplace during recognition campaigns.[10] The combination of circuitous appeals and weak remedies ensure that employers can deploy this devastating weapon with relative impunity. The effects of this lawlessness radiate far beyond the narrow legal confines of the recognition procedure itself. It engenders a climate of fear that shapes widely held perceptions amongst workers that unionisation will exact a heavy toll in terms of job losses, demotion and intimidation.[11] This anticipatory effect would contribute to the resilience of entrenched adaptive preferences.

While the US is an extreme case for adaptive preference effects, it seems likely that there are also adaptive constraints even under British legal procedures. First, with respect to legal delay, the extreme dilatoriness of the National Labor Relations Act (NLRA) procedure has been avoided. There is no right of appeal from Central Arbitration Council (CAC) decisions, and the volume of judicial review proceedings has been low. The Department of Trade and Industry found the median duration of a recognition claim was 19.3 calendar weeks.[12] This has remained relatively stable with the average duration of cases in 2004–2005 at 20 weeks.[13] That said, this still compares very unfavourably with Canadian statutory procedures: in Nova Scotia, for example, the ballot is held within five days of the union's application, and in Alberta the average duration of the statutory procedure is 16 days.[14] Furthermore, employers have successfully utilised a range of dilatory techniques to prolong statutory procedures, including litigation and stalling tactics in the various negotiation pauses designed to facilitate voluntary agreement.[15]

Secondly, the extent to which employers are prepared to resist unionisation will largely determine the successful translation of workers' incipient collective aspirations into support for recognition. There is evidence that union suppression techniques have been deployed during the Schedule A1 procedure, although it is also fair to say that employer resistance lacks the vehemence witnessed in the

[8] Human Rights Watch, *Unfair Advantage: Workers' Freedom of Association in the United States under International Human Rights Standards* (Human Rights Watch, 2000) 24.

[9] WB Gould, *Agenda for Reform: The Future of Employment Relationships and the Law* (Cambridge Massachusetts, MIT Press, 1993) 158–62.

[10] Human Rights Watch, above n 8, 18.

[11] Weiler (above n 7, 117 fn 25) cites survey evidence from a 1988 Gallop Poll indicating that 69% of respondents agreed with the statement that employers sometimes harass, intimidate or dismiss union supporters.

[12] DTI *Review of the ERA 1999* (Department of Trade and Industry 2003), para 2.74.

[13] *CAC Annual Report 2004–2005*, 9.

[14] Gould, above n 9, 216.

[15] KD Ewing, S Moore and S Wood, *Unfair Labour Practices: Trade Union Recognition and Employer Resistance* (London, Institute of Employment Rights, 2003) 30–39.

US.[16] It seems plausible to infer from this that adaptive preference effects are likely to be less pronounced in the UK than in the US. On the other hand, the limited timeframe of the 'unfair practice' provisions, which are only operative during the narrow confines of the Schedule A1 ballot procedure, allows employers a free hand to mould preferences through unfair practices before the question of recognition ever arises. There is currently little scope for countering adaptive distortions in the formation of workers' preferences in the unrecognised workplace.[17] If an adaptive preference effect arises in these circumstances the current legal framework simply defers to the preference regardless of the opportunity constraints on its formation. But if the initial disinterest in collective bargaining is a product of such an adaptive preference effect, it is not clear that the statutory mechanism should defer to the preference.

B Endowment Effects and Collective Bargaining

The endowment effect is another important source of preference distortion. In essence, the endowment effect is to be observed in the frequent disjunction between the price individuals would be willing to pay for an entitlement they lack, and the price they would be willing to accept to relinquish an entitlement they currently hold. Very often individuals will demand more to relinquish a good than they would offer to obtain it. There is a tendency for preferences to adapt to the pattern of current entitlements. The causes of the endowment effect are complex. In part, it is an aspect of cognitive dissonance reduction: valuing what we already have and devaluing what we lack tends to lead to greater satisfaction with our current situation. It also seems rooted in informational asymmetries and risk aversion. We value what we know because we have experienced it. In this respect, it is sometimes less risky to stick with those endowments than trade them for goods that may prove to be less valuable to us. As with the range of feasible opportunities, legal norms perform a constitutive role in the allocation of entitlements. Given the importance of this initial allocation to valuation, the default rules established by the legal framework matter a great deal in framing individuals' desires and aspirations. Accordingly, starting points tend to be inertial and 'sticky',[18] even in the absence of transaction costs. For this reason, the choice of default rule which provides the baseline for bargaining has a significant effect on bargaining outcomes.

The default position for the majority of British workplaces is now non-union. The 2004 Workplace Employee Relations Survey estimates that unions are

[16] TA Kochan, 'A US perspective on the future of trade unions in Britain', in H Gospel and S Wood (eds), *Representing Workers* (London, Routledge, 2003) 166, 169.

[17] Studies of non-union firms highlight the powerful inhibiting effects of ongoing employer hostility on workers' preference formation. See T Dundon, 'Put Up and Shut Up: social mobilisation and employee attitudes in non-union firms' BUIRA Conference Paper (2001).

[18] CR Sunstein, 'Switching the Default Rule' (2002) 77 *New York University Law Review* 106.

recognised for the purposes of collective bargaining in only 30 per cent of workplaces.[19] In the event of a statutory recognition claim, it is the case that 'no collective representation is in place until employees have affirmatively voted for it. The ordinary assumption of the workplace, and hence the default rule, is non-union.'[20] While statutory recognition mechanisms allow some scope for shifting the non-union default position, the endowment effect ensures a 'pronounced tilt against employee attraction to union representation'.[21] To test our intuitions about the endowment effect, Weiler invites us to imagine a world where collective bargaining constitutes the default mode of workplace governance but that workers may affirmatively *opt out* of it if they so choose. He speculates that this would dramatically reverse the declining fortunes of collective bargaining simply by switching the underlying default rule. Workers would be likely to stick with what they knew as the 'natural' union default position.

Recent work on the dynamics of union membership growth lends empirical weight to this endowment effect characterisation. In their analysis of union voting intentions, Freeman and Rogers found a large disparity between current and ex-union members with comparable experiences of union membership: holding the level of satisfaction with the union at a constant, current members in unionised workplaces were much more likely to vote for the union than ex-members in non-union workplaces. The authors postulate this disparity arises out of an endowment effect.[22] This has significant implications given the current state of unionisation. Workers are much more likely to work in a non-union rather than a unionised workplace. Indeed, one of the most striking features of union membership density decline in the UK is the rise in 'never-membership', encapsulating those workers in the labour market having no experience of the representational aspects of union membership. As such 'union density decline in Britain can be almost entirely explained by a lack of uptake on the part of new labour-market entrants rather than by an outflow of existing members'.[23] Indeed, once workers join unions and experience the benefits of representation, union membership proves to be highly durable.[24] The fact that membership status, for both members and non-members alike, has this durable and persistent

[19] B Kersley, C Alpin, J Forth, A Bryson, H Bewley, G Dix and S Oxenbridge, *Inside the Workplace: Findings from the Employment Relations Survey* (London, Routledge, 2006) 117–23.

[20] C Sunstein, 'Human Behaviour and the Law of Work' (2001) 87 *Virginia Law Review* 205, 256.

[21] Weiler, above n 7, 228.

[22] RB Freeman and J Rogers, *What Workers Want* (Ithaca, ILR Press, 1999) 74–6.

[23] A Bryson and R Gomez, 'Buying into union membership', in H Gospel and S Wood, *Representing Workers* (London, Routledge, 2003) 72, 72–3. The authors point out that between 1983 and 2001, the rate of 'never membership' rose from 28% to 48%. This phenomenon is particularly acute among younger workers, with 78% never having had experience of union membership and services. See R Freeman and W Diamond, 'Young workers and trade unions', in H Gospel and S Wood (eds), *Representing Workers* (London, Routledge, 2003) 29.

[24] A Bryson and R Gomez, 'Marching on together? Reasons for the recent decline in union membership', in C Bromley, A Park and K Thompson (eds), *British Social Attitudes: The 20th Report* (2002) 43.

quality indicates an endowment effect at work.[25] Bryson and Gomez postulate that this lies in the experiential nature of the good at stake. Many of the benefits of unionisation, such as the institution of democratic voice through joint regulation in the workplace, cannot meaningfully be evaluated *ex ante* by potential members. Instead, such 'experience goods' can only be evaluated after they have been sampled; this entails that 'membership is risky because it delivers a payoff that is observable only after unionization has been sampled, and hence there is always a chance that joining a union will not deliver its expected return and will leave the worker stuck with his original decision'.[26] This informational asymmetry reinforces the initial non-union endowment.

This experiential perspective on the nature of joint regulation is also consistent with Bain's seminal work on the relationship between union membership and recognition.[27] Bain's analysis demonstrated the positive role that recognition played in stimulating the growth of white collar unionism. This challenged the orthodox assumption that industrial strength, reflected in high levels of union density, was the necessary prelude to recognition. Historically, recognition in white collar industries tended to be conferred by employers in a climate of strong State support for collective bargaining rather than being conceded through the leverage of industrial muscle. Once recognition was conferred, this created a favourable environment for union membership growth, since 'the less recognition an employer is prepared to give a union the more difficult it is for the union to participate in the process of job regulation and thereby demonstrate to employees that it can provide a service for them'.[28] Conversely, then, once recognition is conceded the union is better able to demonstrate its value to workers through the provision of joint regulation through collective bargaining. Recognition and union growth then become mutually reinforcing, although recognition, contrary to the orthodox assumption, is the initial catalyst for this virtuous circle effect. The endowment effect has significant implications for the choice of remedial strategy to counter adaptive preferences. Sometimes it may be insufficient to provide workers with an opportunity to choose the option of which they have previously been deprived, for they may forgo that opportunity even though it might be one that they would value highly had they experienced it. As Sunstein argues, a more intrusive remedy might be justified on the following basis:

> If people do not want an opportunity because they have considered it to be unavailable, the only way to solve the problem is first to make it available and second to force them to take advantage of it.[29]

[25] The endowment effect characterisation is also adopted in A Charlwood, 'Willingness to unionize amongst non-union workers', in H Gospel and S Wood (eds), *Representing Workers* (London, Routledge, 2003) 51, 69.

[26] Bryson and Gomez, above n 23, 83–4.

[27] GS Bain, *The Growth of White Collar Unionism* (Oxford, Oxford University Press, 1970).

[28] *Ibid*, 123.

[29] Sunstein, above n 2, 1149.

This might justify shifting the underlying endowment from non-union to union as a way of precipitating a change in workers' preferences, rather relying on a shift in those underlying preferences as a trigger for changing the default position.

III FIVE CIVIC STRATEGIES FOR COUNTERING DISTORTED PREFERENCES

Preference aggregation is a central element of the current approach to union recognition. As we have seen, adaptive preferences and the endowment effect undermine the legitimacy of preference aggregation as a democratic model. It is possible to identify five legal strategies, some of them immanent features of the current legal framework, which are potentially responsive to the problem of distorted preferences. First, the CAC has interpreted *admissibility criteria* in a manner sensitive to adaptive constraints on preference formation. In particular, the CAC has deployed a flexible timeframe for assessing workers' support for unionisation, looking at the context in which preferences were formed and predicting how they might develop over time through virtuous circle effects. While this ensures that appropriate cases are channelled into the recognition procedure, it does not ensure that unions can transcend adaptive constraints in achieving actual majority support. As such, this must be supplemented with a second strategy, preference transformation through *deliberative democracy*, where workers scrutinise and filter out distorted preferences through the practice of shared deliberation. Again, however, this provides an incomplete remedial response. In particular, workers who have never experienced collective bargaining may be reluctant to place a high valuation on the option even after deliberation. In these cases, preferences may only modify with a State-led shift from a non-union to a unionised governance structure, so that some workers are forced to experience a good that they might not otherwise value.

This highlights the need for endowment shifting techniques as a supplement to deliberative techniques. A third strategy is endowment shifting through *voluntary recognition*. Voluntary recognition deals negotiated in the shadow of the statutory procedure enable a broader pool of workers to experience unionisation than would be feasible through the statutory procedure alone. Unfortunately employers seem reluctant to concede voluntary recognition unless the union has demonstrable majority support. This limits the potential for virtuous circle effects through voluntary recognition. These effects are more likely to occur if proposals for *'staged' recognition* are adopted, allocating consultation rights to unions with less than majority density in the bargaining unit as a stimulus to organisational growth. Finally, the role of workers' own collective agency is explored through the lens of the recent turn to the *'organising model'* in the trade union movement. On this view, union resurgence will only occur in a sustainable form when workers themselves learn to undertake the tasks of self-organisation. The extent to which the legal framework constrains or enables the diffusion of the 'organising model' will be explored.

A CAC Interpretation of Admissibility Thresholds

Schedule A1 is designed so that only recognition applications with a reasonable prospect of success will proceed beyond the threshold of admissibility and validity. To this end the CAC is required to determine whether the applicant union has 10 per cent membership within the proposed bargaining unit and that a majority of the bargaining unit would be likely to support recognition.[30] The interpretive issue faced by the CAC seems straightforward enough: how to measure majority preferences for union recognition. However, as the burgeoning literature on preferences and politics indicates, the gauging of preferences is fraught with theoretical controversy. Liberal conceptions of politics take preference aggregation as their guiding ideal. Whatever preferences are expressed by citizens should simply be respected. When citizens get what they want through satisfaction of their existing preferences then welfare is maximised. By contrast, civic conceptions of politics reject the ideal of maximising satisfaction of current preferences. Certain kinds of preference seem to be driven by external constraints rather than being autonomously endorsed by citizens. If citizens are faced with opportunity constraints in the pursuit of certain goods, their preferences often 'adapt' to those constraints. Whereas liberal accounts of preferences take them as a 'given' to be respected whatever, the civic perspective treats preferences as a socially constructed phenomenon. Where preferences are 'adaptive' to unjust social and economic constraints in their formation, respecting such preferences has a pallid legitimacy.

The CAC's study of the first five years of Schedule A1 demonstrated that unions had been enjoying a large degree of success in the initial stages of the procedure: as of 31 March 2005, 264 applications had been accepted by the CAC and only 50 had not.[31] Of those 50 declined applications the most significant barrier has been the 'majority support likely' criterion.[32] The most recent CAC Annual Report confirms that union success rates in the preliminary stages have continued to improve: in 2007–2008 only 7 per cent of applications were not accepted at the preliminary stage, with the CAC concluding that this reflected increased union familiarity with the relevant criteria.[33] This relative success in the initial stages of

30 TULRCA 1992, Schedule A1, para 36(1)(a)–(b).
31 *CAC Annual Report 2004–2005*, 16.
32 *Ibid.*
33 *CAC Annual Report 2007–08*, 7.

the legislation reflects a cautious and strategic use of the statutory procedure by unions so as to ensure its continuing stability and credibility.[34]

In absolute terms, however, the proportion of workplaces without recognition in the private sector, but with sufficient membership density to satisfy the 'majority support likely' criterion, is small.[35] Evidence suggests the pool of potential statutory recognition claims in the private sector as a whole is limited to approximately 1.7 per cent of workplaces.[36] And this vicious circle is precisely what adaptive preference analysis would predict. Without recognition the benefits of collective voice cannot be experienced in non-recognised workplaces and consequently unions face significant difficulties surmounting the experiential deficit of never-membership in convincing workers to join. Without membership density, unions have no credible opportunity to invoke the statutory procedure to gain recognition, whether voluntary or statutory. Nevertheless, the *reasoning* in CAC decisions under paragraph 36(1)(b) demonstrates considerable awareness of, and an attempt to counter, these adaptive constraints in its application of the 'majority support likely' test.

(i) Union Membership and Support for Recognition: What is the Relationship?

The point has arisen under paragraph 36(1)(b) in determining the link between union membership and support for collective bargaining, and whether an individual's union membership can, on its own, be taken as indicative of his support for union recognition. The CAC has adopted a dynamic interpretation, equating union membership with support for collective bargaining. Thus, the CAC panel in *GPMU and Derwent Information Ltd* addressed the employer's argument that union membership could not necessarily be equated with support for recognition:

> While it is always possible that some Union members may not want the Union to be recognised this is unlikely to be the view of more than a very few people. The Union is not a professional association and membership does not confer particular benefits beyond those achieved through representation with the employer. To be a member and not want recognition for oneself, and by not supporting it make it more difficult for

[34] S Wood, S Moore and P Willman, 'Third time lucky for statutory union recognition in the UK?' (2002) 33 *Industrial Relations Journal* 215. The authors found that 'unions are not prepared to take risks when using the procedure' (228). To this end, 60% of unions in the authors' survey sample indicated they would only use the statutory procedure if they were reasonably sure of majority support at the ballot stage. 29% would only do so if they had majority membership in the bargaining unit.

[35] *Ibid.* The authors take 35% density as the relevant threshold for satisfying the criterion of likely majority support under the Schedule. This is supported by their analysis of CAC decision-making. Without further evidence of support, such as petitions or signed authorization cards, 35% seems to be the outer limit of density taken by the CAC as sufficient to satisfy this admissibility criterion.

[36] *Ibid*, 219.

others to gain collective representation *is unusual if not perverse* in the Panel's opinion.[37] (emphasis added)

The CAC has generally based its decisions on the dynamic assumption that, in the absence of evidence to the contrary, union membership is a legitimate indicator of support for collective bargaining.[38] The CAC has emphasised that it is an 'evidence-based body', so employers' speculations that workers might have joined for reasons other than collective bargaining are not sufficient to meet the evidential hurdle.[39] Rather, the CAC has insisted on specific evidence as distinct from mere assertion that the linkage between union membership and collective bargaining is negated. Contrary evidence has consisted of explicit communications by letter to the employer by union members indicating they did not wish the union to be recognised;[40] and increasing membership density in the context of union-backed litigation for industrial disease compensation.[41] Such cases are, however, rare.[42]

The CAC has also resisted negating the union membership–collective bargaining linkage where the union has offered discounted subscription rates to increase the attractiveness of union membership in non-recognised workplaces. So in *Teknek Electronics Ltd and the ISTC* the employer argued that discounted subscriptions cast

[37] TUR1/72/2001 para 15.

[38] See, eg, *CATU and Industrial Agricultural Engineers* TUR1/358/2004; *TGWU and TVR Engineering Ltd* TUR1/371/2004; *AMICUS and Premdor Crosby Ltd* TUR1/343/2004; *BECTU and BBC River City Production* TUR1/274/2003; *NUMAST and Hoverspeed Ltd* TUR1/433/2005; *NUJ and Champion Newspapers* TUR1/581/2007; *Unite the Union and Harry Lawson Ltd* TUR1/620/2008.

[39] *Unite the Union and Knightsbridge Guarding Ltd* TUR1/624/2008 para 30.

[40] *GMB and F W Farnsworth* TUR1/152/2002. See also *GMB and Capital Aluminium Extrusions Ltd (Capalex)* TUR1/639/2008, where the Panel was scrupulous in its examination of the circumstances in which the letters from workers were collected by the employer. The Panel concluded that the anonymity of the process, and the absence of countervailing petition evidence by the union, provided a justified basis for delinking union membership from support for collective bargaining.

[41] *NUM and Hatfield Coal Company* TUR1/55/2001. Conversely, where increased membership has occurred within the context of a recognition campaign this evidence tends to bolster the union membership-collective bargaining equation, as in *BALPA and Ryanair* TUR1/70/2001. On the other hand, the fact that union membership has been stable over a long period of time in the absence of recognition has not been interpreted by the CAC as negating the union membership-collective bargaining equation, as in *Amicus and H J Heinz Co Ltd* TUR1/556/2007 para 39.

[42] *TGWU and Convatec Ltd* TUR1/346/2004 seems to constitute a departure from this dominant practice of dynamic interpretation. The case manager found membership density of 15.95% and petition support of 44.09%. Some union members had not signed the petition and the union argued this was because union members considered their support for collective bargaining could be assumed in virtue of their paying membership dues. The Panel considered (at para 23) that 'no evidence was given to support the argument that those union members who had not signed could be assumed to support recognition'. With respect, the proper approach seems to be that in the absence of contrary evidence it is reasonable to impute support for collective bargaining to union members. This can be contrasted with, eg, *ISTC and Cornelius Electronics Ltd* TUR1/185/2002 and *Matalan Retail Ltd and the GMB* TUR1/247/2003, where the Panel did not assume that union members' failure to sign a petition indicated a lack of support for recognition. Similarly in *Unite the Union and Sports Direct International plc* TUR1/619/2008, the Panel observed (at para 41) that the failure of union members to sign a petition might indicate that 'those who actually join the union may consider that of itself demonstrates support for collective bargaining'.

doubt on whether workers genuinely supported recognition or had instead joined the union to avail themselves of cheap insurance and loan facilities.[43] This argument was rejected by the CAC. The discounted rate was in accordance with the union rule book and, in the absence of contrary evidence, such discounted membership could be taken as indicative of support for recognition. The CAC's approach demonstrates considerable sensitivity to the recruitment difficulties faced by unions in non-recognised workplaces. Union membership in the expectation of union representation *is* less valuable than union membership under collective bargaining. Discounted membership is one important means by which unions can break the vicious circle of no recruitment without recognition and surmount the experiential deficit of 'never-membership'.[44]

In general, unions have tended to rely on membership evidence alone without the use of supporting petition evidence only in situations of majority membership. That said, whereas membership density in the region of 26 per cent has not been treated as sufficient in itself to establish the 'majority support likely' threshold,[45] the CAC has indicated that membership density of 34.7 per cent might be sufficient to satisfy the threshold in the absence of other supporting evidence.[46]

(ii) Adaptive and Non-Adaptive Conceptions of Preference Formation

Two strands of decision-making can be discerned in the CAC's decision-making under paragraph 36(1)(b) corresponding to non-adaptive and adaptive understandings of preference formation. This emerges specifically in the CAC's identification of the relevant timeframe for gauging workers' preferences. On the non-adaptive conception, preferences are taken as fixed data, impervious to deliberative modification and social constraints. This would tend to be associated with a narrow timeframe for preference measurement. The adaptive conception, however, emphasises that preferences are socially constructed. What we want is often shaped by perceptions of available opportunities, and what we currently value might well be shaped by past deprivations. Moreover, preferences can change. They might do so through shared deliberation as we evaluate and revise

[43] TUR1/267/2003. See also *ISTC and Mission Foods Ltd* TUR1/156/2003; *ISTC and Amicus and Polypipe Building Products Ltd* TUR1/278/2003.

[44] It should be noted that discounted membership has been more problematic in later stages of the procedure. In *AEEU and Huntleigh Healthcare Ltd*, TUR1/19/2000, the CAC ordered a ballot despite majority membership because it considered gratuitous membership engaged para 22(4)(c), raising doubts as to whether a significant number of members wanted the union to conduct collective bargaining on their behalf. It is also important that discounted membership is in accordance with the union rule book. In *MSF and Unipart Group of Companies Ltd*, TUR1/94/2001, the employer successfully argued that the individuals apparently admitted into the union were not in fact members because the union rule book had not authorised reduced subscriptions. The CAC panel then ordered a ballot because there was less than majority membership (which the union subsequently lost).

[45] See, eg, *GMB and WS Britland and Co Ltd* TUR1/593/2007, 26.08% membership density insufficient.

[46] *Unite the Union and Stephens and George Ltd* TUR1/634/2008 para 36.

our preferences in the light of new perspectives. Or, if we are given the opportunity to experience goods from which we have been excluded in the past we might find we value those goods very highly. This adaptive conception of preferences has both a past-oriented and future-oriented dimension. The past-oriented dimension looks to the social constraints that might have shaped current preferences such as prior deprivation of an opportunity. The future-oriented dimension looks to how preferences might modify in the light of deliberative preference-shaping and newly experienced opportunities. The relevant time-frame for assessing preferences is therefore correspondingly broader.

(a) Non-Adaptive Preferences: Narrowing the Timeframe The non-adaptive conception formed the basis to the Panel's decision in *NUJ and Gloucestershire Newspapers Ltd.*[47] The union had 36.1 per cent membership in the bargaining unit. In arguing that this satisfied the requirements in paragraph 36(1)(b) the union based its submissions on the future-oriented dimension of adaptive preferences. Thus, it argued this membership level would translate into majority support due to a projected increase once the union had access to the employer's property. It also drew attention to a wider pattern of ballot support exceeding initial membership density in other CAC-ordered ballots. Moreover, the union contended that membership levels tended to increase after recognition had been awarded.[48] The company insisted that 'the Panel had to assess the matter at the date of the hearing, not at some future unspecified date'.[49] The Panel, in holding the application to be invalid, rejected the future-oriented perspective. Without petition evidence indicating further current support of 15 per cent it could not be said that a majority would be likely to support recognition. Furthermore, 'the union was not entitled to rely on a potential increase in membership or support occurring *after* the ballot'.[50] What was needed was evidence 'that directly reflected the views of the workers within the bargaining unit'.[51]

This insistence on 'directly reflected' preferences precludes the deployment of an adaptive conception, since the past and future trajectory of preferences can of necessity only be a matter of informed speculation. The CAC's approach seemed close to requiring an arithmetical majority of current support demonstrated in petition evidence. In a similar vein, the future-oriented argument based on a 'bandwagon' effect, that support for the union tends to increase in the run-up to the ballot and exceed initial levels of support, was rejected in *TGWU and ConvaTec Ltd.*[52] The Panel observed that no 'evidence was given to support the argument that imminent recognition would of itself generate additional support for

47 TUR1/66/2001.
48 *Ibid*, para 14.
49 *Ibid*, para 21.
50 *Ibid*, para 29 (emphasis added).
51 *Ibid.*
52 TUR1/346/2004.

collective bargaining'.[53] With respect it is difficult to see how any such evidence, relating to the prediction of future events in a specific workplace context, could ever be provided; particularly given the Panel's earlier observation in *NUJ and Gloucestershire Newspapers Ltd* that statistical analysis of what had occurred in other CAC-ordered ballots was irrelevant.[54]

(b) Adaptive Preferences: Broadening the Timeframe There is a rich seam of CAC decisions, however, that are predicated upon an adaptive conception, reflected in a greater elasticity of timeframe in gauging workers' preferences. This encompasses both future- and past-oriented dimensions of the adaptive conception. The future-oriented view was articulated in *MSF and Teachers Management Services Ltd*.[55] Membership density was in flux in the period preceding the union's application, ranging from a high of 76 per cent then dropping back to 36 per cent. These fluctuations occurred in a context of significant labour turnover. The union relied upon its membership density without petition evidence. In a significant statement of principle the Panel observed that 'behind the individuals who have joined the trade union will be workers who whilst supporting recognition prefer not to commit to union membership and others who support recognition but wish to become members of a trade union and pay their union subscriptions once, or if, the union gains recognition'.[56] This looks to potential virtuous circle effects post-recognition on union support and recruitment in its application of the statutory test.

This has largely displaced the non-adaptive conception articulated in *NUJ and Gloucestershire Newspapers Ltd*.[57] In *AMICUS and Baker Oil Tools* the company attempted to resurrect the non-adaptive conception by suggesting a strict test of arithmetical majority support. The CAC rejected this interpretation basing its future-oriented interpretation on the clear statutory wording of the provision. Thus, the Panel stated it was 'required to be satisfied that a majority of the workers constituting the relevant bargaining unit *would be likely to favour* recognition of the union. This construction inevitably requires the CAC Panel to … make an informed decision about how things stand and how they might be likely to develop.'[58] This seems right. What 'would be likely' to happen is future-oriented.

[53] *Ibid*, para 23.

[54] The 'bandwagon' effect was also rejected in *AEEU and Control Techniques Drives Ltd*, TUR1/109/2001, although the Panel suggested that if there had been evidence of upward trajectory rather than stable membership this might have supported the 'bandwagon' argument. See also *TGWU and Jordan (Cereals) Ltd*, TUR1/258/2003, where the 'bandwagon' effect was referred to in company submissions to the CAC. The CAC accepted the union's application on the basis of 16% membership and 46% petition support.

[55] TUR1/57/2001.

[56] *Ibid*, 10.

[57] See, eg, *MSF and Aim Composites Ltd*, TUR1/61/2001; *BALPA and RyanAir* TUR1/70/2001; *GMB and O&H Mobility*, TUR1/302/2003; *NUJ and AOL (UK) Ltd*, TUR1/424/2005.

[58] TUR1/446/2005, para 22. See also *GMB and Caunton Engineering*, TUR1/396/2004, where the CAC drew attention to 'likely' in the statutory formulation. Likely support is not certain support.

And in *Unite—the Union and Cadbury Trebor Bassett* the Panel responded to the employer's assertion that those workers who had not joined the union might be taken not to support recognition:

> The Panel is of the view that there may perhaps be individuals that are unwilling to pay subscriptions in an unrecognised workplace but may well join the Union once recognition has been secured. Another factor could be that there may be individuals that have not joined the Union because they are under the misapprehension that the employer would be informed of that fact and, for whatever reason they do not want this brought to the Employer's attention.[59]

This envisages informed prediction by the CAC in applying the statutory test rather than a strict insistence on arithmetical majority support. In this way, the legal test necessitates a 'light' rather than a 'heavy' touch in terms of the intensity of CAC scrutiny.[60] This seems appropriate since this is only a preliminary threshold with actual support still to be tested later in the legal process.[61]

Acknowledgement of the past-oriented dimension of adaptive preferences has also been a prominent feature of CAC decisions. The CAC has displayed considerable sensitivity to the residual effects of prior employer hostility to unionisation on current preferences. In *AEEU and GE Caledonian Ltd* the employer was, by its own admission, aggressively protective of the non-union status quo.[62] It had utilised surveillance of organisational activity and deployed small group meetings with workers making clear the company's resolute hostility towards and willingness to resist union recognition. In these circumstances the union had mustered 43.8 per cent support in a circulated petition. The Panel had regard to this evidence in applying the statutory test. It considered that this context was likely to have had a dampening effect on workers' preferences. Accordingly the statutory test was satisfied despite the absence of statistical majority support in the petition. Similarly, in *TGWU and Cannon Rubber Ltd,* witness statements from union activists indicated genuinely held perceptions that the company, which claimed a 'tradition of benevolent paternalism' antithetical to collective bargaining, was hostile to unionisation.[63] The union claimed this had the effect of chilling support in the bargaining unit. The Panel accepted that such perceptions were liable to have deterred union support. Accordingly, and adjusting for these

[59] TUR1/582/2007 para 27. For another recent decision that invokes likely virtuous circle effects of recognition on recruitment for the purposes of the statutory test, see *GMB and East Riding Sacks Ltd* TUR1/616/2008, paras 27–8.

[60] *NUJ and City AM* TUR1/638/2008 para 15.

[61] In Wood, Moore and Willman's (above n 34) analysis of ballot results under Schedule A1 up to December 2001 they concluded 'all but one of the successful ballots support the proposition that union membership underestimates support for recognition in the workforce'. This seems intuitively plausible given the employer's duty to grant reasonable access to the union is only triggered once the CAC has ordered the ballot.

[62] TUR1/120/2001.

[63] TUR1/245/2003.

adaptive effects, petition support of 40.64 per cent translated into the likelihood of majority support.[64]

Property rights are also implicated in this adaptive approach to preference measurement. Employer property rights constitute a significant barrier to unions' organisational activities. Without access to the workplace, enabling union organisers to carry their message to the constituent bargaining unit, workers are unlikely to perceive collective bargaining as a realistically available option. Without that kind of personal contact, many workers are likely to know nothing of the potential benefits of collective bargaining. This problem of an experiential deficit in matters of union representation is made more acute by rising levels of never-membership in the labour market. Adaptive preference theory would predict preferences adjusting to these perceptions of unavailability, corresponding to a lack of interest in recognition. Yet without adequate levels of likely support for recognition, the CAC is unlikely to accept the union's application. It is only after acceptance of the application that the union's modest access entitlement is triggered under Schedule A1. As such, property access is a critical condition for breaking into the vicious circle of no recruitment without recognition.

While the CAC has no statutory authority to order access for the union pre-acceptance, some of its decisions have adjusted the 'majority support' threshold so as to offset these proprietary constraints on preference formation. Thus in *POA and Wackenhut (UK) Ltd Escort Services* the CAC noted that the bargaining unit was dispersed across 17 sites throughout the country with workers often travelling between different sites.[65] The union had 35 per cent membership but offered no petition evidence. In deciding that the majority threshold had been reached the CAC referred to the specific organisational barriers faced by the union, which 'made running a recognition campaign more difficult as the union had problems reaching potential members'.[66] Similar adaptive adjustments to offset access difficulties were made in *TGWU and W Jordan (Cereals) Ltd* where the Panel indicated its awareness 'that the petition was circulated during a period in which the union did not enjoy formal access to the workforce', taking petition support of 46 per cent as sufficient to satisfy the statutory criterion.[67]

[64] Similar adaptive adjustments in order to filter out the effects of historic intimidation occurred in *ISTC and Faccenda Group (Corby)* TUR1/200/2002; *BAJ and Mirror Group Newspapers Ltd* TUR1/75/2001.

[65] TUR1/108/2001.

[66] *Ibid*, para 5. See also *GMB and Madame Tussauds* TUR1/299/2003, where the Panel was 'persuaded by the union's evidence that it faced difficulties reaching some workers in the proposed bargaining unit', taking petition support of 45.53% as sufficient to satisfy the statutory criterion. This can sometimes count against the union as in *AMICUS and Ford Motor Company Ltd*, TUR1/447/2005. The employer allowed generous workplace access to the union enabling it to communicate with workers through meetings and work e-mail in the pre-acceptance phase. The union recorded 38.54% support in a petition. Given the degree of access permitted by the employer this level did not satisfy para 36(1)(b).

[67] TUR1/258/2003.

The boldest statement of principle in this regard can be found in *AMICUS and Teconnex Ltd.*[68] Conflicting evidence was provided by union and employer as to the voting intentions of workers in the bargaining unit. The union's petition evidence indicated 65.12 per cent support for the recognition claim. By contrast, the employer had commissioned an independent postal ballot of the workforce which indicated a majority of those voting were against recognition. The Panel noted that 'the Union was severely disadvantaged by not having access to the workforce in order to put its case to the workers ... The Company was then able to put forward its view with no counter argument from the Union'.[69] Without observance of the minimum standards of reasonable access envisaged in the Code of Practice on Union Access,[70] the Panel considered the ballot result could not be taken as a reliable gauge of worker preferences. As such, the union's petition evidence was preferred to the employer's. Although the employer had no legal duty to afford access to the union, the failure to do so undermined the veracity of the employer's evidence in applying paragraph 36(1)(b). This contains the germ of a principle of extended union access whenever an employer adduces ballot-based evidence in the preliminary stages of the procedure.[71]

This leads into a broader problem faced by the CAC in its evaluation of potential support in the bargaining unit. There is no statutorily prescribed method for authoritatively gauging support. Nor is the employer barred from implementing its own enquiries of worker preferences and adducing this as evidence in persuading the CAC that there is insufficient support for recognition. Evidence has tended to include membership density, ACAS co-ordinated ballots,[72] employer sponsored ballots and worker attitude surveys,[73] union petitions,[74] letters from individual workers,[75] and one-to-one interviews between

[68] TUR1/318/2003.

[69] *Ibid*, para 30.

[70] See, now DTI, *Code of Practice on Access and Unfair Practices during Recognition and Derecognition Ballots* (Department of Trade and Industry, 2005).

[71] See also *Unite—the Union and Sports Direct International plc* TUR1/619/2008, para 37, where the Panel drew attention to the difficulties presented in the collation of a union petition where the union was not yet entitled to formal property access.

[72] See, eg, *TGWU and Readmans Ltd* TUR1/96/2001, where ACAS conducted a ballot with the consent of both parties. This established support for recognition of 62.7% which satisfied the statutory criterion.

[73] See, eg, *TGWU and Riverstone Spinning Ltd* TUR1/110/2001, where the company-arranged ballot indicated 73% support for recognition. Similarly, a company-arranged snap ballot backfired in *ISTC and Cornelius Electronics Ltd* TUR1/185/2002 when it indicated majority support for recognition.

[74] See, eg, *TGWU and Stadium Electrical Components Ltd* TUR1/10/2000. The CAC will scrutinise the form of the petition to ensure it provides evidence of support for union *recognition*. In *TGWU and DHL Aviation (UK) Ltd* TUR1/15/2000 one of the petitions in circulation was worded 'Would you like DHL to have a Union?' This made no reference to either the TGWU or the question of recognition. Consequently the petition evidence was unreliable in deciding whether a majority would be likely to support recognition of the applicant union. See also *UNIFI and Nottinghamshire Building Society* TUR1/229/2002 for another example of ambiguous wording undermining the petition's evidential weight.

[75] *GPMU and Sentinel Colour Print* TUR1/37/2001.

management and individual workers.[76] Not surprisingly, employer and union evidence has sometimes conflicted. The CAC's approach has been sensitive to the power imbalance between employers and unions, and the CAC has tended to resolve such conflicts in the union's favour. In *Economic Skips Ltd and TGWU* the company's survey of worker attitudes indicated only four workers had articulated a preference for union recognition, as opposed to 36 against.[77] The union's petition, however, indicated majority support for union recognition. As the Panel observed, 'it is clear that some people have signed both in favour and against recognition at different times'.[78] The CAC opted for the union's petition evidence as a more reliable indicator of potential support. The employer's questionnaire was distributed and had to be completed in one-to-one meetings in the Managing Director's office, during which workers were advised that union recognition would lead to reduced pay. The CAC considered some workers would be intimidated into not revealing their true preferences under these circumstances.

Similarly in *AMICUS and GE Thermometrics (UK) Ltd*,[79] the union submission alleged that an employer sponsored ballot was preceded by one-to-one meetings with veiled threats of closure or relocation in the event of union recognition. Furthermore, the union had no access to the constituent workforce during the ballot period. Under these circumstances the CAC found the union's membership density and petition evidence more persuasive as a guide to potential support.[80] And in *Unite the Union and Stephens and George Ltd* the Panel faced the problem of conflicting evidence as to workers' preferences when comparing the employer's and the union's petition. The Panel concluded that 'the Employer is in a stronger position than the Union to secure expressions of support in its favour from individual workers because of the inducements, positive and negative, it can offer, explicitly or, more likely, implicitly, to those supporting its views'.[81] For this reason, the Panel declined to deduct the total number of dual signatories from the union's petition evidence.

Conversely, where employers have sought to cast doubt on the accuracy of union petitions, such as allegations of peer pressure or intimidation, the CAC has

[76] *TGWU and Mastercare Service and Distribution Ltd* TUR1/275/2003.

[77] TUR1/121/2001.

[78] *Ibid*, para 8.

[79] TUR1/347/2004.

[80] Similarly in *TGWU and Mastercare Service and Distribution Ltd* TUR1/275/2003, the CAC treated the results of one-to-one meetings between management and workers, which the employer argued provided evidence of a lack of support for recognition, with caution. The CAC placed greater weight on the union's petition evidence, which indicated 61% support for recognition. In *Amicus and H J Heinz Co Ltd* TUR1/556/2007 the Panel engaged in very careful scrutiny of the employer's petition evidence, such as the way in which the survey was conducted and the safeguards in place to protect worker confidentiality, in order to evaluate its veracity.

[81] TUR1/634/2008 para 40.

been similarly insistent on the need for specific evidence.[82] In *GMB and Windowstyle (UK) Ltd*[83] the union had sought to encourage workers to discuss the prospects of unionisation by offering a free 'butty and brew'[84] to those workers who met with union representatives in a canteen. The employer alleged that this constituted an improper financial inducement either to join the union or to register a favourable view on the union's petition. The CAC rejected the employer's objections, concluding sensibly that this was nothing more than an attempt by the union to surmount the communicative difficulties for unions in unrecognised workplaces. In short, it was an inducement to talk and nothing more.

In conclusion, the CAC has adopted a bold interpretive stance on the issue of whether workers are likely to favour for the union's recognition claim. This has meant that relatively few applications have failed at the preliminary hurdle on this ground. Nevertheless, it must be acknowledged that this alone can do little to overcome the adaptive preference problem. Even if unions overcome the preliminary hurdle and argue their way into the legal procedure this gives them nothing tangible in substantive terms. They still have to achieve arithmetical majority support either through membership density or through the medium of the ballot before they can achieve recognition. This means that the CAC's interpretive approach needs to be complemented by other strategies designed to overcome adaptive preferences in the actual allocation of bargaining rights. One possible candidate is the ballot procedure itself, which gives unions the opportunity of shaping workers' preferences through shared deliberation.

B Preference Shaping through Deliberative Democracy

The civic tradition places its faith in deliberative democratic procedures that facilitate the *transformation*, as opposed to mere *aggregation*, of preferences. Accordingly, the deliberative perspective rejects the notion that preferences are a fixed and pre-political 'given' that should be counted equally in an aggregative ballot procedure. Rather, deliberative democracy is based on a vision of reasoned dialogue between citizens under conditions of freedom and equality.[85] When institutional frameworks are designed in this deliberative image, 'relations of power and subordination are neutralized, and each [citizen] is recognized as having the deliberative capacities'.[86] These procedural conditions insulate democratic forums from domination by the powerful, so that only the force of the better argument prevails. The shared exercise of deliberative reason tends to

[82] See, eg, *UNISON and Bethany Homestead* TUR1/643/2008, para 31.

[83] TUR1/576/2007.

[84] For those readers unfamiliar with northern vernacular, this is a sandwich and a cup of tea.

[85] See J Cohen, 'Deliberation and Democratic Legitimacy', in J Bohman and W Rehg (eds), *Deliberative Democracy* (Cambridge Massachusetts, MIT Press, 1997) 67.

[86] *Ibid*, 78.

filter out adaptive preferences, thereby promoting the realisation of autonomous preferences as outcomes of the democratic process.[87] As such, citizens are not forced to be autonomous by an intrusively paternalist state. Instead, citizens liberate themselves through the critical scrutiny of their preferences, and the collective rejection of those preferences that fail to withstand deliberative evaluation.

The next question is how far this is consistent with the central emphasis on ballot procedures in Schedule A1, for the act of voting is often characterised as a pluralist alternative to deliberative democracy. Is not the ballot mechanism the institutional embodiment of pluralist preference aggregation as opposed to deliberative preference transformation? In fact, this contrast between voting and deliberation is too sharp, for the vote remains central to most accounts of deliberative democracy. What *does* matter from the civic perspective is whether citizens participate in shared deliberation prior to the ballot taking place. The ballot for determining worker support is not just an aggregative mechanism; access rights also allow citizens the scope for preference transformation through democratic deliberation in anticipation of the ballot being held. In fact, analysis of CAC decisions indicates credible evidence of a deliberative 'uplift' in union support between the determination of the admissibility criteria and the eventual ballot result. In *AMICUS-AEEU and GMB and Liebherr Cranes Ltd*,[88] for example, at the admissibility stage the Panel found there to be 16.4 per cent union membership within the bargaining unit, and 36.1 per cent petition support for recognition. The union then went on to secure recognition in the ballot with 78.41 per cent support; this corresponded to 62.16 per cent of those entitled to vote in the bargaining unit. Similarly in *TGWU and Armchair Passenger Transport Co Ltd* the Panel found 11.58 per cent union membership and petition support of 36.67 per cent at the admissibility stage; at the ballot stage support for the union had rocketed to 92.49 per cent of those voting.[89] These decisions seem to indicate transformative democratic effects between application acceptance and ballot, which fits the deliberative rather than aggregative paradigm of voting.

However, the deliberative transformation of worker preferences as a strategy for countering adaptive preference effects faces two distinct problems in this context. First, the workplace occupies an ambiguous space at the intersection

[87] *Ibid*, 77–9. See also J Elster, 'The Market and the Forum: Three Varieties of Political Theory', in J Bohman and W Rehg (eds), *Deliberative Democracy* (Cambridge Massachusetts, MIT Press, 1997) 3, 11–19.

[88] TUR1/332/2004.

[89] TUR1/291/2002. For other potential examples of deliberative preference transformation suggesting an 'uplift' in union support, see *AEEU and Honda of the UK Manufacturing Ltd* TUR1/129/2001; *ISTC and Cornelius Electronics Ltd* TUR1/185/2002; *GMB and Tristar Cars Ltd* TUR1/338/2004; *AMICUS and Sebden Steel West Midlands* TUR1/357/2004; *UCATT and F W Mason* TUR1/373/2004.

between the market and the forum.[90] This ambiguity arises out of the hierarchical nature of workplace organisation, and the subordination inherent in the employment relation. For this reason, it has been argued that it is mistaken to situate the workplace within the public realm of deliberative communication: the civic 'image of dialogue among autonomous self-governing citizens would be patently out of place' against the backdrop of workplace subordination.[91] On this view, employer domination inevitably violates the core conditions of deliberative discourse. This is a powerful argument. There is no doubt that worker subordination leaves deliberative procedures especially vulnerable to the contaminating influence of employer power. Much depends upon whether legal regulation can effectively neutralise employer domination during the ballot process. If effective neutralisation does not occur then the deployment of coercive tactics by employers during the ballot procedure may actually contribute to the entrenchment of adaptive preferences. Faced with the risk of employer retaliation, workers' preferences adapt to the rational perception that the potential costs of unionisation outweigh its benefits.

These insights have led some scholars to reject the deliberative strategy of preference transformation. As Weiler accounts for it, although

> [A] more informed employee choice would be a freer one, the problem is that when we extend an opportunity to the law-abiding employer to illuminate the issues for its employees, we inevitably create both the opportunity and the incentive for the law-violating employer to intimidate its workers in their decision.[92]

Paradoxically, then, the adaptive preference effect may be remedied by eliminating the opportunities for deliberative preference-shaping and expediting statutory certification procedures, thereby ensuring a less arduous transition to recognition for unorganised workers. There is certainly evidence that British employers have utilised the ballot procedure to their advantage through the deployment of non-deliberative communicative strategies, resulting in a significant decrease in union support between application acceptance and ballot in such cases.[93] Moreover, in every case (bar one) where the union has made an 'unfair practice'

[90] C Estlund, *Working Together: How Workplace Bonds Strengthen a Diverse Democracy* (Oxford, Oxford University Press, 2003) 105–24.

[91] RC Post, 'Racist Speech, Democracy, and the First Amendment' (1991) 32 *William and Mary Law Review* 267, 289.

[92] Weiler, above n 7, 26.

[93] For an example, see *TGWU and Cannon Rubber Ltd* TUR1/245/2003. The CAC accepted the union's allegation at the acceptance stage that there was a perception on the part of some workers that the employer was hostile to unionisation. This may have had the effect of chilling support. Despite this, the union secured 40.64% support in the initial petition. The union lost the ballot, with support dropping to 27.27%. In *TGWU and King Asia Foods Ltd* TUR1/111/2001, ACAS estimated the union membership level at 55%. Nevertheless, against a backdrop of employer interference with worker free choice, the union lost the final ballot, mustering only 25% support. Finally, recognition was bitterly resisted by the employer in *BECTU and Sky Subscriber Services Ltd* TUR1/222/2002. Initial petition support of 51.4% was decimated in the final ballot, which went decisively against the union. For a full discussion, see Ewing, Moore and Wood, above n 15, 19–29.

complaint that has proceeded to a full hearing by the CAC, the union has lost the subsequent ballot despite having demonstrated strong initial support in the early stages of the statutory procedure.[94] While in each of those cases the CAC concluded that there was no 'unfair practice', there is no doubt that the employer had been engaged in 'vigorous' campaigning on each occasion. The limited practical impact of the 'unfair practice' provisions, along with evidence of continuing employer hostility towards unionisation,[95] lends some credence to Weiler's view in the British context.

The second problem relates to specific informational barriers that hinder the spread of unionisation. One of the advantages of deliberative democracy is its tendency to expand the pool of information available in collective decision-making by prompting citizens to engage reflectively with different values and perspectives. However, deliberation may be insufficient to surmount the experiential deficit inherent in the decision whether to opt for unionisation. Workers who have never experienced union representation are often not well-placed to make an informed judgement as to its value. This is reflected in Bain's articulation of the virtuous circle effect, whereby union recognition acts as a stimulant to organisational expansion and increased union density. Persuasion through deliberative dialogue is ill-suited to supplying the necessary information to potential union adherents, for *dialogue is no substitute for concrete experience of union representation.* Rather, the endowment effect predicts that citizens' preferences sometimes shift only in response to a shift in the underlying default position. As Sunstein points out, there is a danger that citizens 'will not take advantage of an opportunity which, because of previous deprivation, they no longer value'.[96] In such cases, deliberative democracy may not allow citizens to transcend their current valuations.

In these circumstances it may be necessary 'not merely to make the opportunity available but also to make it exclusive, so that people try it even if they do not want to do so'.[97] Of course, most of us would recoil from the prospect of State-enforced compulsory conscription of workers into unions. Nevertheless, Schedule A1 has important resources at its disposal that reach beyond the limits of deliberative democracy. In particular, the statutory procedure is conceived of as a last resort. In most cases, the legislative aspiration is that employers will avoid the statutory route by conferring voluntary recognition on unions. One potential consequence of the priority of voluntary over statutory recognition is the

[94] See discussion in ch 5. The exception is The Amalgamated Union and Harrods TUR1/535/2006.

[95] For recent evidence supporting this view, see E Heery and M Simms, 'Constraints on union organising in the United Kingdom' (2008) 39 *Industrial Relations Journal* 24, where the authors observe (at 34) that 'a substantial proportion of UK employers are clearly hostile to unions and resist organising to the extent of victimising activists, involving the police and resorting to anti-union consultants'.

[96] Sunstein, above n 2, 1149.

[97] *Ibid.*

triggering of a virtuous circle effect. As the endowment shifts from non-union to union through the medium of voluntary recognition, workers' preferences also shift in response to the change in default position. As such, the endowment effect is harnessed to support rather than constrain unions' organisational interests. This would offset the informational deficits involved in an exclusive reliance on deliberative preference transformation.

C Shifting Default Arrangements through Voluntary Recognition

The endowment effect points to the reflexive relationship between citizens' preferences and legal norms. Preferences display a tendency to track current allocations of rights and entitlements, and these rights and entitlements are often allocated by legal rules. In many respects the endowment effect is stacked against unions, particularly given the non-union default position that obtains in most workplaces. Nevertheless, the reflexivity that obtains between preferences and legal norms could be a source of organisational support for unions. It suggests the law can have a powerful symbolic role in shaping rather than simply reflecting preferences, attitudes and social norms.[98] The implementation of a statutory recognition procedure, while ultimately deferring to workers' freedom of choice with respect to unionisation, might be understood as a symbolic affirmation of the legitimacy of collective bargaining.[99] We might then expect the signalling effect of legal norms to alter both worker and employer perceptions of unions. If this occurs then workers' propensity to unionise will increase and employer resistance to unionisation diminish. These symbolic legitimating effects would be reflected in the achievement of the legislative aspiration of Schedule A1, that voluntary recognition arrangements are being stimulated by the 'shadow effect' of the statutory procedure.

In support of the thesis that legal norms may shape private preferences through symbolic effects, there is now substantial evidence that the statutory procedure has precipitated attitudinal shifts in key industrial relations actors. With respect to unions, the statutory procedure has galvanised unions' sense of entitlement to recognition. Within the labour movement, this has stimulated a renewed focus on the organisational mission of unions, and a corresponding upsurge in targeted recruitment campaigns as a precursor to requesting recognition. As Gall argues

> a crucial spur to these union activities has been the approach of the recognition provisions, i.e. their 'shadow effect'. They have added to an existing development—that

[98] CR Sunstein, *The Partial Constitution* (Cambridge Massachusetts, Harvard University Press, 1993) 162–94.

[99] For an interpretation of the US recognition procedure as a symbolic legal norm, see M Barenberg, 'The Political Economy of the Wagner Act: Power, Symbol, and Workplace Cooperation (1993) 106 *Harvard Law Review* 1379.

> of an orientation towards organising recognition campaigns, and engendered a sense of urgency and a concentration of minds.[100]

With respect to employers, too, there are positive indications of attitudinal changes generated by the legitimating signals of the legal framework. While it would be misleading to characterise this as the reconstitution of a broad-based pluralist consensus on the legitimacy of collective bargaining, there is evidence that some employers 'were more receptive to union involvement than in the past'.[101] There is no doubt that substantial pockets of vehement anti-union resistance remain.[102] Nevertheless, Gall's recent analysis of CBI surveys suggests that, when presented with a recognition claim, 'a significant section of employers are exhibiting attitudes varying from neutrality to receptiveness when pressed'.[103]

Most strikingly, the preference-shaping effect of legal norms has translated into a significant increase in voluntary recognition deals in anticipation of, and subsequent to, the implementation of Schedule A1. The introduction of the statutory union recognition mechanism has led to some modest recognition gains for unions invoking the statutory procedure. In the first five years of the statutory procedure's operation unions had made 444 applications for recognition and recognition had been declared in 116 cases.[104] During this period nearly 23,000 workers were covered by collective bargaining as a direct result of the statutory procedure. By contrast, the 'shadow effect' of the statutory procedure as a stimulant to voluntary recognition has been much more significant in quantitative terms. According to Gall approximately 3,000 new recognition deals have been signed between 1995 and 2005, and there has been a corresponding diminution in levels of employer de-recognition of unions.[105] These new deals bring an estimated 1.2 million workers within the scope of collective bargaining. Furthermore, statistics from the TUC indicate a sharp increase in voluntary recognition in the run up and subsequent to the enactment of the statutory procedure.[106] It now seems that the peak in new voluntary recognition agreements occurred in 2001, with the levels of new recognition agreements now

[100] G Gall, 'Trade union recognition in Britain, 1995–2002: turning a corner?' (2004) 35 *Industrial Relations Journal* 249, 254. This finding echoes earlier research: S Wood, S Moore and KD Ewing, 'The impact of the trade union recognition procedure under the Employment Relations Act, 2000–2', in H Gospel and S Wood (eds), *Representing Workers* (London, Routledge, 2003) 119, 137. See also J Blanden, S Machin and J Van Reenen, 'Have Unions Turned the Corner? New Evidence on Recent Trends in Union Recognition in UK Firms' (2006) 44 *British Journal of Industrial Relations* 169, 171.

[101] S Oxenbridge, W Brown, S Deakin and C Pratten, 'Initial Responses to the Statutory Recognition Provisions of the ERA 1999' (2003) 41 *British Journal of Industrial Relations* 315, 324.

[102] For an overview, see G Gall and S McKay, 'Facing "Fairness at Work": union perception of employer opposition and response to union recognition' (2001) 32 *Industrial Relations Journal* 94, 104–106. For more recent studies, see Heery and Simms, above n 95.

[103] Gall, above n 100, 255.

[104] *CAC Annual Report 2004–2005* 15.

[105] G Gall, Trade Union Recognition in Britain: An Emerging Crisis for Trade Unions?' (2007) 28 *Economic and Industrial Democracy* 78, 80.

[106] See, eg, TUC, *Trade union trends: focus on recognition* (TUC, 2004).

settling back to the 1998 level.[107] All of this indicates a shift in the relative balance between voluntary recognition and de-recognition cases when comparing pre- and post-1997 data, while also suggesting that unions have now used up the pool of 'easy' recognition targets (high levels of union membership density coupled with supportive or neutral employer response to the union's approach) and are now facing more challenging organisational environments.

As the diminution in new voluntary recognition deals seems to suggest, the scope for harnessing the 'shadow effect' of the legal procedure to promote voluntary recognition is subject to various constraints. Two main criticisms can be levelled at the current statutory framework. First, the legal centrality of majority rule in the statutory procedure has been replicated in social practices, structuring the negotiation of voluntary recognition arrangements. Consequently, many unions are reluctant to press for voluntary recognition unless the support thresholds specified in Schedule A1 have already been reached or even exceeded.[108] It is only under such circumstances that a credible threat of recourse to the statutory procedure can be deployed by unions. In tandem with this, a substantial proportion of employers are reluctant to confer voluntary recognition in the absence of demonstrable majority support.[109] This undermines the potential for significant virtuous circle effects arising out of the 'shadow effect' of the statutory procedure, for even voluntary recognition remains dependent upon high levels of union density as a precursor. As such, workers' preferences must alter *before* there is any prospect of a switch from non-union to a union endowment position. This does little to mitigate the constraining effects of the initial non-union endowment and the informational deficits of never-membership on the union's organisational task.

The historical experience is illuminating in this regard. Kessler and Palmer's analysis of the Commission on Industrial Relations' (CIR) recognition work demonstrated a flexible approach to the allocation of bargaining rights. The CIR would often allocate bargaining rights to unions with less than majority support, in anticipation of the virtuous circle effects that would occur post-recognition.[110] Moreover, the flexible criteria deployed by the CIR had tangible educative effects on the negotiation of voluntary recognition arrangements.[111] This approach was then deployed by ACAS under the 1975 Employment Protection Act (EPA) section 11 procedure.[112] The CAC has already demonstrated that it is capable of applying support criteria flexibly in its interpretation of the 'majority support

[107] Gall, above n 105, 84.

[108] Oxenbridge, Brown, Deakin and Pratten, above n 101, 320; Gall, above n 105, 92.

[109] Gall, above n 100, 263.

[110] S Kessler and G Palmer, 'The Commission on Industrial Relations in Britain 1969–1974: a retrospective and prospective evaluation' (1996) 18 *Employee Relations* 6, 41–5.

[111] *Ibid*, 46.

[112] S Kessler, 'Trade union recognition: CIR and ACAS experience' (1995) 17 *Employee Relations* 52.

likely' threshold, and there seems no reason why it ought not to be given space to do so in the actual allocation of bargaining rights.

One objection might be that the precise specification of fixed quantitative thresholds under Schedule A1 has helped to minimise the risk of intrusive judicial review. Significantly, in *Fullarton Computer*[113] the Court of Session did not overturn the CAC's decision not to order a ballot in a situation of marginal majority membership, though it also observed that 'the shoe pinches tightest for the panel, in relation to the legality of the decision, with regard to the marginality of the majority against the background of the moving target'.[114] As with the major judicial review cases under the EPA 1975 section 11 procedure,[115] the allocation of bargaining rights in the absence of clear and demonstrable majority support continues to be a neuralgic spot for the courts in judicial review proceedings. Nevertheless, the dominant judicial attitude in relation to review under Schedule A1 now seems to consist in an emphasis upon 'the evident legislative intention to reserve a wide margin of discretion to the CAC on most issues'.[116] Accordingly, the CAC might well be able to operate in a more permissive legal framework in this context without attracting intrusive judicial review.

The second major criticism relates to the qualitative character of new voluntary recognition arrangements negotiated in the shadow of Schedule A1. The endowment effect will only be harnessed to the advantage of trade unions if workers have a *positive* experience of joint regulation through collective bargaining. An increasingly common device of union exclusion is to confer voluntary recognition then prevaricate during the negotiation process itself.[117] This might involve 'surface' bargaining in going through the outward motions of negotiation but with a determined intention to avoid agreement, granting no substantive concessions during bargaining, or even attempting to *downgrade* terms and conditions during the negotiation of the first collective agreement. The overall objective is to ensure the shallowness of collective bargaining, thereby undermining positive perceptions of union instrumentality amongst the workforce. The effectiveness of this device was demonstrated vividly in Kelly and Badigannavar's study of an initially successful organisational campaign at a marketing agency call centre. After voluntary recognition had been conceded in the face of a successful union campaign, the employer ensured that bargaining was as hollow as possible by engaging in 'surface' bargaining. This resulted in a collapse in union membership as workers and activists became increasingly frustrated with the union's limited efficacy:

113 *Fullarton Computer Industries Ltd v CAC* [2002] SLT 13, Ct of Session OH.
114 *Ibid*, para 37.
115 RC Simpson, 'Judicial Control of ACAS' (1979) 8 *Industrial Law Journal* 69.
116 B Simpson, 'Judicial Control of the CAC' (2007) 36 *Industrial Law Journal* 287, 293.
117 G Gall, 'Employer Opposition to Union Recognition', in G Gall (ed), *Union Organizing* (London, Routledge, 2003) 79, 92.

> Since most workers join for instrumental reasons, the continuing attachment of new members will be highly sensitive to perceived union effectiveness.[118]

In this case, the employer undermined union instrumentality to great effect. While there is no regulatory silver bullet to eliminate this kind of strategy, legal reforms could certainly curtail the scope for such tactics. One possibility would be the availability of compulsory unilateral arbitration in all cases where the union failed to secure a first collective agreement. Another possibility would be to rethink the multiple restrictions on lawful industrial action so that unions might muster a credible threat of social sanction.

One regulatory option that has been particularly prominent in academic discussion, though not in practical legal reform, is 'staged' recognition. A system of staged recognition would institute union representational arrangements with lower levels of worker support than is necessary for full negotiation rights, for example the allocation of consultation rights to unions with 10 or 20 per cent support in a bargaining unit. As support for the union escalated, the union's process entitlements would also escalate accordingly. Unions would proceed through individual representation, to consultation, to full recognition for collective bargaining purposes as support grew amongst workers in the relevant constituency. This has the potential to harness virtuous circle effects in a very efficient manner. It is to that technique that we now turn.

D Shifting the Default Position through Staged Recognition

The essence of staged recognition is the allocation of consultation rights to 'representative' independent unions with a lower level of union density, (for example 10 or 20 per cent), than is required for the allocation of bargaining rights.[119] In this way, *more* workers get the opportunity to experience *some* form of union representation. Just as importantly, staged recognition also helps to surmount the experiential deficit prevalent amongst employers. According to Bryson, Gomez, and Willman's study of employers' propensity to unionise, the authors concluded that the majority of employers hold attitudes that might be characterised as 'indifference, or neutrality, that is born of limited experience with unions and the potential costs of switching from one voice regime to

[118] J Kelly and V Badigannavar, 'Union organizing', in J Kelly and P Willman (eds), *Union Organization and Activity* (London, Routledge, 2004) 32, 42. See also G Gall, 'The National Union of Journalists and the provincial newspaper industry: from derecognition to recognition to fraught bargaining', in G Gall (ed), *Union Recognition: Organising and Bargaining Outcomes* (London, Routledge, 2006) 115.

[119] KD Ewing, 'Trade Union Recognition: A Framework for Discussion' (1990) 19 *Industrial Law Journal* 209. More recently, see PL Davies and C Kilpatrick, 'UK Worker Representation after Single Channel' (2004) 33 *Industrial Law Journal* 121.

another'.[120] We might expect this shift to a union default position to have positive effects on both employers' and workers' preferences for unionisation. Consultation rights give the union a representational foothold in the workplace, thereby harnessing the endowment effect and initiating a virtuous circle between representation and organisation.

The issue of union involvement in consultative workplace structures has always prompted a ubiquitous ambivalence on the part of organised labour. It is a fierce debate that has generally straddled two distinct sets of questions. The first might be termed the 'union substitution' dilemma: are consultative structures liable to 'capture' by union activists so offering an organisational gateway into non-union enterprises? Or, conversely, is it more likely that consultative structures such as works councils will present a 'substitution' effect by displacing union voice mechanisms and reducing the incentive to unionise? The second might be termed the 'union instrumentality' dilemma: does union involvement in consultation mechanisms provide an opportunity for unions to demonstrate their representational value to a much broader class of employers and potential union adherents, thereby offsetting the experiential deficit in the provision of collective voice? Or is it more likely that union involvement in 'a weak consultative body, without negotiating powers, may present unions themselves as weak organizations incapable of securing real improvements at work', thereby undermining workers' perceptions of union effectiveness?[121] In truth, stated at this level of abstraction the answer to each of these questions is 'yes, perhaps'. As Hyman points out, 'any institutional experiment in British industrial relations will have results which are in large measure uncertain … and these would be significantly conditioned by the precise content of any legal innovations: the devil is in the detail'.[122] These concerns have assumed a pressing contemporary significance with the recent enactment of a general framework for consultation in national-level undertakings.[123]

(i) The Dilemma of Union Substitution

The organisational risk at the heart of the 'union substitution' dilemma is well articulated by Ewing:

> The danger with mandatory consultation through works councils or enterprise committees is that employers would be happy to create such institutions which would simply be

[120] A Bryson, R Gomez and P Willman, 'The end of the affair? Employers' propensity to unionize', in J Kelly and P Willman (ed), *Union Organization and Activity* (London, Routledge, 2004) 129, 144.

[121] S McKay, 'Representation or Recognition', in A McColgan (ed), *The Future of Labour Law* (London, Cassell, 1996) 34.

[122] R Hyman, 'Is there a case for statutory works councils in Britain?', in A McColgan (ed), *The Future of Labour Law* (London, Cassell, 1996) 79.

[123] Information and Consultation of Employees Regulations 2004 SI 2004/3426.

> another way to undermine trade union organisation ... For rather than encourage the growth of trade unionism, such devices may serve only to chill support.[124]

One solution to this dilemma would be to endorse a single channel approach to staged recognition. Consultation rights would be allocated to non-recognised trade unions with a specified threshold of support, say 10 per cent membership density in the workplace, but there could be no consultation without union involvement. Such an approach has now been effectively precluded by the European Court of Justice in *Commission v UK*,[125] which requires universal provision for consultation even where there is no trade union presence. Since single channel staged recognition is no longer a viable regulatory option, at least in the context of European law, it is important to elucidate the factors that tend to heighten 'union substitution' effects. In this respect, a comparative perspective is crucial.

European systems of industrial relations exhibit a high degree of convergence in fixing upon a dualistic pattern of worker representation. The institutional detail displays a rich variety, but in general terms this dualism corresponds to a functional division between union representation and works council representation. Distributive conflicts are channelled through the trade union mechanism of collective bargaining; this operates in tandem with works council institutions designed to facilitate the cooperative resolution of production-related matters at enterprise level. In predicting substitution effects, the critical issue lies in the degree of co-ordination and integration between the two channels.

European experience indicates a broad spectrum of possibilities. In Germany the relation between unions and works councils is highly symbiotic. External unions provide technical expertise, training and advice to works councillors, thereby ensuring the effective implementation of co-determination procedures. In turn, works councils function as 'union workplace organizations that operate within the legal form . . . Works councils also provide for easy de facto union recognition and are used by unions as a convenient device for recruiting members.'[126] The institutional base of the works council has contributed to the organisational resilience of enterprise unionism.[127] By contrast, the failed attempt in France to emulate this representational symbiosis is striking. Its variant of the works council system is now widely regarded as having deepened 'an ongoing crise du syndicalisme (crisis of unionism)'.[128] One effect of the Auroux reforms in 1982 was to have works council-type structures and enterprise-level collective bargaining located in the same regulatory space. With an ideologically

[124] Ewing, above n 119, 220–21.

[125] Cases C-382–92 and C-383–92, [1994] IRLR 392 and [1994] IRLR 412.

[126] J Rogers and W Streeck, 'Workplace Representation Overseas: The Works Councils Story' in RB Freeman (ed), *Working Under Different Rules* (New York, Russell Sage, 1994) 97, 117.

[127] R Adams and CH Rummel, 'Workers' participation in management in West Germany: impact on the worker, the enterprise and the trade union' (1977) 8 *Industrial Relations Journal* 4.

[128] BE Brown, 'The Rise and Fall of *Autogestion* in France', in M Donald Hancock, J Logue and B Schiller (eds), *Managing Modern Capitalism* (New York, Greenwood, 1991) 195, 209.

fractured union movement unable to exploit the new institutional opportunities, and works council structures vulnerable to employer domination due to relatively weak juridical guarantees of consultation rather than co-determination, the organisational base of French enterprise unionism has suffered spectacular and unprecedented erosion.[129] The resulting organisational vacuum at enterprise level has been colonised by a variety of employer-led individualised modes of worker participation, such as quality circles, that are less threatening to managerial prerogative.[130] The comparative lesson is clear: 'without the constraints of autonomous collective bargaining, managerial prerogative can turn consultation into a highway for "personalised contracts".'[131] Similar 'union substitution' effects have also occurred, albeit less dramatically, in the Netherlands and Spain.[132]

Works councils, then, are no panacea for strong enterprise unionism; the German success story is certainly not typical. How might this success be replicated? First, much depends upon the history, structure and values of a country's union movement. Union substitution tends to occur in those countries with an ideologically pluralist union movement, as in France, Spain and the Netherlands. Centralised and unitary union structure minimises inter-union competition, leaving unions better placed to utilise works councils as an organisational platform in the enterprise. Secondly, the juridical form of the works council's procedural rights matter to union substitution. Legally guaranteed co-determination rights are less vulnerable to employer domination than weaker consultation rights. Further, substitution is avoided where works councils are excluded from bargaining functions. Finally, the stronger the degree of institutional separation, the less likely that substitution will occur. This 'bright line' differentiation often manifests itself as a difference in regulatory level. In Germany, distributive conflicts are channelled predominantly through national level collective bargaining, while representative consultation is channelled through enterprise level council structures. Strict demarcation ensures regulatory mechanisms do not compete for the same regulatory space.

Unsurprisingly, decentralised collective bargaining is strongly associated with union substitution by works councils. Decentralised bargaining structures are characteristic of the UK and North America. The US provides an illuminating comparison in assessing the threat posed to unions' organisational strength by

[129] R Tchobanian, 'France: From Conflict to Social Dialogue?' in J Rogers and W Streeck (eds), *Works Councils: Consultation, Representation, and Cooperation in Industrial Relations* (Chicago, Chicago University Press, 1995) 115.

[130] See Brown, above n 128.

[131] Lord Wedderburn, 'Consultation and Collective Bargaining in Europe: Success or Ideology?' (1997) 26 *Industrial Law Journal* 1, 32.

[132] For a comparative overview, see M Terry, 'Workplace Unionism: Redefining Structures and Objectives', in R Hyman and A Ferner (eds), *New Frontiers in European Industrial Relations* (Oxford, Blackwell, 1994) 223.

enterprise level consultative structures under a system of enterprise level collective bargaining. The most striking feature of the US pattern of worker representation is its repudiation of dual channel worker representation. This is reflected in one of the cornerstones of the statutory edifice, the section 8(a)(2) ban on 'company unions'. Thus, it is an 'unfair labor practice' for an employer to 'dominate or interfere with the formation of any labor organization, or contribute any financial or other support to it'. At the time of its enactment, section 8(a)(2) was considered an inseparable corollary of the statutory guarantee of employee free choice of bargaining representative. During the inter-war period 'the company union had become firmly established as an alternative to collective bargaining with self-organized employee associations'.[133] These consultative committees proved highly durable and effective devices of union substitution, offering the promise of collective voice within the enterprise but without the 'costs and risks associated with collective bargaining. Consequently, they hold an allure against which it is difficult, if not impossible, for conventional unions to compete.'[134]

Recent research lends further empirical weight to these historical concerns with union substitution by workplace consultative committees; Freeman and Rogers' wide-ranging analysis of worker preferences demonstrates that 'employee involvement' schemes significantly 'reduce interest in unions by giving workers more say at the workplace outside the union venue'.[135] Accordingly section 8(a)(2) was critical in eliminating anti-union employers' weapon of choice against workers' right to self-organisation. In so doing, section 8(a)(2) sealed the fate of dual channel as a viable pattern of worker representation, embodying instead a preference 'for the private ordering of the employment relationship that is based on collective bargaining through self-organized and autonomous employee associations'.[136]

The evidence mustered by Freeman and Rogers indicates that many workers prefer the consultative option over collective bargaining where it is available. The obvious response is, 'so much the worse for collective bargaining'. Perhaps representational forms should simply track workers' preferences. Freeman and Rogers argue powerfully that the principal consideration in deciding matters of workplace governance ought to be what workers themselves want. If workers prefer workplace consultation to collective bargaining, then why should the State tell them they ought to prefer collective bargaining instead? From this perspective, section 8(a)(2) smacks of State paternalism, disrespectfully overriding workers' preferences by promoting a particular representational form—collective

[133] TC Kohler, 'Models of Worker Participation: The Uncertain Significance of section 8(a)(2)' (1986) 27 *Boston College Law Review* 499, 523.

[134] Note, 'Collective Bargaining as an Industrial System: An Argument against Judicial Revision of section 8(a)(2) of the National Labor Relations Act' (1983) 96 *Harvard Law Review* 1664, 1679.

[135] Freeman and Rogers, above n 22, 113.

[136] Kohler, above n 133, 533.

bargaining through independent trade unions. This also points to a deeper interpretive puzzle in relation to the legislative structure. The Wagner Act scheme is predicated on respect for workers' free choice of whether to institute joint regulation through collective bargaining. The choice to remain non-union is respected to the same degree as the choice to unionise. The apparent paternalism of section 8(a)(2), in limiting the range of workplace governance options available to workers, sits uneasily with this liberal framework.

The quest for interpretive coherence has precipitated some imaginative judicial treatment of section 8(a)(2) to bring it into line with the liberal cast of the legislation. This has been achieved through the fashioning of preference-sensitive standards of domination under s 8(a)(2). So in *Hertzka & Knowles v NLRB* the Court of Appeals (Ninth Circuit) emphasised the significance of workers' preferences in determining whether company sponsorship of a consultative committee amounted to unlawful 'domination, interference or support'.[137] Thus, the 'enthusiastic acceptance' of such committees by the workforce negated any section 8(a)(2) violation. To hold otherwise would undermine 'the purpose of the Act as a whole—fostering free choice—because it might prevent the establishment of a system the employees *desired*'.[138] This seems to leave section 8(a)(2) on the horns of a tricky interpretive dilemma. Endorsing 'preference insensitivity' as the touchstone of 'domination' imperils legislative coherence because of the difficulty in reconciling a strong paternalist restriction with an overarching liberal commitment to free associational choice. Endorsing 'preference sensitivity' entails a far laxer standard under section 8(a)(2) than its framers envisaged, whereby 'free-choice becomes the freedom not to self-association, but to ratify an "organization that is not free" and [is] thus incapable of functioning in the collective bargaining process.'[139] Neither prospect is an attractive one.

Fortunately there is a more subtle rationale for the 'preference insensitive' standard consistent with the liberal purposes of the legislation. At its inception section 8(a)(2) was conceived as a measure to ensure the autonomy of workers' governance choices by preventing *manipulation* of those preferences. Employer-sponsored consultative committees were inherently manipulative. They promised a democratic liberty that was counterfeit, the appearance without the reality of joint regulation; furthermore, these consultative structures 'penetrated the social infrastructure of the workforce. That penetration illegitimately distorted group deliberation and coerced worker choice more systematically than did the non-union workplace.'[140] Section 8(a)(2) sought to prevent this manipulation by removing its source—the 'company union' itself. In this way, 'the ban on

[137] 503 F. 2d 625 (9th circuit 1974).
[138] *Ibid.*
[139] Kohler, above n 133, 545.
[140] Barenberg, above n 99, 1459.

company unions therefore protected, rather than paternalistically overrode, workers' free group choice'.[141]

It is therefore not illiberal to disregard workers' preferences favouring 'company unions' because preferences formed in such manipulative contexts are not autonomous. This is supported by the adaptive understanding of preference formation. On this view, preferences ought to be respected only if they are formed autonomously, and this necessitates a normative evaluation of the context in which those preferences are formed. Given the similarities in bargaining structure, the absence of a functional equivalent to section 8(a)(2) in British labour law is remarkable. Lacking any substantive criteria of domination, there is a risk that consultation measures stimulated by the Information and Consultation of Employees Regulations (ICER) 2004 framework might precipitate the spread of employer-dominated consultative structures leading to union substitution at enterprise level.

It is still too early to tell whether ICER 2004 will prove to be a threat or an opportunity for trade unions. The early signs are that the Regulations have had a very limited impact on the representational landscape.[142] What is certainly problematic is that ICER 2004 accords no preferential rights of involvement to trade unions, whether recognised or otherwise. Trade unions cannot even pull the 'trigger' to initiate the negotiation of a 'negotiated agreement' under ICER 2004. It therefore departs from the staged recognition model which would advocate allocating preferential rights of involvement in consultation procedures where unions have levels of membership density lower than the 50 per cent threshold for statutory union recognition. This minimises the potential for ICER 2004 to catalyse virtuous circle effects for trade union growth, and it heightens the risks of union substitution by alternative voice mechanisms.

(ii) The Dilemma of Union Instrumentality

The assumption underlying staged recognition is that the allocation of consultation rights to representative (but non-recognised) unions enables them to expand their membership through the provision of valuable representation to a broader pool of workers. In shifting the default position from non-union to union representation, we should expect this to be reflected in altered worker preferences which would adapt to the newly unionised status quo. However, this strategy rests upon a critical assumption: that involvement of representative unions in consultative procedures will promote positive perceptions of union instrumentality by portraying the union as an effective guardian of workers' interests. As we have seen in relation to voluntary recognition arrangements, this cannot simply be

[141] M Barenberg, 'Democracy and Domination in the Law of Workplace Cooperation' (1994) 94 *Columbia Law Review* 753, 776.

[142] M Hall, 'A cool response to the ICE Regulations? Employer and trade union approaches to the new legal framework for information and consultation' (2006) 37 *Industrial Relations Journal* 456.

assumed. Where the employer effectively neutralises the trade union's role through 'surface' bargaining or prevarication, this can have deleterious effects on workers' willingness to continue supporting the union.

One line of radical criticism levelled at consultative structures argues that 'the "social partnership" ideology inscribed in works councils could undermine the serious and credible alternative of militant trade unionism';[143] as such, union involvement in works councils is 'ideologically disarming'.[144] On this view, instrumental effectiveness is better served by unions vindicating workers' interests through strike action and industrial pressure. Where strike action is deployed visibly and successfully, 'non-union workers have been encouraged to join in unusually large numbers'.[145] The underlying assumption here, that ideologies are inscribed into particular institutional forms, seems far too categorical. The inadequacy of some of the new voluntary bargaining arrangements, and the increasing elision of the distinction between collective bargaining and consultation, undermines the view that different processes can be compartmentalised in this neat way.

Ultimately, the effectiveness of worker representation depends upon the balance of power within the enterprise, and the potential for enterprise-based union locals to mobilise social pressure through grassroots activism. As Terry points out, 'without strong organization in the workplace, works councils are effectively taken over by management, whatever the legal rights conferred on employees'.[146] Even in the context of the German system, with its strong juridical guarantees of co-determination rights, Adams and Rummel have observed that 'in the last resort, its effectiveness is dependent upon union power'.[147] We should therefore be cautious in embracing the threshold of 10 per cent density as a basis for allocating consultation rights. Where the union is organisationally weak, as in a situation of low union density, there is a risk that the union could lose rather than gain support through an inability to function as an effective guardian of workers' interests. These risks can be mitigated by ensuring that the legal framework facilitates rather than obstructs the process of worker mobilisation. This suggests the need to think carefully about the possibilities and limits of staged recognition. Staged recognition is based upon an implicit market-based view of the relation between unions and workers. Unions are conceived of as suppliers of representational services vying to 'sell' their product to workers in the marketplace. Unions will succeed in the marketplace to the extent they can demonstrate their value and attract the loyalty of consumers.

143 J Kelly, 'Works Councils: Union Advance or Marginalization?', in A McColgan (ed), *The Future of Labour Law* (London, Cassell, 1996) 58.

144 *Ibid*, 60.

145 J Kelly, *Rethinking Industrial Relations* (London, Routledge, 1998) 64.

146 Terry, above n 132, 245–6.

147 Adams and Rummel, above n 127, 20.

This consumerist vision rests upon a distorting view of the relationship between unions and their members.

Unions will only be effective representatives to the extent that *workers themselves* are prepared to act collectively in defence of their own interests. Without the foundation of an effective 'right to organise' at its base, and without workers prepared to shoulder the burdens of collective action, staged recognition will be deficient as a legal technique for resolving the problem of adaptive preferences. We must therefore turn to British labour law's regulation of workers' organisational activity.

E The Right to Organise

In recent years, the project of union revitalisation has been spurred by the thought that unions need not simply wither in the face of persistent decline. Rather, the deployment of effective organisational strategies has the potential to stem or even reverse the pattern of decline. This repudiation of passivity is emblematic of the 'organising model' paradigm, which holds that the fate of unions is not sealed by some mechanistic calculus of economic and social vectors beyond workers' control. Rather, organisational trajectories can be determined by unions' strategic choices and the deployment of specific organisational methods. Paradigmatically, the 'organising model' consists in the conduct of 'aggressive and creative campaigns utilizing a grass-roots, rank-and-file intensive strategy, building a union and acting like a union from the very beginning of the campaign'.[148] This has encompassed a range of methods: planned organising campaigns and workplace 'mapping' to identify potential union supporters and activists in the workforce, personal contact through house calls and small group meetings to stimulate union support, professional 'lead organisers' developing a core of activist rank-and-file leaders in the workplace and building a rank-and-file organisational committee around this core group, the use of internal and external pressure tactics on management to augment worker solidarity and stimulate worker resistance to managerial anti-union tactics, and the framing of campaign issues in terms of justice, respect and dignity at work. This new paradigm is now exerting some influence on the strategic choices of British unions, reflected in the TUC's institutional commitment to its 'Organising Academy'.[149]

The 'organising model' emphasises the primacy of workers' collective agency in rebuilding the union movement. In many respects, the diffusion of organising values and techniques will be shaped by factors *internal* to the trade union

[148] K Bronfenbrenner and T Juravich, 'It Takes More Than House Calls: Organizing to Win with a Comprehensive Union-Building Strategy', in K Bronfenbrenner, S Friedman, RW Hurd, RA Oswald and RL Seeber (eds), *Organizing to Win* (Cornell, Cornell University Press, 1998) 19, 24.

[149] E Heery, M Simms, R Delbridge, J Salmon and D Simpson, 'The TUC's Organising Academy: an assessment' (2000) 31 *Industrial Relations Journal* 400.

movement itself: formal policy commitments, financial investment in organising, development of specialist organisational functions, and the political will to innovate and transform union priorities and methods.[150] Nevertheless, this emphasis on union agency should not obscure the importance of legal norms in enhancing or constraining the opportunities for effective collective action. Legal rules inevitably shape, at least to a certain extent, the effectiveness of workers' collective agency. Evaluation of the legal framework suggests a mixed picture as far as the law's role in facilitating the 'organising model' is concerned. We shall first consider the constraining effects of legal norms, focusing on the law's inadequate protection of union activists and its suppression of vigorous picketing activity. Then we shall consider the enabling effects of legal norms, focusing on the CAC's interpretation of the bargaining unit concept under Schedule A1.

(i) Legal Constraints: Union Activists and Confrontational Tactics

Trade union activists are central to the process of effective mobilisation of workers in the bargaining unit.[151] Well trained activists can help to construct a sense of collective identity amongst the work group, they can ensure that workers attribute blame for grievances and injustices to the employer rather than impersonal market forces, and they can encourage a sense of effective collective agency. According to Kelly's influential theorisation of union mobilisation, each of these elements marks a critical stage in the process.[152] While the main emphasis in the 'organising model' is on rank-and-file activism, professional union organisers are particularly important in ensuring the effective penetration of 'greenfield' sites that possess little or no union presence—the prime targets in the recognition context. As Gall has pointed out, 'in the absence of a wider milieu of local lay activists in each union and throughout the union movement to assist workers, alongside workers' lack of self-confidence and self-belief relative to previous periods, the skills, experience, and resources of full-time officers are increasingly important'.[153]

This is supported by Heery et al's analysis of a typical 'greenfield' organisational campaign, where the authors concluded that 'the green nature of the workforce and activists has also made them heavily reliant on external support'.[154] It is unsurprising that one of the most potent weapons in stifling

[150] E Heery, M Simms, R Delbridge, J Salmon and D Simpson, 'Union organizing in Britain: a survey of policy and practice' (2000) 11 *International Journal of Human Resource Management* 986. For a recent evaluation of the internal and external constraints on the successful deployment of organising methods, see E Heery and M Simms, 'Constraints on union organising in the United Kingdom' (2008) 39 *Industrial Relations Journal* 24.

[151] M Simms, 'Interest formation in greenfield union organising campaigns' (2007) 38 *Industrial Relations Journal* 439.

[152] Kelly, above n 145.

[153] G Gall, 'Conclusion', in G Gall (ed), *Union Organizing* (London, Routledge, 2003) 233.

[154] E Heery, M Simms, R Delbridge, J Salmon and D Simpson, 'Organizing unionism comes to the UK' (2000) 22 *Employee Relations* 38, 46.

incipient union organisation is 'decapitation' of the lead activists through dismissal or redundancy.[155] Once this occurs the organisational momentum can be effectively stopped, and other workers are reluctant to risk the loss of employment that comes with undertaking the tasks of organisation. The law is deficient in shielding and nurturing the civic activism of workers in three ways.

First, the law provides inadequate safeguards against the victimisation and dismissal of workers who are union activists. While it is automatically unfair to dismiss an employee for the reason that they participated in trade union activities at an appropriate time,[156] the remedies for the unfairly dismissed activist are not sufficient to provide an effective deterrent against such egregious conduct. Unlike 'whistleblowing' dismissals, for example, the level of compensatory award in the trade union context is subject to restriction.[157] Furthermore, even if individuals secure legal redress to compensate for their own losses, there is no way for unions to secure a collective remedy if the effect of the dismissal is to derail the organisational process. Under the 'unfair practice' provisions that operate during the ballot procedure under Schedule A1, the union can obtain an order for recognition in cases of serious breach. However, the 'unfair practices' are only operative during the timeframe of the statutory ballot procedure.[158] What is needed is a freestanding unfair practice provision operating independently of Schedule A1 able to provide an effective collective remedy in situations where activists have been dismissed.

Secondly, the inability of professional union organisers to obtain access to the employer's property for organisational purposes continues to place significant constraints on the capacity of trade unions to organise in 'green' contexts.[159] The limited access rights under Schedule A1 apply once the union has surmounted the preliminary support thresholds.[160] At the very least, there is a strong case for a right of periodic access for professional union organisers to the employer's

[155] Gall, above n 117, 87.

[156] TULRCA 1992, s 152. Workers are protected from 'offers' and 'detriment' on that ground under TULRCA 1992 ss 145A and 146.

[157] S Deakin and G Morris, *Labour Law*, 4th edn (Oxford, Hart Publishing, 2005) 778.

[158] For discussion, see AL Bogg, 'Employment Relations Act 2004: Another False Dawn for Collectivism?' (2005) 34 *Industrial Law Journal* 72.

[159] In Heery and Simms' recent study (above n 95, 34), they found that two thirds of surveyed union organisers identified lack of access as a significant problem hindering their organisational efforts in targeted workplaces.

[160] See TULRCA 1992, Schedule A1 para 26. The CAC has not been reticent in ordering access for full-time union officials in the event of a disagreement between the parties over access arrangements: see *TGWU and King Asia Foods Ltd* TUR1/111/2001 and *TGWU and TVR Engineering Ltd* TUR1/371/2004. In organizational terms, however, this modest entitlement is too little too late, since the union is granted access only after the union has mustered substantial support at the outset of the statutory claim (for the union's application to be admissible a majority of the bargaining unit must be likely to favour recognition).

property that is 'consistent with reasonable "time, place, and manner" restrictions'.[161] Finally, the design of organisational rights continues to be guided by the legislative purpose of buttressing established bargaining arrangements against erosion by inter-union competition, thereby avoiding fragmentation of bargaining structures. This is reflected in the specification of *recognition* as a trigger for enhanced legal support for the union's workplace activities. Thus, rights to time off for union officials and union members are confined to situations where the union is already recognised.[162] While the current legal structure has its uses in enabling 'in-fill' recruitment where the union recruits non-members in recognised workplaces,[163] it is of little use to unions trying to establish recognition in unorganised workplaces. Proposals for union *membership* as a trigger for enhanced organisational facilities, such as rights of reasonable union access and use of the employer's property to hold meetings, would seem to be more attuned to the particular difficulties faced by trade unions seeking to garner activism in workplaces without recognition.[164]

Another facet of the 'organising model' approach is its preference for confrontational strategies to ratchet up external pressure on employers hostile to unionisation. This includes mass picketing and public protest, and use of the media to shame recalcitrant employers through negative publicity. Such picketing is often designed to be as disruptive and militant as possible.[165] These tactics have sometimes been spectacularly effective in achieving organisational success for unions in situations of extreme adversity. For example, the 'Justice for Janitors' (JFJ) campaign in Los Angeles is emblematic of the militant resurgence of organised labour in the US.[166] The union deployed a highly visible campaign of public protest, targeting both the cleaning contractors employing non-union labour and the building owners that contracted with them. This became 'a war against the employers *and* the building owners, waged on all fronts [without] leaving any stone unturned'.[167] Given the structure of the local labour market,

[161] KE Klare, 'Workplace Democracy and Market Reconstruction: An Agenda for Legal Reform' (1989) 38 *Catholic University Law Review* 1, 48.

[162] TULRCA 1992, ss 168–70; this pattern is replicated with respect to 'union learning representatives', where paid time off is similarly confined to situations where the union is recognised: see TULRCA 1992, s 168A.

[163] On which, see S Oxenbridge, W Brown, S Deakin and C Pratten, 'Initial Responses to the Statutory Recognition Provisions of the Employment Relations Act 1999' (2003) 41 *British Journal of Industrial Relations* 315, 320.

[164] See the proposals in KD Ewing (ed), *Working Life: A New Perspective on Labour Law* (London, Lawrence & Wishart, 1996) 223.

[165] See the vivid account of effective organizational mass picketing in R Milkman and K Wong, 'Organizing the Wicked City: The 1992 Southern California Drywall Strike', in R Milkman (ed), *Organizing Immigrants* (Ithaca, Cornell University Press, 2000) 169.

[166] See CL Fisk, DJB Mitchell and CL Erikson, 'Union Representation of Immigrant Janitors in Southern California: Economic and Legal Challenges' in R Milkman (ed), *Organizing Immigrants* (Ithaca, Cornell University Press, 2000) 199.

[167] R Waldinger, C Erikson, R Milkman, DJB Mitchell, A Valenzuela, K Wong and M Zeitlin, 'Helots No More: A Case Study of the Justice for Janitors Campaign in Los Angeles', in K

secondary picketing of building owners was essential for organisational success. Organising cleaning contractors one-by-one would have been a pyrrhic victory for unions if this led to the cancellation of service contracts by building owners, and the shifting of work to cheaper non-union service providers. Through the deployment of mass secondary picketing, the union was highly successful in organising the entirety of the local labour market.

As yet, there are few signs that British unions are prepared to organise with this degree of militancy.[168] Once again, however, unions' strategic choices are subject to various external legal constraints. The kind of vigorous public protest that was instrumental in achieving organisational success for Californian janitors would undoubtedly be unlawful in Britain. First, *mass* picketing is almost certain to take protest activity outside of the statutory immunity and involve the simultaneous commission of a range of torts and crimes, with normative guidance in the Code of Practice on recommended maximum numbers of pickets now seemingly crystallised into a fixed rule of law.[169] Secondly, the tactic of *secondary* picketing of service users' premises would also fall outside of the statutory immunity, since the immunity is confined to workers' picketing at their employer's premises.[170] Furthermore, the use of lay union activists from other unionised firms to picket on behalf of the unorganised would also fall foul of the legal strictures on secondary action. As Wedderburn has argued, 'the only indisputably lawful pickets are those who attend near their own workplace in small numbers and who keep out of the way'.[171] These external constraints have placed important limits on the process of union mobilisation.

(ii) Legal Support: The Case of Bargaining Unit Determination

By contrast the CAC's interpretation of the bargaining unit concept has tended to facilitate the process of mobilisation. The tension between competing conceptions of worker community is ubiquitous in collective labour law.[172] On the one hand, managerial ideologies characterised the workplace as a unitary community yoked together by common values and overarching managerial authority to realise the 'general will'. On the other hand, pluralist ideologies identified the workplace as a site constituted by a multiplicity of legitimate sectional interests

Bronfenbrenner, S Friedman, RW Hurd, RA Oswald and RL Seeber (eds), *Organizing to Win: New Research on Union Strategies* (Ithaca, Cornell University Press, 1998) 102, 114.

[168] E Heery, M Simms, R Delbridge, J Salmon and D Simpson, 'Trade union recruitment policy in Britain: Form and Effects', in G Gall (ed), *Union Organizing* (London, Routledge, 2003) 56, 65.

[169] See *Code of Practice on Picketing* (PL928, Revised 1992) paras 48–51.

[170] TULRCA 1992, s 220.

[171] Lord Wedderburn, *The Worker and the Law*, 3rd edn (Harmondsworth, Penguin, 1986) 548. Similar sentiments may be found in Bercusson's Marxist critique of picketing law, where he concludes that 'militant picketing which seeks to achieve its purposes is bound to be held unlawful': B Bercusson, 'One Hundred Years of Conspiracy and Protection of Property: Time for a Change' (1977) 40 *Modern Law Review* 268, 276.

[172] A Fox, *Industrial Sociology and Industrial Relations* (London, HMSO, 1966).

with overlapping foci of loyalty centred on functionally differentiated groups within the workplace. From this pluralist perspective, conflicts of interest in the workplace were a natural outgrowth of the diverse communal attachments arising under conditions of free association. Since one of the key determinants of successful mobilisation is workers' shared realisation that the interests of 'their' community are often in legitimate conflict with the interests of management, bargaining unit determination straddles this ideological clash between competing union and employer claims to authority in delineating the locus of solidarity.

Unions have asserted the centrality of workers' perceptions as authoritative, with solidarities based on occupational or geographical distinctiveness. Employers have often rejected this, arguing instead for a unitary conception of community based around an organic, 'whole company' ethos. Analysis of CAC decision-making discloses an approach that prioritises the perceptual authority of workers themselves. This has been supported by the *Kwik-Fit* decision which accords a large margin of discretion to the union's proposed bargaining unit.[173] Compatibility with effective management is not a comparative exercise involving a search for the most compatible bargaining unit: the union's proposed unit must simply be capable of co-existing with effective management. The effect of this is to give a pronounced tilt to the union's initial proposal, insulating it from easy displacement by employers' counterproposals. This has been crucial in offsetting the countervailing tilt in the statutory criteria for unit determination prioritising managerial interests in 'effective management'.[174] Furthermore, the CAC has also emphasised that even though separate collective bargaining arrangements within a company might be inconvenient, time consuming or create friction between distinct groups of workers, this would not be sufficient to constitute incompatibility with 'effective management'. The effect of this is to entrench further a high threshold for displacement of the union's initial unit proposal.[175] The rebalancing by the Court of Appeal in *Kwik-Fit* has been reflected both in levels of voluntary agreement and CAC endorsement of the union's proposed unit. Early analysis of the legislative structure concluded that 'the employer will therefore have considerable influence in determining the scope of the workforce balloted for recognition'.[176] Yet in the first five years of the Schedule's operation, the bargaining unit had been agreed in 58 per cent of cases; where the unit was contested the union's proposal was followed in 62 per cent of cases.[177] The most

[173] *R (on the application of Kwik-Fit Ltd) v CAC* [2002] ICR 1212. This approach has recently been reaffirmed in *R (on the application of Cable & Wireless Services UK Ltd) v Central Arbitration Committee* [2008] ICR 693, by the Administrative Court.

[174] TULRCA 1992, Schedule A1 para 19 (3) (a).

[175] *TGWU and Tyco Electronics* TUR1/521/2006.

[176] T Novitz and P Skidmore, *Fairness at Work: A Critical Analysis of the ERA 1999 and its Treatment of Collective Rights* (Oxford, Hart Publishing, 2001) 90.

[177] *CAC Annual Report* 2004–05, 16.

recent CAC Annual Report indicates that voluntary agreement on the bargaining unit still exceeds significantly CAC determinations of that issue.[178]

With respect to the geographical dimension, this perceptual clash was played out in *ISTC and Teknek Electronics Ltd*.[179] The union's proposed bargaining unit encompassed a single site in which there was concentrated union support. From the union's perspective, this constituency constituted a natural boundary given the workers' *self-perception* of their community of interest, which did not extend to the employer's other site. By contrast, the employer's perception of community was based on a unitary, 'whole company' ethos encapsulating all production workers across both sites. This better reflected its 'team' philosophy based upon an integrated system of production with both sites yoked together by shared interests and values. In a significant articulation of principle, the CAC prioritised workers' self-perception of community in delineating the bargaining unit:

> it was a particular group of workers, identified as the Union's proposed bargaining unit, who recognised that there were issues relating to terms and conditions, who rather than approaching the Company chose to raise the issues with the Union. This indicates that *those workers consider themselves as sharing a clear community of interest distinct from other workers in the company*. It also indicates that the production workers at Inchinnan do not fully subscribe to the 'Teknek Team' ethos.[180]

This conclusion was bolstered through an appreciation of objective, work-related characteristics of workers in the bargaining unit. Distinctive working practices and substantive terms and conditions, limited mobility between sites, and differences in skills all supported the workers' own sense of their communal distinctiveness. The unitary argument in favour of a 'whole company' bargaining unit has been deployed frequently by employers in this context.[181] The CAC has adopted a strict, evidence-based approach in scrutinising the employer's counter-proposals based on such arguments, distinguishing unitary assertions from unitary realities. A range of objective, evidential factors supporting geographically limited bargaining units have been identified by the CAC: single site or regional bargaining units are located in distinct labour markets;[182] units operate

[178] *CAC Annual Report* 2007–08, 7.
[179] TUR1/267/2003.
[180] *Ibid*, para 17.
[181] See, eg, *TSSA and Culina Logistics* TUR1/236/2002; *Unison and Craegmoor Group Ltd* TUR1/249/2003; *GMB and Magna Kansei Ltd* TUR1/471/2005.
[182] See, eg, *TGWU and Grosvenor Casinos Ltd* TUR1/188/2002; *TGWU and Gala Casinos Ltd* TUR1/206/2002. Both decisions identify the London region as a distinct labour market in support of a geographically limited bargaining unit. See also *TSSA and Culina Logistics* TUR1/236/2002.

in practice with a degree of decision-making autonomy independent of centralised control,[183] or that centralised control could co-exist in future with decentralised bargaining;[184] limited labour mobility between sites;[185] substantive differences in terms and conditions between sites;[186] and spatial proximity of different sites within the employer's organisation.[187] Where objective criteria cannot be identified in support of the employer's unitary arguments, the union's proposed unit is not easily displaced.[188] Conversely, where such objective criteria do exist, such as centralised pay-setting and policy formulation, the CAC will be reluctant to accept what seems to be an arbitrary geographical boundary drawn simply to reflect existing pockets of union support.[189] Generally, however, the resilience of the union's initiative in proposing the bargaining unit has been bolstered by the *Kwik-Fit* decision.[190]

With respect to the occupational dimension of unit determination, the CAC has had to resolve similar tensions between employer and worker perceptions of the appropriate worker constituency. Employer arguments have been largely predicated upon a unitary, 'whole company' conception of the appropriate constituency, encompassing distinct occupational groups within the workplace. By contrast, union proposals have tracked workers' perceptions of a shared community of interest. In *AMICUS and Baker Oil Tools* the union's proposed unit covered hourly paid production staff, excluding monthly paid workers engaged in administrative or technical work from the unit.[191] As the union pointed out, *workers themselves* had identified this as the relevant unit. In reflecting workers' preferences, the proposed unit provided a natural locus of solidarity along functional lines. Against this, the employer asserted an 'all for one', unitary culture encompassing monthly paid workers. The CAC endorsed the union's

183 See, eg, *Unison and Craegmoor Group Ltd* TUR1/249/2003. Conversely, limited local decision-making autonomy can block a union's proposed unit, as in *TGWU and Mastercare Services and Distribution Lied* TUR1/275/2003.

184 See, eg *TGWU and Grosvenor Casinos Ltd* TUR1/188/2002; *TGWU and Gala Casinos Ltd* TUR1/206/2002; *TGWU and Royal P&O Nedlloyd* TUR1/400/2004.

185 The CAC will look beyond the existence of formal contractual mobility clauses to ascertain the degree of labour mobility in practice, as in *TSSA and Culina Logistics* TUR1/236/2002.

186 This was an extremely important consideration supporting the union's proposed unit in *Amicus and Sebden Steel Services Centres Ltd* TUR1/357/2004.

187 This led to a modification of the union's proposed unit in *CATU and Industrial Agricultural Engineers* TUR1/358/2004, generating a CAC imposed three-site unit severable from the employer's other sites on the basis of physical proximity.

188 See, eg, *Connect and Vodafone Ltd* TUR1/564/2007 where the union's proposal for a bargaining unit consisting of Regional Operations North was upheld by the Panel because the employer had not raised sufficient objective evidence to challenge it as 'inappropriate'. The union indicated that this was a staging post on the way to a whole company bargaining unit, and that it had confined its application to this geographical area because of a concentration of union membership and support for recognition. This did not count against its geographically circumscribed proposed unit.

189 See *Unite—the Union and The College of Law* TUR1/563/2007.

190 For pre-*KwikFit* CAC decisions going against the union's proposed unit, see *BFAWU and Seabrooks Crisps* TUR1/54/2001; *TGWU and Gala Casinos Ltd* TUR1/119/2001.

191 TUR1/446/2005.

proposal. Once again, the CAC adopted a strict, evidence-based approach in scrutinising the employer's assertion of a pervasive unitary culture. Where objective criteria such as task differentials indicate an alignment between workers' perceptions of collective identity and patterns of work organisation, the union's proposal will not be displaced.

While worker perceptions are dominant in setting the CAC's interpretive parameters, concentration of union organisation within a specific segment of the workforce is not in itself a relevant consideration.[192] Moreover, the proposed unit must itself be supported by objective criteria. These have included: existing structures of consultation mirroring distinct occupational constituencies;[193] uniforms as badges of occupational distinctiveness;[194] differences in substantive terms such as payment mechanisms and time arrangements;[195] separate lines of managerial accountability;[196] and little practical mobility between occupational groups.[197] The CAC has also been receptive to the need for managers to be excluded from occupational bargaining units in order to eliminate undesirable conflicts of interest, so that the union does not sit on both sides of the bargaining or disciplinary table.[198] Conversely, where objective criteria support the employer's claim of a 'one company' ethos then that may be sufficient to block the union's proposed bargaining unit. In *Unite—the Union and Kettle Foods Ltd*,[199] the union proposed a bargaining unit of production operatives, on the basis that this was an occupationally distinct group that self-identified as such. The employer pointed to its utilisation of a common contractual platform for all its workers, with its 'one company' ethos extending even to the architectural design of its canteen. In this case, the Panel noted that the employer's claims were neither aspirational nor rhetorical but were supported by actual management practices,

[192] In *AMICUS and CCL Label* TUR1/473/2005 the CAC considered that a dilution of membership density implied by the employer's counterproposal was not 'a relevant consideration for determining the appropriateness of the bargaining unit'. Similar sentiments were articulated in *URTU and First Line Contracts* TUR1/454/2005.

[193] *GMB and URTU and Ultraframe (UK) Ltd* TUR1/313/2003; *GMB and TRW Automotive* TUR1/597/2007, para 37.

[194] *AMICUS and Baker Oil Tools* TUR1/446/2005; *Unite—the Union and Cadbury Trebor Bassett* TUR1/582/2007, para 32.

[195] See, eg, *TGWU and Adfil Ltd* TUR1/423/2004; *AMICUS and Fibrothetford* TUR1/435/2005;*GMB and Windowstyle (UK) Ltd* TUR1/576/2007.

[196] *AMICUS and JW Froehlich Ltd* TUR1/393/2004.

[197] *GMB and Caunton Engineering Ltd* TUR1/396/2004; *Unite—the Union and Kamns Paper Mill Ltd* TUR 1/615/2008, para 45.

[198] This fits very crisply with the concerns of the 'organising model' approach. See, eg, *CWU and Cable & Wireless* TUR1/570/2007, para 44; *Unite—the Union and Sports Direct International plc* TUR1/619/2008, para 43. It is also important to observe that the CAC has stated there is no fixed industrial relations principle that managers and supervisors may not be included in a legitimate occupational bargaining unit: *BECTU and Royal Shakespeare Company Ltd* TUR1/540/2006. The enquiry is fact-sensitive.

[199] TUR1/557/2007.

and this was sufficient to negate the union's proposed bargaining unit. Nevertheless, CAC decisions have tended to defer to the union's initial proposal where objective criteria are consistent with that proposal.

IV CONCLUSION

Any legal structure that takes preference-sensitivity as its guiding ideal must take the problem of distorted preferences seriously. If it does not, the allocation of bargaining rights will lack legitimacy. We have seen that Schedule A1 is deficient in this respect. While the CAC has performed an important role in mitigating the problem of preference distortion, both in its interpretation of the 'majority support likely' threshold and in the determination of bargaining units, the potential of more radical 'endowment-shifting' techniques such as the promotion of voluntary recognition or 'staged' recognition have not yet been exploited fully. In the final analysis, however, the organisational fate of trade unions will depend upon the preparedness of individual workers to undertake the civic task of trade union activism in the workplace. Gall's sobering assessment of the prospects for union revitalisation in the UK is very pertinent: 'renewing and growing the networked grassroots activist base of trade unionism is . . . important and this may be usefully approached through deploying social democratic or socialist ideologies, which seek to attain social justice within and without the workplace'.[200] This envisages nothing less than the civic project of creating citizens fit to rule and be ruled in turn. As civic republicans are keen to point out, the task of creating citizens is fraught with difficulties. The life of active citizenship is not an easy one; civic torpor is commonplace. Nevertheless, the stakes could not be higher for the trade union movement or indeed for the wider polity. While the law alone cannot inculcate the virtues and practices of good citizenship, there is much more that could be done through smart legal reform to make this civic goal more attainable. It is a goal that is worthy of our allegiance.

[200] Gall, above n 105, 105–106.

7

The Political Theory of Collective Bargaining: Pluralism, Deliberation and the Duty to Bargain

I INTRODUCTION

ONCE BARGAINING RIGHTS have been allocated, the question of collective bargaining then arises. This raises a host of normative issues. What is collective bargaining's democratic nature, pluralist or deliberative? Which interpretation is most compatible with the ideology of social partnership? What role should the State have in regulating the bargaining relationship through the medium of a duty to bargain? In this final chapter, a deliberative understanding of collective bargaining is defended against some common misconceptions. Then, the model of good faith bargaining in North America is evaluated as a possible blueprint for the deliberative turn in collective labour relations. Having identified the weaknesses in the concept of good faith bargaining, the recent emergence of 'social partnership' ideology in the UK is appraised. While social partnership seems to be aligned with the values and concerns of deliberative democracy, New Labour's conception of social partnership misunderstands the institutional implications of a deliberative theory of democracy. Consequently, the duty to bargain in Schedule A1 is ill-suited to promoting deliberative governance in the industrial sphere. While the deliberative ideal is worthy of our allegiance, it is likely to remain elusive without systematic legal reform.

II TWO CONCEPTIONS OF POLITICS: PLURALIST AND DELIBERATIVE DEMOCRACY

The ideal of democratic citizenship has attracted widespread support in law and political philosophy, connected as it is to values of freedom and equality. Nevertheless, the contours of this ideal remain contested. This is reflected in the underlying tension between two different conceptions of politics. On the one hand, pluralist conceptions of politics conceive of democratic citizenship as a natural corollary of self-interested interaction in the marketplace. Citizens associate together and promote their interests through interest-group bargaining. This results in a kind of democratic equilibrium in the political marketplace. On the other hand, deliberative conceptions of politics emphasise the discontinuities between the market and the forum. The demands of democratic citizenship are more stringent in the forum than in the marketplace. Citizens do not simply enter the forum with fixed interests that they try to maximise through bargaining. Instead, they are expected to deliberate together in a quest for consensus on the common good. This involves shared dialogue, with citizens committed to the public exchange of reasons that differently situated citizens could reasonably accept. The essence of the distinction between pluralist and deliberative conceptions is captured in the distinction between prudence and reciprocity:

> Prudence aims at only a modus vivendi whereby self-interested citizens can deal with their disagreements through various forms of bargaining. Reciprocity aims at deliberative agreement, whereby citizens are motivated to justify their claims to those with whom they must cooperate.[1]

In historical terms the pluralist conception was dominant in law and politics. In recent years, however, the deliberative turn in democratic theory has been in the ascendant.

At its inception the pluralist conception was based upon the virtue of political competition in ensuring respect for citizens' preferences. Political parties were conceived of as suppliers of goods in the democratic marketplace, vying for the allegiance of citizen consumers. The magic of the invisible hand would ensure that individual self-interest worked to the benefit of all, with parties adjusting their policies to track citizens' preferences. The resulting consumer sovereignty was a robust democratic safeguard against tyranny. Citizens were also free to associate together to promote their interests in the democratic marketplace. This permitted a vibrant associational culture, with groups in civil society promoting their interests through pressure, threats and bargaining. Interest group activities ensured that public decision-making was open to influence by a broad range of interested parties. As with the system of competitive party politics, pluralists were also optimistic about the democratic virtue of these associational freedoms. While it was not assumed that all groups would exercise equal influence on policy outcomes, defenders of the pluralist vision concluded that interest-group bargaining would generally result in stable compromise and equilibrium.

It is easy to understand the tenacious hold of the pluralist conception on political thought. In normative terms, the pluralist conception seemed rooted in values of freedom and equality. Pluralists envisaged 'a process of competitive bargaining between different interest-groups, which involves no attempt to

[1] A Gutmann and D Thompson, *Democracy and Disagreement* (Cambridge Massachusetts, Harvard University Press, 1996) 54.

evaluate the propriety of any of the interests represented'.[2] Consequently, citizens were free to define their own interests without interference by the State, and this was based on the liberal understanding that citizens were generally the best judges of their interests.[3] Furthermore, associational freedoms allowed all citizens equal access to the democratic marketplace to promote their interests. As Cohen argues, the process of competitive bargaining appears well-suited to the realisation of the democratic ideal, for it provides a procedural framework 'that gives equal weight to the interests of citizens in part by enabling them to present and advance their interests.'[4]

Despite its normative appeal, the pluralist conception has been subjected to a trenchant critique from the deliberative perspective. First, interest group bargaining proceeded from the existing baseline of proprietary entitlements as its axiom. Accordingly, it rested on a formal and impoverished account of political equality; its assumption of equilibrium belied the distorting effects of economic inequalities on effective opportunities for political influence. In taking preferences and interests as sovereign, moral appeals to principles of justice in distribution were foreclosed in the democratic marketplace. Yet it is only in these terms that the distributive injustice can be exposed and challenged. Secondly, interest group bargaining fails to provide an attractive basis for the legitimacy of democratic decisions. If my interests are disregarded because of insufficient bargaining strength, that decision fails to honour my equal standing as a citizen. From a deliberative perspective it is necessary to *justify* decisions to citizens in terms of reasons that they could reasonably accept. Only then can the decision be regarded by citizens as democratically legitimate.

Thirdly, interest group bargaining is ill-suited to the instrumental goal of improving the quality of public decision-making. Where citizens engage with each other in competitive bargaining, with an orientation towards maximising their relative advantage, outcomes will mirror the balance of power between citizens. Where citizens engage with each other in the exercise of deliberative reason, with an orientation towards offering mutually acceptable reasons, decisions will be better informed, public spirited and more likely to represent the common good. Fourthly, the pluralist ideal of democratic citizenship 'rests on too thin a conception of what citizens owe one another in an increasingly interdependent society'.[5] The practice of public reasoning inculcates civic dispositions, ensuring 'deliberators are amenable to changing their judgements, preferences, and views during the course of their interactions'.[6] This transformative dimension of deliberation might narrow the civic distance between citizens, enabling

[2] P Pettit, 'Reworking Sandel's Republicanism', in AL Allen and MC Regan (eds), *Debating Democracy's Discontent* (Oxford, Oxford University Press, 1998) 40, 44.

[3] J Cohen, 'Procedure and Substance in Deliberative Democracy', in J Bohman and W Rehg (eds), *Deliberative Democracy* (Cambridge Massachusetts, MIT Press, 1997) 407, 411.

[4] *Ibid*, 411.

[5] Gutmann and Thompson, above n 1, 58.

[6] JS Dryzek, *Deliberative Democracy and Beyond* (Oxford, Oxford University Press, 2000) 1.

them to transcend differences based on narrow understanding, partial perspectives and incomplete information.

This critique has led to the ascendancy of the deliberative conception in contemporary political thought. The main elements of deliberative democracy stand in contrast to those of interest group pluralism. From the deliberative perspective, 'outcomes are democratically legitimate if and only if they could be the object of a free and reasoned agreement among equals'.[7] First, the democratic process demands the justification of collective decisions in terms of *reasons* that all those subject to the decision could accept. This rejects the pluralist vision of democratic outcomes generated by competitive bargaining amongst fixed interests. Accordingly, democratic communication should be 'free from coercion, deception, self-deception, strategizing, and manipulation', which is the very lifeblood of pluralist bargaining.[8] Secondly, the demands of deliberative citizenship are rigorous and exacting. Citizens must engage with each other with a mutual commitment to *reciprocity*: 'to justify imposing their will on you, your fellow citizens must give reasons that are comprehensible to you. If you seek to impose your will on them, you owe them no less.'[9] Reciprocity is a complex ideal, encompassing democratic virtues, cognitive abilities, and the emotional capacity for empathy across difference. Its realisation depends in part upon political action to promote the deliberative capacities of citizens, such as civic education. Yet active deliberative engagement itself has an educative effect on citizens, compelling the participant to 'weigh interests not his own; to be guided, in the case of conflicting claims, by another rule than his private partialities; to apply, at every turn, principles and maxims which have for their reason of existence the common good'.[10] Thirdly, deliberative democracy requires a far richer and more substantive ideal of political equality. This requires the egalitarian redistribution of social and economic advantages to insulate deliberation from the distorting effects of economic inequality on political influence. Thus, deliberative democrats are hospitable to a range of political measures to achieve political equality, such as campaign finance regulation, the welfare state, and workplace democratisation.[11]

The richness of the deliberative conception of politics provides a striking contrast with the starkness of the pluralist conception. It is easy to see why the retreat from the pluralist conception has been joined by so many lawyers and

[7] J Cohen, 'Deliberation and Democratic Legitimacy', in J Bohman and W Rehg (eds), *Deliberative Democracy* (Cambridge Massachusetts, MIT Press, 1997) 67, 73.

[8] Dryzek, above n 6, 22.

[9] A Gutmann and D Thompson, *Why Deliberative Democracy?* (Princeton, Princeton University Press, 2004) 4.

[10] JS Mill, *Representative Government* (1910) 217, cited in C Pateman, *Participation and Democratic Theory* (Cambridge, Cambridge University Press, 1970) 30. The educative effects of deliberative engagement are also stressed in Dryzek, above n 6 169: 'The only way to learn civility and reciprocity is through practice in deliberation itself.'

[11] See, eg, the policy proposals in C Sunstein, 'Beyond the Republican Revival' (1988) 97 *Yale Law Journal* 1539, 1576–90.

political philosophers. The next section analyses the pluralist-deliberative dichotomy in the conceptualisation of the collective bargaining process. Historically, at least, interest group pluralism exercised a pervasive influence on the terms of the debate. For Clegg:

> trade unions act as pressure groups both in politics and in industrial relations. There are many similarities between collective bargaining and the political processes of compromise and concession … The rules of collective bargaining can be seen as the industrial equivalent of the political rules governing the operation of pressure groups.[12]

This complemented his democratic affirmation of the oppositional role of unions in the industrial sphere, echoing Schumpeter's competitive model of democracy.[13] These pluralist values also had a pervasive influence on Kahn-Freund's conception of labour law.[14] As we have seen, this pluralist model of collective bargaining did not achieve total dominance even at the height of its influence. Allan Flanders defended a deliberative conception of collective bargaining, though this never had more than a marginal impact on industrial relations practice.[15] However, in line with recent shifts in public law and political philosophy, we might now expect the deliberative turn to exert a more profound influence upon new theorisations of collective bargaining. As we shall see, the eclipse of the interest-group pluralist conception has been strongly resisted in the sphere of labour law. Most notably, Tonia Novitz has offered some powerful arguments against the deliberative conception as a model for reshaping collective bargaining.[16] It will be necessary to address those arguments before endorsing the deliberative turn in collective labour relations.

III A DELIBERATIVE CONSTITUTION OF INDUSTRIAL DEMOCRACY: DELIBERATION DEFENDED

The centrality of reasoned dialogue to deliberative democracy has a powerful intuitive appeal. How could one object to the democratic priority of reasoned arguments over threats and the naked pursuit of self-interest in the political sphere? Within the context of collective bargaining, however, Novitz invites us to resist this temptation, identifying the deliberative conception as allied with a unitary conception of social partnership in the workplace. First, the deliberative commitment to consensus ignores the reality of conflicts of interest within the employment relation. Instead, deliberation connotes a unitary common good

12 HA Clegg, 'Pluralism in Industrial Relations' (1975) 13 *British Journal of Industrial Relations* 311.

13 HA Clegg, *A New Approach to Industrial Democracy* (Oxford, Blackwell, 1960) 19–30.

14 For discussion, see Lord Wedderburn, 'Otto Kahn-Freund and British Labour Law', in Lord Wedderburn, R Lewis and J Clark (eds), *Labour Law and Industrial Relations: Building on Kahn-Freund* (Oxford, Oxford University Press, 1983) 29.

15 See ch 2.

16 T Novitz, *International and European Protection of the Right to Strike* (Oxford, Oxford University Press, 2003) 20–22.

that requires worker citizens 'to lay aside their perceptions of divergent interests, and instead work together in "partnership" with management to achieve ends which are of mutual benefit to both'.[17] To the extent that deliberative democracy silences voices of justified dissent in the quest for consensus, this unitary dissolution of conflict is ideologically distorting. Conflicts of interest in the employment relation are perennial and intractable. Moreover, perhaps it is unrealistic and naive to expect interest groups such as trade unions or employers' associations to behave as impartial deliberators when partisanship is the lifeblood of industrial politics.[18] In these circumstances, bargaining is a more appropriate mode of procedural resolution than deliberation.

Secondly, deliberation can mask the effects of oppressive discourses and power disparities. With power relations occluded from view, deliberative democracy 'represents a danger to the extent that its application can be used to cloak, and thereby legitimize, underlying cultural assumptions, economic discourse, and other sources of skewed power dynamics'.[19] By contrast, bargaining renders power relations more transparent. It also avoids the slippage into market liberalism as a dominating ideology structuring the contours of the deliberative consensus. Moreover, perhaps workers' discursive engagement with alien values of market liberalism is a normative gulf that cannot be crossed by deliberative procedures, marking a divide between mutually incompatible values and closed discourses that simply speak past each other.[20] This makes the pluralist conception particularly well-suited as a theoretical underpinning to collective bargaining. Finally, deliberation appears to leave the right to strike otiose. The conduct of industrial warfare is anathema to the reasoned resolution of disagreement. Rather, it is intimately tied to the pluralist bargaining conception of industrial politics. Consequently, under the deliberative conception 'industrial action comes to be seen as too confrontational to foster the trust needed for deliberation. It becomes redundant.'[21] Without the right to strike, however, workers have no means at their disposal to vindicate effectively their legitimately divergent interests against employers.

Each of these criticisms poses a significant challenge to the deliberative conception. Cumulatively they present a devastating case against the deliberative conception if they are justified. However, despite the cogency of these arguments, each of the points can be countered. Three counter-arguments will be made. First, the assumption that the deliberative conception rests upon a unitary

[17] Novitz, *ibid*, 21. See also T Novitz and P Skidmore, *Fairness at Work: A Critical Analysis of the Employment Relations Act 1999 and its Treatment of Collective Rights* (Oxford, Hart Publishing, 2001) 17–18.

[18] For an argument along these lines, see J Donaghey, 'Deliberation, Employment Relations and Social Partnership in the Republic of Ireland' (2008) 29 *Economic and Industrial Democracy* 35, 58.

[19] Novitz, above n 16, 22.

[20] 'One is reminded here of Wedderburn's analysis of the failure to counter Hayek's neo-liberal "economic" discourse with principles established in labour law, because they do not share the same moral precepts or notions of value' in Novitz *ibid*.

[21] *Ibid*, 21.

conception of the common good is based upon a misinterpretation of the role that consensus plays in deliberative democracy. Secondly, the deliberative conception is more attuned to distorting effects of power and oppression in the democratic process; the real danger of legitimating unjust power relations is posed by a continuing adherence to the pluralist bargaining conception. Thirdly, far from being otiose, the right to strike would in fact be critical to the realisation of the deliberative conception in collective labour relations.

A Consensus and Disagreement: Unitary or Pluralist?

It is tempting to dismiss the deliberative quest for reasoned consensus as misguided in pluralistic societies. The sources of political disagreement seem too multiple to render consensus an attractive aspiration. Inevitably, material resources are scarce and this provokes conflicts as to their appropriate distribution. Furthermore, and as is to be expected in a pluralistic community, citizens differ reasonably in their tastes, experiences and conceptions of the good. To the extent that deliberative democracy is tied to a unitary conception of the good, it denies the circumstances of reasonable pluralism amongst citizens. In its pursuit of the homogenising uniformity of a shared common good, deliberative democracy seems to take on a stifling and even authoritarian quality.

Such criticisms are targeted at a mischaracterisation of the deliberative conception, which rests upon a faulty conflation of two senses of pluralism in the democratic sphere. It is true that deliberative democrats place faith in the ability of deliberative procedures to enable citizens to work together towards a political common ground. Citizens with an orientation towards deliberative engagement are reflective and open-minded to changing their preferences in the light of reasoned arguments. This involves a rejection of the pluralist *process* of interest-group bargaining, in the sense of unreflective citizens engaging with each other in order to maximise their pre-political interests. This does not lead deliberative democrats to reject pluralism in a second sense: citizens disagree persistently and reasonably about moral values, along with 'differences of preference and ability, life chances and biological endowment, ethnicity and rhetorical style'.[22] The central terrain of deliberative democracy is occupied by pluralists in this second sense, and this is manifest in widespread rejection of the unitary view of a common good in the deliberative conception.

Deliberative democrats acknowledge that consensus may not be the outcome of deliberative procedures even under ideal conditions.[23] Given the fact of reasonable pluralism, intractable conflicts between incompatible values will often

[22] J Cohen, 'Democracy and Liberty', in J Elster (ed), *Deliberative Democracy* (Cambridge, Cambridge University Press, 1998) 185, 188.

[23] Cohen, who counts as a pluralist deliberative democrat, is explicit on this point: 'even an ideal deliberative procedure will not, in general, produce consensus': see Cohen, above n 3, 414.

be too deep for consensus to obtain. The inability of deliberation to yield consensus is heightened in the real world of politics, where time constraints preclude open-ended dialogue. Moreover, deliberation 'may actually crystallise bases for disagreement' by bringing irreconcilable moral positions into sharper relief.[24] While deliberative democrats prize the achievement of a consensus that may be the object of rational assent by diverse citizens, they do not prize consensus at any price. For this reason, there is ample space in deliberative democracy for other modes of collective decision-making such as voting, bargaining and workable compromises to achieve closure in the absence of consensus. Moreover, a prime virtue of the deliberative conception is its inculcation of certain virtues to allow citizens to live respectfully with each other in circumstances where reasonable *disagreements* cannot be resolved rationally. In particular, the deliberative virtue of civic magnanimity requires citizens to engage with each other in a spirit of respectful open-mindedness to an opponent's position. While civic magnanimity might not bridge the chasms of moral disagreement in a pluralistic community, it embodies a notion of civic friendship that encourages citizens to live with reasonable disagreement in conditions of mutual respect.

As such, deliberative procedures presuppose rather than denigrate differences between citizens. Instead, difference is better conceived of as a deliberative resource, enriching the terms of deliberation through its inclusion of a plurality of views and perspectives. Citizens do not leave their partial perspectives at the gateway to the deliberative forum. If they did, there would be nothing to deliberate *about*. Instead, deliberative democracy offers the hope that partial interests may connect with more general interests during the process of deliberative engagement between citizens. This undermines Novitz's portrayal of the deliberative conception as leading ineluctably to a 'unitary' frame of reference in industrial relations, with workers yoked together by a common purpose defined by management, co-opting them into a skewed accord based on economic efficiency.[25] This unitary frame of reference is neither deliberative nor democratic. Deliberative democracy does not enjoin worker citizens 'to lay aside their perceptions of divergent interests' in deliberating with employers, for 'partial interests can also be legitimate, so purging partial interests should not be at issue'.[26] Moreover, the demands of reciprocity would apply equally to workers *and* employers. This mutuality ensures that employers, too, are enjoined to engage with workers' interests and perspectives in the deliberative process.[27]

[24] S Besson, *The Morality of Conflict: Reasonable Disagreement and the Law* (Oxford, Hart Publishing, 2005) 230.

[25] For the classic account of pluralist and unitary frames of reference in industrial relations, see A Fox, *Industrial Sociology and Industrial Relations* (London, HMSO, 1966).

[26] Dryzek, above n 6, 169.

[27] Cohen, above n 3, 421. In a similar vein, the deliberative conception articulated by Gutmann and Thompson is robustly egalitarian in its articulation of deliberative outcomes to the democratic process.

B Real Politics is about Interests and Power—Deliberation is a Sanitising Distraction

The second of Novitz's criticisms, that deliberative democracy obscures intractable conflicts of interest and asymmetric power relations from view, parallels broader criticisms of the deliberative conception. Thus, Shapiro points to the workplace as a site of conflict where deliberation might 'lead workers to discover that they share interests that are fundamentally at odds with those of employers'.[28] Worse still, the deliberative conception avoids robust engagement with the economic forces that constrain the realisation of deliberation. Under these circumstances, the deliberative conception is a dangerous palliative in the ugly sphere of real politics, for it attends 'too little to the degree to which moral disagreements in politics are shaped by differences of interests and power'.[29] Any conception of politics, and particularly one in the industrial sphere, must speak to these twin elements of interests and power if it is to attract our allegiance. In its foregrounding of these elements, the interest-group pluralist conception seems more attuned to political realities.

With respect to interests, however, the deliberative conception provides a superior account of the nature of the conflicts mediated by collective bargaining. The canonical position in our labour law was articulated by Kahn-Freund, who argued powerfully for the view 'that the legitimate expectations of labour and of management belong to those which are inevitably in conflict'.[30] These conflicts were essentially distributive, such that 'the distribution of the social product between consumption and investment can only be determined by a constant and unending dialogue of powers'.[31] Given that these distributive conflicts of interest were both pervasive and intractable, the best that could be hoped for was a process of ongoing adjustment and compromise between the collective parties through interest-group bargaining. There is much that is attractive in this view, but an over-emphasis on parties' self-interest fails to do justice to the moral nature of this conflict. Income, skills and security in employment can all be characterised as basic opportunity goods for citizens. These basic opportunity goods furnish citizens with the resources needed to enable them to lead decent and civilised lives. And what constitutes an appropriate pattern of distribution of these basic opportunity goods is a moral question.

[28] I Shapiro, 'Enough of Deliberation: Politics Is about Interests and Power', in S Macedo (ed), *Deliberative Politics* (Oxford, Oxford University Press, 1999) 28, 31.

[29] *Ibid*, 29.

[30] PL Davies and MR Freedland (eds), *Kahn-Freund's Labour and the Law*, 3rd edn (London, Stevens and Son, 1983) 66.

[31] *Ibid*, 27.

So collective wage bargaining does not simply engage deliberation with respect to 'factual matters such as the financial well-being of the firm and the productivity of the labor force'.[32] Instead, deliberation speaks to the moral dimension of the decisions that employers make daily that affect the life chances of citizens through the medium of basic opportunity. While self-interest and relative bargaining strength will undoubtedly influence distributive outcomes in collective bargaining, the view that this ought to be the sole determinant should be resisted. To the greatest extent possible, moral conflicts ought to be settled on moral terms. Within the field of industrial relations, this reconstruction of pluralism in terms of values rather than interests suggests that deliberative discussion is a more appropriate process for resolving conflict than interest-group bargaining.[33] These insights have led deliberative democrats to argue for the extension of deliberative principles beyond the horizons of the State to the realm of 'middle democracy', inhabited by unions, corporations and other actors implicated in determining citizens' basic liberties and opportunities.

With respect to power, critics of the deliberative conception have pointed to the exclusionary biases inherent in the deliberative process. Thus, Young has argued that in deliberative situations involving interaction between privileged and disadvantaged groups 'the perspectives of the privileged are likely to dominate the definition of that common good' on account of their superior material and cultural resources.[34] Clearly we should be cautious in endorsing the deliberative conception as a panacea in these circumstances, and the practice of deliberation may well perpetuate disadvantage in its structuring of the common good. Nevertheless, it is difficult to see how interest-group bargaining avoids these difficulties, dependent as it is on relative bargaining strength. One of the weaknesses of the interest-group pluralist conception was its assumption of equilibrium in the democratic process, and its failure to engage critically with underlying distributions of power. In these circumstances, weaker groups are unlikely to bargain their way to distributive justice through the exercise of power politics and self-interest.

In contrast, the deliberative appeal to reciprocal reasons furnishes the disadvantaged with the kind of moral language needed to mount an effective critique of distributive injustice. Unlike the interest-group pluralist conception, equilibrium is not taken as axiomatic. As Gutmann and Thompson argue, 'to the extent that the political struggles take place on the basis of deliberation rather than power, they are more evenly matched. Because moral appeals are the weapon of

[32] J Elster, 'Introduction', in J Elster (ed), *Deliberative Democracy* (Cambridge, Cambridge University Press, 1998) 1, 7.

[33] C Provis, 'Unitarism, Pluralism, Interests and Values' (1996) 34 *British Journal of Industrial Relations* 473, 484–7.

[34] Iris Marion Young, 'Communication and the Other: Beyond Deliberative Democracy', in S Benhabib (ed), *Democracy and Difference: Contesting the Boundaries of the Political* (Princeton, Princeton University Press, 1996) 120, 126.

the weak, a deliberative playing field is more nearly level.'[35] One is reminded here of the radical critique of industrial relations pluralism developed by Fox.[36] For industrial pluralists, as for their political pluralist counterparts, equilibrium and consensus in the bargaining relationship was assumed rather than argued for. These assumptions of equilibrium and consensus 'increasingly tended to serve as a conservative legitimation of established institutions'.[37] Industrial relations pluralism served to mask large scale structural inequalities inherent in the incidents of private property and the logic of capitalist production. Accordingly, as the radical critique demonstrated, a simple retrieval of interest-group pluralist commitments may itself serve to conceal conflict and disequilibrium from critical exposure.

C A Deliberative Conception of the Right to Strike

The most troubling allegation levelled at the deliberative conception is that it would render the right to strike 'redundant'. We have already seen this tendency in Flanders' protean deliberative theory of collective bargaining, where he comes close to the view that strike action is inconsistent with the *reasoned* solution of industrial disputes. The deployment of coercive threats in the collective bargaining process is more akin to interest group bargaining, not deliberation. Consequently, the right to strike seems to be anathema to the constitution of deliberative democracy.

In fact, the right to strike is critical to the realisation of deliberative democracy for two reasons. First, Cohen has defended a rich ideal of political equality as an aspect of deliberative participation. This embraces a principle of 'equal opportunities for effective influence'.[38] In public policy terms, this necessitates redressing social and economic inequalities between citizens in order to diminish inequalities in political influence. But this kind of move does not involve slippage back into the interest group pluralist conception. Rather, enhancing the social power of disadvantaged groups renders their political equality manifest to other citizens, and 'by reducing inequalities of power, reduces the incentives to shift from deliberative politics to a politics of bargaining'.[39] In the industrial sphere, this translates into a deliberative justification for guaranteeing an effective right to strike. Without the right to strike, the political inequality of workers is manifest to employers, and this heightens the risk that deliberative engagement will be a sham. With the right to strike, deterrent-based incentives for genuine deliberation based on reciprocity are created, for employers are faced with the potential of

[35] Gutmann and Thompson, above n 1, 50.
[36] A Fox, *Beyond Contract: Work, Power and Trust Relations* (London, Faber, 1974) ch 6.
[37] R Hyman, 'Pluralism, Procedural Consensus and Collective Bargaining' (1978) 16 *British Journal of Industrial Relations* 16, 35.
[38] Cohen, above n 3, 422.
[39] *Ibid*, 423.

serious economic harm if they are exposed as manipulating the deliberative process in bad faith.

In situations where employers eschew reciprocity, unions may legitimately respond with economic countermeasures, for 'individuals and groups are not obligated to deliberate if others refuse to do so, and if doing so would put them at a further disadvantage'.[40] It is not only the deterrent value of strike action that renders it attractive from a deliberative perspective. Sometimes the deployment of such direct action, while non-deliberative in form, can itself promote deliberative ends. As Gutmann and Thompson observe, 'those who speak on behalf of the disadvantaged can ill afford to ignore the need to be effective'.[41] Direct action such as 'sit-ins and workers' strikes' can sometimes be justified deliberatively if they precipitate public deliberation on issues of serious injustice that might otherwise be marginalised or ignored.[42]

Secondly, bargaining continues to have an important but residual role in the constitution of deliberative democracy.[43] As we have seen, consensus may not be attainable in the face of deliberative disagreements over conflicting values and interests. Even where there is broad agreement on moral ends, intractable disagreement on the appropriate means to achieve them might remain. In these circumstances, decisional closure necessitates bargaining to a mutually acceptable resolution. For this reason, the right to strike remains central to the deliberative conception for it is a guarantor of fairness in any bargaining process that might follow deliberation. Nevertheless, even if strategic action cannot be eliminated from industrial politics because of the continuing role that bargaining must play, this should not lead us to conclude that deliberation adds nothing to interest group pluralist conception. As Dryzek points out, 'deliberation can multiply dimensions and options' at the bargaining table, and this 'proliferation increases the possibilities for stable and non-arbitrary agreement'.[44] This enables collective parties to respond to an apparent bargaining impasse in creative ways, for 'introducing additional dimensions can make social choices *more* tractable'.[45] In this way, while deliberation may not have the resources to displace bargaining entirely in many cases, it certainly has the resources to make bargaining a more enlightened exercise.

Novitz's arguments are effective in challenging some versions of the deliberative model as appropriate in the industrial sphere. However, she underestimates the richness of the deliberative tradition, and the extent to which deliberative democracy may incorporate agonistic elements without sacrificing its core

40 Gutmann and Thompson, above n 1, 72–3.
41 Gutmann and Thompson, above n 9, 51.
42 *Ibid.*
43 Gutmann and Thompson, above n 1, 69–73.
44 Dryzek, above n 6, 41.
45 *Ibid*, 73.

commitment to the democratic exchange of reasons.[46] Accordingly, proponents of the deliberative conception have pointed to the potential of deliberative democracy as a blueprint for extending and enriching democracy in the industrial sphere. This has coalesced under the banner of 'associative democracy'.[47]

In associative democracies the State promotes the formation of secondary associations in civil society and underwrites their participation in the tasks of regulation and governance. These secondary associations enhance the representation of under-represented interests, thereby offsetting political inequality, and augment public competence in promoting the common good. The regulatory activities of unions and employers' associations provide an example of associative democracy in action. On account of their greater competence, unions and employers' associations might be better placed than the State to participate in the authorship, diffusion and enforcement of standards relating to training, skills and health and safety in the workplace. The associative State actively intervenes to enable civic associations to do what it cannot in certain contexts because of its limited competence to promote the common good. Associative democrats are hopeful that 'it may be possible to use the associative strategy to advance the principles of participation and the common good without thereby encouraging particularistic group identities that turn politics from deliberation to bargaining'.[48] In the next section, the North American concept of the duty to bargain in good faith shall be evaluated, tracing the different ways in which legal norms have constrained the promotion of deliberative elements in the collective bargaining process.

IV THE US DUTY TO BARGAIN IN GOOD FAITH: PLURALIST OR DELIBERATIVE?

The duty to bargain in North America enjoins employers and unions to engage with each other in good faith. This mutual obligation of 'good faith' seems redolent of a deliberative conception of politics. Thus Shapiro argues that through its enforcement of good faith bargaining obligations 'government seeks to mandate deliberation through an affirmative duty to bargain'.[49] Certain judicial statements reinforce the sense that there is an alignment between good faith obligations and deliberation: 'collective bargaining requires that the parties involved deal with each other with an open and fair mind and sincerely endeavour to overcome obstacles or difficulties existing between the employer

[46] See J Mansbridge, 'Conflict and Self-interest in Deliberation', in S Besson and J Luis Marti (eds), *Deliberative Democracy and its Discontents* (Aldershot, Ashgate, 2006) 107.

[47] J Cohen and J Rogers, *Associations and Democracy* (London, Verso, 1995).

[48] Cohen, above n 3, 431.

[49] I Shapiro, *The State of Democratic Theory* (Princeton, Princeton University Press, 2003) 46.

and the employees',[50] or that 'there is a duty on both sides, though difficult of legal enforcement, to enter into discussion with an open and fair mind, and a sincere purpose to find a basis of agreement'.[51] These statements denote a particular state of mind necessary for good faith bargaining; one that is open to the possibility of resolving differences of interest for the sake of agreement. In this respect, the specification of good faith bargaining resembles the deliberative virtues of reciprocity and civic magnanimity, with deliberative participants striving to be reflective and open-minded in the mutual search for a moral accommodation of divergent perspectives.[52]

On closer analysis, however, legally regulated bargaining in North America falls short of the deliberative ideal in three respects. First, legal standards of good faith in the bargaining process have been fashioned in a pluralist rather than a deliberative image. Secondly, the subject-matter of collective bargaining has been interpreted so as to be highly solicitous of managerial prerogatives. Thirdly, the one-sided restriction of unions' economic weaponry entails a significant power imbalance between employers and unions. This disequilibrium is inconsistent with the demands of manifest and substantive political equality necessitated by the deliberative conception.

A Good Faith Bargaining: The Ascendancy of Pluralist Politics

At its inception the interpretive parameters of the duty to bargain in good faith straddled both pluralist and deliberative conceptions of politics. This corresponded to a distinction between two functions ascribed to the legal duty.[53] On the one hand, the *passive* function necessitated mutual recognition by the parties for bargaining purposes. The law merely guided the collective parties to the bargaining table and required them to confer with a view to striking a mutually acceptable bargain. Beyond this the State would not intrude upon the autonomy of the bargaining process. The passive duty was therefore minimalist in what it required of the bargaining parties; the substantive contours of the collective agreement would simply reflect their relative bargaining strengths and acumen, with each party seeking to maximise its self-interest. Its main elements were intimately bound up with the interest group pluralist conception of politics.

On the other hand, the *active* duty to bargain was more deliberative in tone. Collective bargaining was not merely 'a brute contest of economic power somewhat masked by polite manners and voluminous statistics'.[54] Instead, the active duty envisaged that the parties 'must explain their respective positions,

[50] *NLRB v Boss Manufacturing Company* 118 F.2d. 187, 189 (7th Circuit 1941).

[51] *Globe Cotton Mills v NLRB* 103 F.2d. 91, 94 (5th Circuit 1939).

[52] Gutmann and Thompson, above n 1, 79–94.

[53] HH Wellington, 'Freedom of Contract and the Collective Bargaining Agreement' (1964) 112 *University of Pennsylvania Law Review* 467.

[54] A Cox, 'The Duty to Bargain in Good Faith' (1958) 71 *Harvard Law Review* 1401, 1409.

listen to reasoned arguments, and pursue the search for agreement with sincerity and in genuine good faith'.[55] This countenanced much greater State involvement in the collective bargaining process. To ensure compliance with the active duty, the State might need to scrutinise the reasonableness of bargaining practices, even extending to evaluation of whether the parties had adopted reasonable substantive positions or made reasonable concessions during the collective bargaining process.

In theoretical terms, the interpretive choice might seem easy enough. Given the alternatives of collective bargaining based on brute bargaining strength, or collective bargaining based on deliberative reason, should we not prefer the deliberative version and its corollary of an active duty to bargain? In normative terms, the deliberative turn in democratic theory seems utterly compelling. Yet the weight of academic and judicial opinion came down firmly in favour of the passive duty. This preference was based upon two kinds of argument, one *normative* and the other *institutional*.

The best version of the *normative* argument in defence of the passive duty was offered by Harry Wellington. According to Wellington, enforcement of the active duty would constitute an undue encroachment on the parties' collective freedom of contract. Of course, statutory recognition involved some sacrifice of negative freedom of contract, in that the employer could no longer refuse recognition to the union as its bargaining adversary. But beyond this, the State should respect the parties' positive freedom of contract in fashioning bargains of their own making to the greatest possible extent. The virtue of collective freedom of contract rested upon an anti-paternalist critique of the State, reflecting broader elements in pluralist political philosophy. The parties themselves were better placed to negotiate substantive terms and conditions appropriate to their context, for they had a better sense of what lay in their respective interests. The State was simply not competent to engage in controversial value judgements as to which bargaining positions were reasonable. Furthermore, an active duty to bargain would embroil the State in substantive influence over the outcomes of collective bargaining: 'the enforcement of reasonable behaviour results in control over the substantive terms of the collective agreement'.[56] In heightening State control over autonomous regulatory processes in civil society, the democratic virtue of dispersed power amongst a plurality of competing interest groups would be compromised.[57] With the passive duty to bargain, however, the State's role was procedural in its orientation; bargaining outcomes would be shaped predominantly by the parties themselves.

Even on the passive understanding of the duty, its proponents were cognisant that

[55] Wellington, above n 53, 472.
[56] *Ibid*, 473.
[57] *Ibid*.

> the bargaining status of a union can be destroyed by going through the motions of negotiating almost as easily as by bluntly withholding recognition ... As long as there are unions weak enough to be talked to death, there will be employers who are tempted to engage in the forms of collective bargaining without the substance.[58]

As such, some scrutiny of the quality of negotiations would be needed to distinguish 'hard' bargaining from 'surface' bargaining. In hard bargaining there is a resolute and stubborn pursuit of self-interest such that any ensuing agreement is mainly on one's own terms. From the perspective of a passive duty to bargain, this is legitimate bargaining conduct. In 'surface' bargaining, by contrast, there is an outward pretence of bargaining coupled with an inner resolve to obstruct agreement. Even from the minimalist vantage point of the passive duty, this was illegitimate bargaining conduct. The distinction was a fine one, but it marked the boundary between lawful and unlawful bargaining conduct in separating 'employers who are seeking to talk a union to death from those who are merely stubborn negotiators exercising their full bargaining power'.[59] Nevertheless, defenders of the passive duty could point to the fact that 'an employer or a union can be very unreasonable without violating the statute'.[60] Only where the employer had flatly refused to make any concession or counterproposal to the union during negotiations,[61] or 'advanced demands so obviously intolerable to the union as to suggest a purpose to obstruct negotiations',[62] would an inference of subjective bad faith be warranted. Legal enforcement of the passive duty thus continued to give significant latitude to the parties' collective freedom of contract. This commitment to collective freedom of contract was a natural corollary of the pluralist conception of politics. The philosophical repudiation of a deliberative, active duty was confirmed by the Supreme Court:

> It must be realized that collective bargaining, under a system where the government does not attempt to control the results of negotiations, cannot be equated with an academic collective search for truth—or even with what might be thought to be the ideal of one. The parties—even granting the modification of views that may come from a realization of economic interdependence—still proceed from contrary and to an extent antagonistic viewpoints and concepts of self interest. The system has not reached the ideal of the philosophic notion that perfect understanding among people would lead to perfect agreement among them on values.[63]

[58] Cox, above n 54, 1413.

[59] *Ibid*, 1417.

[60] Wellington, above n 53, 476.

[61] *NLRB v Reed & Prince Manufacturing Company* 205 F.2d 131, 134–5: 'If an employer can find nothing whatever to agree to in an ordinary current-day contract submitted to him, or in some of the union's related minor requests, and if the employer makes not a single serious proposal meeting the union at least part way, then certainly the Board must be able to conclude that this is at least some evidence of bad faith, that is, of a desire not to reach an agreement with the union ... The employer is obliged to make some reasonable effort in some direction to compose his differences with the union'.

[62] Cox, above n 54, 1422.

[63] *NLRB v Insurance Agents' Union* 361 US 477, 488–9 (1960).

The legal contours of the good faith bargaining duty have been shaped by these pluralist assumptions. This is reflected in the dominance of a contractual paradigm, articulated by the Supreme Court, in delineating the requirements of good faith.[64] The National Labor Relations Board (NLRB) has inferred unlawful 'surface' bargaining in circumstances disclosing extreme intransigence at the bargaining table, as in a 'take it or leave it' stance at the bargaining table,[65] or insistence on substantive conditions 'so consistently and predictably unpalatable to the other party',[66] often involving the broad retention of unilateral managerial rights under the collective agreement in conjunction with 'no strike' clauses during its subsistence. Such inferences always take their colour from an investigation of all the circumstances; consequently 'each case is unique and generalization hazardous'.[67] Consistent with the passive nature of the duty and its pluralist underpinning, however, both the NLRB and the courts have been astute to assert the continuing legitimacy of hard bargaining and the resolute pursuit of self-interest by the bargaining parties. Such resoluteness is plainly anathema to the deliberative conception of politics. This position was put most starkly by the Court of Appeals for the Fifth Circuit, in its reversal of an NLRB finding of employer bad faith:

> In our opinion the matter at hand resolves itself into purely a question of hard bargaining between two parties who were possessed of disparate economic power: a relatively weak union encountered a relatively strong company. The company naturally desired to use its advantage to retain as many rights as possible. We do not believe, however, that that desire is inconsistent with good faith bargaining.[68]

The *normative* argument was also complemented by an *institutional* defence of the passive duty to bargain. As an exemplar of this institutional argument, Archibald Cox rejected the dogma of collective freedom of contract and based his argument instead on the inherent limitations of retrospective adjudication.[69] As a technique for promoting deliberative engagement, retrospective adjudication was insufficiently supple to track the dynamic quality of political relationships. Worse still, legalism 'may cause negotiators to bargain with a view toward making the strongest record for NLRB scrutiny'.[70] This was echoed in later critiques of the NLRB's transition from a non-legalistic ethos based on voluntary settlement to its

[64] See, eg, *H K Porter v NLRB* 397 US 99, 108 (1970). For critical discussion of 'contractualist' values guiding the explication of the duty to bargain in Supreme Court jurisprudence, see K Klare, 'Judicial Deradicalization of the Wagner Act and the Origins of Modern Legal Consciousness, 1937–1941' (1978) 62 *Minnesota Law Review* 265, 293–310.

[65] The classic instance is of 'Boulwarism', where the company made a 'first, firm and final offer' to the union accompanied by widespread publicity advertising its bargaining position. See *NLRB v General Electric Company* 418 F.2d 736 (2nd Circuit 1969).

[66] *NLRB v Mar-Len Cabinets* 659 F.2d 995 (9th Circuit 1981).

[67] RA Gorman and MW Finkin, *Basic Text on Labor Law, Unionization and Collective Bargaining*, 2nd edn (St Paul Minnesota, Thomson West, 2004) 651.

[68] *Chevron Oil Company v NLRB* 442 F. 2d 1067 (5th Circuit 1971).

[69] Cox, above n 54.

[70] *Ibid*, 1441.

adoption of a legalistic, adjudicative role in collective labour relations. This 'legalistic judicial method does not sit easily with a flexible industrial relations problem solving approach'.[71] Legal enforcement of the passive duty to bargain minimised the extent to which third party agencies were embroiled retrospectively in the minutiae of bargaining relationships, because retrospective review of bargaining conduct was not conducted intensively. In other words, it was only in cases of seriously egregious bargaining malpractice that the reviewing agency would be likely to find a breach of the passive duty to bargain. By contrast, an active duty to bargain would necessitate much more intensive review as a precursor to its enforcement. This was something that labour boards and courts were institutionally ill-equipped to doing.

Can the normative and institutional arguments in defence of the passive duty (and, implicitly, against the active duty) be surmounted? With respect to the normative argument, Langille and Macklem have argued powerfully against the pluralist assumption that 'self-interest remains the definitional rationale for behaviour'.[72] Instead, they defend the view that collective bargaining should be understood as a mechanism for ensuring certain substantive outcomes in workplace governance, associated with the ideal of democratic citizenship. Accordingly, the legal concept of good faith should be extended to include a duty to implement workplace institutions limiting the arbitrary exercise of unilateral employer power, such as seniority rules, just cause limits on discipline and dismissal, and fair grievance procedures. While the detail of these institutional arrangements may be shaped creatively by the parties, their very existence ought not to be eliminated through hard bargaining by powerful employers. This offers an alternative vision of the duty to bargain that is more closely aligned with the 'active' version of the legal duty. More generally, deliberative democrats would be less solicitous of collective freedom of contract, and therefore less reticent about the idea that the objective reasonableness of parties' bargaining conduct might be scrutinised by an agency of the State. For example, where one party refuses to make any concessions during bargaining this might be evidence that there has been a refusal to engage reflectively in the deliberative process with at least open-mindedness to changing preferences in the light of new information and new perspectives. Or where a party consistently refuses to provide supporting evidence to justify its proposals or refusals to change position, this might be evidence that there has been no attempt to engage in the deliberative process of evidence-based argumentation.

With respect to the institutional argument, Cox's concern with the limits of legal norms echoes recent contributions to the debate on how to institutionalise

[71] B Townley, 'Union Recognition: A Comparative Analysis of the Pros and Cons of a Legal Procedure' (1987) 25 *British Journal of Industrial Relations* 177, 191.

[72] B Langille and P Macklem, 'Beyond Belief: Labour Law's Duty to Bargain' (1988) 13 *Queen's Law Journal* 62, 74.

deliberative democracy. For Dryzek, for example, courts are ill-suited to promoting the kind of free discourse characteristic of deliberative engagement. They are primarily

> devices for adjudicating disputes and elaborating rules; they are not mechanisms for solving problems ... The severe constraints of law's language game are deadly to freely discursive democracy.[73]

Deliberation is more likely to occur in situations involving third-party mediation.[74] Mediation is facilitative, encouraging the parties themselves to explore possible bases of consensus through open-ended dialogue and exchange of information. Mediators 'can also take actions to reduce rigidities in the bargaining positions of adversaries' by injecting novel perspectives into discursive debate, or encouraging the dissemination of relevant information.[75] Most importantly, perhaps, 'the product of mediation is not a verdict, but consensus among the actors involved, sensitive to the central concerns of these parties'.[76] On this view, deliberative aspirations may be better realised through the vehicle of prospective third party mediation instead of retrospective adjudication by labour boards and courts. As such, institutional concerns do not rule out an active duty to bargain; they merely indicate the need to be more imaginative in choosing appropriate institutional forms to ensure that the active duty is implemented.

B Subjects of Bargaining: The Mandatory/Permissive Distinction in the Duty to Bargain

One of the central issues in evaluating the democratic potential of the duty to bargain concept is the extent to which it extends across the full frontier of managerial prerogative. Critics of pluralist political philosophy often pointed to its failure to penetrate the many ways in which structural power relations operated invisibly to limit the scope of democratic agendas. This occurs when powerful interest groups devote their energies 'to creating or reinforcing social and political values and institutional practices that limit the scope of the political process to public consideration of only those issues which are comparatively innocuous'.[77] This is pertinent to a critical evaluation of the scope of bargaining in the US legal procedure. Mandatory topics of bargaining, which are subject to bargaining duties, are encapsulated in the statutory formulation in section 9(a) which refers to bargaining collectively 'with respect to wages, hours, and other terms and conditions of employment'. This has been interpreted to include

[73] J Dryzek, *Discursive Democracy* (Cambridge, Cambridge University Press, 1990) 83.
[74] On the deliberative properties of mediation, see *ibid*, 45–6.
[75] *Ibid*, 45.
[76] *Ibid*, 46.
[77] P Bachrach and MS Baratz, 'The Two Faces of Power' (1962) 56 *American Political Science Review* 947, 949, discussed in D Held, *Models of Democracy*, 2nd edn (Cambridge, Polity, 1996) 212–13.

bargaining over hourly pay rates, overtime premiums, paid vacations, profit-sharing plans, pensions, and hours of employment.

The crux of controversy, however, has centred upon those managerial decisions lying at the heart of entrepreneurial control, but involving significant threats to job security: sub-contracting, automation of the productive process, plant relocation, and plant closure. As we shall see, the Supreme Court has fashioned a distinction between mandatory and permissive subjects of bargaining that has the effect of placing many of these decisions beyond the reach of democratic influence. In so doing, subsisting employer property rights have been systematically privileged over the statutory promise of industrial democracy.[78] This has created a situation where, along the spectrum of managerial decisions, 'roughly speaking, the least significant are subject to bargaining; the most important—those involving basic changes in the scope of the enterprise and many jobs—are not'.[79]

The parameters of this interpretive task were set in *Fibreboard Paper Products v NLRB*.[80] The question was whether sub-contracting of bargaining unit work was a mandatory subject of bargaining. In a superficially pro-labour holding, the Supreme Court determined that it was. In involving 'a problem of vital concern to labor and management' the issue was ripe for discussion through collective bargaining. There were three main elements in the Court's reasoning. First, since the employer's concerns related to labour costs, collective bargaining would not be a futile exercise. The union ought to have the opportunity to bargain since it might make concessions that could materially influence the ultimate decision. Secondly, this conclusion was bolstered through an appreciation of prevalent industrial practices. The fact that many collective agreements dealt with the issue of sub-contracting indicated it was apt to characterise it as a mandatory subject. Finally, sub-contracting 'did not alter the Company's basic operation … to require the employer to bargain about the matter would not significantly abridge his freedom to manage the business'.[81] This latter concern was pivotal in the concurring opinion by Mr Justice Stewart. According to him, 'managerial decisions which lie at the core of entrepreneurial control', such as 'decisions concerning the commitment of investment capital and the basic scope of the enterprise', were beyond the scope of mandatory bargaining.[82] Any other conclusion 'would mark a sharp departure from the traditional principles of a free enterprise economy'.[83] In fact, the robust affirmation of inherent property

[78] For an illuminating critical analysis in these terms, see JB Atleson, *Values and Assumptions in American Labor Law* (Amherst, University of Massachusetts Press, 1983) 111–59.

[79] CL Estlund, 'Economic Rationality and Union Avoidance: Misunderstanding the National Labor Relations Act' (1993) 71 *Texas Law Review* 921, 944.

[80] 379 US 203 (1964).

[81] *Ibid*, 213.

[82] *Ibid*, 223.

[83] *Ibid*.

rights in Mr Justice Stewart's concurrence would have a pervasive influence on future doctrinal development.

In the face of conflicting Board and Courts of Appeal decisions subsequent to *Fibreboard*, the Supreme Court revisited the mandatory/permissive distinction in *First National Maintenance Corporation v NLRB*.[84] This involved a decision even closer to the 'core of entrepreneurial control', a partial plant closure. The court concluded this was not a mandatory subject of bargaining. The restrictive potential of *Fibreboard's* three elements conspired to trump the union's democratic claims. First, the employer's economic concerns were unrelated to labour costs. Consequently, this was an instance where bargaining would be futile. Since the employer's need for unencumbered decision making was 'weighty', and this was not offset by any instrumental procedural benefits in submitting the decision to joint resolution, it was inappropriate to characterise the decision as a mandatory subject. Secondly, current bargaining practices indicated that the extent of bargaining over the decision to close a plant, as opposed to mitigation of its effects, was 'relatively rare'. Thirdly, the Act's purposes were intended 'to foster in a neutral manner a system in which the conflict between these interests may be resolved'.[85] Statutory incursion upon core managerial prerogatives would not advance the neutral purposes of the Act. Those neutral purposes would be best served by holding the balance in favour of the employer's subsisting prerogatives left intact by the legislation, insulating 'the core of entrepreneurial control' from erosion by State action. In the words of the court, 'Congress had no expectation that the elected union representative would become an equal partner in the running of the business enterprise'.[86]

From a deliberative perspective, these two decisions rest upon flawed premises and fallacious reasoning. Two lines of critique are especially germane. First, the 'property rights' and 'extant bargaining practice' claims are vulnerable to the objection that existing preferences and social practices, or the common law allocation of property and contract rights, do not constitute a privileged constitutional baseline from which to measure the legitimacy of State action. Secondly, the 'bargaining futility' element misunderstands the instrumental and expressive dimensions of deliberative procedures. With respect to the instrumental dimension, it fails to give sufficient weight to the dynamic potential of deliberative participation; with respect to the expressive dimension, it ignores the intrinsic value of deliberation, such that deliberative procedures might be

[84] 452 US 666 (1981).
[85] *Ibid*, 680–81.
[86] *Ibid*, 676.

justified as expressive of civic respect even where deliberation makes no difference to outcomes. Each line of critique will be discussed in turn.

(i) Challenging 'Status Quo' Neutrality

What is striking about the Supreme Court's interpretive framework is its robust defence of inherent employer property rights, tied to an understanding of neutrality in the legislative framework. Decisions at the 'core of entrepreneurial control' fall within a sanctified proprietary zone lying beyond statutory encroachment;[87] State interference with that proprietary exclusion zone is characterised as a violation of its duty to be neutral towards the parties in dispute. In this way, 'existing distributions and the common law provide the benchmark from which to measure intervention',[88] and Sunstein characterises this position as 'status quo neutrality'. It is vulnerable to the objection that the common law and property rights are not natural, pre-political concepts. As much as employees' statutory right to collective bargaining, the employer's property rights are a product of law, reflecting specific regulatory choices by the State to recognise and enforce certain rights with certain distributive consequences. The Supreme Court's endorsement of status quo neutrality is accordingly hollow. State enforcement of property rights is neither more nor less neutral than if the Court had extended the reach of employees' democratic influence through a broader statutory interpretation. It represents an active regulatory choice to prioritise private property over industrial democracy. The neutrality/partiality distinction clouds the reality of this choice. Ironically, the New Deal that spawned the legislation marked a constitutional revolution, whereby the mystification of the common law status quo 'as an unanalyzed given' was decisively rejected.[89] Legal entitlements such as the right to private property were stripped of their mystical force, and stood or fell in their contribution to compelling human values and social policies. In these terms, the limited scope for democratic influence over plant closure decisions engendered by *First National Maintenance* must be found wanting, ill-befitting the constitutional origins of the US legal framework.

The 'status quo neutrality' myth also infects the court's appeal to extant bargaining practices as a method for determining the legal boundary of mandatory subjects. In *Fibreboard*, the social prevalence of subcontracting as a subject of bargaining justified its inclusion as a mandatory item; in *First National Maintenance*, the social rarity of plant closure as a subject of bargaining justified its exclusion. In this way, the law functions as a 'mirror' of social practices and preferences.

[87] On the centrality of inherent private property rights in the Court's reasoning, see Note, 'Mandatory Bargaining and the Disposition of Closed Plants' (1982) 95 *Harvard Law Review* 1896; see also Note, 'Subjects of Bargaining under the NLRA and the Limits of the Liberal Political Imagination' (1983) 97 *Harvard Law Review* 475, 485–7.

[88] CR Sunstein, *The Partial Constitution* (Cambridge Massachusetts, Harvard University Press, 1993) 75.

[89] *Ibid*, 60.

From a deliberative perspective, however, the notion of preference mirroring as a justification for legal rules can be distorting. It rests upon the mistaken idea that it is meaningful to think of preferences and social practices existing 'pre-legally'.

In fact, and as Sunstein's republican perspective emphasises, preferences are often a product of legal rules. This is the insight offered by adaptive accounts of preference formation. What we want is often shaped by our perceptions of which options are realistically available; and those perceptions are in turn framed by legal rules allocating rights and entitlements. Take the example of bargaining over partial plant closure. Prior to *First National Maintenance,* and in the face of conflicting NLRB decisions, most courts of appeal had determined this was a permissive rather than mandatory subject.[90] In designating it as such, it is hardly surprising that there was not a prevalent social practice of bargaining about plant closure. Quite naturally, preferences and social practices adapted to the perception that this was not a mandatory subject. The eventual justification for the legal rule in those terms is guilty of a vicious circularity. Legal rules can be defended in terms of the values or policies they promote, not in terms of 'respect for private preferences'. If there is an adaptive preference effect at play here, such that workers' preference for less self-government in industry is 'a product of a belief that self-government in the workplace is unavailable',[91] the rule cannot be justified by reference to the social practice or ostensibly 'private' preferences.

(ii) The Intrinsic Value of Deliberation

Another strand in *First National Maintenance* is the view that, within the context of partial closure decisions, the encumbrance of a duty to bargain would impede realisation of the public interest in economically efficient decision-making. In these situations, management is portrayed as the epitome of economic rationality, and an agent of the public interest in the efficient allocation of capital investment; organised labour, by contrast, 'cannot objectively evaluate an employer's economic decision when that decision results in loss of employment'.[92] Where labour costs are not directly implicated in a particular decision, bargaining is characterised as 'futile', with no countervailing social benefit to offset the social costs arising out of union involvement in managerial decision-making. Unions can bring nothing but delay, obstruction and distorting irrationality to the process. Inevitably, these tenets have filtered through into NLRB decision-making and its fashioning of standards related to bargaining over plant

[90] Gorman and Finkin, above n 67, 685.

[91] C Sunstein, 'Legal Interference with Private Preferences' (1986) 53 *University of Chicago Law Review* 1129, 1148.

[92] MA Goldman, 'Partial Terminations—A Choice between Bargaining Equality and Economic Efficiency' (1967) 14 *University of California at Los Angeles Law Review* 1089, 1091.

relocations. In *Dubuque Packing Company*,[93] for example, the NLRB considered that a presumption of mandatory bargaining could be rebutted by an employer where labour costs were not a factor in the decision to relocate, or where it could be demonstrated that bargaining would make no difference to the employer's decision. The deliberative conception presents three challenges to this received understanding of the collective bargaining process.

First, judgments by courts of the futility of deliberative procedures ignore the epistemic virtue of deliberation. Deliberation is a dynamic process whereby new information emerges during the course of democratic dialogue, and a multiplicity of perspectives is brought to bear on issues of shared concern. As such, '*coherent* judgements cannot precede deliberation; deliberation allows for the expression of arguments in the light of which opinions and beliefs can then be revised'.[94] This implicit denial of unions' rational capacities rests upon a cluster of outmoded and dubious assumptions that should be rejected.[95] There is overwhelming evidence that unions can make a valuable epistemic difference to rational decision-making and not merely in the narrow sense of labour cost concessions.[96] The dynamic potential of deliberative engagement was captured perfectly by Archibald Cox in his influential explication of good faith bargaining:

> Participation in debate often produces changes in a seemingly fixed position either because new facts are brought to light or because the strengths and weaknesses of the several arguments become apparent. Sometimes the parties hit upon some novel compromise of an issue which has been thrashed over and over. Much is gained even by giving each side a better picture of the strengths of the other's convictions. The cost is so slight that the potential gains easily justify legal compulsion to engage in the discussion.[97]

Secondly, the court's restrictive equation of decisional rationality with economic efficiency is unwarranted and arbitrary from a deliberative perspective. The economic dislocation associated with such matters as plant closure and automation all have profound effects on the democratic citizenship interests of employees. The inevitable deprivation involved in the loss of income and self-respect are of profound importance for workers' citizenship, undermining their ability to pursue diverse and valuable forms of life. It is one thing to allow for the possibility that an employer's economic liberty might trump workers' competing basic opportunity claims against that employer in a specific instance; it is quite

[93] 303 NLRB 386 (1991).

[94] Besson, above n 24, 227.

[95] See Atleson, above n 78, 158: the implicit assumption of the Court 'denigrates the capacity and intelligence of workers.'

[96] See, in particular, RJ Rabin, 'Fibreboard and the Termination of Bargaining Unit Work: The Search for Standards in Defining the Scope of the Duty to Bargain' (1971) 71 *Columbia Law Review* 803, 823–6; Note, 'Duty to Bargain about Termination of Operations: Brockway Motor Trucks v NLRB' (1979) 92 *Harvard Law Review* 768; JB McArthur, 'Enforcing the NLRA: The Need for a Duty to Bargain over Partial Plant Closings' (1982) 60 *Texas Law Review* 279.

[97] Cox, above n 54, 1412.

another to assume without argument, as the court does, that basic opportunity considerations should not figure at all in managerial decisions relating to plant closure. Such a perspective is incompatible with the deliberative viewpoint. Given that these kinds of decision 'significantly affect people's basic liberties and opportunities in the society', deliberative democrats argue that corporate power exerts 'a kind of control that is properly considered political, not only economic'.[98] Translated into the idiom of collective bargaining law, all managerial decisions that touch upon workers' basic opportunities should be characterised as mandatory subjects, regardless of the 'core of entrepreneurial control'.[99] This would not lead to an effective veto by workers of economically necessary closures; after all, the relevant duty is a duty to bargain in good faith, not a duty to agree. But it would at least ensure that employers are compelled to consider the basic opportunity costs of their decisions before implementing them.

The 'futility' bar to mandatory characterisation also ignores the *expressive* significance of deliberative procedures.[100] According to the courts and the NLRB, it is pointless to compel bargaining where that process would make no difference to the decisional outcome. The deliberative conception would resist such a 'no difference' rule. It is true that deliberative procedures are often justified on epistemic grounds, in their instrumental contribution to wise decision-making. But this is not exhaustive of deliberative democracy's justificatory basis. The deliberative practice of reasoned dialogue is also intrinsically valuable, treating those subject to a political decision as equal citizens worthy of a reasoned explanation of why things are as they are. Thus, deliberative practices embody a form of mutual civic respect between citizens, regardless of their instrumental contribution to decisional outcomes. Where worker citizens are deprived of their jobs without any opportunity to deliberate they are treated as objects of political decision-making rather than citizens. The corrosion of civic respect entailed by this state of affairs is a palpable loss for deliberative democrats. For this reason, the 'no difference' rule denies the expressive dimension of deliberative reasoning.

C The Demands of Political Equality: Bolstering the Right to Strike

As we have seen, an effective guarantee of the right to strike is a necessary condition for the realisation of deliberative democracy. Without this, there can be

[98] Gutmann and Thompson, above n 9, 34.

[99] Reform proposals in this vein are defended in CW Summers, 'Questioning the Unquestioned in Collective Labor Law' (1998) 47 *Catholic University Law Review* 791, 806–809: 'we should seriously consider opening up the subjects for collective bargaining by recognizing that circumscribing bargaining is contrary to the original premises of the Wagner Act. We should reject the rule that one party can refuse to discuss a subject which the other considers of mutual concern.'

[100] Gutmann and Thompson, above n 9, 21–3.

no substantive equality between employers and unions, and the resulting disequilibrium undermines the potential for meaningful deliberation between them. The assumption that there is a natural equilibrium between management and labour is pervasive in judicial thinking,[101] reflecting broader currents in pluralist political philosophy. Nevertheless, analysis of legal protection for the right to strike discloses a 'prevailing inequality of economic weapons', systematically privileging the employer's position in labour disputes.[102] Once again, State neutrality is measured from the baseline of subsisting employer property rights and inherent managerial prerogatives. As such, employees' statutory right to strike has attracted a restrictive interpretation, reflecting deep rooted judicial solicitude for this common law backdrop. This has had a predictably constraining effect on the boundaries of legitimate strike action. In its deference to employers' proprietary entitlements and inherent prerogatives, this interpretive approach 'can hardly be said to exhibit legal neutrality regarding the results of the contest'.[103] As Stone has argued:

> If there is a structural inequality of power between management and labor based upon the incidents of private property as the law has defined it ... the law must intervene actively to alter the definitions of property rights to create true equality.[104]

Yet this structural inequality has simply been perpetuated by the courts through the process of statutory interpretation, negating the pluralist assumption of equilibrium in the collective bargaining relationship.

The most notorious doctrinal feature exemplifying this tendency is the Supreme Court's decision in *NLRB v Mackay Radio & Telegraph Company*.[105] In the face of a seemingly broad statutory protection of employees' right to strike, the court affirmed the employer's inherent 'right to protect and continue his business'.[106] This inherent employer right, which was nowhere specified in the statute, encompassed the hiring of *permanent* strike replacements. This had the effect of displacing striking employees from their jobs at the end of the strike. Thus, while strikers were protected from dismissal for participation in protected strike action, they were not protected from permanent replacement. From the strikers' perspective, this is a fine legal distinction without a difference; the practical upshot with respect to the extinction of their job security is the same in

[101] See, eg, *American Ship Building v NLRB* 380 US 300 (1965), where the Court stated that the NLRA 'established a system of collective bargaining whereby the newly coequal adversaries might resolve their disputes' (at 317). This is echoed in the work of pluralist scholars; see, eg, Wellington, above n 53, 497: 'there is no felt inequality of bargaining power between union and employer ... The countervailing pressure of a bargaining imbalance is absent.'

[102] PC Weiler, 'Striking a New Balance: Freedom of Contract and the Prospects for Union Representation' (1984) 98 *Harvard Law Review* 351, 387.

[103] *Ibid.*

[104] KVW Stone, 'The Post-War Paradigm in American Labor Law' (1981) 90 *Yale Law Journal* 1509, 1579–80.

[105] 304 US 333 (1938).

[106] *Ibid*, 345.

both situations. The *Mackay* doctrine is testament to the tenacious grip of 'status quo neutrality' on the judicial imagination. While the courts have scrupulously denied the propriety of explicitly regulating the parties' economic weapons in the interests of balancing bargaining strength,[107] the seamless continuity of common law values woven into the statutory fabric ensures this balance is already set decisively in the employer's favour.[108] The employer's weapon of permanent replacement renders the lofty statutory protection of employees' right to strike illusory. The eclipse of employees' statutory rights by inherent employer property rights has been pervasive; other instances include the characterisation of sit-ins[109] and go-slows[110] as unprotected activities, and the stringent statutory constraints on secondary industrial action.[111]

The illusory character of employees' right to strike is testament to the pluralist myth of bargaining equilibrium. This persistent imbalance in parties' economic weaponry is inconsistent with the deliberative ideal of substantive political equality. In the absence of collective countervailing power, meaningful deliberation depends upon the civic goodwill of employers. Coupled with a passive duty to bargain and weak procedural remedies for bad faith bargaining, it is unsurprising that newly certified unions fail to achieve a collective agreement in about a third of cases.[112] The failings of the US system are well documented.[113] There is now a wide range of compelling reform proposals aimed at the restoration of equilibrium in the balance of economic weapons. The most pressing priority is a reversal of the *Mackay* doctrine, rendering the use of permanent strike replacements unlawful;[114] other proposals for reform include expanding the definition of protected activities to encompass go-slows, and liberalisation of the strictures on secondary boycotts during economic disputes. Without root-and-branch reform of the legal framework to ensure greater parity of bargaining strength, the deliberative aspiration will remain unrealised.

[107] *NLRB v Insurance Agents' International Union* 361 US 477 (1960).

[108] Atleson, above n 78, 19–34.

[109] *NLRB v Fansteel Metallurgical Corporation* 306 US 240 (1939). Klare (above n 64, 324–5) decries the repression of communitarian sentiment through the Court's invocation of over-riding employer property interests in its treatment of the sit-in: 'The logistics of the sit-down required the constant participation of all in decision-making and fostered a spirit of community, cooperation, and initiative. The sit-downs nurtured a new psychological and emotional experience.'

[110] *NLRB v Montgomery Ward & Company* 157 F 2d 486 (8th Circuit, 1946).

[111] PC Weiler, *Governing the Workplace* (Cambridge Massachusetts, Harvard University Press, 1993) 397–404.

[112] Weiler, above n 102, 354. See also JR Grodin, 'Some Thoughts on the American Model' (1998) 20 *Comparative Labor Law and Policy Journal* 29, 30.

[113] For a recent critique of strike law in the US, see Human Rights Watch, *Unfair Advantage: Workers' Freedom of Association in the United States under International Human Rights Standards* (Human Rights Watch, 2000) 31–2.

[114] Summers, above n 99, 813–22.

V THE DUTY TO BARGAIN IN BRITISH LABOUR LAW: PLURALISM, DELIBERATION AND SOCIAL PARTNERSHIP

In understanding the trajectory of third way industrial politics, the concept of social partnership is of central importance. With its emphasis on trusting cooperation and civic responsibility, the ideology of social partnership seems naturally aligned with a deliberative conception of industrial politics. This deliberative alignment resonates with broader themes in third way thinking. The renewal of social democracy necessitates the renewal of civil society and a vibrant public sphere, mediating between the State and markets.[115] Nevertheless, there are two major points of divergence between the conditions of deliberative democracy and New Labour's particular interpretation of social partnership. First, deliberative cooperation is predicated upon equilibrium of social power between civic associations. As Cohen and Rogers argue, 'genuine cooperation is based on mutual respect, which typically depends on recognition of mutual power'.[116] Without strong union organisation, the social bases of cooperative deliberation are absent. In the North American context, the authors indicate this has undermined the deliberative potential of collective bargaining. The organisational erosion of unions ensures that 'employees are commonly incapable of extracting from employers the sorts of institutionalized respect for their interests … needed to elicit genuine cooperation'.[117] This indicates the first deliberative limitation of social partnership: reluctance to promote *collective* strength as the appropriate basis for cooperation in the workplace. This is reflected in New Labour's continuation of labour law's restrictive function placing strict limits on legitimate industrial action, and the individualistic bias of its conception of social partnership.[118]

Secondly, many deliberative democrats reject the idea that patterns of associative interaction are determined by 'nature, or culture, or some other unalterable substrate of a country's political life'.[119] Instead, they point to the 'artifactual' nature of associational life. The extent to which associations are able to participate deliberatively in the tasks of economic governance depends upon 'opportunities and incentives that are induced by the structure of political institutions and the substance of political choices and so can be changed through public policy.'[120] In this way, the State can and should be active in altering those opportunities and incentives to ensure that the right kinds of association flourish, and that institutional arrangements are in place to facilitate deliberative governance in civil society. This indicates the second deliberative limitation of social

[115] A Giddens, *The Third Way and its Critics* (Cambridge, Polity, 2000) ch 3.
[116] Cohen and Rogers, above n 47, 79.
[117] *Ibid*, 79–80.
[118] For a powerful critique of social partnership in this vein, see Novitz and Skidmore, above n 17, ch 1.
[119] Cohen and Rogers, above n 47, 46.
[120] *Ibid*, 47.

partnership: its notion that the law should mirror rather than shape social practices in industrial civil society. This is reflected in the centrality of voluntary agreement between employers and unions: the law 'can reflect a new culture, can enhance its understanding and support its development', but presumably it cannot change it.[121] Social partnership is therefore 'anti-artifactual' in its orientation. From a deliberative democratic perspective, however, it matters a great deal *what* the law is reflecting. If social practices are neither deliberative nor democratic, or there is systematic disequilibrium between the 'social partners', then the law must be used to refashion the associational framework to enable the tasks of deliberative governance. These two features of social partnership have constrained the deliberative potential of the legal duty to bargain in British labour law.

The next section will consider the wisdom of according primacy to voluntary recognition between employers and trade unions from a deliberative perspective. Two problems will be considered. First, the increasingly shallow nature of voluntary collective bargaining arrangements seems inconsistent with the need for equilibrium as a precondition of genuine deliberation. Secondly, the priority given to voluntary over statutory recognition in Schedule A1 has allowed employers to confer voluntary recognition on weak and unrepresentative organisations that are ill-equipped to engage in genuine deliberation from a position of equality with the employer. While both of these features of the legal framework are implications of New Labour's conception of social partnership, each demonstrates the failure of social partnership as a vehicle for promoting genuine deliberation.

A The Primacy of Voluntary Practices: Undermining Deliberative Democracy

There are two modes of recognition available to unions; voluntary and statutory. Voluntary recognition is based upon the principle of employer consent; statutory recognition is based upon the principle of worker consent, reflected in the majority support thresholds necessary to the statutory allocation of bargaining rights. It is important to emphasise that these two methods are interlinked by design. First, the statutory method is conceived as a last resort to compel recalcitrant employers to come to the bargaining table; the legislative aspiration is that in most cases the parties will, perhaps stimulated by the possibility of a statutory duty to bargain, decide their own recognition arrangements voluntarily. In this respect, the statutory mechanism has been very successful in achieving its stated aims, with voluntary recognition deals far outstripping the levels of

[121] *Fairness at Work* (Cmnd 3968, 1998) Foreword.

recognition secured directly through the legislation.[122] Secondly, employer consent is given normative priority in the statutory framework. Thus, where an employer has anointed a union and conferred voluntary recognition upon it, this precludes a competing statutory claim by another union. This is regardless of whether the applicant union has substantial worker support within the bargaining unit.

Both these aspects are a direct result of New Labour's 'anti-artifactual' perception of the relationship between legal norms and social practices. On this view, the law should respect social practices and private preferences rather than shape them through legal intervention. This is simply another version of the idea of 'status quo neutrality', so dominant in North American legal discourse. As we shall see, its effect is to legitimate and entrench social practices that are profoundly non-deliberative and undemocratic, undoing the deliberative aspirations of social partnership.

(i) The Nature of Voluntary Collective Bargaining

In accordance with the British tradition of voluntarism the principal method of recognition is still voluntary in nature. The concept of voluntary recognition is based upon employer consent. Sociological analysis indicates a procedural transformation in the nature of voluntary collective bargaining over the last four decades. This has corresponded to a dilution of the union's regulatory function within the enterprise. In procedural terms, joint regulation has been progressively eroded and this has been substituted by greater unilateral control of the employment relationship by employers. This has been manifested in two tendencies. First, the scope of dialogue has contracted significantly. Whereas in the mid-1960s joint regulation extended to issues such as work distribution, recruitment and the implementation of new technologies, more recent research points to 'a very substantial decline in union representative involvement in the regulation of employee obligations and work organization aspects of the employment contract'.[123] In tandem with this, dialogue with unions is increasingly assuming a consultative character. This shift to consultative interaction leaves the managerial prerogative intact.

The 'shallowness' of voluntary collective bargaining is reflected most strongly in the erosion of union influence over pay bargaining. Even where unions are recognised, payment mechanisms are often arranged on the basis of performance-related pay. As pay awards increasingly track individual appraisals, the extent of union involvement is diminished. The widespread exclusion of recognised unions from the core activity of pay determination is emblematic of

[122] See G Gall, 'Trade union recognition in Britain, 1995–2002: turning a corner?' (2004) 35 *Industrial Relations Journal 249*.

[123] W Brown, S Deakin, D Nash and S Oxenbridge, 'The Employment Contract: From Collective Procedures to Individual Rights' (2000) 38 *British Journal of Industrial Relations* 611, 617.

their social weakness in voluntary arrangements.[124] This has led to some reorientation in union function within the enterprise, with greater emphasis on the role of unions in enforcing individual statutory rights rather than the more traditional regulatory function of normative standard-setting.

In theoretical terms, the preference for voluntary arrangements was always based upon an assumption of power equilibrium in the collective bargaining relationship. This clear pattern of declining union influence suggests the assumption of equilibrium no longer holds true. This casts serious doubt on the legitimacy of a legislative strategy that steers union recognition, as far as possible, outside of the statutory framework. Its practical effect is to entrench the status quo in voluntary collective bargaining, augmenting managerial property rights and unions' relative bargaining weakness. The theory of deliberative democracy poses two challenges to this strategy. First, genuine deliberation depends upon a balance of power between the parties. Yet the shallowness of voluntary collective bargaining is a powerful reminder that this equilibrium cannot simply be assumed as a state of nature. Secondly, neither does deliberative governance arise naturally without appropriate regulatory support. Where the voluntary associational life of a political community is neither deliberative nor democratic, as is currently the case with many voluntary recognition arrangements, the State has a duty to intervene actively to reshape that associational context to promote deliberative governance. This might consist in various 'institution-building' measures such as the reconstruction of sectoral bargaining forums. However, the 'anti-artifactual' dimension of New Labour's conception of the law's role in collective labour relations is a significant barrier to the kinds of interventionist measures envisaged by the deliberative conception.

Even then, we need to be cautious in evaluating the detail of specific legal measures, for there is a danger that 'anti-artifactual' assumptions might be built into the very structure of legal intervention. As an example, the statutory provisions providing recognised unions with information for collective bargaining purposes are critical to the realisation of deliberative governance. The epistemic virtue of deliberation rests upon its propensity to 'impart and increase necessary information', making it more likely that 'the truth will prevail over prejudice'.[125] Yet the current statutory framework tracks voluntary practices in significant ways. Duties of disclosure are anchored to the current scope of recognition enjoyed by the union. Where the information relates to matters outside of that scope it need not be disclosed: consequently the reach of the statutory obligation waxes and wanes in tandem with the extent of recognition. Furthermore, relevant information need not be disclosed if it is not 'in accordance with good industrial relations practice' to disclose it for collective bargaining, a clear gesture towards social

124 S Oxenbridge, W Brown, S Deakin and C Pratten, 'Initial Responses to the Statutory Recognition Provisions of the Employment Relations Act 1999' (2003) 41 *British Journal of Industrial Relations* 315, 327.

125 Besson, above n 24, 227.

practices in setting the parameters of disclosure.[126] The Central Arbitration Council (CAC) conceives of its role as reflecting prevailing social practices such that 'it cannot act as a trail-blazer or standard-setter'.[127]

Again, if those social practices are developing in such a fashion as to limit the union's role in joint regulation, the point of legal intervention should not simply be to reflect an unjust status quo. Rather, legislation should be harnessed to specify and enforce generous deliberative standards of information provision with the aim of augmenting the union's democratic role in the workplace. The 'adversarial' tenor of the legislation is predicated on an interest-group pluralist conception of the bargaining process, with the employer portrayed as a 'reluctant divulger of secrets rather than active participant in information transmission and social partnership at work'.[128] Given its heritage as a pluralist measure introduced when industrial relations pluralism was in the ascendant, this tone is unsurprising. Such reticence does not, however, fit the notion of trusting cooperation that lies at the heart of deliberative reciprocity.

(ii) The Priority of Subsisting Voluntary Recognition Arrangements

The legacy of voluntarism is also unattractive in other respects, particularly with regard to the admissibility criteria in Schedule A1. An application is not admissible if there is already a collective agreement in force that encompasses any of the members of the bargaining unit. This is based on the priority of voluntary over statutory recognition and the need to protect existing voluntary bargaining structures from destabilisation. This has created two distinct problems. First, an employer may block the statutory procedure by voluntarily recognising an independent trade union even where that union is not representative of the constituent bargaining unit. This remains so even where there is a competing union with substantial support within the bargaining unit. The representative union is precluded from bringing a statutory claim in virtue of the voluntary arrangement.

This occurred in *R (NUJ) v CAC*,[129] where the employer accorded voluntary recognition to a 'sweetheart' union with little support in the bargaining unit, blocking the statutory claim of another union with substantial organisational strength. Indeed, the voluntarily recognised union had (at most) one member within the bargaining unit, in comparison with the majority membership enjoyed by the National Union of Journalists (NUJ). This gives an employer considerable opportunities for avoiding effective collective bargaining through the manipulation of 'sham' voluntary agreements. Evidently, the Court of Appeal was

126 TULRCA 1992, s 181(2)(b).

127 H Gospel and G Lockwood, 'Disclosure of Information for Collective Bargaining: The CAC Approach Revisited' (1999) 28 *Industrial Law Journal* 244.

128 *Ibid*, 247.

129 [2005] IRLR 28.

reluctant to engage with the argument that the agreement was a sham and consequently not 'in force'. Instead, it focused on the subjective perceptions of the British Association of Journalists (BAJ) and the employer that the agreement was meaningful. The suggestion that 'in force' might equate with something like 'capable of being enforced' was given short shrift by the court, as were the submissions on breach of Article 11 of the European Convention on Human Rights. This is particularly problematic since there is no statutory derecognition mechanism available in situations where there is a voluntarily recognised independent union.

Secondly, the employer is entitled to confer recognition on a non-independent union under employer domination, so blocking a statutory claim by an independent union.[130] Although Schedule A1 provides for cumbersome de-recognition machinery in this specific situation this is not satisfactory and in most cases the status quo is unlikely to be displaced given the high thresholds required for an order of de-recognition.[131] This is particularly acute given the 'stickiness' of default arrangements on account of the endowment effect and adoptive preferences. This has been reflected in the very low incidence of statutory derecognition claims during the life of Schedule A1 in this specific situation.

The priority of voluntary over statutory recognition embodies a legislative choice to prioritise employer consent over worker consent in the determination of recognition arrangements. This cannot be defended from a deliberative perspective. Where voluntarily recognised unions are organisationally weak, with little support in the bargaining unit, this is unlikely to lead to a situation where employees are able to extract 'from employers the sorts of institutionalized respect for their interests … needed to elicit genuine cooperation'.[132] What is needed is a more substantive approach, fashioning legal criteria for identifying 'representative' unions and the development of an unfair labour practice jurisdiction targeting sham organisations under employer domination and control. This approach rejects the rather fatalistic perception in New Labour's idea of social partnership that legal norms should simply track social practices, regardless of their substantive merits.

B The Statutory Duty to Bargain: Pluralist or Deliberative?

Once the CAC has declared the union as entitled to be recognised by the employer then the parties must try to agree, perhaps with assistance from the

130 TULRCA 1992, Schedule A1 para 35(4); see KD Ewing, 'Trade Union Recognition and Staff Associations—A Breach of International Labour Standards?' (2000) 29 *Industrial Law Journal* 267. For a recent example of shallow collective bargaining with a non-independent union that was sufficient to block an independent union's application under Schedule A1, see *Unite—the Union and DSG Retail Ltd* TUR1/567/2007.

131 TULRCA 1992, Schedule A1 Pt VI.

132 Cohen and Rogers, above n 47, 79–80.

CAC, a bargaining procedure. If the parties fail to agree a procedure then the CAC is required to impose a legally binding 'default procedure agreement' (DPA), which specifies a procedure for the conduct of negotiations on pay, hours and holidays. While the form and content of the DPA is to be determined by the CAC, in practice the 'model' DPA laid down by the Secretary of State has been adopted by most CAC panels. The exclusive remedy for breach of a CAC-imposed procedure agreement is an order of specific performance directed against the recalcitrant party, which must be obtained in the ordinary courts.

We should be cautious in ascribing too much direct practical significance to the specification of legal duties in this context. In the CAC's study of the first five years of Schedule A1, there had been 94 voluntary procedure agreements and only 11 cases where the CAC has imposed a legally binding DPA.[133] This trend has continued with voluntary procedure agreements continuing to exceed by a significant margin legally imposed DPAs. Nevertheless, the legal duty has a symbolic importance that should not be under-estimated. The 'anti-artifactual' perspective assumes a separation of legal norms from social practices; the best that can be done is that legal norms track those social practices faithfully. The deliberative perspective makes the opposite assumption: social practices take their shape from legal norms and institutional structures. Accordingly, social practices cannot be taken as an autonomous and independent datum. The artificiality of the 'anti-artifactual' perspective is underscored by recent research on the contours of voluntary arrangements negotiated in the shadow of Schedule A1. These arrangements are remarkably congruent with the statutory minima prescribed in the model DPA, with voluntary negotiations extending to pay, hours and holidays on an annualised basis.[134] As such, voluntary social practices seem to be tracking legal norms, reversing the assumptions of social partnership.[135] With this in mind, it is important to distinguish two dimensions of the legal duty to bargain in Britain: its *scope* and its *procedural nature.*

(i) The Legal Duty to Bargain I: Scope

The most striking feature of the statutory bargaining agenda is its limited scope, extending no further than 'pay, hours and holidays'. This aspect of the DPA has embroiled the CAC in an interpretive dispute over the meaning of 'pay'. In *UNIFI and Union Bank of Nigeria* the question arose whether 'pay' encapsulated bargaining over pensions;[136] the Panel concluded that 'the obligation to negotiate on "pay" includes all matters relating to the levels or amount of employer's

[133] *CAC Annual Report 2004–2005*, 18.

[134] S Moore, S McKay and H Bewley, *DTI Employment Relations Research Series No 43: The Content of new voluntary trade union recognition agreements 1998–2002, Volume 2* (Department of Trade and Industry, 2005).

[135] S Moore, 'The relationship between legislation and industrial practice: A study of the outcome of trade union recognition' (2006) 28 *Employee Relations* 363.

[136] [2001] IRLR 712.

pension contributions', although this did not encompass management or administration of the pension scheme itself. The decision rested upon two distinct arguments. First, the argument from ordinary language stressed the relative breadth of the term 'pay', as distinct from other narrower formulations such as 'wages' or 'remuneration'. Reasoning by analogy with the Equal Pay Act 1970, where Parliament used the word 'pay' but expressly excluded pensions from its ambit, the CAC concluded that the ordinary meaning of 'pay' was sufficiently broad to encapsulate pension contributions. Secondly, the argument from voluntary practices was based upon the CAC's perception that the social practice of voluntary bargaining often included pensions within its scope. Accordingly, the CAC's interpretive task under the legally binding DPA was bound up with an assessment of social practices, with those social practices setting outer limits to the boundary of the legal duty.

Despite the seeming boldness of the Panel's decision, the argument from voluntary practices set very modest parameters to the CAC's interpretive task. Its 'anti-artifactual' tenor was aligned with New Labour's perception of the relation between legal norms and social practices, with the law's role conceived as standard-reflecting rather than standard-setting. With the fate of voluntary and statutory bargaining so closely intertwined, the decision was vulnerable to the counterargument that the waning democratic reach of voluntary bargaining should lead to a corresponding diminution in the reach of the statutory duty. This is precisely what occurred in the *DTI Review of the ERA 1999*. Proposals for the extension of the bargaining agenda to encapsulate training and equality issues were rejected on the basis that these items were not typically bargaining subjects in voluntary practices.[137] Moreover, while the Government regretted that pensions were not generally included in voluntary negotiations, it was important that the DPA did not become 'more comprehensive in scope than voluntary bargaining arrangements'.[138] Accordingly, Schedule A1 was amended to exclude pensions from the statutory bargaining agenda,[139] while reserving a power for the Secretary of State to include it in the event of more widespread voluntary bargaining in future.[140]

In empirical terms, the Government's perception of the content of social practices seems more accurate than that of the CAC in the *Union Bank of Nigeria* decision. Pensions, training and equality do not tend to figure as subjects of bargaining in voluntary negotiations.[141] Yet it seems as likely that this limited

[137] DTI, *Review of the Employment Relations Act 1999: Government Response to the Public Consultation* (Department of Trade and Industry, 2003) paras 2.45–2.53.

[138] *Ibid*, para 2.56.

[139] TULRCA 1992, Schedule A1, para 171A(1), inserted by ERA 2004, s 20.

[140] TULRCA 1992, Schedule A1, para 171A(3)–(7).

[141] S Moore, S McKay and H Bewley, *DTI Employment Relations Research Series No. 43: The Content of new voluntary trade union recognition agreements 1998–2002, Volume 2* (Department of Trade and Industry, 2005).

voluntary agenda is in fact being shaped by the contours of the DPA.[142] Similar effects have been noted in employer responses to the union's request for voluntary recognition, where employers are increasingly insisting upon evidence of majority support as a precursor to voluntary recognition.[143] As the North American experience in *First National Maintenance* indicates, this leaves the union's bargaining rights stranded between two equally unpalatable interpretive possibilities. On the one hand, the CAC might take social practices as its interpretive touchstone, as in *Union Bank of Nigeria*. As Rideout has argued, 'a major point for consideration by the CAC should be whether it is normal in the United Kingdom to negotiate … collectively. If it is not, there is clear support for the view that the legislature did not intend compulsory recognition to set new standards for voluntary bargaining.'[144] From the deliberative perspective, it is doubtful whether such an interpretive approach is even coherent, given the dependence of social practices on legal norms.

On the other hand, the CAC might decline jurisdiction to decide the point, leaving the dispute to be settled by the High Court in an action for specific performance. This seems to be the approach adopted in more recent CAC decisions. In *Amicus and Epichem Ltd*,[145] there was a continuing dispute between the employer and the union as to whether discretionary bonuses fell within the scope of 'pay' in the statutory DPA. While noting the disagreement, the CAC concluded that 'these matters are not for the CAC to adjudicate upon'.[146] Litigation in the ordinary courts is unlikely to be an attractive prospect for unions. The vivid testament of *First National Maintenance* is that where industrial democracy and employer property rights collide, the ordinary courts will jealously safeguard the employer's 'core of entrepreneurial control'. With interpretive alternatives as stark as this, the DPA cannot augment deliberative democracy within the workplace.

(ii) The Legal Duty to Bargain II: Procedural Nature

With respect to the procedural nature of the legal duty to bargain, it is important to ascertain whether the 'model' DPA embodies a passive or an active duty to bargain. This enquiry is necessarily speculative, for the nature of the legal duty depends upon judicial rather than CAC interpretation and no party has yet sought an order of specific performance to enforce the DPA. Nevertheless, the legislature explicitly rejected any requirement of good faith bargaining. Instead, it was envisaged the parties would merely be under a legal duty to 'meet and

[142] S McKay, S Moore and H Wood, 'The nature of collective bargaining achieved through the statutory procedure', in G Gall (ed), *Union Recognition: Organising and bargaining outcomes* (London, Routledge, 2006) 98.

[143] Gall, above n 122.

[144] R Rideout, 'What shall we do with the CAC?' (2002) 31 *Industrial Law Journal* 1, 31.

[145] TUR1/380/2004.

[146] *Ibid*, para 23.

talk': in the words of the CAC, the 'model' DPA is 'purely procedural' in nature, not substantive.[147] This is reflected in the structure of the 'model' DPA. The specified bargaining procedure envisages a sequential exchange of proposals and employer counter-responses, initiated by the union in anticipation of the employer's annual decisions on 'pay, hours and holidays'. While the employer is required to make a reasoned response to the union's proposals, there is no requirement that an employer make counter-proposals in the event of disagreement.[148] Furthermore, despite the deliberative tone of reasoned and sequential dialogue implied by the bargaining procedure, it is notable that the 'model' DPA does not improve upon the weak informational duties specified in TULRCA 1992.[149] In the spectrum of possibilities between active and passive conceptions of the duty to bargain, the 'model' DPA embodies an extreme variant of the passive approach. This is consistent with the 'anti-artifactual' nature of social partnership. Enforcement of the active duty would necessitate heightened judicial scrutiny of the reasonableness of bargaining procedures and substantive proposals. By contrast, enforcement of the passive duty leaves bargaining autonomy largely intact.

The attractiveness of the law's approach in this regard is questionable. One of the institutional preconditions of deliberation is equilibrium between the parties. Without this, deference to bargaining autonomy can easily become a mask for employer domination of the bargaining process. This is inconsistent with genuine deliberation between equals. As Simpson observes, 'growth in the restrictive function of labour law has not been reversed', and this has undoubtedly led to 'a reduced source of bargaining power' for unions.[150] Two features of the DPA are likely to erect further obstacles to the achievement of collective solidarity in the workplace. First, the DPA makes provision for the union to make 'reasonable' requests to the employer for workplace meetings between the union and workers to discuss aspects of the bargaining process. However, where such meetings are held in working time the employer is under no obligation to pay workers for the time off.[151] This is unlikely to promote democratic discussion amongst workers, which is integral to those workers acquiring the sense of cohesive solidarity. In *GMB and AJ Cheetham Ltd*,[152] the union argued for a modification of the 'model' DPA such that the employer would be obliged to pay workers for time off to attend these meetings. The CAC rejected the union's request, considering that

[147] *Union Bank of Nigeria*, above n 136, para 4.

[148] The Trade Union Recognition (Method of Collective Bargaining) Order 2000 (SI 2000/1300) para 15, step 3(b): '*If* the response contains any counter-proposals, the written communication shall set out the reasons for giving them' (emphasis added).

[149] *Ibid*, para 27.

[150] B Simpson, 'Trade Union Recognition and the Law, a New Approach—Pts I and II of Schedule A1 to the Trade Union and Labour Relations (Consolidation) Act 1992' (2000) 29 *Industrial Law Journal* 193, 221.

[151] Trade Union Recognition Order, above n 148, para 23.

[152] TUR1/159/2002.

'this is an issue best determined by the two parties in direct negotiations with each other'.[153] Accordingly, the DPA was modified to leave it silent on the issue of payment for time off.

Secondly, the DPA continues to assert the primacy of the individual contract in tracing the normative effect of collective agreements.[154] This has been bolstered by the wide latitude for flexibility through individual contract permitted in TULRCA 1992, section 145B. This posits an individual right for a worker who is a member of an independent union not to have an offer made to him by his employer if that union is recognised or seeking recognition; and where the 'sole or main purpose' of the offer is that workers' terms of employment will not (or no longer) be determined by collective agreement. The restrictive 'sole or main purpose' criterion ensures that employers can escape liability through the assertion of ostensibly neutral purposes such as promoting flexibility in individual pay determination. Yet individually bargained advantages 'are a fruitful way of interfering with organization and choice of representatives; increased compensation … is often earned at the cost of breaking down some other standard thought to be for the welfare of the group'.[155] Conferring legitimacy on employer strategies designed to 'divide and rule' the workforce is unlikely to institutionalise the social bases of deliberative cooperation.

VI CONCLUSION: COLLECTIVE BARGAINING IN THE DELIBERATIVE IMAGE

The ideology of social partnership promised a new dawn in collective labour relations. In many respects, this ideology seemed to invoke many of the best elements of deliberative democracy: trust, cooperation and the reliance on reasoned dialogue. This chapter has argued that the deliberative democratic ideal is worthy of our allegiance in the industrial sphere. Many of the criticisms levelled against it have rested upon an unduly narrow understanding of the preconditions of deliberative engagement. Nevertheless, New Labour's understanding of social partnership is radically deficient as a framework for realising the deliberative ideal in the workplace. How, then, can collective bargaining be refashioned in the deliberative image? It is suggested that six reform strategies would help to realise the deliberative potential of collective bargaining.

A Constructive Mediation

As we have seen, deliberative democrats have stressed the deliberative qualities of mediation as a form of dispute resolution. It is suppler than either arbitration or

[153] *Ibid*, para 24.
[154] Trade Union Recognition Order, above n 148, para 18.
[155] *JI Case Co v NLRB* 321 US 322 (1944) at 337–9.

legal adjudication. Its aim is 'not a verdict, but consensus among the actors involved, sensitive to the central concerns of these parties'.[156] In this way, it can 'stimulate discourse and reflection about goals, interests, and values and reciprocal education'; in this respect, it contains 'intimations of discursive politics in the form of both a search for reasoned consensus and understanding of the legitimate, if different, interests of other parties'.[157] An interesting and ready-made set of institutional proposals in this vein can be found in McCarthy and Ellis' outlining of a system of 'constructive mediation' in labour relations, which they proposed as an alternative to the Industrial Relations Act 1971.[158] Another deliberative possibility can be found in the old system of Industrial Courts of Inquiry. These institutions were often used in particularly difficult industrial disputes where mediation had failed and arbitration had been refused by the parties. Their reliance on fact-finding and publicity, above all their typical reliance on attempts to mobilise 'the influence of informed public opinion' in resolving intractable disputes, meant that these public forums were classically deliberative in their operation.[159] Their disappearance from the industrial relations landscape is regrettable, given their alignment with deliberative forms of public reasoning. The power to set up such Courts, though long fallen into disuse, still exists under section 215 TULRA 1992.

The next question that arises is whether these deliberative modes of dispute resolution should be voluntary or compulsory. It is unlikely that they will have a significant impact in difficult cases where the employer is hostile to joint regulation if they are conceived as voluntary forms of intervention. Novitz has objected that compulsory schemes of dispute resolution might become a cloak for State promotion of particular values within the bargaining process.[160] However, such an objection seems misconceived. While we might object to the promotion of *faulty* values by the State, it seems difficult to sustain an objection to State promotion of values per se. If State-led mediation and inquiry is guided by the values of democratic participation and joint regulation, for example, this should be welcomed rather than deplored.

B Expanding the Bargaining Agenda

An enriched and expanded bargaining agenda has two main deliberative virtues. First, it allows citizens the opportunity to exercise collective democratic control over the social and economic forces that shape their lives. Secondly, multiplying the dimensions of democratic control helps the tractability of disputes by

[156] Dryzek, above n 73, 46.
[157] *Ibid.*
[158] WEJ McCarthy and ND Ellis, *Management by Agreement* (London, Hutchinson, 1973).
[159] WEJ McCarthy and BA Clifford, 'The Work of Industrial Courts of Inquiry' (1966) 1 *British Journal of Industrial Relations* 39.
[160] See Novitz, above n 16, 52–4, discussing the dangers of the partisan State in arbitration and mediation procedures.

multiplying the possibilities for imaginative and stable compromise and agreement. The statutory agenda of 'pay, hours and holidays' in Schedule A1 is impoverished. At the very least, to extend the scope of the statutory duty to encapsulate 'the recent and probable development of the undertaking's activities and economic situation',[161] reflecting the formulation in the Information and Consultation of Employees Regulations 2004, would enrich the deliberative potential of the bargaining duty. More radically, there is something to be said for McCarthy and Ellis' proposals for a system of 'management by agreement', where the authors proposed that there should be no 'area of management decision-making where management itself could claim an absolute and unilateral right to resist union influence in any form. In other words there would no longer be any room for a doctrine of "reserved rights" or "managerial prerogatives".'[162] Instead, trade unions (with the assistance of constructive mediation) would be empowered to negotiate on *any* area of managerial policy (although the employer would only be compelled to negotiate rather than agree). This seems preferable to the arbitrary strictures that currently constrain workers' democratic participation in economic governance based either on deference to employer's property rights (as in the US) or deference to social practices (as in the British case).

C Expanding the Employer's Informational Duties

The current law relating to information disclosure is hedged with restrictions, limited to the reach of existing bargaining arrangements, and hobbled by a conservative approach to standard-setting by the CAC.[163] Deliberative reform would focus on liberalising duties of disclosure, perhaps along the lines of Swedish law. Gospel's comparative analysis of the Swedish law on informational disclosure points to important deliberative advantages over the British approach. Swedish employers are under a legal duty to keep the union continuously informed about a wide range of matters, including 'production, general economic, and personnel matters'; the employer is required to provide any information that is requested by the union during the negotiation process, and this extends to any specific documents requested by the union that are in the employer's possession; the employer must allow the union access to its accounts and any other documents it wishes to inspect, with the employer under an obligation to assist the union in the analysis of such documentation; and finally Swedish law and collective agreements restrict the scope of exceptions and defences to the employer's obligations of disclosure.[164] This positive use of legal norms, harnessed to pursue a *standard-setting* role in collective labour relations, is

[161] Information and Consultation of Employees Regulations 2004, Reg 20(1)(a).
[162] McCarthy and Ellis, above n 158, 96.
[163] Gospel and Lockwood, above n 127, 135.
[164] HF Gospel, 'Trade Unions and the Legal Obligation to Bargain: An American, Swedish and British Comparison' (1983) 21 *British Journal of Industrial Relations* 343, 347.

in striking contrast to the limitations of the British *standard-reflecting* approach. It is more attuned to the needs of deliberative governance based on the exchange of *reasoned arguments* supported by *evidence-based justification*.

D A Deliberative Conception of the Right to Strike

New Labour's conception of social partnership endorsed the existing balance of power between trade unions and employers. This existing balance of power could fairly be described as 'unionization weakened and atrophied, particularly in the private sector of the economy and especially in the private services subsector'.[165] This was reflected in New Labour's enthusiastic endorsement and retention of many of the Conservative Government's restrictive reforms of strike law, such as strike ballots, notice requirements, limits on lawful picketing, and the ban on secondary and sympathetic industrial action. While New Labour modified certain elements of this framework, Novitz was right to conclude that these 'tend to tinker with the detail of the previous statutory framework and do not necessarily make it any easier for unions to call industrial action'.[166] As we have seen, deliberative democracy is based upon a rich ideal of political equality with respect to the democratic participants. This current imbalance of social power between employers and trade unions erodes the basic preconditions of deliberation in the industrial sphere, and this highlights a fatal flaw in New Labour's conception of social partnership. At a minimum it is imperative that the UK ensures its legal framework on industrial action is finally brought into line with basic International Labour Organisation standards.[167]

Moreover, we might usefully invoke Phelps Brown's distinction between legislation aimed at restricting industrial action in the interests of 'balance' or 'equilibrium' between the parties, and legislation aimed at restricting 'unreasonable' industrial action that inflicts excessive social costs with no countervailing social benefit. Phelps Brown rejected the first rationale as misguided. From the deliberative perspective (which Phelps Brown defended in a protean form), 'it is the uses of the trade union power, rather than the power itself, that should form the object of policy'.[168] Trade union disempowerment was not a sound pathway to trade union responsibility, and deliberation between unequal parties was no

[165] G Gall, Trade Union Recognition in Britain: An Emerging Crisis for Trade Unions?' (2007) 28 *Economic and Industrial Democracy* 78, 79.

[166] T Novitz, 'A Revised Role for Trade Unions as Designed by New Labour: The Representation Pyramid and "Partnership"' (2002) 29 *Journal of Law and Society* 487, 505; see also P Smith and G Morton, 'Nine Years of New Labour: Neoliberalism and Workers' Rights' (2006) 44 *British Journal of Industrial Relations* 401.

[167] For reform proposals that take account of ILO standards, see T Novitz, 'International Promises and Domestic Pragmatism: To What Extent will the Employment Relations Act 1999 Implement International Labour Standards Relating to Freedom of Association?' (2000) 63 *Modern Law Review* 379.

[168] H Phelps Brown, *The Origins of Trade Union Power* (Oxford, Oxford University Press, 1983) 293.

deliberation at all. So legislation aimed at restricting the social power of trade unions, such as the ban on secondary industrial action, is more likely to undermine rather than promote deliberation. By contrast, legislation aimed at securing a compulsory pause for 'constructive mediation' or public inquiry might be defensible as part of a deliberative framework for the right to strike.[169] Currently, however, the cumulative effects of restrictions on the exercise of industrial action in the UK are destructive of the deliberative ideal.

E National and Sectoral Bargaining Structures

One feature of the current approach to trade union recognition in the UK is that it is predicated upon a model of single employer bargaining based around relatively small bargaining units. In bargaining terms, this has led to a democratic vacuum at other regulatory levels such as the district or other geographical region level, at sectoral level, or at national level. The development of a multi-level approach to industrial governance seems essential from a deliberative perspective. First, there are certain matters that cannot be regulated effectively where structures are excessively decentralised. As an example, collective action problems mean that the formulation and implementation of training and skills strategies cannot be pursued through a series of firm-specific collective agreements. This could only be done effectively at sectoral or regional levels where the problems of free riding can be reduced by strong trade unions and employers' associations.

Secondly, more centralised bargaining structures can promote more encompassing behaviour by producer groups because these groups are forced to argue in public forums. Put simply, the discipline of public dialogue and argumentation constrains the way in which political positions are articulated and defended. Participants cannot simply invoke their self-interest as a sufficient reason to persuade others to endorse a course of action; they must reach out for justifications that could reasonably be endorsed by differently situated others. In turn, the deliberative hope is that participants will eventually begin to think (as well as speak) in a more impartial way when engaged in political talk.

There are signs that trade unions are keen to develop their regulatory capacities at the sectoral level,[170] but such structures are unlikely to emerge naturally without State intervention and support. The lesson of the 'artifactual' theory of associative governance is that the State enjoys a unique capacity to support and steer the actions of actors in civil society, and that well-designed regulatory initiatives can be very effective in the implementation of new

[169] There would need to be careful scrutiny of the social effects of such legislative initiatives. In respect of compulsory mediation, Novitz has pointed to the impact of compulsory mediation provisions in South Africa which diminished unions' bargaining power: see Novitz, above n 16, 53–4.

[170] See *Labour Research*, October 2008, 18–20.

frameworks of governance. Despite some tentative suggestions that the State might underwrite new sectoral forums for trade unions and employers to discuss matters of shared concerns such as training or low pay in the Warwick Accord of 2004,[171] there is little evidence that the project of institutional construction has begun in earnest.

F An Active Duty to Bargain?

Finally, there is scope for developing an 'active' legal duty to bargain in British labour law. A crucial first step would be to give the CAC jurisdiction to adjudicate upon alleged failures to bargain in good faith, as opposed to the High Court. The CAC is better placed to make the controversial normative judgements necessary to enforce an active duty to bargain. Enforcement of an active duty would necessitate scrutiny of the objective reasonableness of the parties' conduct from a deliberative perspective. This might include drawing inferences from a party's failure to make concessions, for example. Where a party has failed to make reasonable concessions, this might suggest a failure to engage reflectively with the deliberative process since one distinctive element of deliberation is the transformation (as opposed to aggregation) of preferences through reasoned debate and dialogue. Or a failure to justify proposals by reference to supporting evidence might also constitute evidence of a failure to deliberate through the exchange of evidence-based reasons. This would be preferable to the current position based on the passive duty to bargain, where the State leads a weak union to the bargaining table and stands aside while the employer capitalises on its economic strength and talks the union to death. In any political system that cares about deliberative democratic values, such a position would be entirely unacceptable.

[171] See KD Ewing, 'The Function of Trade Unions' (2005) 34 *Industrial Law Journal* 1.

Index